THE CODE OF OPPOSITES ·

A Sacred Guide to Playing with Power and Not Getting Burned

MAHALENE LOUIS

with

MICHAEL WOLF

BOOK 2: NO SELF-DOUBT

Copyright

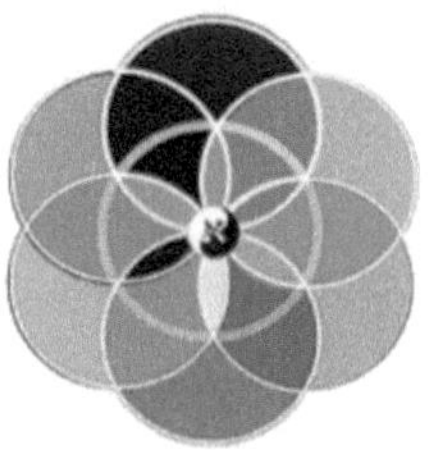

www.GoldenXPR.com
www.emPoweringNOW.com
www.thecodeofopposites.com

Paperback ISBN: 978-0-9824605-5-9
eBook ISBN: 978-0-9824605-7-3

Dedication

To reality, a.k.a. "God," my nemesis

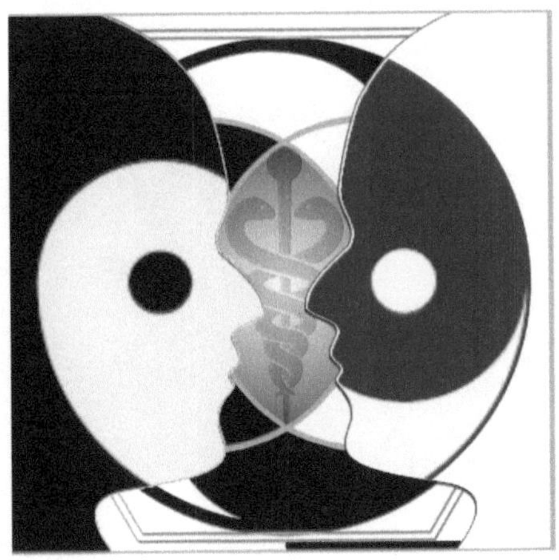

Mission of TCO

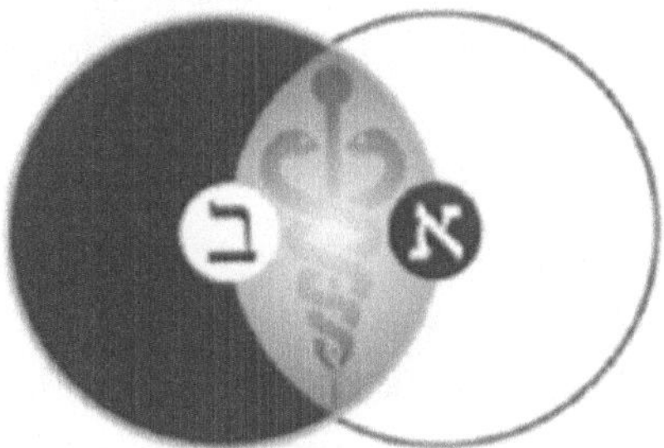

TCO's mission is to heal our relationship to Power.
To do so, it reveals the force of a sacred language that guides us to the field in between, where to transcend our beliefs of right and wrong, and know in our blood that the divine has no religion and no elect. By becoming fluent in "God's" language – in the paradox, feeling and sensing the all-pervading realities that beckon us now, we open to the Love that has no opposite, and experience Health in all levels of our communication.

A Sacred Guide to Wholesome Power

"Power doesn't corrupt people, people corrupt power." *William Gaddis*

Adopting a water-like path of least resistance heals my relationship to Power. When yet to be an amphibian (able to breath while going through intense emotions), I'm like a little engine who wants to think I can, which is not quite the same as *actually* thinking I can. Henceforth, I shall capitalize the sentence "I CAN" to remind me that emPowerment is a matter of perspective, but also, of self-esteem. Being unconditional in offering my gifts is how to like myself and "believe" in myself. I also see that the letters I CAN reorder as CAIN – the prophet who killed his brother, despaired and enraged to see that "God" favored his brother's offerings and disregarded his.

The story of Cain and Abel is so deeply archetypal and crucial to liberation that the Hebrew names find their perfect tone in English as brothers "I can't" and "I'm able." The transmission corroborates life's universal purpose: to offer our gifts in a way that they can be received. It is clear that, while Abel's offering was accepted, Cain's offering was dismissed by "God." Cain must have had strings attached to his gift. He wanted something in the exchange, which is how he couldn't allow for *QKabbalah* "receptivity" to occur. Consider: when I love myself, I don't hunger for your love, approval and recognition. I trust me. I hear me. I see me. Giving it all (no strings attached) makes me lovable in my eyes. It is fundamentally how to "receive" me, but also you.

Conversely, I do harm when my mind wages a personal war against its own creation of unrequited love. When I perceive that you don't love me, I want to make you pay. Same for "God." But since there's no one out there, I am the one who's regularly vanquished by the enemy (the part of me that resists Love). In that space, I'm the loser, but only all the time! If it is my sincere desire to participate in the work of transformation, I will seek to be congruent, and reconcile the split parts of me. When the two are One, there is no push/pull. I feel a Love so pure that it naturally extends to my family, my community, my nation; the world.

AB | BA

I NOW RECOGNIZE THAT THE BEST WAY TO ESTABLISH ORDER IS BY OFFERING RESPECT, AND NOT DOMINATION OR EVEN DEBATE.

RESPECT, DOMINATION, DEBATE: THESE ARE ISSUES OF POWER.
THEY ORIGINATE FROM MY SENSE OF JUSTICE AND OF THE LACK THEREOF.
WHEN I GIVE FREELY, I AM MOVED BY THE LOVE OF JUSTICE, AS I AM
NEITHER LOOKING FOR REWARD NOR PUNISHMENT.
MY RECEIVING A REWARD IS IN THE GIVING.

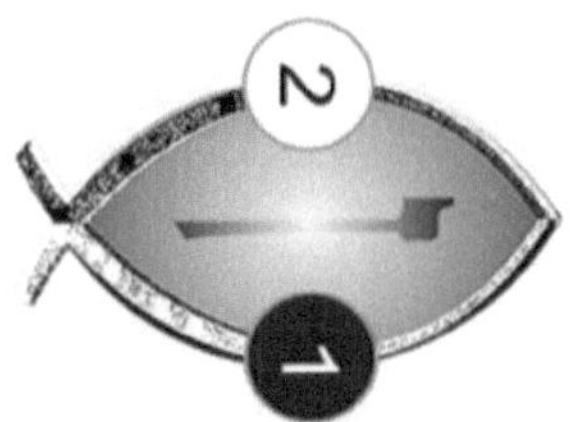

"The map is not the territory." *Alfred Korzybski, philosopher & mathematician*

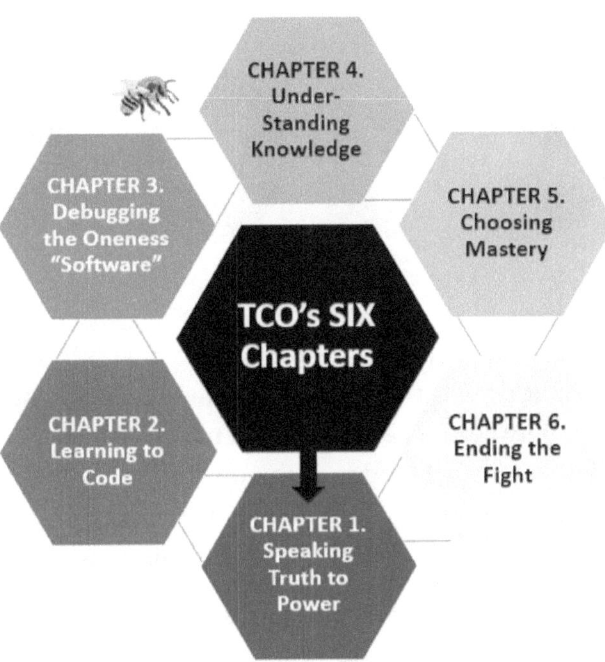

In my search for the kind of usability that would give me practical results, I tend to confuse the model with reality. I forget that reality is a lot messier. I even want to ignore that chaos is part of life! Thus, while my mind creates maps of reality in order to understand reality, I still won't understand the limits of my maps. **But what if I stumbled upon a map that would inspire me to walk the territory?**

Book 2 – in Context

"The snake which cannot cast its skin has to die. As well the minds which are prevented from changing their opinions; they cease to be mind." *Friedrich Nietzsche*

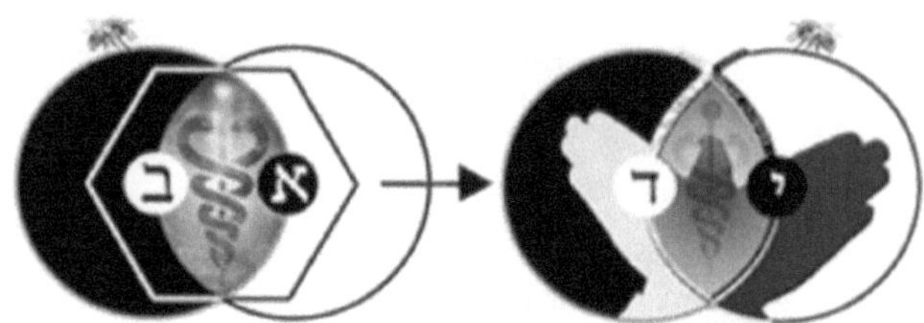

The primary purpose of TCO—the Series is to heal our relationship to Power. To do so, it reveals the force of a sacred language that guides us to the field in between, where to transcend our beliefs of right and wrong, and know in our blood that the divine has no religion and no elect. This field in between is also known as the middle path. It is the caduceus' rod onto which the two snakes of my mind are entwined.

Book 1—no push/pull invokes such caduceus: in the beginning was the end, when I deliberately choose peace and rest while working. This book lays the foundation for me to recognize the existence of a meta-language as a sacred guide to using Power. Power is a big deal (thus the capital "P"). It is wholesome when I am unbridled in my expression, and yet, do not need to accuse myself of either speaking too much or not enough. Therein is the healing I seek.

Book 2—no self-doubt now superimposes "my eagle hands" over the caduceus. Eagle teaches me to return to childlike innocence. The same eagle who inspires me to reach for the sky grounds my action by suggesting a master code. Its head and wings are the digits of my two hands united in giving/receiving. When I feel the freedom of reciprocity, I know the kind of faith that makes everything well. Henceforth, this book invites me to inquire on why I do not trust myself.

AB | BA

ALL ANCIENT TRADITIONS ALLUDE TO A GREAT POWER THAT LIVES IN
EVERYONE AND EVERYTHING, A POWER BY WHICH TO TRANSCEND ANY
CHALLENGE. BUT IT IS AS IF A GLOBAL EVENT WIPED OUT OUR MEMORY OF
IT, LEAVING US DISCONNECTED. NO POWER!
WHERE IS THE LOST SYMBOL BY WHICH TO INTERFACE
WITH THE COSMIC FORCES, HEAL OUR BODIES, AND ABORT THE GREAT
TRAGEDIES THAT HUMANKIND IS NOW FACING?

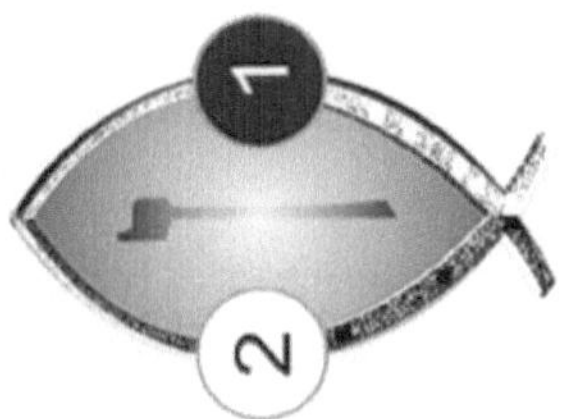

AT A TIME OF EPIC TRANSFORMATION WHEN THERE IS AN URGENCY IN
STEPPING INTO A FORM OF AUTHENTIC LEADERSHIP, COMMUNICATION IS OF
THE ESSENCE. TO HAVE A COMPLETELY NEW WAY TO AUTHENTICALLY
COMMUNICATE ABOUT THE MANY DIMENSIONS OF REALITY — AND THUS
SPEAK TRUTH TO POWER, WE NOW REQUIRE THE VISIONARY REVELATION OF
A METALANGUAGE, A LANGUAGE BEHIND ALL LANGUAGES.

The Happenstance of Book 2

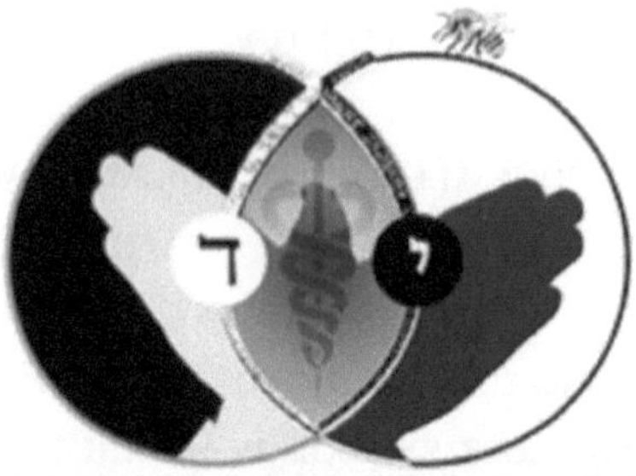

Book 2	Book 1	Book 3
My Eagle Hands	A Caduceus	Our Eye of Providence
No Self-Doubt	No Push-Pull	No Yearning
Individual Power	Symbolic Power	Collective Power

Book 2 places a caduceus over "my eagle hands." It adopts the "I, my and mine" perspective of individual Power. Eagle models this Power by teaching me to connect to my heart and return to childlike innocence. The same eagle who inspires me to reach for the sky grounds my action by suggesting a master code: its head and wings are the digits of my two hands united in giving/receiving. When beyond the illusion of separation, there is no one left to doubt myself as I feel the freedom of Oneness. I am walking the talk, talking the walk, and my speech and actions results in harmony.

- **As it happens,** the two hands are those of the second son of Michael Wolf, Thomas, who agreed to lend a hand or two, for *Golden XPR* to be seen.
- **As it happens,** the name Thomas comes from the S/Hebrew word *Teomim*.
- **As it happens,** *Teomim* is also the word for the astrological star known as "Gemini" – the twins that are in each of us and behind The Code of Opposites.
- **As it happens,** the Gemini astrological star lives in the 3rd house – the house of communication. Moreover, Gemini is an Air / mental sign, ruled by the fickle planet Mercury. The mind

is that which I seek to heal. When I do, I understand how Roman Mercury is also known as Greek Hermes – the god of communication, commerce and healing.

- **As it happens,** one of the most celebrated and yet mysterious quotes of the Gospel of St Thomas (the Good News of the Twins – a code of opposites in itself) is: "If you bring forth what is within you, what you bring forth will save you. If you do not bring forth what is within you, what you do not bring forth will destroy you."

- **As it happens,** this is a most revolutionary verse, as it implies that either I do not need Jesus to be saved, or that Jesus is another word for fulfilling my potential by falling into my folly, which heals me by "bringing forth the wisdom that is within me."

- **As it happens,** my hands and my actions will be divided until I hear from within that, in magical English, TWINS spell: "Thy Will Is Not Separate." Hearing it, I will reach my goal, simply because it is no longer me minus "God" that does the work. The work is done through me – by "IT."

- **And when that happens,** the doubting Thomas in me will have died. For I will have owned fully my desire to be somebody (me) and allow myself to be that person deliberately, rather than forbid it. Yep, I'll eventually give myself the permission to live in accordance with my true nature, even if it means to not be spiritually correct and/or what I was expected to be. I will know that seeking authenticity first leads me to find the QKingdom, when I am enough, body and soul. Being "enough" is to no longer doubt myself, which also means that I don't need to convince you to believe certain things about myself. Strangely, now that I "buy" me, I'm no longer for sale.

AB | BA

PISCEAN MESSAGE – IN SUPPORT OF "I BELIEVE:"
THE TRICK TO HAVING FAITH IS TO BE **100%** CERTAIN.
100 STARTS WITH BEING I WITH EVERYTHING,
AND ENDS WITH HAVING **0** DOUBT.

THEN FROM THE PISCEAN "I BELIEVE,"
I NATURALLY MOVE INTO THE AQUARIAN "I KNOW."
"I KNOW" IS THE KEYWORD OF THE AGE OF AQUARIUS,
A.K.A. THE INFORMATION AGE OF ZEROES AND ONES.
WILL I DARE KNOWING THE JOY OF BEING (1) AND NOT BEING (0), FOR
THAT WOULD BE THE END OF THE YEARNING...

Table of Contents

Words Of Power

This book includes Sacred Names that have been held for eons to be charged with the Power of Creation. If it were true that the Hebrew alphabet is imbued with non-biological sentient life, it would be our responsibility to treat it with as much respect as other life forms.

To this end, there is an ancient law that protects books inscribed with such Names, preventing any of its pages from being recycled as secular writing. It asks that any hard copies would be treated as holy and returned to the Earth when complete.

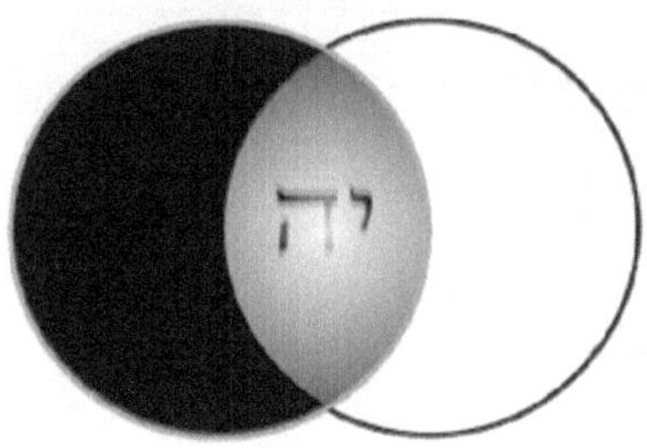

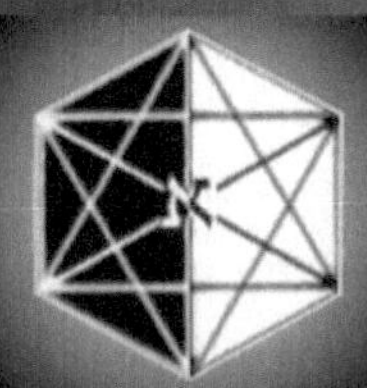

ONE

Speaking Truth to Power

AH... I'm still dealing with the same agenda to warp the law by making it into a coercive device so that I could do what I darn well please, and indulge my greed for Power. The problem with that strategy is that it makes me a fraud; a loser. No longer believing in myself, I tend to lose patience and perspective which makes it hard to make sound decisions. Bummer! I am now reminded that the gold is in the shadow, but in a brand new (and not so new) way. I meet a group of deities of the ancient Sumerians, Akkadians, Assyrians and Babylonians, giants who were said to have come to Earth some 200,000 years ago to harvest gold. Called the Anunnaki, their names held a symbol by which to interface with great Power, and either fall into perdition, or descend as the incarnated soul of divine teachers. The gold they sought to harvest may have been the sense of enough; the deliverable of the path of *Golden XPR*. This path breaks open the seals placed on ancient prophecies for me to feel why I am so intent on destroying my potential. The question leads me back to Cain – potentially the greatest prophet that ever lived and never died, for me to understand what the heck is going on between free will, karma and destiny. Will I ever be able to stop worshipping false "golds?"

PART I: THE SOURCE OF MY DISCONTENT

- The truest part of me aspires to be and do the beauty I'd like to be and do. However, to meet that part of me, I must dive deep into myself, which results in elevating the soul.
- Possibly, the hardest thing for me to forgive is that I won't do as well or greater than the greatest models that lived, e.g.; Jesus, Buddha or Krishna. And yes, it is a tall call, to say the least. It feels so hopeless that, instead of dying to my sins, I continue to live for them. It's easy: I just have to shut off the voice of my conscience which gives me my law, moment by moment... That voice can be so annoying! :-)
- To further ensure that I did turn off my intuition, I go one step further. I make "God" into a tyrant, and pretend that I was coerced to obey the law. I can now remain a child, taking no responsibility and deliberately refusing to grow up into the leader I was born to be.
- Eventually the pain behind the question "how long, O LORD" will lead me to come out of nothingness with the will and desire for a new story – a story by which the concealed and the revealed complement each other for me to connect body and soul. And then, I'll feel it. I'll feel that I've become real.

AB | BA

THE SOURCE OF MY DISCONTENT:
I KNOW WHAT TO DO, I JUST DON'T WANT TO DO IT.
THE DECISION TO BREAK MY OWN LAW IS WHAT CAUSES MY MISERY, AS IT
SEPARATES ME FROM "GOD." YEP, I TURN OFF GOD'S VOICE, A.K.A. MY
INTUITION, AND ENTER "SCARE CITY."

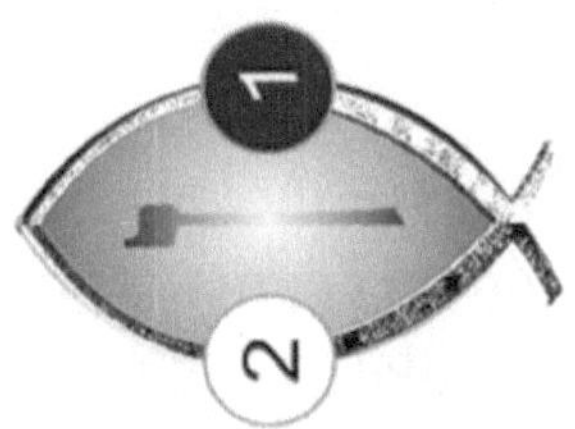

I'M NOW SO LONELY I COULD DIE! I LIVE IN FEAR AND IN LACK...
NEXT TIME I RESIST FEELING LONELY, SAD, SHAMED, FEARFUL OR EVEN
ANGRY, I COULD ASK MYSELF: "WHAT LAW DO YOU NOT WANT TO HONOR
AND RESPECT? BESIDES YOURSELF, WHO ARE YOU TRYING TO PUNISH
BY BEING AN OUTLAW?"

Intuition, the Alphabet and the Law

"Shallow men believe in luck or in circumstance. Strong men believe in cause and effect." Ralph Waldo Emerson

My intuition gives me the law; moment by moment. As such, it is the Law of laws, and also the law without law, as I can never know what my next command will be. Yes, it can be disturbing to think of myself as a soldier being given orders, especially when my ego wants to be the general! However, isn't my story the story of Lucifer; an angel who fell from grace after he rebelled against the rule of God? Devilish? Yes! Archetypal? You bet!

So, why can't I obey (a big word) when the consequences are so dismal? In this age of quantum physics, it is baffling to me to realize that I don't understand Newton's 3rd law: "for every action, there is an equal and opposite reaction." If I did, I would stop doing the same insane thing while pretending to expect different results! Indeed (and in misdeed), I appear to be in dire need of a code of opposites for me to triumph over the inner enemy I created!

As for my intuition, it speaks to me in numbers, sounds, images, and/or words. I will soon see that each Hebrew letter corresponds to a number (e.g.; Aleph is #1), a sound (Aleph can be pronounced as either a, e, i, o, or u), a hieroglyph (Aleph is א), and by extension, a word (*Aleph* is the word for "ox"). From there, archetypes can be deduced (Aleph the "ox," the primal force that moves the herd, is the Fool of the tarot deck as the blessed child who does not hesitate – a born leader. I will also soon realize that the Hebrew Bible speaks of "10 Words," and not as what we were led to believe of "Ten Commandments." These 10 Words stretch from 1st Word Aleph to 10th Word Yod.

And it makes me wonder... Could it really be that the entire wisdom teaching of the Bible would be distilled in the *hieroglyphs* and/or "sacred signs" of a simple alphabet? Might it mean that, if I could only understand how the 22/27 letters are patterned after the first 10, I'd be able to stop rebelling against my own "God" as my own "Good?" Not only would this mean the end of my communication issues, but also and foremost the end of my Power issues...

***

AB | BA

DO I WISH TO BE A QKABBALIST, THAT IS, TO UNDERSTAND KNOWLEDGE IN MY BLOOD AND MY BONES? IF SO, I WILL BEGIN BY LISTING 1 OR 2 SUPER-PAINFUL EXPERIENCES
THAT KEEP ON REPRODUCING IN MY LIFE:

1)

2)

A TRUTH DIFFICULT TO HEAR: COMPLETE NULLIFICATION OF THE EGO, WHETHER IT IS DONE THROUGH INQUIRY OR SURRENDER, IS THE PREREQUISITE TO TRANSCENDING DESTINY — A DESTINY PARTLY ENGRAVED BY THE SUPER-PAINFUL EXPERIENCES ABOVE.

10 Digital Words

"Moses was there with the LORD forty days and forty nights without eating bread or drinking water. And he wrote on the tablets the words of the covenant—the 10 Words." *Exodus 34:28.*

ON THE NOTE OF TEACHING WISDOM, HOW COULD WE HAVE MISSED THAT the Hebrew alphabet gave the code of enlightened action? It is surreal! And yet, Jesus didn't have an iPad. :-) We had to wait for the information age to perceive that Hebrew is a metalanguage. Similarly, to hear the dictates of my heart, would it help me to realize that the Torah does not speak of "Ten Commandments," but of "10 Words?"

Since each Hebrew letter is also a word and a number, the "10 Words" refer to the first 10 letters of the alphabet. These 10 words mean what they say and say what they mean. The sense of their symbols go a long way to shed light on the supposed "Commandments." They are so real that they will eventually inspire me to surrender, and join my hands in service to Love. Yep, the word digit does come from Latin *digitus,* to help me be true to my word – accountable.

Looking at the image below, I see my palms engraved with the tablets of the law. Each tablet has 5 letters: 5 for my yin side and 5 for my yang side. When I no longer split the letter of the law from the spirit of the law, I no longer observe that the law is coercive. Instead of wanting to run, I stand in awe, touched beyond belief!

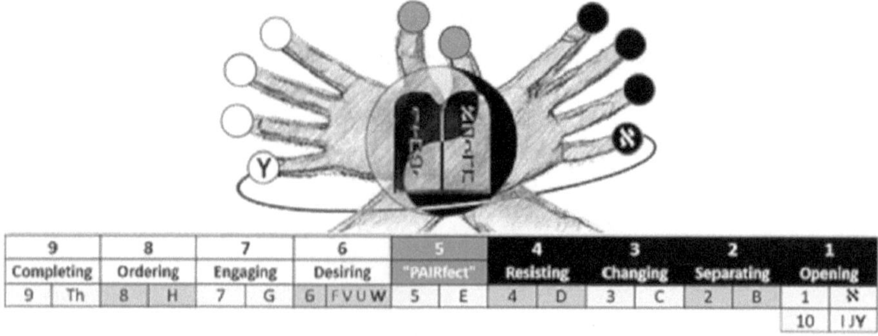

9		8		7		6		5		4		3		2		1	
Completing		Ordering		Engaging		Desiring		"PAIRfect"		Resisting		Changing		Separating		Opening	
9	Th	8	H	7	G	6	FVUW	5	E	4	D	3	C	2	B	1	א
																10	I JY

AB | BA

ON THE PREVIOUS PAGE, THE CHART DESCRIBES HOW EVOLUTION COMPELS ME TO MOVE HORIZONTALLY, FROM THE PAST OF 1-OPENING TO THE FUTURE OF 9-COMPLETING, AND BACK. ON THE NEXT PAGE, THE DIAGRAM SHOWS HOW EVOLUTION NOW COMPELS ME TO MOVE VERTICALLY, FROM 7 "INFERNAL" SPHERES TO 3 "SUPERNAL" SPHERES, AND BACK. THESE TWO WAYS TO "DO" TIME (HORIZONTAL AND VERTICAL) CAN COMPLEMENT EACH OTHER, ONCE I RECEIVE THE KEY TO ENLIGHTENED ACTION.

THIS IS WHEN THE LEFT HAND OF 7-ENGAGING JOINS THE RIGHT HAND OF 3-CHANGING. ENGAGING IS WHEN I TAKE ACTION TOWARDS ACHIEVING MY VISION AND FULFILLING THE NEED FOR CHANGE THEREOF.

The Depth of Vertical Time

"Time is the horizontal dimension of life, the surface layer of reality. Then there is the vertical dimension of depth, accessible only through the portal of the present moment." Eckhart Tolle

Do I know what motivates my action? For my "write" hand to no longer know what my left hand is doing, I must have turned off my conscience. Henceforth, I'm all lonely, abiding in "Scare City," and believing in lack.

The tree of life offers me a way out when viewed as a code of opposites. On the top is the light of 3 supernal spheres (rungs of the crown and 3rd eye chakras). When I hear my conscience, I am in "the Promised Land." In turn, resonating with the 3 supernals allows me to inhabit the whole tree, from crown to root; in the "QKingdom." But when I turn off my guidance, I'm stuck in the darkness of 7 infernal spheres (rungs of the throat, heart, navel, sex and root chakras). I am now in bondage to my own misery – in "the Land of Egypt." To make my exodus, I must enter the sphere where the taijitu is. This sphere is traditionally named *Daath* for a "knowledge" that is sexual as it calls me to drop my judgments of what I think is "good" and/or "evil." It is the mouth chakra, thus far ignored. When I have sufficiently "eaten" my desires and resistances, I receive the key to the QKingdom.

The QKingdom

The Key to the QKingdom		
3 Supernal Spheres	Sphere of Knowledge	7 Infernal Spheres
"The Promised Land"	The Exodus	"Ego-Egypt"
Freedom	Shadow Work	Bondage

AB | BA

THE TREE OF THE KNOWLEDGE OF OPPOSITES IS REVEALED BY TCO AS THE CRUX OF THE MATTER, AS IT IS THE LINK BETWEEN ABOVE AND BELOW, WITHIN AND WITHOUT. ENERGETICALLY, IT IS THE MOUTH CHAKRA. THE SPHERE IS NAMED *DAATH* FOR A "KNOWLEDGE" THAT, ONCE EATEN, LEADS ME TO DIE TO WHO I *THINK* I AM. WHEN MY JUDGMENTS ARE METABOLIZED, I SEE THAT THE MOUTH IS A TRANSCENDENTAL CHAKRA. ITS ACTIVATION IS COMPLETE WHEN I NO LONGER MISUSE THE THREE PRIMAL ACTS OF POWER — EATING, SPEAKING, AND KNOWING (SEXUALLY). I CAN NOW TAKE FULL RESPONSIBILITY FOR MY HEALTH, WEALTH AND RELATIONSHIPS.

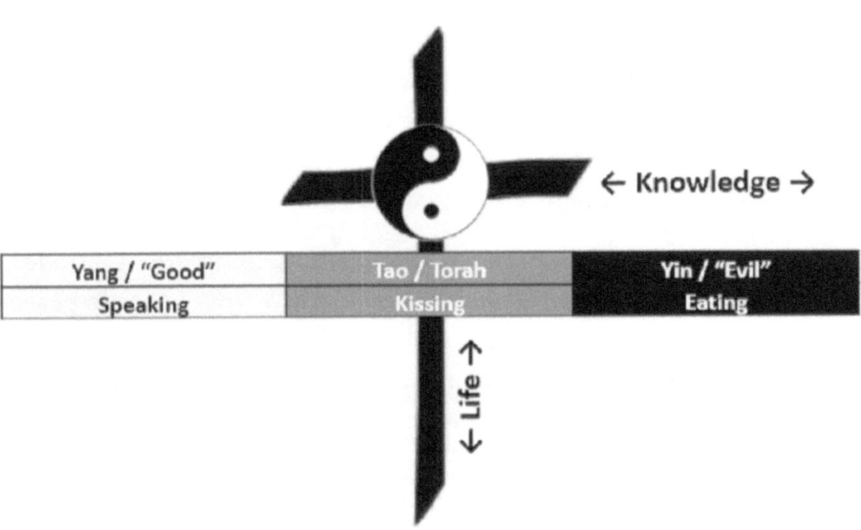

Daath is "crucial" as it marks the intersection of two trees – life and knowledge.

WHEN YANG OR OUTWARDLY DIRECTED, I USE MY MOUTH TO SPEAK.
WHEN YIN OR INWARDLY DIRECTED, I USE MY MOUTH TO EAT.
WHEN CENTERED IN BIBLICAL KNOWLEDGE, I USE MY MOUTH TO KISS.

Hear! Hear!

"Hear, O you who IS-REAL, LOVE is our God. LOVE is One." *TCO's Transmission of Deuteronomy 6:4*

I suffer from a very real hearing loss when the twins – the part that knows what to do to succeed, and the part that doesn't want to do it – fight in my psychic womb. In that ambivalent space, I can't relate to how the *Shema* – a word that means "hear" and thus obey – would be the foundation of the three Abrahamic religions. Here is the traditional translation of the verse above: "Hear, O Israel! the LORD is our God, the LORD is One." Surely, if I could only understand oneness in my blood, I would know the Love that has no opposite, and wouldn't feel that "God" has forsaken me!

While meditation, fasting, sex, yoga or making art can and does give me a felt sense of what it means to be One, and thus to rest while working, inquiry and surrender are the only two keys that were given toward sustaining such state of enlightenment. **Either option, provided it is practiced in totality, opens me to peace immediately.**

Therefore, when I am not at peace, there is something I do not understand. My inquiry is incomplete. If it were done, I would choose peace. The Power to choose peace in any and all circumstances is to surrender the fight. It is no less than having my attention fully disciplined; under my control. Being successful in my creation is now matter-of-fact, as I do not let doubt enter my mind. This results from reconciling the two opposite parts of me, and thus allowing for my heart and my mind to be in alignment.

My work is to inquire until I come into complete understanding on why I can't seem to stop fighting my own law – which is my own good. Understanding why I once chose to do harm is understanding everyone and everything. It is the *Shema*. Its decoding as perspective (or the seer) and interaction (or the seeing and the seen) traces a direct line to the observer effect of quantum physics. This will unfold in Chapter 3 –

Choosing Oneness. Cracking this code changes the way I look at things such as "the Law." Such sentience guides me on the ways of wholesome Power.

Indeed, when I make contact with truth, surrendering "my" free will is matter-of-fact. Moreover, once I surrender it all, I have no more questions. I can finally live without a why. This natural motion unravels the symbolic significance of inquiry being announced as a first key by Buddha (~500 BCE), and surrender as a second key by Jesus (~33 CE). I found the QKingdom – his justice and her sense of enough.

The "QK" of a QKosmocentric QKabbalah

"But seek first the QKingdom – his justice and her sense of Enough, and all these things will be given to you as well." *Transmission of Matthew 6:33 in Aramaic*

It is believed that the laws are revealed as the body of the Torah, and the QKabbalah, concealed as the soul of the Torah. This explains how, even though the Talmud states that "the Law speaks in the language of men," I can't hear it: poor reception!

Taking the laws of the body as an example, they can be summarized as hygiene, wholesome nutrition, exercise and rest. I may know that I "should" exercise. But if my soul is not into it, it is unlikely that my workout will benefit me. If it is clear that body and soul must be together for the law such as exercise to be revealed (i.e.; for me to have my results), it is equally true for laws such as "Thou Shalt Not Kill." Judging by how I sabotage and kill my potential, my soul is yet to "grok" that law.

The split of body and soul is behind a number of violations – and maybe all of them. Curiously, the same split also shows up at the symbolic level, where the Hebrew word קבלה which begins with the sign Qoph (ק) is transliterated as "Kabbalah," as if it began with the sign Kaph (כ). Here's the gist:

- Qoph (the 19th letter of the Hebrew alphabet) evolved into Q (the 17th letter of the English alphabet) and Kaph (the 11th letter of the Hebrew alphabet) evolved into K (also the 11th letter of the English alphabet).
- This is Qoph: ק. This is Kaph: כ. Different shapes. Different frequencies.

On that note, there are two schools that base their studies on the Hebrew scriptures: the school of Rabbinical Kabbalists (prophets, healers, legalists, priests, rabbis, Zionists, etc.) and the school of Hermetic Qabalists (Greek philosophers, theurgists, alchemists, astrologers, pagans, Christian Gnostics, freemasons, etc.). The former transliterates the Hebrew word with a "K;" the latter, with a "Q."

As for me, I am here to return to being a child at heart, and enter the "QKingdom" as Queen & King. This sacred marriage is eased by a "QK" love spell that weaves together the codes of two opposites. **This QK, however, intimates a bigger question: might the English language be playful enough to stand as the best conveyor thus far of the multi-modality of the S/Hebrew language?**

Coercion & Hierarchies

"He suspended the mountain over them as a barrel." *Talmud, Shabbat 88a*

A merging of the Kabbalah and Qabalah can only help me integrate the body and the soul of the Torah. I would then be as water, resisting nothing. On that note, could the K of letter Kaph be associated to rabbinical Kabbalah in light of Kaph's meaning?

Kaph is the 11th letter. As a noun, it means "palm of the hand;" as a verb, "subdue, coerce." The Talmud offers that, when the Torah was given on Mt. Sinai, "He suspended the mountain over them as a barrel." Whereas the colossal revelations were an expression of Divine Love, the people resisted as they felt "coerced" into accepting the yoke of Heaven. It was too much light, too soon, and the "palm of the hand" closed up. Thus, while the Law was given, it was not quite "received:" no QKabbalah!

It is said that, when the Law was given, all the souls were present in Mt. Sinai. This may explain how we would all be ambivalent in regards to the law – a part of us knowing what to do, the other part feeling coerced and resisting doing it.

Moreover, the word *Kaph* (כף) is formed by the two letters Kaph (כ) and Peh (ף) which can be read as an acronym: Kaph stands for *Koach* (the "force" of divine potential) and Peh for *Poel* (the "Power" of applied capability). Therefore, Kaph represents the possibility to actualize my divine and emerging potential in the human realm, a concern of great resistance to my ego personality, and of great interest to the contemporary sciences of adult development.

These sciences have evidence of two kinds of human capabilities: applied capability as per my present performance, and potential capability. For my present performance to show the light body's applied capability – when I resist nothing and experience absolute Truth, I must know that the Force is with me. This implies that I no longer misuse Power.

This is the developmental stage when I transcend and include world-centrism and enter QKosmocentrism. This transition is of particular concern to a demographic that is identified as "cultural creatives." They live mostly in the realm of pluralism: "I have my truth. You have your truth. And neither can be challenged." While this meme is at the root of movements such as feminism, social justice, environmental concerns, ecology and diversity, it can also cause confusion, disorientation and dissociation. Difficulties with self-actualization can occur, when I either compulsively attend self-growth seminars or start denigrating the quest for self-development.

Moreover, I experience a marked allergy to anything representing order, structure, or organization, as I link these values to intellectualism, capitalism, business, profit, ranking, hierarchy and meritocracy. I want to see that all people are born equals, and recoil at anything having to do with accomplishment or even excellence. I see these as coercive, as if some Power "suspended the mountain of success over me as a barrel."

This is how I contradict myself, claiming that my view is morally superior, all the while preaching that all "should" be equal. When attached to this story, I project all my hate and resentment of hierarchy onto any and all forms of excellence and achievement, condemning businesses or enterprises that I judge to be mean, arrogant and Power-driven. I ignore that, just as I had critiqued institutionalized religion for being fallacious and stifling in their fundamentalism, I have become the very oppressor whom I had formerly denounced. While confusing dominator hierarchies (which are factually oppressive) with growth hierarchies (which are the way of Nature), I block myself from going to the next stage of evolution. **And this may actually be the point – to keep me from dying to who I *think* I am!**

I make it all about me and play the nihilist game by attaching to the belief that all truths are cultural constructs and thus, contextual and relative. Furthermore, I hold that there is no big picture, no QKosmic narrative, no universal metatheory and certainly, no metalanguage to support any of it. And here I am – stubbornly refusing to grow up!

Childhood Unlearning

"The mind is slow to unlearn what it learnt early." *Seneca*

As complexity increases in the way we communicate and even isolate in this information age, I am now finding myself in somewhat of a dilemma. Being inexorably faced with the urgent need to grow up, I must now find a theory of adult learning whose territory is empirical enough to provide sustainable change. Whether I am aware of it or not, adulthood engages me in a form of learning that is unparalleled by the developmental stages of childhood. By having a curriculum that educates me on the stages I must transcend and include to function as a leader, I could lay claim to a set of practices that paves the initiatory path. I would then make a pivotal difference for the planet, as I would bypass the risks of being accused of fraud and/or intellectual opportunism. In Gandhi's words, I'd "be the change I wish to see in the world."

What about being the change I wish to see in the word? Am I true to myself, meaning what I say and saying what I feel? Experiencing the changes that I advocate is the only way that my voice can find a trust and a hearing, and the gifts I bear, a receiving. Such realness awakens me to a mode of knowing that plugs me directly into the ground of all being – that which quantum physics calls the "zero-point field" and religion, "God."

This learning is in fact an unlearning of the beliefs that I borrowed in my childhood. It makes room for the distinctive schooling of adult life and for four capacities and/or intelligences that are heightened in adulthood:

- **To know** when I received an intuitive hit, and to willfully follow it as an accurate guide to what I say and do.
- **To think** dialectically and make decisions by balancing universal rules against the contextual imperatives of a given situation.
- **To leverage** emotions into critical reflection to assess the effectiveness, the accuracy and the validity of the belief systems I accept.
- **To understand** the context of a situation (be it deciding to have surgery or placing a bet), using a common sense that is experiential and inferential.

Consider: when I know, think, leverage and understand, I am no longer as a child asking "how long?" I have patience; I CAN wait!

I CAN'T WAIT

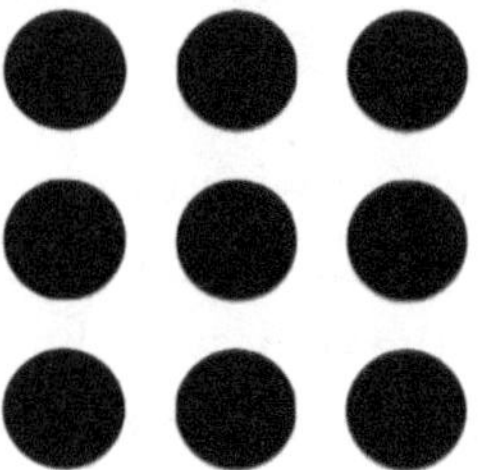

I CAN'T WAIT. That's my problem! When conflicted, I am like a frightened child running to my mommy. I compulsively try to find the comfort I need in sex, food, drugs, money, work, social media... And while I may know that healing comes from within, I'm still looking for love in all the wrong places – *out there!*

What will it take for me to courageously turn within where truth lives?

I spent lifetimes trying to please here or run there just to feed the hunger for love. And while I seem to leave no stone unturned, I keep on dodging a simple question: are you ready for how truth will change your life?

Yes, I ignore what is true for me and engage with you in deceptive games where I violate your boundaries or let you violate mine, just to avoid stepping into my Power. I'm so terrified that you'll reject me that I reject what I am called to be, do, have. I refuse to grow up, and simply attach to the belief that I'm not enough – a belief which eventually flips into "I'm special..." Oyveh!

If only I could wait, I would feel the infinite intelligence which knows nothing of obstacles and come to the Love that has no opposite. I'd stop fighting, and my special/not enough pendulum would center in peace.

But that would mean to come to the root of my addictions and my allergies, and understand the Power games I play. This would lead me to reclaim the feminine and be in touch with the wisdom of my body. I would understand *in my blood and my bones* the fundamental truth of oneness. Knowing that the force is with me (smiles), I would automatically transcend the fear of being emPowered.

Hear, hear! Evolving consciousness is the work of acquiring wholesome Power. Acquiring wholesome Power is the work of evolving consciousness. It is enlightenment, as there is no one left to try to control the show.

So, yes! I write in the "I" perspective because I am called to turn within, where my Power is. No matter how challenging, I am compelled to shift from collective Power (when I let the tribe decide for me) to individual Power (when I'm really me).

... And back into collective Power: I invite you to see if you can relate.

For starters, did you also set up a battlefield between the part of you that knows what to do to succeed, and the part of you that doesn't want to do it?

Caveat—TCO's words are live food. Ingesting them is becoming a part of this mysterious tale. It is claiming the Power to change!

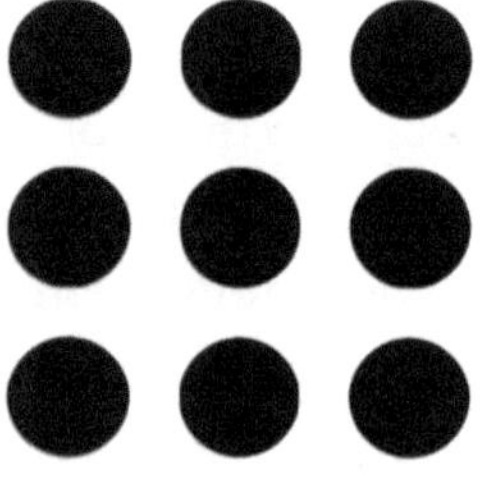

Patience, Power and Perspective

"The real voyage of discovery consists not in seeking new lands but in seeing with new eyes." *Marcel Proust*

PERSPECTIVE IS THE WAY I CHOOSE, CONSCIOUSLY OR NOT, TO SEE something. The level of evolution of my "I" is the filter through which my eyes see and interpret reality. This is how I can reread the same book and see it the second time with entirely new eyes. Applying this principle to obstacles, I can change the reality I see by changing the way I look at reality. **The more perspectives I can take, the more I evolve, and the more Power I have.** Thus, mastering the art of changing viewpoints is the goal of spiritual practice, as it leads me to adopt perspectives so infinite that I can just be. In turn, the choice to be more inclusive, tolerant and compassionate unleashes my creativity.

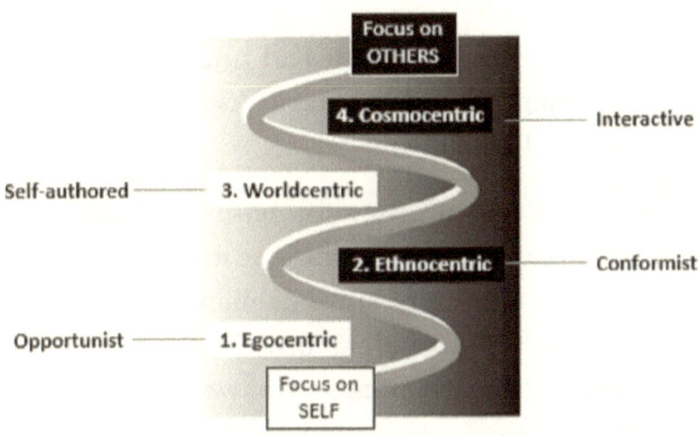

From the bottom up...

1. Focus on SELF: the egocentric stage of being an opportunist.
2. Focus on OTHERS: the ethnocentric stage of being a conformist.
3. Focus on SELF: the worldcentric stage of being self-authored.
4. Focus on OTHERS: the cosmocentric stage of being interactive.

The illustration above shows a pattern of evolution that moves the focus from the SELF to OTHERS, in four distinct stages. While the opportunist and the self-authored parts of me are both focused on the SELF, there is a marked difference in their altitude and breadth of perspectives. The same difference in altitude and breadth exists between the conformist and the interactive parts of me, although they are both focused on OTHERS.

This is just one of the models of research in human development that shows several structures unfolding the ever-increasing ability to adopt multiple perspectives. And it makes me wonder... Can we continue to have science evolving, while religion stopped its development at the ethnocentric level? Religion has now become a force that contradicts itself, preaching love and justice while calling for holy war on all those who disagree with its beliefs on the divine. It is absurd! How could something that teaches love, wisdom and understanding continue to cause so much suffering, all in the name of "God?" Agree with me, and I'll love you. Argue, and I'll kill you!

When there is a very real urgency for both the individual and the collective to reach the cosmocentric stage, it may be wise not to throw out religion with the bath waters, since its mandate (however yet to be fulfilled) is to take us beyond judgments. On the note of fulfillment, most traditions divide their teachings into two forms – "exoteric" and "esoteric." Exoteric are the "outer teachings" meant for the masses as a series of parables and indoctrinated beliefs, such as "believe and you'll be saved!" This is the level where wars are waged. Esoteric are the "inner teachings," kept mostly secret and only shared with the pure of heart. This is the level that concerns TCO, the level where all mystics across traditions are in agreement. Consider: when of One heart, I have no need to push you or pull away from you. A dialog can now begin.

It's about time!

> "You do not need to leave your room. Remain sitting at your table and listen. Do not even listen, simply wait, be quiet, still and solitary. The world will freely offer itself to you to be unmasked, it has no choice, it will roll in ecstasy at your feet." *Franz Kafka*

Why postpone having a consensus within my society of cells, when it is what Health is? This is a great paradox: on the one hand, I can't wait, on the other, I fear speed. Why? Would I resist reaching my goal if I trusted myself to use my energy for the greater good? Instead, I remain a child, powerless to have what I want, continuously asking "how long?" Surely, evolving consciousness will lead me to develop such Power of attention that I won't let anything enter my mind that opposes my goal. When focused on the goal, I AM the AIM, having unlearned my creation of time. The novel credibility inspires the appreciation and perseverance needed to go from stage to stage, until I can sustain the choice of Peace. Patience! I will eventually resist nothing, no longer create unconscious time and not experience a delay interposed between what I want and what I see created. Surrender does make things easy!

Meanwhile, my work is to use the instances where I can't hold the tension between opposites to probe the sea of the unconscious until I get to the pearl in consciousness. I will then understand why I could not wait for life to take care of itself. The more I make the unconscious conscious, the more I repair the broken compass of my instinct, and the more patience I have. Instinct can now sync time by way of images – the foundation of all symbols.

As for how symbolic Power is ordered and conveyed by a meta-language, the Voice of TCO lives to clarify it, one page at a time. To be clear and unequivocal, it originates from the zero-point field as the Living Word moved by one desire and one will: to connect body and soul. This is the only way that I'd hear the law. I would then drop the need to control the environment and be at ease with the law being concealed until it is revealed to me.

Code Body and Soul - MY / YM

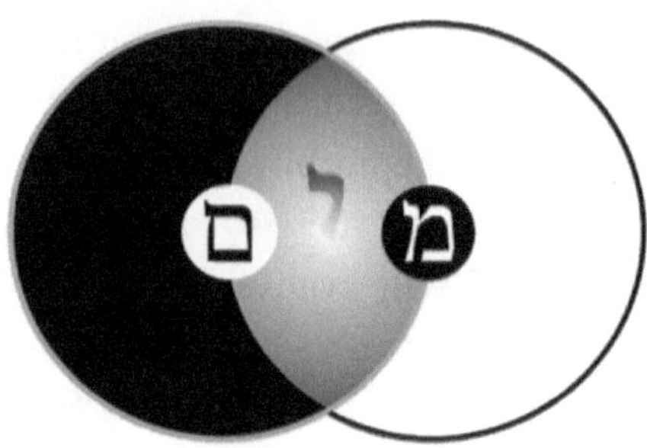

Imagine a language so pure and so sacred that it can reconcile opposites in just three letters...

Right: Hebrew letter Mem (מ) → M in Roman Script

In the middle: Hebrew letter Yod (י) → I, J, Y in Roman Script

Left: Hebrew letter Mem final (ם) (when at the end of a word) → M in Roman Script

Here is how S/Hebrew inscribes the code "Body and Soul:"

- **MY:** from right to middle, I read *Me* (מי) for "Who [am I]?"
- **YM:** from middle to left, I read *Yam* (ים) for "ocean, sea."
- **MYM:** from right to left, I read *Mayim* (מים) for "pairs of waters."

The Decoding: water is the most receptive (or feminine) of the four classical elements. This is how I must jump into the **ocean** of my being where the fragmented self awaits cohesion, which is when I answer the ultimate question (**who am I?**). The fragmentation occurs on Day 2 (*Genesis 1:6*), when there's a division between the pair of waters (above vs. below), effectively splitting my mind from my heart, and my body from my soul. "The pair of above" refers to mind and heart; "the pair of below" refers to body and soul.

I now start having boundary issues, and a need for protection. Will I have the courage to dive into the abysmal depths of the emotional body so as to quench my thirst for Love? Will I fish for the symbols of the dreams in the murky and turbulent waters of my repressed emotions? Water symbolizes the Torah. Just as water is cleansing and restores the soul, so does the Torah: "the water I give them will become in them a spring of water welling up to eternal life" (*John 4:13-14*). "Come, all you who are thirsty, come to the waters" (*Isaiah 55:1*). *Mayim* or **Mem** is the middle letter of the alphabet, inviting me to center and be as water, adopting the path of least resistance. Water also symbolizes the Tao. "The highest good is like water. Water gives life to the ten thousand things and does not strive. It flows in places men reject and so is like the Tao." *Lao Tzu, Tao Te Ching, Chap. 8.*

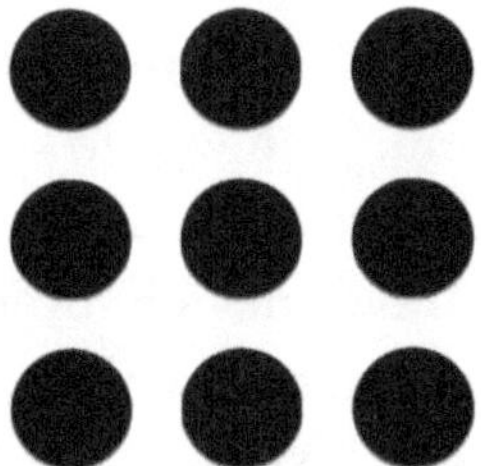

THE NECESSITY

THE NECESSITY comes from the fact that we are at a crossroad. There is now an urgency, for the individual and the collective, to make the evolution of consciousness a priority. Finding sustainable solutions requires facing our fear of being emPowered.

On that note, isn't it strange how, throughout history, we end up calling forth the great purging which we seem to simultaneously fear and yearn for? We may be sensing that being humbled to our core is a necessary step to quicken wholesome Power. It prepares us to wholeheartedly participate in a planetary movement that transitions our world from greed into grace, one person at a time.

As for me, as I do the work and move from stage to stage (and some stages may require years of work), I find that most transitions occur through rough waters. Each new level of Power bends me, and even shatters me. There is now a wound through which "God" may enter. Once passed, the initiation is a sure way to show me that a level doesn't own me anymore. This change in parameter is terrifying as I must now resonate with a higher frequency in order to heal. When I shift my vibrational mode, life changes with me.

The unlearning completes in a full recovery of sentience - the ability to feel and sense. When sentient, I can wait to know what love wills. I then realize that Love is my Nature. Love will transform our religious institutions, our educational system, our government, our economy, our military, our health care system by ennobling them and making them real. The solution must emerge from the problem – our inability to hear and understand each other – let alone, ourselves.

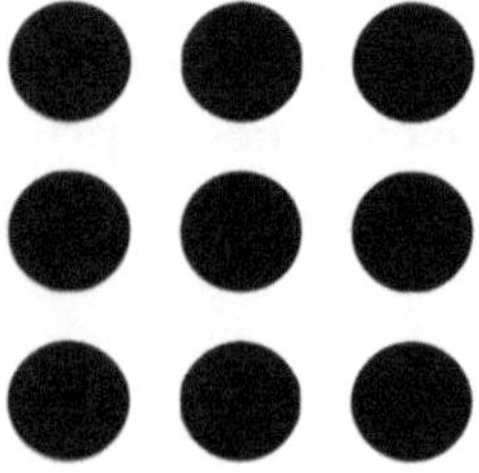

PART II: THE GOLD IS IN THE SHADOW

- This section begins with the question: what's the rush? Is the misdirected love of money –which is said to be at the root of all evils – that which creates my distortion of time? Would it help me emPower the NOW if I could let go of my obsession with silver and gold?
- I am now ready to meet a people who came to Earth some 200,000 years ago to harvest gold. Whether these people were real or not, nobody knows. Called the Anunnaki, they held a symbol in the core of their name by which to interface with great Power, and either fall into perdition, or descend as the incarnated soul of a divine teacher.
- This symbol is the S/Hebrew letter Nun – the sign at the core of their name (A-Nun-aki). Whether they knew it or not, the gold they sought to harvest was the sense of enough. This sense is the deliverable of the psycho-technology known as the path of *Golden XPR.*
- XPR breaks open the seals placed on ancient prophecies for me to understand Cain – the greatest prophet that ever lived and never died, for me to understand what's going on between free will, karma and destiny. At last, I can be free of my attachment to the material world and my yearning for more.

AB | BA

"During the gold rush is a good time to be in the pick and shovel business." *Mark Twain*
Either way, there's still the risk
that I'll end up worshipping a golden calf.
Would I be in a rush to get my slice of the pie
if I knew that I was enough?

Gold Is in the Shadow

"Socrates said the unexamined life is not worth living, but the examined one is no bargain." *Woody Allen*

The gold is in the shadow. When the Jews left Egypt, they took all sorts of gold with them, which they eventually used to build a golden calf, but also a tabernacle. Clearly turning within and going in the dark is frightening. And yet, it is where I lost my keys. I must go into the dark night of the soul – in "Ego-Egypt" – to retrieve the precious gold of a sane mind. This is the invitation issued by the alchemical process – to visit *Al-Khemia*, Arabic for "the land of black Earth."

I really wish to liberate me from the slavery I accepted! And here is my ethical dilemma: I cannot become conscious without the shadow, and I cannot become conscious of the shadow without massive moral effort. Shadow work demands a rigorous honesty, endurance and the willingness to uncover what I call "snake beliefs," the beliefs that, unbeknownst to me, hide in the dark. I may be aware of surface beliefs behind my resisting being emPowered, e.g.; "I'm not worthy." But am I aware of the deeper fears surrounding who I may become once I acquire wholesome Power?

Elevating the repressed, dissociated, disowned, unconscious parts of self into the light of the soul can be humiliating, just like it would be to be seen after partying too hard. The more I bury the energy of a desire that was shamed each time it tried to emerge, the more active this thought-form is in the unconscious. The somber pattern acts as the guardian of my destiny. Unless I recognize and embrace the emotions behind it, I can't uncover the treasure of self-knowledge – the gold, and can't come into my Power.

Shadow work is not for the faint of heart, since, as a rule, the ego personality will meet it with great resistance. I must be willing to painstakingly visit and revisit the same energy pattern, feeling how it and I move in different places in the spiral. Hear! Hear! Having a meta-language eases the work of clearing up, since my dark secrets are in an entanglement relationship with the secret codes of the Torah. This mirror effect is no less than surreal. And yet, as within, so without: the more I expose my dark games, the more the QKosmos reveals the secrets of its QKabbalah to me, and the more I harvest the gold of a sane mind that equally accepts blame or praise, honor or dishonor.

AB | BA

GOLD IS ALSO INHERENT TO "THE GOLDEN MEAN," THE PERFECT MODERATE POSITION BETWEEN TWO EXTREMES AND, AS SUCH, A CODE BALANCING THE OPPOSITES OF EXCESS AND DEFICIENCY. IT IS THE EXPERIENCE OF EMBRACING THE PARADOX AND IMAGINING NO BOUNDARIES, WHICH MAKES ME A CHILD AT "heART." WHEN I KNOW THAT ENOUGH IS "IN OFF," I LIVE BY THE GOLDEN RULE, AND FIND THAT THE COHERENCE OF MY HEART FUELS THE FAITH OF MY MIND. BEING AWAKE *ENOUGH* TO NOT DO UNTO OTHERS WHAT IS HATEFUL TO ME, I DON'T FEAR POWER. INSTEAD, I FEEL THE LOVE THAT HAS NO OPPOSITE.

The Gold in the Anunnaki

"Since the dawn of time, you have sought enlightenment through understanding language. Riddles scribbled into the stones of time have been made more accessible by the advent of cybernetics, which permit scrutinized cross-reference analysis of keywords interwoven throughout various Semitic tongues. By correlating etymologies, you have 'hoped' to relate to your ancestral history, as a way to know who you are." *Michael Tellinger, Slave Species of the Gods*

New archaeological and genetic evidence suggests that Sumerians and Egyptians inherited their knowledge from the Anunnaki, a people who lived more than 200,000 years ago. These were said to be our ancestors, ancient astronauts who came from a faraway planet to Earth in search of gold. "They biologically engineered the first humans as a slave race to mine the gold," Tellinger continues. This may be the cause of our greed and obsession with gold; of our shifting back and forth from bestial dominance to slave-like submission. This may also explain how we made "God" our tyrant.

The attribution of the ancient Sumerian culture to the Anunnaki is at the core of Zechariah Sitchin's books. His work – which is translated into more than 25 languages – has been dismissed by scientists and academics as pseudoscience and pseudohistory. Sitchin proposes that the Anunnaki came from Nibiru as "the twelfth planet," because it is the planet that follows the Sumerian gods-given conception of the Solar System counting the seven classical planets plus Neptune, Pluto, Uranus and Earth. Nibiru means "crossing" or "point of transition," which is also the exact meaning of *Yvrit,* the S/Hebrew word for "Hebrew" (Hibiru?). The planet was the home of the technologically advanced human-like extraterrestrial race. The same Anunnaki, Sitchin states, are known in Genesis as the Nephilim or the "fallen ones."

As for me, provided I feel worthy of tapping into my giant Power, I believe that seeing the codes embedded in ancient languages would help me to do so. If my intentions are pure, I may just be able to energize the trees of (my) life and of (my) knowledge of good and evil by resolving the riddle of the "God" Names. Instead of being a victim of my DNA, I would then reprogram my genetic information and heal my ancestry. Whether it would lead me to unravel "giant" mindbenders such as immortality, space-time travel, remote viewing, quantum word entanglement is an intriguing proposition...

AB | BA

But why S/Hebrew, when the cuneiform script of Sumer is the earliest known system of writing? Why the Bible, when the Bible seems to be the most prejudiced book of all? It is because the symbiotic relationship between the cure and the poison is needed for an authentic solution to emerge.

This is best expressed in the letter Nun in the core of the Vesica Piscis below but also in the A-Nun-aki's name, a letter that signifies both the fall of man and the descent of an incarnate divine teacher. To transcend my fear of falling, I must go deep into the abysmal waters of the unconscious. I will then befriend *Nun*, also the word for "fish" – the mighty dragon of desire.

As for the codes, rabbis have asked why the Torah begins with the letter Beth (ב) and not with Aleph (א), the first letter of the alphabet? To answer, I must mine the gold of Aleph...

The Gold of Aleph

"It's not what goes into my mouth that defiles me; I am defiled by the words that come out of my mouth." *Matthew 15:11*

HERE IS ANOTHER THING I FORGOT: MY SOUL IS PURE! MY BELIEF IN PURITY lost is how I defile myself by speaking words that are either too severe or falsely kind. If S/Hebrew is the metalanguage by which to hear my conscience and trust my use of Power, it must mean that the alphabet is the law of laws and, even more so troubling, *the law without law*. Indeed, the results of my communication show my true intentions, which may be conscious or not. Seeing the word "alphabet" archetypally helps me mine the gold.

The first part *alpha* is linked to the Fool and the second part *bet*, to the Magician – the Fool and the Magus being the first two letters and archetypal initiations of the hero, as represented by the tarot. Thus, the "alpha-bet" reconciles *bet* (the mind divided by conflicting desires) to *alpha* (the mind that can think, wait and fast, as it does not hunger for anything). Aleph's magic is gold. Its trust is so pure that it resists nothing and succeeds in everything. To be "IT," I am invited to fall down the AlphabeT from stage A to stage T, and then rise back up to A. Aleph and Beth (the first and second letter) are the first pair of non-biological sentient animals to have entered Noah's Ark. It is the pair portrayed on the cover of *TCO—Book 1*. Aleph-Beth also clarifies the nature of two concepts that tend to be confused: awareness and consciousness.

Aleph is pure and choiceless as the awareness that the choice is already made, since creation happens *through* me. Beth is decisive or indecisive as the consciousness that thinks that creation happens *by* me. "Being the body," asks Beth, "am I not also a separate doer?" Thus, Aleph is the Eternal Now, and Beth is the beginning of time, which is the beginning of mind.

To free me from a mind that is either boasting ("look at the earth I've just created") or putting myself down ("bad me; I shouldn't have..."), I have Aleph, a primal force that takes nothing personally. If Beth initiates "in the beginning" – the first word of the Torah, Aleph is the first Word of the 10 Words, a.k.a. the Ten Commandments. Here is its prompt: **"I am the LORD your God, who brought you out of the land of Egypt, out of the house of bondage."** *Exodus 20:2.* The verse begins with *Anokhi*, a four-lettered S/Hebrew word which starts in letter Aleph and means "I, myself." Consider: when freed from my bondage to materialism, I yearn no more. This translates as the end of dissatisfaction and of my addiction to serving false idols.

AB | BA

WHAT DOES MY NUN FISH DESIRE?
INDEED, DO I KNOW WHAT I REALLY WANT?

"THE DESIRE OF GOLD IS NOT FOR GOLD.
IT IS FOR THE MEANS OF FREEDOM AND BENEFIT."
RALPH WALDO EMERSON

The Gold of Freedom

"And you [Moses] support yourself by your sage's statement more than all of them, since you are the Leviathan of the sea of the Torah, the master of all fishes called Leviathan." *Zohar 48, vs. 66.*

ONE DAY, I WILL JUST WANT FREEDOM – NOT FREEDOM FROM A LONG LIST of perceived ailments and but just freedom. And on that "day," I will be response-able and have the courage to face the Mighty Dragon; yep, the very Leviathan. This is the Great Beast of Desire that bars me from freedom by having each of its scales inscribed with a "should." The fact that I have two ideations of two monumental Pisces – Moses & Jesus – does neither preclude me from desiring freedom, nor from doing what they did (or better) to will it into being.

When in enough pain to have robbed me from the permission to be, I will inquire on the "shoulds" that I accepted and yet resent. I will then eventually feel the sense of these masterful words: "I shall not cease from exploration, and the end of all my exploring will be to arrive where I started and know the Aleph place for the first time." *T.S. Eliot, revisited.* Indeed, I start in Aleph, move to Beth, and continue to fall as "light-bringer" Lucifer until I reach last letter Tav, the word for "sign" – the place where, having crucified my illusions, I turn a leaf. I then rise back to Aleph, where freedom awaits. Thus, Aleph is not only the 1st of the 10 Words; it is THE Word of the decalogue (Greek "10 Words"), if only because Aleph is the unity which is the Mystery of mysteries, and the door to all wonders.

When spelling out the Nun in *Anokhi* (אנכי) for "I, myself," I pronounce the Sumerian name *A-nun-aki*. Both words have the letter "Nun" in their core – the letter associated with "falling" as a destitute angel and of "descending" to earth as an Avatar, when I am the Aleph Word made flesh.

The letters of *Anokhi* reorder as *K'Ani* "like me" and *K'Ain* "like nothing." Indeed, I am mostly myself when I let go. Emptying out is how to let creation happen through me. When there's no one left to believe that "I" could make an error, I don't try to protect myself from being shattered by Love. Such selflessness is a giant Power – a "God" bringing me out of the House of Bondage. It opens me to sentience, and restores the information I lost when thinking of myself as a slave.Finally, I am awake.

Aleph therefore is just another word for "nothing left to lose…"

AB | BA

WHEN ADDING THE VALUES OF THE LETTERS OF *ANOKHI* (ALEPH 1 + NUN 50 + KAPH 20 + YOD 10), I OBTAIN THE NUMBER **81**.
AND IT MAKES THE **QK**ABBALIST IN ME WONDER…
WHAT'S THE PSYCHIC LINK? AND SO, I SEARCHED THE DATABASE FOR ANOTHER WORD OF THE SAME VALUE, AND CAME TO *LEAVDIL* (FOR "TO DIVIDE"). THE WORD ASKED ME: WHY NOT DIVIDE YOURSELF FROM YOUR ATTACHMENTS? WHAT ARE YOU AFRAID TO LOSE?

DO YOU NOT SEE THAT YOU EXIST IN A STATE OF ABSOLUTE FREEDOM SINCE OPPRESSION AND BONDAGE ARE OF YOUR OWN CHOOSING?

The Gold of Decision-Making

"Suffering is going to happen in life. The question is whether you'll make enough meaningful choices to justify living through it." *Jordan Peterson*

DECISION-MAKING IS A DICEY POWER. THIS IS HOW I TEND TO WORRY about making a choice: shall I go right or left? I fear to incur a loss. The similar sounds of "profit" and "prophet" come to mind. To ensure that I'd make a profit, I would need to see into the future – and become a prophet. But then again, prophets abide in the Now. They are not into predictions. Moreover, they're not afraid of losing it all, since they already did lose it all!

Life is made up of an infinite number of choices, each choice being a creative act determining which consequence I will set up. I know that the word "deciding" comes from Latin *de-caedere* for "to cut off." There's Power behind making a choice, which is why choosing terrifies me.

When avoiding the changes that my "cuts" would generate, I speak and act out of fear, and lose connection with what I communicate. I thus can't be heard, which sources more suffering. Eventually, I'll go to the edge and make "THE decision" – the decision to work in consciousness and strive to acquire self-knowledge (or wholesome Power). This decision is the gold of decision-making; the Rolls-Royce of choices. It is made for me when my heart is bursting with Love or when it is so shattered by it that I pass the threshold of enough pain. Little by little, I begin to do what I couldn't or wouldn't do before. I feel my pain, experiencing more compassion with myself and others as I go. The story then magically drops on its own, making room for silence.

Will I be big enough to decide to take full responsibility for the results of my communication? If life is about making conscious choices, consciousness is the job I've signed up for, whether I am conscious of it or not.

This whole discussion makes me wonder... What would it be like if I decided to see that every event, interaction, emotion, or thought is the result of something "I" once put into motion? Would remembering that I signed up for it as my specific sacred contract help not to take (my) destiny personally and free me to know who I Am?

Ah, once again, I am confronted with the puzzle of free will, karma, destiny... Do I decide or do I not decide? Would someone explain this to me?

AB | BA

On THE Decision...

'The only freedom man has is to strive for and acquire the *jnana* ("self-knowledge") that will enable him not to identify himself with the body. The body will go through the actions rendered inevitable by *prarabdha* ("destiny") and a man is free either to identify himself with the body and be attached to the fruits of its actions, or to be detached from it and be a mere witness of its activities.' *BE AS YOU ARE: The Teachings of Sri Ramana Maharshi.*

The Gold of *Golden XPR*

"What consciousness does is to manipulate information in the form of at least numbers, alphabet letters and most generally symbols." *Dr. William Tiller, Some Sciences Adventures with Real Magic*

If I understand the words of physicist Tiller (who was in the *What the bleep do we know?!* movie), "XPR" may just be the ultimate symbol in consciousness. XPR is the transliteration in Roman script of the Hebrew root ספר. This root-verb branches into words that encompass the nature of information: *sappir* for "sapphire" (and by extension, light), *mispar* for "numbers," *sephirah* for "sphere, wheel, chakra," *sepher* for "book" (and by extension, letters), and *sippur* for "story" (and by extension, sounds).

Golden XPR is an ancient path that came back from the future to give a no non-sense approach to scriptures. It reveals a unifying equation that makes the consciousness universe sensible. While walking on the XPR path, I am at once the scientist, the guinea pig and the laboratory. As I move back and forth from deduction to revelation, I begin to experience that the scriptures are not out there, but in here and *in ear*.

Feeling S/Hebrew's codes doesn't require that I'd learn Hebrew (I will soon see that Isaiah agrees). To feel and understand, I have English – the best conveyor of Hebrew thus far. The two languages are woven together to inspire me to do what it takes to be true to my word, and authentic in my relating. Besides compensating for the loss in translation (which could be done in any language), the playfulness of English gives me a felt-sense of S/Hebrew's multimodality. It allows for the loss in translation to be found as a transmission. **For example, this is how English spins the many senses of ספר as they sustain the work in consciousness: to eXPloRe, eXPeRience and eXPiRe to my limitations, so that I can eXPRess my true Self.**

As above, so below. As within, so without. Everything I do for me I do for the whole. The highest contribution I can make may just be to believe that it is possible for me or anyone sincerely desiring freedom to transition from greed (when giving is split from receiving) into grace (when the gift is so pure that you and I resonate with St Francis of Assisi's words: "it is in giving that we receive"). The question remains: how much do I trust in the goodness of the cosmic narrative; of "God" and ultimate reality?

AB | BA

THE TRICK TO BELIEVING – OR TO HAVING FAITH – IS TO BE **100%**. SUCH ENTIRETY IS BIG **LOVE** – THE LOVE THAT HAS NO OPPOSITE. IT IS KIND. IT DOES NOT JUDGE. IT IS A COMPLETE, PERFECT, UNCONDITIONAL AND SERENE ACCEPTANCE OF REALITY.
IT FULFILLS THE MANDATE OF RELIGION BY INSPIRING ME TO INVITE THE HOLY ACCIDENT, WHEN SOMETHING SO HUMONGOUS HAPPENS THAT I SURRENDER (MY) JUDGMENTS.

The Gold of Honey

"XPR, the final frontier... This is the initiatory journey of the Soul. Its continuing mission is to explore strange new WORDS, to seek out new life and new civilizations, to boldly go where no mind has gone before, in the obscure INTERPRETATION of the Judeo-Christian scriptures – a shadow that is anchored in the collective unconscious and has worked for eons to split spirit and matter." *Adapted from Star Trek – the Series*

Is XPR the philosopher's stone – a mythic alchemical substance capable of turning base metals such as mercury into gold? Can I use it for rejuvenation or to achieve immortality? To find out, I will look into what alchemists called *Magnum Opus,* "the Great Work." Here is a most curious fact: to understand how mind moves into feeling and feeling into matter (the experience of a goal being tangible), alchemists of old used Hebrew symbols, regardless of their religious persuasion. Why not use Arabic or Greek or Sanskrit?

Going with the hypothesis that S/Hebrew is a language of Nature, I take the root-word דבר (DBR) which branches into the word *Debarim. Debarim* refers to the 10 "Words" or *"matters"* of the Ten Commandments. Once evolved into Greek, 5 of these 10 Words have been used to designate brainwaves and related mental states (e.g.; Theta wave induces the dreaming state). The next page's exercise leverages the Greek name of a specific brainwave (e.g.; the Gamma wave) by supporting it with the meaning of the parent letter and word (e.g.; Gamma came from S/Hebrew Gimel for "camel"). Surprisingly and not, the S/Hebrew word corroborates what the wave expresses. Even more so surprising, the Commandments prompted by the S/Hebrew letters support the latest scientific findings on brainwaves:

1. **Alpha wave** connects to the witness state (a relaxed yet wakeful state, akin to meditation and held to be the ideal level of performance). This state is derived from the *matter* of Aleph

(the word for "ox"): "I am the God who took you out of the Land of Egypt and the House of Bondage." This is when I am free to do the next "write" thing!

2. **Beta wave** connects to the waking state (a state where I stress out as I tend to separate matter from spirit). This state is derived from the *matter* of Beth (the word for "house" or that which divides inside from outside): "You shall not make a graven image." When I do, I stand a much better chance not to be possessed by my possessions.

3. **Gamma wave** connects to the suchness state (a state when I am highly alert and conscious). This state is derived from the *matter* of Gimel (the word for "camel" or the movement of change): "you shall not take the Name of the LORD your God in vain." When I do not not burn myself out of misusing Power (the Name), I experience high levels of presence and energy.

4. **Delta wave** connects with the deep sleep state (a state when the personal or the unreal disappears, for me to detach from objects versus subjects). This state is derived from the *matter* of Dalet (a word for "door"): "you shall remember to keep the Shabbat holy." When I do, my mind is so open that I can rest while working and sleep while sleeping (no agendas).

5. **Theta wave** connects to the dreaming state (where I still see objects, yet vibrating faster). This state is derived from the *matter* of Teth (the word for "Snake," which is the most recurrent dream symbol): "you shall not bear false witness." When I do, I wake up from my illusion of separation and from the dream of karma.

DBR also forms *Deborah,* the word for "bee," an insect whose genius is in organization which is the foundation of all creativity. While honeybees build a honeycomb to serve as storage vessels, *Golden XPR* assembles its fractals in hexagonal shapes to leverage information and optimize the receiving of meaning.

XPR's honeycomb offers the following SIX gifts – to be unwrapped on the next page:

1. AWESOME CODES: to eternally stretch me to the sacred.
2. POWER NAMES: to understand and transcend my fear of emPowerment.
3. "SCIENCE-FRICTION:" to reframe the indigestible dogma into a personal training in non-resistance.
4. TOE: a Theory Of Everything (TOE) to allow for multiple viewpoints, common sense, compassion and reciprocity.
5. A SMART BIBLE: to see patterns by which to connect to my soul's "inner-net," recognize the universal slave narrative, and finally feel my pain.
6. ACCOUNTABILITY: to be true to my word and be the change.

Q: how do I reconcile the fact that there are five brainwaves and 10 words, matters or commandments?

A: the 10 Words are written on two tablets of the law; each tablet being encrypted with five S/Hebrew letters and/or words and/or brainwaves. This hints to the fact that the letters work in polarity for me to come to the LOVE that has no opposite.

Q: since there are only five brainwaves, how will XPR fill in the SIXth hexagon?

A: while there may not be a missing brainwave, there is a place "in-between," when I shift from wave to wave (or state to state), e.g.; from Delta (deep sleep) to Theta (dreaming). Fifth word *Heh* for "breath, window, womb" is where the passage occurs, as Heh is the letter invoking the silence between the notes or the white space between the letters. It is the quantum spacetime when that which understands has an understanding of "God." Note: to mark that there is no actual "Epsilon" brainwave – Epsilon being the evolution of Heh in Greek, TCO follows the word Heh with a question mark (see map next page).

The SIX Honeyed Gifts of XPR

Prepare to DIE: to access the online inquiry tool, click the BEE Map below or visit www.goldenxpr.com/tco_gifts_xpr/.

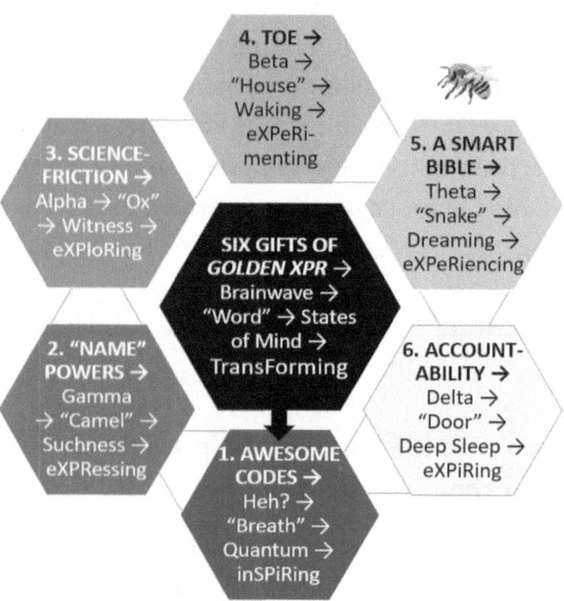

- **Step 1:** I fill in the blank: I want to know WHY I would choose to think I CAN'T _______ (e.g.; find a job, be patient, etc.).
- **Step 2:** I ask for truth and generate a number.
- **Step 3:** I find my number on the map and then use the words in the given hexagon to fill in the brackets: when I receive the gift of [**GOLDEN XPR**], my brain naturally resonates with the [**Brainwave**] imaged as [**"Word"**]. This leads me to enter the [**States of Mind**] state of mind. Soon enough, I am the [**TransForming**] I wish to be.
- **Step 4:** what most surprised me in this process is _______.

AB | BA

THE S/HEBREW WORD FOR "GOLD" IS *ZAHAV*.
ADDING THE VALUE OF ITS LETTERS (ZAYIN 7 + HEH 5 + BETH 2), I COME
TO 14. ANOTHER WORD VALUED 14 IS *DAI* (DALET 4 + YOD 10).
THE MESSAGE: THE SENSE OF ENOUGH IS GOLD.

DALET YOD (יד) IS THE PAIR OF LETTERS ON THE COVER OF BOOK 2.
GOING FROM RIGHT TO LEFT, I READ *DAI* FOR "ENOUGH."
FROM LEFT TO RIGHT, I READ *YAD* FOR "HAND."
WILL I BE BIG ENOUGH TO JOIN MY HANDS
IN SERVICE OF **LOVE?**

The Gold of Enough

"He who knows that enough is enough will always have enough."
Lao Tzu

I once heard that a true artist is defined by the capacity to know when enough is "in off," and stop. Sounds simple, doesn't it? And yet, how many endeavors got ruined, either because the creative agent went too far or not far enough? Indeed, the difference between "to run a business" and "to ruin a business" is an "I." However, when I let "IT" do the doing, I am sentience, and have the capacity to feel and sense. Such intimacy understands that which has an understanding of "God," and is symbolic Power at its best. It *is* beautiful – a way of being that carries justice in all affairs, knowing that justice is another word for "giving it all to LOVE."

Indeed, Art is an act of generosity. This is why beauty is symmetry and why the beautiful of Art adheres to the middle path. When I am an "artist" – no matter what my Art is, I experience the humility to let go and be a conduit for "IT." By receiving the gift of anonymity, I resonate with a frequency so pristine that it allows for mutuality by touching everyone I meet.

But giving it all? I can only imagine how disarming it would be to let the thought "not good enough" go... Whatever the moment would ask of me, I would do it. Since there would be nothing's left but the kindness of "God," I'd stop hiding behind excuses and give birth to the Word. "IT" would be done; my potential, fulfilled. I would hear and see the reciprocity of life, and know myself to be whole, complete and "PAIRfect." However, for now, I am split between the desire to be enlightened and the resistance to being enlightened! And it is this exact lack of integrity that prevents me from knowing when to stop.

TCO's poetry comes from the depth of the abyss to uplift the soul and give her a universal voice. How does it work? For its Art to communicate sentience in a sustainable way and inspire me to be willing to be real, it offers the following three qualities:

- **Mastering a skill:** TCO is the result of a 40-year wax-on wax-off process in learning to let go of the idea "I am the writer," so that the writing could offer itself freely as a guide to freedom. Indeed, the emptier "I" become as a vessel, the more the written word is fit to resonate with the individual and the collective.
- **Innovating the form of the message:** while the message ("let go and let God") has remained the same for eons, the form in which TCO delivers it sparkles with originality. It gives codes that are awe-provoking in their depths, codes that reveal ancient cosmic secrets to help us transmute newly acquired shame. It also uncovers "G-d" Names or Names of Power that provide a context on how you and I co-create our reality. Lastly, it presents mind-mapping patterns to provide immediate understandings by which to become accountable.
- **Voicing compassion:** neither the mastery of a craft nor the ground-breaking message would make a difference if M&M hadn't made the vow to live life consciously, in service to the community. The compassion that emanates from the writing communicates realness. By being the energy of liberation made flesh, the work fulfills the assignment of Art – to be a healing force and a catalyst for awakening.

This is how Art is the first wisdom teaching and the last. Indeed, "every child is an artist. The problem is to remain an artist once we grow up." It invites me to recognize that I was born to create my "Master Peace," for that recognition alone will nullify any possible fear of not being enough.

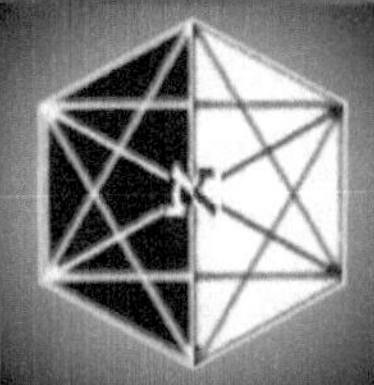

TWO

Learning to Code

"If you can't explain it simply, you don't understand it well enough." Albert Einstein

I KNOW that there is a hidden code that can unlock the laws of the universe, patterns that connect everything from the ancient past to the far future. But is there a code to give me a reliable way to do shadow work? Numbers have long been intrinsically linked to the divine. They were said to come from "God" because they obeyed laws that no one could change. More than abstract entities, numbers are the key to making sense of the world. Codes emerge from the ground of being, as exemplified by the nautilus shell and/or the swallows' flying patterns. To feel that light travels in codes, I now have smartphones and texting. These wondrous events make the impossible possible – a code to connect me to the ground of being and to the clear Self observing the creative process as it unfolds. It begins with one basic rule – the Rule of Plus One which sustains the integrity of "the Physics of Belief." To see this code, I let the child in me receive an "image" which my physical senses cannot see. The patterns never lie. And as the pieces start fitting together, I am inspired to increase my quota of honesty, doing what I do because that's what I do. No explanations, no justifications.

PART I: WHAT'S THE POINT?

Below are the "practical" topics of this section:

- The meaning and the sense of *QKabbalah* – to make room for the absolute Truth that sets me free.
- The GR-Code – to move from "GReed" into "GRace."
- The Physics of Belief – to understand how mind moves into matter and matter moves into energy.
- The Measure of Enough – to know when to stop and make of life an Art.
- The QKabbalah of 9 Chambers – to go beyond ambivalences, be total in my actions and succeed in my creation.
- Sacred Geometry – to trust that my inquiry can be complete as it is founded on patterns that are ecological, universal and radical.
- 10 Words – to free me from "the House of Bondage" by taking the mirror to the next level and leading me to pure awareness.
- Noah's Art – to give me a vision of the profound and enlightening decoding that is behind a very "cute" story.

The Sense of *QKabbalah*

Once upon a Zen time, a philosophy professor went to a Master to ask about God. The professor talked and talked, until the Master said: "Let me first serve you tea." The professor was at a loss: how could all his questions be answered by drinking tea? The Master brought the kettle, poured tea in the cup, and kept on pouring. "Stop!" said the professor. "What are you doing? Do you not see that the cup is full?" The Master said, "That's exactly how your mind is: so full of questions that there is no space for an answer to come in. Go back, empty your cup, even break it: when you are no longer, there will be no one left to stop the wholeness of LOVE to flow into you."

There is no avoiding it: to come to Self-knowledge, the mind has to be totally cleared of any and all obstructing concepts. Emptying the cup determines how much I am able to *QKabbalah* or "receive" the various phenomena that can appear. This is where shadow work is at its most purposeful. It makes room to include what the personal unconsciously represses – the "shadow." It is a paradox: the more "negative" I allow myself to be, the more I "positively" flourish. The greater the nothing, the more space I have for the something. It is a numbers game – a quantification.

Shadow work goes hand-in-hand with life's evolutionary processes. It can be expected that at any junction of transcending and including (that is, of going beyond my issue by embracing it) something could go wrong and form a shadow phenomenon. This is how cleaning up needs to support every stage of development that I endure. If, for example, I remain identified to the oral stage, I would develop an eating addiction, using food as a substitute for contact. But if the disidentification goes as far as disowning, I'd go to the opposite pole, developing an allergy and an eating disorder such as bulimia or anorexia. A food personality is now created that owns me.

I suffer from an acute case of mistaken identity. Unable to own the shadow, I can't withdraw the projection on an "out there" I see as my enemy. I don't know who I Am as I deleted my memory of the light body, and identified instead with this skin – the shame body which weighs heavily on me and confirms my inadequacy. Henceforth, I don't have the gumption to transcend my self-imposed limitations. I'm just a slave to the material world, fragmented, torn, tortured and broken.

The GR-Code & 11001001

"If at first you don't succeed, call me version 2.0." *Version 1.0*

Since stages are a calculation, what if enlightenment was a code? What if synchronicity could be graphed? What if destiny had a formula? Mathematics is the language of nature. Everything can be represented and understood via numbers. If I graph the numbers of any system, patterns begin to emerge. These patterns are hidden in plain sight, in nature and also in the Torah which uses a numerical alphabet. I just have to know where to look. Then what I normally see as chaos (be it in galaxies, plants, trees, seashells, humans, beliefs systems) reveals itself to actually follow subtle laws of behavior – what *Golden XPR* calls "the Physics of Belief."

There's an ancient kabbalistic myth about an ethereal red thread of wisdom that binds the letters whose energies are destined to touch. While this mystical thread may stretch or tangle, it will never break. It is woven with the mathematical probability by which to crack the **GR**-code, transition from **GR**eed into **GR**ace, when I know that it is in **G**iving that I am **R**eceiving. This code grants the male and female sides of my brain the exact measure of being whole, "PAIRfect," complete and connected – enough!

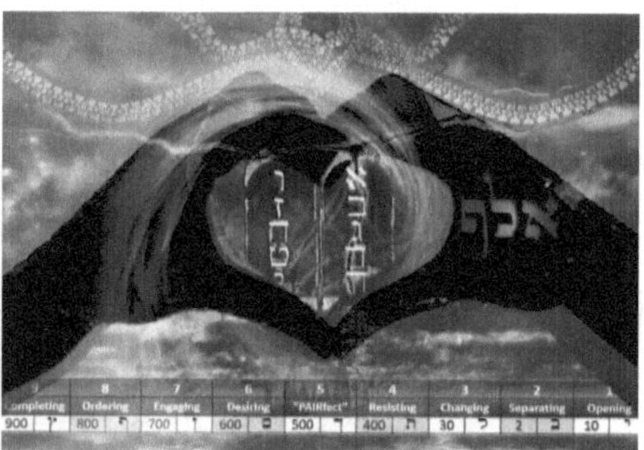

Binary Hands at One (0/1)

The Physics of Belief

"Tis true without lying, certain & most true. That which is below is like that which is above & that which is above is like that which is

below to do the miracles of one only thing." Emerald Tablet, Isaac Newton's translation.

Ancient alchemists worked with principles such as "as above, so below; as within, so without." These laws became more sensible with the advent of psycho-energetic physics which can be seen as the modern unfolding of ancient alchemy. Quantum experiments showed that what is being observed in nature depends on the choices made by the observer: as within, so without; as above, so below.

Here is a most curious fact: to understand how mind moves into feeling and feeling into matter, alchemists used Hebrew symbols, regardless of their religious persuasion. Why not use Arabic or Greek?

The Hebrew alphabet originated from Cuneiform – the oldest known form of writing which was invented by the Sumerians in Mesopotamia in the fourth and fifth millennia B.C.E. As stated by linguist and rabbi Marc-Alain Ouaknin, in *Mysteries of the Alphabet:* "The names of the letters still continue to be "ox," "house," "camel," "door," etc.: aleph, beth, gimel, daleth... and so on. These Hebrew and Semitic names can be found in Canaanite, then in Greek in the barely concealed form of alpha, beta, gamma, delta."

Since Hebrew has not changed form since its inception, this alphabet must be a force of Nature. Its signs are multimodal, they are a glyph just as letter A is a glyph in English. They are also words: e.g.; Aleph means "ox." Backed up by a numerical value, these words mean what they say and say what they mean: Aleph is valued at 1, as it is the "ox" or the primal force that moves the herd of non-biological lettered animals. Beth is valued at 2, as it is the "house" or that which divides inside from outside.

Using their "common" sense, a sequence of physical and metaphysical transformations can be traced. Once I understand the physics of my belief system, that is, how mind moves into feeling and feeling into matter, I can practice the alchemy of changing lead into gold (or my self-imposed limitations into pure awareness). This involves feeling how consciousness plays with information by way of numbers, alphabet letters, and most generally symbols since the words I use construct the worlds I see. Eventually, I find that I am enough which resolves my own measurement problem.

The Measure of Satisfaction

The Buddha's Four Noble Truths: life is _Dukkha_, Sanskrit for "dissatisfaction." The cause of dissatisfaction is craving. There is an end to the dissatisfaction. There is a path to the end of dissatisfaction.

"How do you know when a painting is finished?" is a question often asked to artists. And it is intriguing. By which magic does a painter know that she painted the last stroke? This sense – the sense of enough – is the Buddha's third noble truth: "there is an end to the dissatisfaction" (from Latin _satis_ "enough"). Although subtle, the sense of enough is a very real measure. If there is a code behind the Hebrew alphabet that can help me have this sense (not only in what I view as my "art," but in all parts of life), then I'm all for it, as it would make of life an art – a true "master peace."

To begin, here is a truth difficult to hear and understand: coming to the end involves a complete nullification of the ego personality, whether the death is brought about through inquiry or surrender. It is the prerequisite to transcend dissatisfaction – the belief that I am "not enough." On the way, I will pass through a series of initiations, each initiation being a death – a place where I must face the truth. Life as I have known it is finished. The partnership is over. The body is ill. The job is done. The money is gone. Something has happened that changes everything. The "holy accident" shatters my heart, leaving me wide-open, sobered. I am in-between – in an unknown space – a nobody awaiting a new appointment. I don't know who I am or where I'm going. I just know that somewhere, a sacrifice had to be made.

There is a price I must pay to feed the soul and complete each initiation rite. When I surrender and give up my attachment, I move to the next rung – a rung affording more abundance, a greater perspective that transcends and includes what I used to hold as true. A huge reconstruction follows.

While states are given, stages are earned (that is the price I must pay). But also, while states are temporary, stages, once earned, are permanent.

The journey calls me to the other side – where I am whole. Wholeness is found in the totality that rings like truth. Eventually, the consciousness that thinks in opposites merges into the pure awareness of oneness, asking "just how infinite can I allow myself to be?" As the cellular body receives the fundamental truth of oneness, it is nourished by it. The frequencies of matter and spirit begin to resonate and move with each other. The body can now reveal the Mystery of death by opening to Love and feeling connected to every other body and to life itself. And while it becomes an antenna instinctively receiving and transmitting the frequencies of the way and the truth of life and death (no opposites), I know what being "the Word made flesh" means.

When I perceive that there is a universal code to experiencing the soul of perennial truths, I am not afraid of receiving a kiss of truth which is also a kiss of death as it changes (my) life. If there is such a thing as absolute Truth, it must be found across cultures. This brings me to Code East & West.

Code East & West – AM / MT

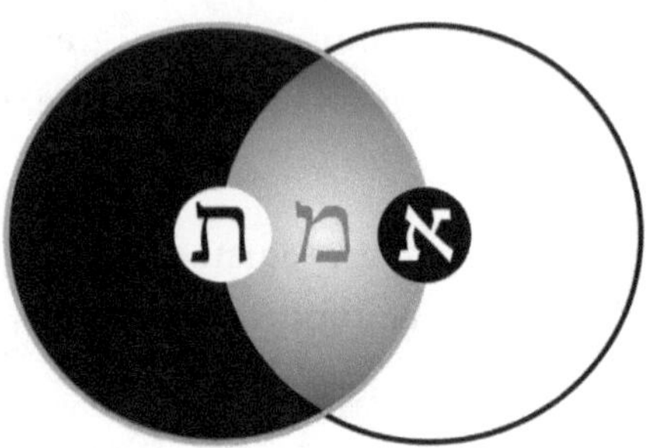

Imagine a language so pure and so sacred that it can reconcile opposites in just three letters…

Right: the alphabet's first letter – Aleph (א) → A in Roman Script
Middle: the alphabet's middle letter – Mem (מ) → M in Roman Script
Left: the alphabet's last letter – Tav (ת) → T in Roman Script.

Consider: when East meets West, my feminine and masculine sides are reconciled at the planetary level. Here is how S/Hebrew inscribes "Code East & West:"

- **AMT:** from right to left, I read the word *Emet* (אמת) for "truth."
- **AM:** from right to middle, I read the word *Im* (אם) for "mother."
- **MT:** from middle to left, I read the word *Mat* (מת) for "death."

The Decoding: there is truth in death just as there is "**death**" in "**truth**." The word *Emet* for "truth" invokes the nobility of the first truth ("life is dissatisfaction") by encompassing the entire alphabet as the beginning, the middle and the end. Surely, the whole alphabet writes the book of life, as I go from the beginning (the pain of birth) to the middle (the pain of illness) to the end (the pain of death). Taken separately, each of the three letters is also a name, a hieroglyph and a signifier, each letter invoking one of the next three Noble Truths as follows:

- Signifying "ox, primal force," *Emet's* first letter Aleph (א) says "I am the cause of dissatisfaction, when I crave" to have a consequence – an outcome.
- Signifying "pair of waters," *Emet's* middle letter Mem (מ) says "there is an end to dissatisfaction," when I am as water, adopting a path of least resistance.
- Signifying "sign, mark, note," *Emet's* last letter Tav (ת) says "there is a path to the end," which I mark by being the keeper of the crossroad.

Understanding that there is "death" in "truth" is becoming ready for how truth is about to change my life. As the change becomes real, I also understand in my body (and not just in my head) how profound this metalanguage is that includes the word *Im* for "**mother**" in the word *Emet* for "truth," for me to embody truth.

THE PATH TO THE END – THE "FINAL" SENSE OF ENOUGH.

Golden XPR is a newly revealed path to the end. It uses a metalanguage that sustains all wisdom teachings. Its stages are marked by 10 numbers and 22 letters. Five of the 22 basic letters (כ, מ, נ, פ, צ) are also called "final" letters and look as follows (ך, ם, ן, ף, ץ). They are final physically, when placed at the end of a word. They are final spiritually, when the letters' decoding transmits an image that circulates in my blood to convey the end of an unwholesome mental state; e.g.; Mem final unites the split waters of my emotions to usher the end of desire. The end of desire is also the start of fulfillment. I see the basic Mem (מ) in *Emet* (אמת) for "truth," and the final Mem (ם) in *Im* (אם) for "mother." True and certain it is, there is an end to dissatisfaction and a path (or two) to the sense of enough.

The QKabbalah of the Nine Chambers

"The great question of philosophy remains: If life is meaningless, what can be done about alphabet soup?" *Woody Allen*

9		8		7		6		5		4		3		2		1	
Completing		Ordering		Engaging		Desiring		"PAIRfect"		Resisting		Changing		Separating		Opening	
9	ט	8	ח	7	ז	6	ו	5	ה	4	ד	3	ג	2	ב	1	א
90	צ	80	פ	70	ע	60	ס	50	נ	40	מ	30	ל	20	כ	10	י
900	ץ	800	ף	700	ן	600	ם	500	ך	400	ת	300	ש	200	ר	100	ק

Above are the letters of the Hebrew alphabet, organized within what the elders called "the Kabbalah of the Nine Chambers." The first row (under the two title rows) contains the single digits; the second row, the tens, the third row, the hundreds. When a letter is capitalized, its value is multiplied by 1000, which makes for a full accounting system. S/Hebrew being read from right to left, the first chamber (#1) is to the right, and the last chamber (#9), to the left. The associated value is marked next to each letter, e.g.; 2 | ב.

Golden XPR takes one more step by clarifying the progression that occurs (e.g.; from 1-Opening to 2-Separating) by way of an ancient rule known as the "Rule of Kolel." *Kolel* means "God of Integrity." **The spirit of its law is to integrate divisiveness of speech by imparting and transferring the unity of letter Aleph to each letter and word, whether that letter or word visibly contains an Aleph or not.** As for the letter of the law itself, it stipulates that any word can be equal to any other word by plus one. Therefore, a word valued at, e.g.; 73 can be linked to any words equal to 74.

Inviting Aleph as my plus one moves the spirit of unity from Aleph (א) to Beth (ב) to Gimel (ג) until the 9th letter Teth (ט) completes the first cycle, each time adding 1 Aleph dot. The second and third rows simply expand the same cycle. This process traces the movement of energy, each stage preparing the terrain for the next stage to occur:

- **1** dot. This is my mind **Opening** to the awe and humility to be part of the vast QKosmos, while contributing my unique starlight.
- **2** dots. Yep, this is where I draw the line, and go into **Separating** – a necessary step to creating anything.
- **3** dots. I draw a triangle which elevates my perspective beyond any possible conflict of opposites, for me to be **Changing**.
- **4** dots. I draw a square – a massive form for me to be **Resisting** what my intuition tells me is "no good" for me.
- **5** dots. I draw a double pentagram (up-pointed and down-pointed), making me yin to yang **"PAIRfect"** and able to hold the tension.
- **6** dots. I draw a hexagram whose interlaced triangles suggest and invoke the tantric energy of **Desiring**.
- **7** dots. I draw a heptagram, guiding me to be **Engaging** in every day of the seven days of the week, moment by moment.
- **8** dots. I draw an octagram, whose eight interrelated concepts are **Ordering** my affairs and my sense of reality.
- **9** dots. I draw an enneagram whose typology allows me to be **Completing** what I started and die to who I *think* I am.

9	8	7	6	5	4	3	2	1
Completing	Ordering	Engaging	Desiring	"PAIRfect"	Resisting	Changing	Separating	Opening

Horizontal States: The Nine Chambers are female when horizontally linking the STATES in pairs, around 5 that is "PAIRfect." For example, when joining 3-Changing and 7-Engaging, I hold the tension of opposites. This ability speaks of consciously holding a STATE. To do so, I move through STAGES, beginning in Opening. I soon find that I can't help moving to Separating. From Separating, I can't help moving to Changing, etc. It is the way of Nature, bringing me to Completing. The more I move sequentially through the nine, the more I can rest and stay "in-between." The same movement is reproduced within the second row of tens and the third row of hundreds.

Vertical Stages: The Nine Chambers are male when vertically ranking the STAGES of my process by developing a growth hierarchy from ones to tens to hundreds. In each chamber (for example, in 8-Ordering), the numbered letters move down from one realm to the next, to enact the "order of creation" as 1) think, 2) feel, 3) have. The first row gives me information on the mental part of ordering, the second row, on the emotional part, and the third row, on the physical part.

8	
Ordering	
8	ח
80	כ
800	ך

The Cathartic Power of the Ego Triangle

"If the triangles made a god, they would give him three sides."
Montesquieu

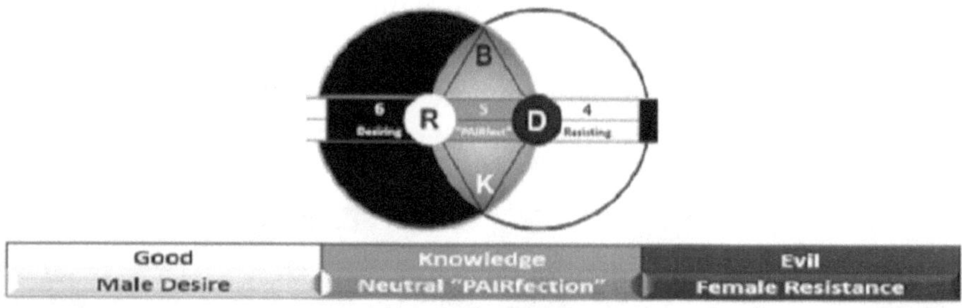

Gentle warning: this page is **so cathartic that it may need guidance in order to be fully received.**

At the apex of my ego triangle is the letter **B** for the "Belief" that there's an "out there" out there. I am now in Scare City, afraid that "you" won't give me what I want or that you'll take what I have. **At the base of my ego triangle** are the letters **R** and **D**, swinging me back and forth from one pole (Resistance) to the other pole (Desire):

- Resistance is a Desire to be without what is evil, e.g.; money.
- Desire is a Resistance to be without what is good, e.g.; money.

At the apex of my inverted ego triangle is the letter **K** for the Knowledge of Opposites. Understanding my Beliefs in "good" and "evil" helps balance Desire and Resistance from within. When these **Beliefs** are metabolized (an experience known as "forgiveness"), I **Know** to be created male/female and center in "PAIRfection." I am now out of Scare City. I neither fear emptiness nor "being without:"

- Resisting evil is how my inner female knows fulfillment.
- Desiring good is how my inner male knows freedom.

Therefore, the trick to the ego triangle is to flip it vertically, turning within to hold the tension between Desire and Resistance. This catharsis is supported by the Power of Three (tripled in the Nine Chambers), for me to investigate why I choose to believe what I **Believe**, until I Know the Self beyond doubt (an experience called "Faith").

The Sacred of Geometry

"I love the simplicity of the Cube because it's a very clear geometrical shape, and I love geometry because it's the study of how the whole universe is structured." *Erno Rubik*

When I realize that everything in the Universe is geometric, be it people, animals, planets, solar systems, stars, etc., I am motivated to measure my belief systems on a geometric scale. S/Hebrew letters being also numbers, they give me the ideal tools to practice the art of making the numerals speak. In becoming a *geo-meter*, the measure I choose to feel cellularly is the sense of enough, which naturally transitions me out of greed.

Self-esteem matters. Unless I have complete faith in what I choose to believe, it won't become my experience. It is only when I am 100% certain (zero doubt) that I see my creation manifested. However, which numbered path do I pick: the four kinds of leadership, the seven steps to success, the five secrets of abundance, the ten strategies to wellness?

I wish to have a measure I can trust. That wish is fulfilled by the felt sense that, since my inquiry is sourced in sacred geometry, it becomes universal, radical and therefore credible.

Geometry: the measure of the Earth by way of the mathematics of the properties, measurement and relationships of points, lines, angles, surfaces, and solids.

geOMetry: word coined to include the sacred marriage of sound and form sanctified in *Om*, the supreme Sanskrit syllable consisting of the 3 mother-sounds (a·u·m) and linking the total world of Brahman as the triad of creation, preservation and destruction via the electromagnetism (EM) of the word. The EM force was first studied by Galileo and made popular by Hans Jenny's work, termed "Cymatics" to address the physical patterns produced by the vibratory interaction of waves.

Gematria: the QKabbalistic art and science of sensing, transposing and inquiring on S/Hebrew codes, e.g.; the psychic links between words of equal value. Opening the seals placed on ancient prophecies reveals the order in the information thus far scrambled. It inspires me to be honest – the surest way to knowing that I am enough.

Readability and Usability

"**Music is the arithmetic of sounds as optics is the geometry of light.**" *Claude Debussy*

Egyptians and Greeks felt that "geometry is frozen music." When sound changes, matter changes. If all things are only an expression of something numeric or harmonic (if God is a geometer), I'd like to play with the word as if it were a musical instrument tuned to that which contains it. To this end, the shapes of geometry make visible the harmonic modules that uplift the soul. **When I can see what my intuition tells me, I am less likely to ignore it and more likely to make "sound" choices.** Geometry may just be the ultimate poetry as it includes the golden mean by which to hold the tension between two extremes. At one end is excess, at the other deficiency. Finding a moderate position (which is the sense of enough) is at the foundation of pure action.

The S/Hebrew alphabet unfolds evolution by way of geometry and algebra. However, to feel the letters' vibration from within, I must still be able to know what these letters are. Just having the transliteration (a transfer of words from one alphabet into another) is not enough. Taking the word סוד as an example: transliterating it as *Sohd* helps me read it. But the letters of *Sohd* lead me to believe that I am looking at a four-lettered word, when the S/Hebrew word סוד only has three letters. Moreover, the sound "S" can come from the letter Samekh (ס) or from the letter Shin (ש). Which one is it?

To clear possible ambivalence and avoid miscalculations, *Golden XPR* gives me the table below which replaced each Hebrew sign with the Roman script into which it evolved (source: rabbi and linguist Marc-Alain Ouaknin, *Mysteries of the Alphabet*).

9		8		7		6		5		4		3		2		1	
Completing		Ordering		Engaging		Desiring		"PAIRfect"		Resisting		Changing		Separating		Opening	
9	Th	8	H	7	G	6	F V U W	5	E	4	D	3	C	2	B	1	א
90	Z	80	Ph P	70	O	60	X	50	N	40	M	30	L	20	K	10	I J Y
900	Z f.	800	P f.	700	N f.	600	M f.	500	K f.	400	T	300	S Sh	200	R	100	Q

I can now calculate a specific gematria and hear a word's frequency accurately as I have: 1. the word's transliteration, 2. a parenthesis holding the evolution in English of the S/Hebrew signs, e.g.; *Sohd* (XWD), 3. the meaning, e.g.; "secret." I simply use the table to locate the signs X, W, D, and calculate that *Sohd's* value is 60 + 6 + 4 = 70. I may even hear XPR telling me "I got your number!" :-)

The Four Gematriot (pl.)

There are several methods for "making the numeral speak." The following gematriot are the four that are most often used:

- **Absolute gematria:** each letter is given the value of its accepted numerical equivalent. The first set of 9 letters are for the single digits, the second set are for the tens, the third set are for the hundreds (see previous page). Note: the five final letters –Kaph (K f.), Mem (M f.), Nun (N f.), Peh (P f.), Tzaddi (Z f.) – can take the value of the standard letter or of the final letter, e.g.; Nun final can be equal to 50 or to 700.
- **Ordinal gematria:** each of the 22 letters is given an equivalent according to its rank, one to twenty-two. Aleph (A) equals 1, but Lamed (L), whose absolute value equals 30, has an ordinal value equal to 12 as Lamed is the 12th letter. Kaph final (K f.) equals 23, Mem final (M f.), 24, Nun final (N f.), 25, Peh final (P f.), 26 and Tzaddi final (Z f.) equals 27.
- **Reduced gematria:** each letter is reduced to one single digit. Aleph (A) equals 1, Yod (Y) equals 1 (10=1+0=1), Qoph (Q) equals 1 (100=1+0+0=1). Beth (B) equals 2, Kaph (K) equals 2 (20=2+0=2), Resh (R) equals 2 (200=2+0+0=2). Therefore, the 27 letters have only nine equivalents, rather than twenty-seven. This reduces the three rows of numbered letters to the first row from 1 to 9.
- **Great gematria:** each letter involved in the full-out spelling of a letter is accounted for. The letter Kaph, for example, is spelled Kaph (K) Peh (P), giving it a value of 20 + 80 = 100.

In both the ordinal and reduced codes, the five final letters are generally equivalent to their value when they appear within a word. However, they are sometimes given an independent value, e.g.; the ordinal value of the final Peh is at times considered 16, and at times, 26. Similarly, its reduced value is at times 7, and at other times, 8.

The word *Chokmah* (HKME) for "wisdom" is measured in four ways:

- Absolute gematria: H8 + K20 + M40 + E5 = 73.
- Ordinal gematria: H8 + K11 + M13 + E5 = 37.
- Reduced gematria: H8 + K2 + M4 + E5 = 19 = 1+9 = 1

- Great gematria: HYT418 + KP100 + MM80 + EA6 = 604

Envisioning Wisdom

"Deep inside you are ten thousand flowers. Each flower blossoms ten thousand times. Each blossom has ten thousand petals. Each petal sings ten thousand sounds. — You might want to see a specialist." *David M. Bader, Zen Judaism: For You a Little Enlightenment.*

When reordering the letters of *Chokmah* (HKME) for "wisdom," I come to *Mah Koach* (ME KH) for "what force?" This is a question about respecting Power.

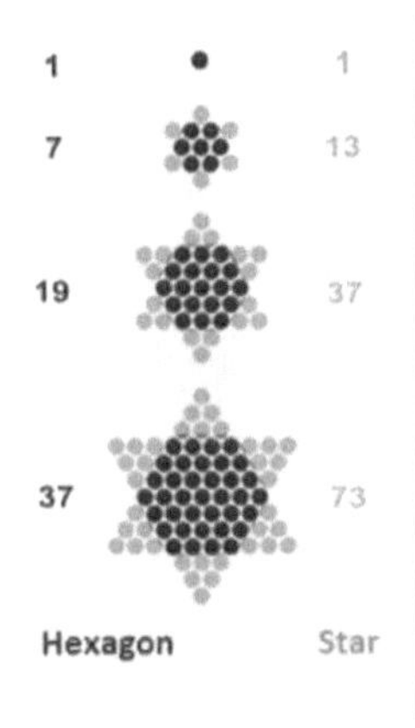

The value of *Koach* (28) is present in the first sentence of the Torah that has 28 letters and 7 words. The absolute gematria of the entire sentence is 2701, which is equal to 37x73 and also the sum of all numbers from 1 to 73. 37 and 73 are both prime numbers (numbers that never divide). To embody wisdom is to be primary, beyond divisiveness. This consciousness is shown here in the interplay of the numbers of dots in the stars and hexagons:

- *Chokmah* "wisdom:" absolute gematria = **73 (dots)**. Ordinal gematria = **37 (dots)**.
- *Halev* (ELB) for "the heart:" absolute gematria is **37 (dots)**. Ordinal gematria = **19 (dots)**.
- *Echad* (AHD) for "One:" absolute gematria = **13 (dots)**, moving into **One dot** as pictured above.

Envisioning Power

> *"What for centuries raised man above the beast is not the cudgel (weapon) but the irresistible power of unarmed truth." Boris Pasternak*

My Power issues are boundary issues. Fearing speaking "the unarmed truth," I go into excesses or deficiencies which enforces the belief that I am powerless. The gematriot of *Yirah* (YRAE) for "fear" and *Geburah* (CBWRE) for "Power" are both equal to **216**, which is 6x6x6. Might I be avoiding my leadership by giving my Power away because I am afraid that my 666-beast would have me violate borders?

Seen geometrically, Power is powerful. From a small triangle formed by three satellites of 6 dots (3x6=18), a core of 10 dots (the composite of 28) and 3 borders of 6 dots (the triangle's periphery comprising 18 dots), I continue growing the pattern. I will then come to the big triangle on the right which has three satellites of 666 dots (666x3=1998), a core of 703 dots (the composite of 2701 dots), and 3 borders of **216 dots**.

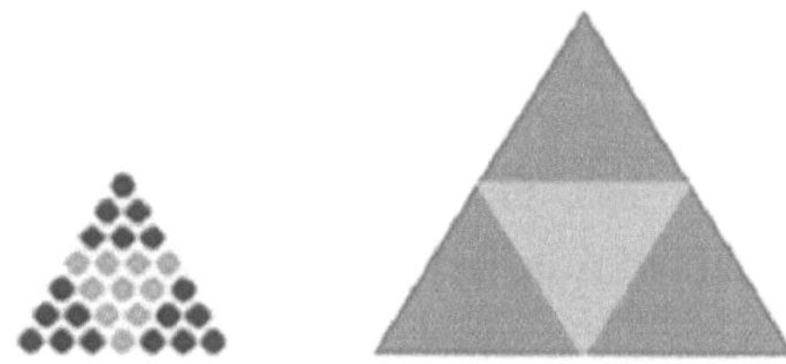

	Satellite	Core	Composite	Border
Small Triangle	6	10	28	6
Big Triangle	666	703	2701	216

The 666 satellites contained within the boundaries of the 216 borders evoke a wholesome use of Fire-Power. The 2701 dots and the 703 core dots resonate with the 73 of "Wisdom" – when "the force" is with me. I have seen how 2701 is the sum value of the letters in *Genesis 1:1*. It is also 73 x 37, both measures of "Wisdom." The "PAIRfection" of these geometries encourages me to inquire on my use of Power, and embody wisdom. This is the surest way to end the war of the sexes and come to the LOVE that has no opposite.

Envisioning the combined geometries of Power and wisdom brings a new light to TCO's inquiry: what if wisdom was the partner of Power (and not kindness)? Would the shift restore the proper functioning of the throat center?

The Numbers of the Law

"The tablets were the work of God; the writing was the writing of God, engraved on the tablets." *Exodus 32:16*

A world without writing is unimaginable. There would be no record keeping, no tax returns, but also no literature, no advanced science, and no history. Of all humanity's discoveries, the development of writing has had possibly more impact on the evolution of society than any other invention. But where and how did it start? Sumer is said to be the birth place of a form of writing called cuneiform for "wedge shaped." It seems to have been invented not for literature or holy scripture, but for accounting purposes. Could it be that writing is as unavoidable as death and taxes?

Indeed, my troubles begin when my accounting is divorced from "God's" accounting. I plan and "God" is laughing. This may be how there is a need for lessons in ethics, as given in the masonic rituals that use a ruler and a compass: "the square, to square our actions; the compasses, to circumscribe and keep us within bounds with all mankind."

The same idea is found in Chinese mythology via the first sovereigns Fu-Hsi and Nü-wa whose serpent bodies are intertwined as opposite forces. Fu-Hsi holds the square as he rules over the four-cornered earth. Nü-wa holds the compass pointing up to the circling heaven over which she rules. Square and compass are explained in the modern

Chinese phrase *kuci chü* meaning "the way things should be – the moral standard."

There seems to be a universal need for some form of divine law to regulate the human tendency to calculate for its own advantage. This is also how the birth of the Semitic alphabet (which became our modern alphabet) is linked to the revelation and the giving of the law: "the writing was of God." To transition from polytheism to monotheism and birth "God," a frontier had to be crossed. This Exodus needed the Phoenicians and Aramaeans to fervently assure the alphabet's widespread diffusion.

Thus, the Hebrews left Egypt and were given the tablets of the law in Sinai. This law allowed them to create a social structure based on the birth of a non-pictographic alphabet – an alphabet that would become the law of laws. Consider: communication is the *result* of what is said and done, and as such, the law of cause and consequence. However, while the writing was given, it was and is yet to be received.

The Letters of the Law

"Moses was there with LOVE forty days and forty nights without eating bread or drinking water. And he wrote on the tablets the words of the covenant—*the 10 Words.*" *Exodus 34:28*

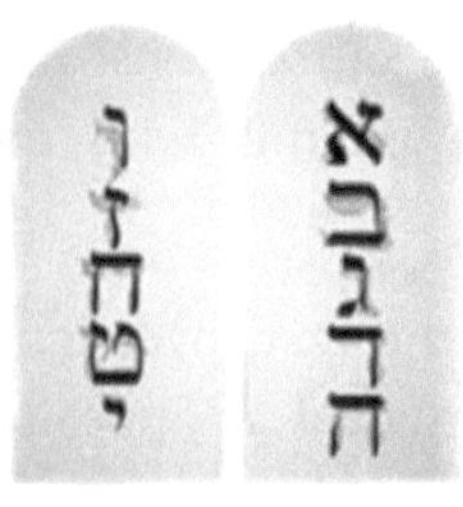

I set myself up to resist what I judge as an oppressive force when I think of "Ten Commandments" whereas the Bible speaks of *Esseret HaDebarim* – "the 10 Words." The idea of being commanded feels so coercive to me that I want to run. Even when I try to obey, my urges are so strong that I end up doing harm. Splitting the letter of the law from its spirit is how I become a slave to the material world.

Meanwhile, the "10 Words" simply refer to the first 10 letters engraved on the tables of the law (see previous page). These words say what they mean and mean what they say. Here is another example: Gimel – value 3 – is the "camel." It moves me to adopt a 3rd perspective by which to rise above the first two in conflict. The 10 are for me to join my 10 fingers in service to LOVE.

I still must address the difference in between being given the law and receiving it. I already spoke of the contraction that occurs when my letter Kaph (K) and "palm of the hand" closes in a fist and won't receive. As the 11th letter, Kaph follows Yod, the 10th letter. Yod is the giving "hand" symbolizing surrender and saying to the Self: "my actions are yours. I will not follow my private agendas anymore. I'll speak on your behalf, as your messenger." For the 11th to go to the 10th, I must ascend the alphabet and not just "fall" into it. When Kaph rises up to join Yod, my palm opens to "receive" the law. I can now be both: fulfilled and free. I just needed to return to innocence by rising back into Aleph's pristine unity one letter at a time, from Yod the 10th letter to Aleph – the First in the descent and the Last in the ascent, at my own rhythm.

THE 10 WORDS

1	
Opening	
1	א
10	י
100	ק

"And he wrote on the tablets the words of the covenant—the 10 Words." Aleph (א) is the 1st of the 10. Yod (י) is the 10th. These two words – Aleph and Yod – live in the same chamber of 1-Opening. As such, they work to open my mind and my heart to Self-knowledge.

When owning the projections, Aleph says: "I Am the LORD my God who freed me from the Land of Egypt and the House of Bondage. I shall not have other gods before the Self." Yod says: "I shall not covet…" (a long list follows). When seeing that Aleph and Yod are in the same chamber – on the same boat, so to speak, it occurs to me that the end of jealousy is the beginning of silence, when I am free to listen to my intuition – the "God" which ends all addictions. Surely, when I know who I Am, I don't covet anything. The rest of the "commandments" are details.

Could it be that simple? Would understanding the Power of 10 Words reveal the soul of the teachings (the QKabbalah) so completely that I could sense in my blood the body of the teachings (the laws) at work? That would be the end of suffering!

The 10th letter (י) is the word *Yod* for "hand," value 10. When fully spelled-out, the word *Yod* looks like this: יד. I can immediately see how small *Yod's* script is. Opposite to the tallest letter Lamed, Yod is the smallest. **However tiny, its flame has an immense purpose: to illuminate the writing of every letter, so that reading it would turn on the light. Thus the 10th letter initiates, sparks and is part of the story of every sign.**

Code Satisfaction Guaranteed - DY / YD

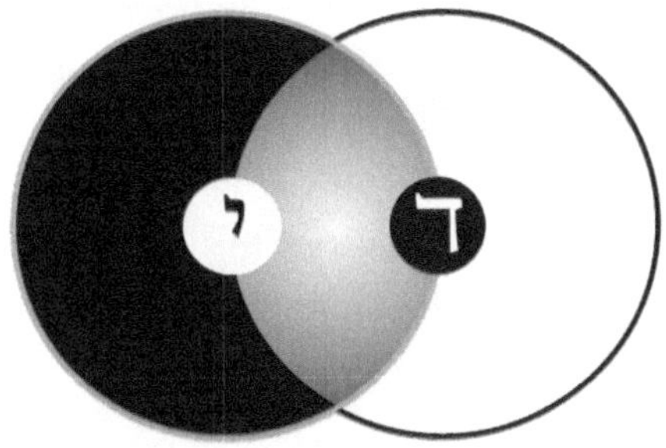

***Imagine a language so pure and so sacred that it can
reconcile opposites in just two letters...***

Right: Hebrew letter Dalet (ד) → D in Roman Script
Left: Hebrew letter Yod (י) → Y in Roman Script

Here is how S/Hebrew inscribes "satisfaction guaranteed:"

- **DY:** In one direction, I read *Dai* (די) for "enough."
- **YD:** In the other direction, I read *Yad* (יד) for "hand."

THE DECODING: "IF YOU WANT TO BE CREATIVE," SAYS JEAN PIAGET, A psychologist known for his work on child development, "stay in part a child, with the creativity and invention that characterizes children before they are deformed by adult society." Picasso concurs: "every child is an artist. The problem is how to remain an artist once he grows up." Might the problem also be how to grow up into a servant leader while remaining a child at heart? Growing up is to give my *Yod* **hand** and "sacrifice" (big word) my personal desires to make room for a greater vision. For me to know what St Francis of Assisi knew ("it is in giving that I am receiving"), I must evolve consciousness until I am **enough**, when satisfaction is guaranteed. The more I delay gratification, the more wholehearted is the offering of my gifts, and the more they are accepted. Sensing in my body that "less is more," I am able to hold the tension. Rather than insisting on getting my pound of flesh, I rejoice at experiencing the bliss of enlightened action. When I can sense that enough is "in off," I also sense when something is complete.

Noah's "Art"

> "What physics tells us is that everything comes down to geometry and the interactions of elementary particles. And things can happen only if these interactions are perfectly balanced." *Antony Garrett Lisi*

Since karma is no less than an accounting system, it is helpful to have a numerical alphabet that spells out how to do no harm. The letters being also numbers, they can assist me to be accountable to my word, and thus grow in self-esteem. Altogether, I'll eventually drop the shame body and reveal the light body that is beneath it. As for the GR of "GReed" that Gives and Receives fear, and the GR of "GRace" that Gives and Receives Love, it is the English code to transmit S/Hebrew נח (NH) for "Noah."

The pair of letters נח (NH) is also the first pair of "animals" that entered Noah's ark. As always, the pairings of S/Hebrew letters join opposites for me to see the miracle of one only thing - as above, so "belove."

Noah's "Art" was to listen to his heart, no matter how absurd it may have sounded to be directed to build an ark. His choosing to go within and hear the truth is marked by the letters themselves as the pair NH for "Noah" turns around to write HN or *Chan* for "grace." This mirror effect is at the core of *Genesis 6:8:* "But Noah (NH) found grace (HN) in the eyes of LOVE." I see it when I see with "the eyes of LOVE."

The story: observing that the earth is corrupted with greed, "God" decides to destroy all life via a flood. Noah was spared, as "he was a wise man, who walked with God." He is instructed to build an ark, and bring on it "two of every sort [of animals], male and female" and their food.

The decoding: several elements in the story allude to the medium of S/Hebrew being the message. The living word is the source of Noah's liberation from bondage to the material world (no need for greed or hunger), as it prompts a turn within:

- The word *Tevah* itself means "ark" but also "word." Noah entering the Ark is Noah entering the Living Word, that is, being authentic in his relating.
- The word *Basar* that is extrapolated in most translations as "animal" means "flesh" of the proverbial "Word made flesh," when my male and female sides (the pair of animals) balance giving and receiving.
- "Every living thing of all flesh, two of every sort" speaks of the letters going in pairs as non-biological sentient animals. Their message is consistent: "the way in is the way out. This is how to open to childlike wonder!"

The more I see how the non-biological lettered animals subsidize "the Word made flesh," the more my communication is like Noah's: coherent and "PAIRfectly" synced to my heart. I know what to do (build an ark!), and I do it as I know I am enough.

Noah – A Children's Story

"Poetry is as precise a thing as geometry." *Gustave Flaubert*

I remember being a child and projecting a light on my hands to form the shadow of an eagle... Since ancient times, Eagle has taught me to connect to my heart and see that which is invisible to the eyes. Its feathers are a most sacred healing tool, as Eagle flies closest to the Sun, illuminating a Truth that will set me free.

This same eagle, who inspires me to reach for the sky, grounds my action by suggesting a master code. Its head and wings are the digits of my left hand and of my right hand united in giving/receiving.

When the palms are facing me, the fingers of my left hand are to the right, and of my right hand, to the left. If I can't see the "PAIRfection" of what is given and received, it can only be because I want to fly solo, apart from Spirit's guidance. My right hand no longer knows what my left hand is doing, as my thumb (digit **#6**) chose to detach out of **Desiring** to pursue its own private goals. Incidentally, palmists hold that the thumb is the instrument of will.

Code Parental Guidance - AM / AB / BM

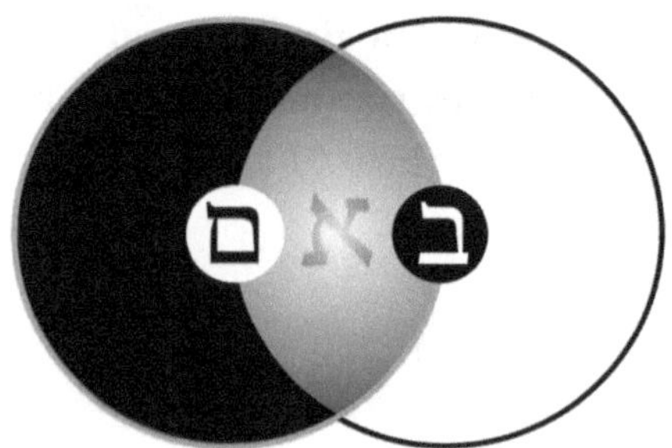

Imagine a language so pure and so sacred that it can reconcile opposites in just three letters...

Right: Hebrew letter (ב) Beth → B in Roman Script
Middle: Hebrew letter (א) Aleph → A in Roman Script
Left: Hebrew letter Mem final (ם) → M in Roman Script

Here is how S/Hebrew inscribes the code "parental guidance:"

- **AM:** from the middle to the left, I read *Im* (אם) for "Mother."

- **AB:** from the middle to the right, I read *Ab* (אב) for "Father."
- **BM:** joining right to left, I read *Bam* (בם) for "into them."
- **BAM:** from right to left, I read *Boam* (בּאם) for "they come."

The Decoding: I am Aleph (א) – invisible because I don't plan. I stopped moving long ago and have no conflicting desires. Indeed, my trust is so pure that I resist nothing and succeed in everything – even when it means to fail. I am simply grateful to be **"into them,"** as I listen to and follow their guidance. **Mother** is my body. She speaks to me in the voice of instinct. **Father** is my heart. He speaks to me in the voice of intuition. At last, I am in my sanctuary, emPowering the Now. I have built my inner temple, believing that if I did, **they would come.** And they did. The more I tune **"into them"** – and hear the communication of my instincts and intuition in my body and my heart, the more I read "FAMILY" as code for "Father And Mother I Love You!"

The Mother, the Father & the Child

It takes being a child at "heART" to see that the nine digits are the ten fingers of my two hands joined in pure action. This child may also be a little bit of a scholar and know that Latin *digitus* for "digit" first means "finger." When I imagine that each of my fingers is touched by the flame of Yod, I recognize that the nine chambers are also the nine-branch candelabrum which is only lit at *Chanukah* to celebrate the miracle of enlightenment. This miracle is the birth of the divine child – the anointment of a miraculous synchronicity, when I am no longer counting time but making time count.

The Father				The Child	The Mother			
9	8	7	6	5	4	3	2	1
Completing	Ordering	Engaging	Desiring	"PAIRfect"	Resisting	Changing	Separating	Opening

5 - "PAIRfect" and the Child

The numbered letters move in pairs as sentient animals for me to receive the 10 Words. Around the core chamber 5 – "PAIRfect" (the

Child) are four pairs, each adding to a 10: 4+6 | 3+7 | 2+8 | 1+9. **4+6** is the biggie, as I must balance my male and female sides (Father & Mother) in order to transcend and include **desire** and **resistance**. As these opposites harmonize, I shift from the motion of stages to the stillness of states. I am now simultaneously Changing *and* Engaging, Separating *and* Ordering, Opening *and* Completing, knowing the peace of Shabbat when the work is done through me.

As "fate" would have it, the word *Chanukah* also means "they rested on the 25th," referring to the fact that the Jews ceased fighting on the 25th day of the Hebrew month of Kislev. It makes me smile, as I see that both holidays – Chanukah and Christmas –are linked to the number 25, that they both occur in the midst of winter, during the darkest night of the soul, and that they both herald to the birth of a divine child.

The divine child of *Chanukah* is in number 44 – the number of candles lit throughout the eight nights of Chanukah. 44 is also the value of *Yeled* (YLD) for "child" and the sum of *Im* (AM = 41) + *Ab* (AB = 3) for "mom and dad." I am now well-equipped to begin my inquiry of 5th Word Heh which commands: "honor your father and mother." To feel such depth of honoring, I must relate to the words Jesus spoke to his parents: "why were you looking for me? Didn't you know I had to be in my Father's house? But they did not understand what he said to them." (*Luke 2:49-50*). To understand, the parents and the child in me must open to Code Enlightenment.

Code Enlightenment - DY / YD → E

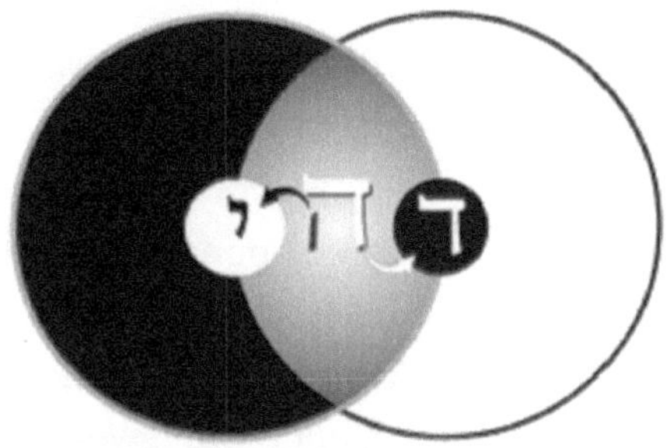

Imagine a language so pure and so sacred that it can reconcile opposites in just one letter...

Right: Hebrew letter Dalet (ד) → D in Roman Script
Middle: Hebrew letter Heh (ה) → E in Roman Script
Left: Hebrew letter Yod (י) → Y in Roman Script

Dalet and Yod combine to write the sign Heh (ה). This is how S/Hebrew inscribes the code "Enlightenment:"

- **DY:** In one direction, I read *Dai* (די) for "enough."
- **YD:** In the other direction, I read *Yad* (יד) for "hand."
- **E:** center, I read *Heh* (ה) for "window, breath." Heh includes both signs – Yod and Dalet – to say "being enough, my action is total. My action being total, I am enough to include both signs – male Yod within female Dalet."

The Decoding: to include it all is to open to the miracle of enlightenment, knowing that all is done *through* me and not *by* me or even *to* me. I am no longer identified to the body – no longer that which is dying. As I transcend the fear-based belief that time is money, I stop selling myself to the highest bidder just to make a living. I rest into being and experience right livelihood. At last, I stop recreating the "sins of the parents" – the voices I grew up with which I repressed and denied. I turn within and hear where I introjected them. Doing so eventually silences them. Taking back the projections, I find that I am no longer a victim of my biology. I am fulfilled and free, and SO grateful!

Persevering to the end is the greatest honoring I will ever extend to my genetic parents and, by extension, to life itself. This is the work – to grow up! When ready for how truth will change my life, I drop my story and forgive. The Heh (ה) "window" opens for me to "breathe," both "window" and "breath" being conveyed by the name Heh. I feel whole and complete. I relate to how Heh is the Hebrew equivalent of the Sanskrit mantra *Om Mani Padme Hum* ("the Jewel is in the Lotus"). It is the Supreme Container that holds the code of opposites and honors mother and father, on Earth as in Heaven.

The value of Heh is 5, five dots by which to trace the geometry of a pentagram. When the pentagram is doubled (5 + 5), I transcend and include the 10 Words – 5 for the left hand (the female side of the brain), and 5 for the right hand (the male side of the brain). This perfect pairing is conveyed by the story of patriarch Abram (אברם) and his wife Sarai (שרי) who became Abraham (אברהם) and Sarah (שרה) after a letter Heh became part of each of their names.

I have seen how Sarai was so angry to be barren that she became a worse patriarch than her husband. She abruptly sent away Hagar, the maid whom she had given to Abram to conceive an heir. She couldn't love the "stranger" – the meaning of *Hagar*. And yet, to create a double Heh, she must have

softened, taken a breath and willingly surrendered her love / hate relationship to the male (the Yod in *Sarai*). Yod's value (10) is equal to two Heh (5x2). With a double Heh, the couple could get pregnant and have a legacy. When this force is with both my male and female sides, I have a container, and don't fear being emPowered. Being enough, I succeed in my creation.

PART II: LIGHTS & SHADOWS

Below are the "enlightening" topics of this section:

- Sunlight and moon shadows – the male and female sides.
- The essence of shadow work – to return to innocence.
- The bumpy turnaround of *Teshuvah* – first, I initiate the turnaround (going from 10 to 9 to 6). Second, I understand a few basic "divine" perspectives (going from 6 to 4). Third, I feel and sense a "God" technology (going from 4 to 3 to 2 to 1). Lastly, I realize that resistance is futile. I will be assimilated (going from 1 to 0).
- Passing through the 11:11 Gate – the DNA of identities.
- The hidden map – how to transform the snake into a messiah.

The Sun & the Moon

"If the Sun and Moon should ever doubt, they'd immediately go out." *William Blake*

I am the sun and the moon – an electric being working with opposite poles that attract and repulse each other. For now, my wires are so crossed that I am not conscious of the nature of the feminine or the masculine. It is my ignorance of the code of opposites that makes me an addict, unable to hold the tension when the going gets tough. My attachments prevent me from working with the immense energy derived from having both my lunar feminine side and my solar masculine side developed to the point that they can give rise to each other. This inner marriage makes the outer marriage possible, as it gives me the sense of being connected to my heart, to nature, to friends, to life itself, to LOVE.

The harmonic balancing is reflected in symbols such as the yin and yang of a taijitu, the intersection of the arms of a cross, the two interlaced triangles of a tantric or Jewish star, and/or the snakes intertwined on a caduceus. These two snakes are the pillars of my temple; the sun and the moon illuminating how the feminine and the masculine interact. Both snakes evolve, until they can see face-to-face.

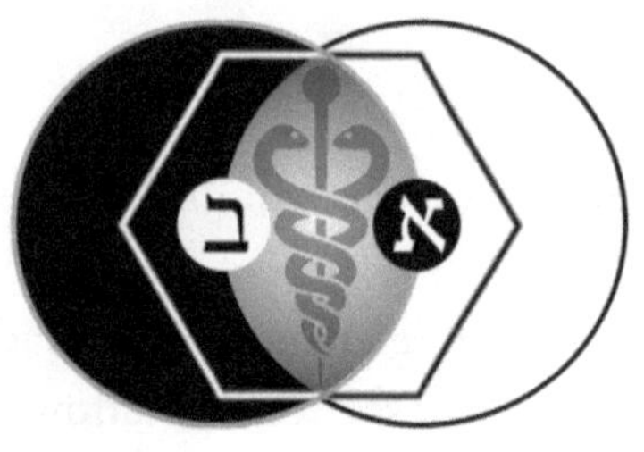

The message is universal: healing comes from within. The key to stop the fight is to embrace the shadow. Rejecting my darkness is also rejecting my humanity, pushing it down into the unconscious to then project it out for someone else to be the carrier of my own negated flaws. I will eventually meet truth face-to-face. For example, if we are One and everything is One, the world must be a reflection of me. Here's looking at you, kid! Also, since I create the world using my words, then the Word is equally a reflection of me. This is how I direly need to listen to the story I tell or squelch.

The above information has been known to mystics for centuries. Kabbalists use gematria in order to connect to perennial truths, and gain wisdom and wholesome Power. Far from being "airy fairy," the point of these calculations that join opposites is to ease an embodied sense of the paradox, e.g.; the value of the word *Nachash* (נחש) for "snake" is equal to the value of the word *Mashiach* (משיח) for "messiah." Yes, it is the same Snake that appears in Genesis 3. Here is a table for me to check it out:

9		8		7		6		5		4		3		2		1	
Completing		Ordering		Engaging		Desiring		"PAIRfect"		Resisting		Changing		Separating		Opening	
9	ט	8	ח	7	ז	6	ו	5	ה	4	ד	3	ג	2	ב	1	א
90	צ	80	פ	70	ע	60	ס	50	נ	40	מ	30	ל	20	כ	10	י
900	ץ	800	ף	700	ן	600	ם	500	ך	400	ת	300	ש	200	ר	100	ק

My First QKabbalistic Calculation

- The word *Nachash* (NHS) for "snake:" 50+8+300=**358**

- The word *Mashiach* (MSYH) for "messiah:" 40+300+10+8=**358**

The snake is "the craftiest of all animals" as it tells partial truths: "you won't die. Your eyes will be opened, and you will be like God, knowing good and evil." What it doesn't say is that it will take eons of working in consciousness to become so fluent in the language of paradox that I know good and evil. Such heartfelt knowledge gives me the "God" Power to embrace the evil in me and change. The same awakening is present in the Eastern teaching known as *Kundalini Shakti*, Sanskrit for "Serpent Power." Kundalini is represented symbolically as a serpent coiled at the base of the spine; a dormant energy waiting to be released through meditation techniques.

The Snake is the Devil. Both are known by many names. One of them – "the other" – came from the medieval ages. This name fills me with fear as corroborated by the Upanishads, "wherever there is other, there is fear." To wake up from the dream of separation, I must now make "THE decision" and choose to clear up shadow places. This is no less than awakening my inner messiah, who, for now, is asleep.

ONE DECISION

ONE DECISION; I'm always one decision away from a different life. I have that Power! Decisiveness may require real brokenness in order to arise. It will be hard. It'll get dark, messy and murky. I will have to face my demons, and yes, I will want to quit. That's shadow work. It's not about being perfect. It's about endurance, and also about freedom. I must love myself enough to free myself from the low self-esteem that lets *the other* be the author of my life. **"Low self-esteem" is the meaning of *Belial*, one of the S/Hebrew names for the Devil.**

———

The cycle by which I'll come to surrender is orchestrated by YEWE; the "LORD" of Karma and Power of Accountability giving me the same challenge until I remember that I am here (and "hear") to transcend my bond to the material life. Will I ever stop counting time or money? Will I ever stop calculating for the little self alone?

———

I am still resisting going out of business. I fear that, if I were to stop pushing to make things happen, I'd lose my shirt. I think that I'm the doer, boasting when I succeed, scolding me when I fail. I save or spend money out of obedience or rebellion against my programming, and then blame you for my poor ROI. I inhabit the realm of karma, a theory common to many oriental religions.

———

The word karma means both "action" and "consequences of actions." It is held to be a universal accounting system in which I must experience the consequences of my actions. These consequences are like a debt that can be carried over into future lives.

———

These are three types of karma:
1. **Portfolio** or the karmic debts accumulated from previous births.

2. **Redemption** or the debt I take out of my portfolio to work out in this lifetime.

3. **Acquisition** or new debt incurred in the present life.

Isn't it interesting how the vocabulary of the soul is mirrored by the financial lingo: bonds, trust, equity? The "LORD," it appears, calls me to "redeem" myself and "save" my soul by cleaning up my dangerous liaison to *Mammon*, S/Hebrew for "1. money, 2. yearning."

Small print: "the laws of karma are binding as long as one imagines to be separated from the Self. This separation feeds the yearning."

While in this dream-like illusion, I will go through a series of pre-ordained experiences, all consequences I have placed in motion through previous words and actions.

My only freedom is to realize that there is no one acting and no one experiencing. This is witnessing the eternal and all-observant I Am – the Self. At that time, the whole structure of karmas becomes obsolete, since there is no ego left to suffer from the consequences of my actions. My work is simply to remember who I Am.

Code Leadership - ESM / MSE

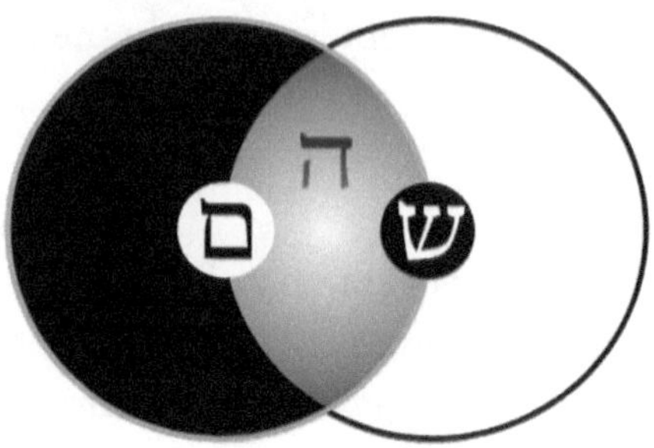

Imagine a language so pure and so sacred that it can reconcile opposites in just three letters...

Right: Hebrew letter Shin (שׁ) → S, Sh in Roman Script
Middle: Hebrew letter Heh (ה) → E in Roman Script
Left: Hebrew letter Mem Final (ם) → M in Roman Script

Here is how S/Hebrew inscribes the code "Leadership:"

- **ESM:** In one direction, I read *Hashem* (השם) for "The Name."
- **MSE:** In the other direction, I read *Moshe* (משה) for "Moses."

THE DECODING: LET'S SAY THAT MY NAME IS MOSES, A BIBLICAL NAME meaning "pulled out of the waters" of the unconscious. I am a motivational speaker about to give a talk on how to get free from slavery. Although I know that I am a born leader, here to inspire others to change, I find myself doubting my heart: "suppose I go to my people and say to them that you sent me. They'll ask me what your Name is." To which my heart said: "I Am that I Am. That's all you need to say. I Am sent me to you" *Exodus 3:13-14. Ehyeh* (AEYE) for "I Am" resonates with YEWE – the four-lettered Name that is so potent that it is casually referred to as *Hashem* "**the Name.**" For me, Moses, to be in my Power, I must turn around and go within. *It is the only way to know that I Am, literally.* "The medium is the message." The famous words from communication theorist Marshall McLuhan apply perfectly to a metalanguage that uses pairs of letters to model what I must do to be a leader: turn within to meet the Name (the call of my destiny).

Time and Money

"The power of mathematics is often to change one thing into another, to change geometry into language." *Marcus du Sautoy*

To change geometry into language helps me measure the height, depth and width of my motivations. By inquiring on why I do what I do, I go within and meet "the Name." This is how the letters of *Moshe* (משה) for "Moses" reverse into *Hashem* (השם) for "the Name." This is also how *Shemot* for "names" is the Hebrew title of *the Book of Exodus*.

S/Hebrew word *Shem* comes from Sumerian *Shumu* for "a rocket ship to heaven." It first appears in *the Epic of Gilgamesh,* a poem from ancient Mesopotamia that is held to be the earliest surviving great work of literature and the second oldest religious text, after the Pyramid Texts. Understanding *Shem/Shumu* is rocket science: how can words have the Power to fly me free me from the slavery of "Ego-Egypt?"

The gematria of *Shem* (SM) is 340, equal to the XPR root-verb that branches into words supporting the expression of consciousness: *Sephor* for "number," *Sippur* for "story" or sounds, *Sepher* for "book" or letters. The way into the "Name" is the way out of the story: fulfilling my destiny is how I rewrite my script!

As for the numbers, first came "the time code" that originated in Mesopotamia as the Babylonian sexagesimal (base-60) numeral system. This is how I calculate 60 seconds in a minute, 60 minutes in an hour, 24 hours in a day, and 360 degrees in a circle. Then came the "money code" which first appeared in Chinese and in Hebrew numerals as the decimal numeral system (base-10). Ten fingers on two hands is the likely origin of decimal counting. These two systems – the sexagesimal system of time and the decimal system of money – are entangled in the Nine Chambers:

- **10—decimal** becomes 1 by way of reduced gematria, 1 being the first of the Nine Chambers. The nine digits can also be organized as a square that elders called "magical," since each row, each column, and both diagonals all add to 15, 15 being the "magic constant" (see image below).
- **60—sexagesimal** becomes 6 by way of reduced gematria. 6 is the "problem area" as it is when the will (or right thumb) is compelled by the force of Eros – 6-Desiring. Consider: when I desire to serve the ego, I create unconscious time.

The "magic constant" of 15 also becomes 6 by way of reduced gematria (1+5=6). No matter whether I choose to view the Nine Chambers as a line or a square, I have a tool that can help me understand the beliefs I borrowed about time (60) and money (10), and begin to feel how these beliefs are just constructs.

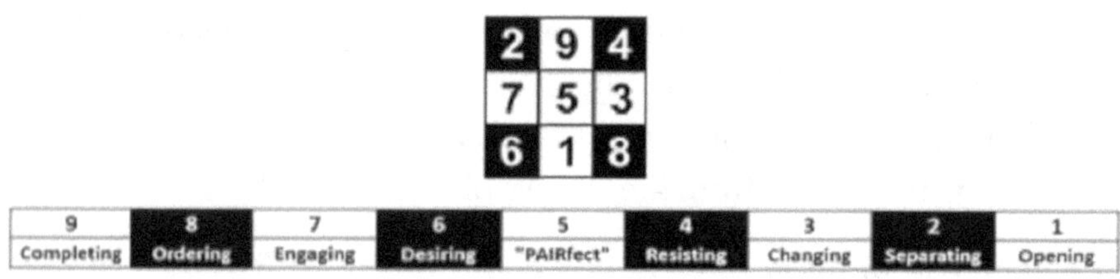

Fair and Square Accounting

As I become sentient in these two codes – the 60-based time system and the 10-based money system, I am more likely to drop the plan and return to being a child at "heART," open to Give and Receive by way of GRace, no longer GReed. Just like a part of "me" was compelled to emerge out of nothingness to be something, I am equally compelled to return to innocence.

This return is marked by a turnaround of the letters and the numbers, which sustain a hidden map for me to transcend and include mind, time, space and *Mammon* / money. Imagine... No more hankering or yearning; just the sense of enough!

When the letters turn around...

"It is not the strongest of the species that survive, nor the most intelligent, but the one most responsive to change." *Charles Darwin*

The words below "grew" out of rabbi Chananya's teachings, which are part of *Sepher HaZohar* – "The Book of Splendor" – a mystical commentary on the Torah. This inquiry, which I visited in *TCO—Book 1*, concerns the intentionality of the letters in creating change. Here is the story, reviewed.

When S/Hebrew was still embryonic and concealed as an object of divine delight, the Sovereign of o/i had contemplated how to play at creating a world with the letters. When o/i was ready, all the letters presented themselves in reverse order. Last letter Tav advanced in front, pleading to be placed first in the creation of the world in light of being the final letter of *emeT* for "truth." Since o/i was called "truth," it would be becoming to create the world by Tav. o/i (blessed be the Name) said: "You, Tav, are certainly worthy, but I can't create the world by you; for you are destined to be the associate of *maveT* ("death"), of which you are the final letter. Therefore, the creation of the world cannot and must not be through you." After Tav had disappeared, Shin, the sign before last, ascended and said: "I pray you, o/i! In light of Your great name being *Shaddai* ("S/He who is enough"), let it please you to create the world by me, by the holy Name that becomes you only." Said o/i: "oh, Shin, you are worthy, pure and true; but the letters of the word *Sheqer* for "falsehood" will associate themselves with you in order that you may be credited only with the appearance of truth. For this reason, I cannot create the world by you."

All the letters presented themselves in turn, and all were rejected: Ayin because it started *Avon* for "iniquity." Samekh, because its role was to "support" Nun the "fallen." This went on until came Beth's turn, who enthusiastically said: 'create the world by me, as I am the initial letter of *B'rachah* for "blessing." Through me, all will bless o/i, both in the world above as in the world below.' Said o/ı: "I hear you, Beth, and I will surely create the world by you only." This is how o/ı started the Torah with the upper-case Beth of *Bereshit* for "in the beginning" (it's very rare to see upper-case letters).

During all that time, first letter Aleph had remained silent. Said o/ı: "Aleph, Aleph, why didn't you come before me as all the other letters did?" Aleph replied: "o/ı, I observed that, Beth excepted, all have returned as they went, without success. Why, therefore, should I come before you, since you have already given to Beth the precious gift of creation so many of us crave and desire? Moreover, it becomes not the monarch of the universe to take back his presents from one subject and give them to another."

To these words o/ı responded: "Aleph, Aleph! You shall be the first of all letters and my unity shall be symbolized only by you. In all conceptions and ideas human or divine, in every act and deed begun, carried on and completed, in all of them shall you be the unity that precedes any beginning."

What would happen if I didn't try so hard to create "my" reality?

The Bumpy Turnaround

"When the truth gets buried deep beneath a thousand years of sleep, time demands a turnaround. And once again the truth is found." *George Harrison*

Most of the time, I am so hard on myself! Deep down, I think I'm a failure; never good enough! I just have to try harder, make things happen, conquer and never stop. Just reading these words is exhausting! So, when my insane severity drives me to burn out, I flip into indulgence. That's the only way I know to relax.

So why the obsession about creating the world? Don't I know that there's nothing "out there?" This is why o/ı (blessed be the Name) went through all the letters of the alphabet to finally arrive at the letter that initiates "Blessings," as Beth the Magician does. "My formula *Abra-cadabra* ("I create as I speak") works. However, there is a price to pay for using magic. For my conceptions to be immaculate, I must complete my ascent and reach Aleph. That is the only way that I will eventually let it B."

As long as I am split by conflicting desires, my work is not finished. I must dive into my shadow, deep enough to see my own light. The more I feel how I make the other my enemy, the more I can hold the tension between opposites. Shadow work is the practice to remain in the middle, learning from sign Mem – the "pairs of waters" that adopt the path of least resistance and succeed in everything. When my mind centers and stops moving, I can feel my Power. I can think, I can wait and I can fast.

The turnaround of the S/Hebrew letters eases my transformation. I simply accept these two things: 1. the WORLD is a reflection of me, 2. so is the WORD. By having the courage to look in the mirror and write down my judgments, I can tune in to the letter and/or archetype that is in the shadow and correct the places that need editing. Admittedly, this is hard work. Moreover, it never stops.

To make my accountability easier and *even possible*, the letters are also numbers. Feeling the archetypal soul of 10 numbers gives me an impeccable map and structure to do my turnaround. Moving me from 10 to 0/1, it leads me to embrace my binary black and white way of thinking, while ensuring that I won't miss a step.

10 to 9 to 6: Initiating the Turnaround

'After you've been doing inquiry for a while, if you have the thought "she doesn't love me," you just get the immediate turnaround with a smile: "oh, I'm not loving myself in this moment."' *Byron Katie*

The idea of *Teshuvah* is so essential to well-being that it is one of the three pillars of the Jewish religion. However, the word is often translated as "repentance" when it really means "turnaround." This turn is, indeed, when I take full responsibility for the results of my communication, stop blaming others for my failures, and open to love it all – "God" or reality, my neighbor and the stranger. I will soon see how the S/Hebrew word for "neighbor" speaks of my projections (the stuff I deny and repress), and how the word for "stranger" speaks of my introjections (the voices I borrowed).

XPR's turnaround occurs via a countdown from 10 to 0, using the physics and metaphysics of numbers. I begin with 10, go to 9, then curiously find that I jumped to 6. What happened to 8 and 7?

Number 6 happened! It is the force of Eros (the Vav of 6-Desiring) that splits my hands and prevents me from knowing the bliss of total action – when I am so absorbed by the action that I am free of the action.

- **How number 6 eclipses 7:** 7 cannot be separated from SIX, since the SIX "days" of creation complete in the seventh day known as the Shabbat for "rest."
- **How number 6 eclipses 8:** 8 is 4x2, four universal shadow archetypes and four universal light archetypes. These four are invoked by the Four-lettered Name, which *Elohim* (the Name that is created-SIX) includes and transcends. On that note, TCO's next chapter – Debugging the Oneness "Software" – will explore the DREaM code and the LOVE code as eight archetypes that transmit the Four-lettered Name.

As for "me," I must be real with what I create out of believing in lack and forced labor. Being locked in 6-Desiring freezes me into the egocentric stage, when I care only about myself and want what I want because that's what I want, regardless of how it may affect the whole.

The Mark of the Beast

"The perfect man employs his mind as a mirror; it grasps nothing; it refuses nothing; it receives, but does not keep." *Chuang-tzu*

When **6-Desiring** is not in a "PAIRfect" union with **4-Resisting**, I am miserable because I desire what I *believe* I can't have, and resist what I also *believe* I can't have. The operating word is "believe." I am yet to investigate why I chose to believe what I believe – in this case, that I am in lack! Desire now becomes a resistance to be without (the money, the girl, the food), while resistance becomes a desire to be without (the money, the girl, the food). Either way, I won't turn within nor do a turnaround to understand why I would choose, albeit unconsciously, to be in Scare City.

It seems absurd, as my ignorance leads me into temptation, increasingly making me a slave to my desires. I don't know that the fulfillment and the freedom I seek depend on my meeting and including the beast. This is what "she" looks like in code:

6	
Desiring	
6	ו
60	ס
600	ם

666: Vav (ו) is the line. Samekh (ס) is the circle. Mem Final (ם) is the square. 666 vs. 444 is psychologically what the squaring of the circle is mathematically: an impossible riddle! How could I join the circle and the square, that is, bring heaven on earth? How? I see the S/Hebrew alphabet as an ark hosting PAIRS of animals for me to be the life of One (10 = 1 + 0 = 1), e.g.; male 4-Resisting marrying female 6-Desiring (4 + 6 = 10 = 1).

I now have a real measure to transcend and include each stage. Eventually, the right and left sides of my brain merge, and the left and right hands unite into pure action. Free to be (1) and not to be (0), I succeed in my creation.

There may just be a code for life's perfection, a communication code by which to hear and understand myself. I just had to read the first word of the Torah. It was right there, "in the beginning," explaining to me everything I ever wanted to know about the number SEX, yet never dared to ask...

Code Communication - AT / TA

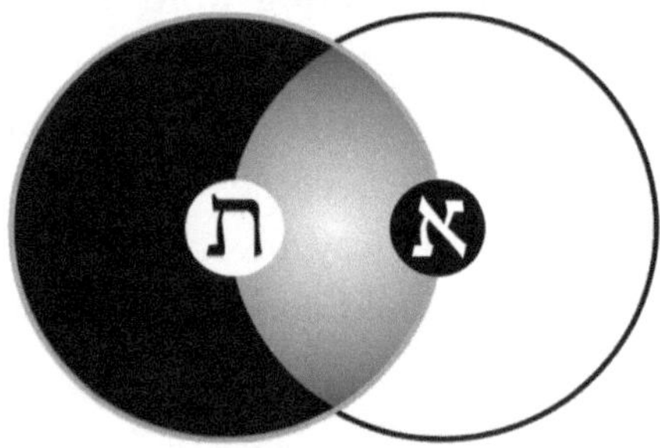

Imagine a language so pure and so sacred that it can reconcile opposites in just two letters...

Right: Hebrew letter Aleph (א) → A in Roman Script
Left: Hebrew letter Tav (ת) → T in Roman Script

Here is how S/Hebrew imprints the code "communication:"

- **AT:** in one direction, I read *Et* (את) for "untranslatable."
- **TA:** in the other direction, I read *Tah* (תא) for "cell."

The Decoding: authentic communication is epitomized in two letters, which happen to be the first and the last of the Hebrew alphabet. Being "the first and the last" is allowing me to transcend time, as I come to the end of dissatisfaction and thus the beginning of integrity. I am emPowering the Eternal Now. I don't plan. I just follow the Voice. Such detachment is evoked by an **"untranslatable"** particle as if to say: "The Torah that can be told is not the eternal Torah." The Torah's grammar places a particle before a direct object as if to remind me not to objectify the other. Surely, when at the end of greed, I have no wish to control anything. And since I no longer project scarcity or enmity, I don't misuse Power by playing games of dominance or submission. I am whole, "PAIRfect," complete and connected, cellularly. Each "**cell**" is now free to transmit and receive a message of appreciation for the privilege and the joy of being the Word made flesh.

John 101

"In the beginning was the Word, and the Word was with God, and the Word was God." *John 1:1*

Below is the original version of *Genesis 1:1* – "in the beginning, God created the heavens and the earth." The verb "created" has two direct objects: "the heavens" and "the earth." Both words are preceded by *Et* (את), the particle of Code Communication, untranslatable as I can't predict the Logos or the result of my communication. To optimize it, I must wait to feel it and see it in my cells, as *Et* reverses into *Tah*. I now hear "in the beginning, God created the Logos of the heavens and the Eros of the earth."

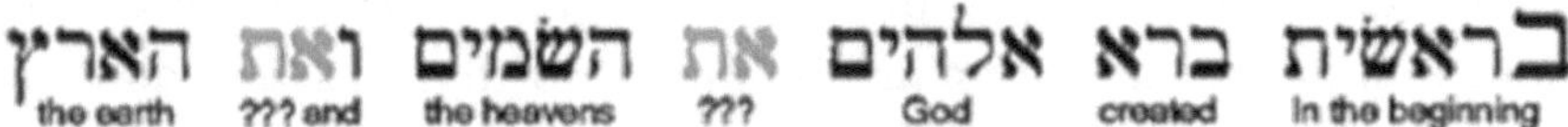

The True *Genesis 1:1*

It takes courage to face life's big questions and go deep enough to find answers. When I don't want to know the truth, I tend to stay on the surface. Either give me pre-digested answers or let someone else do the work – a Buddha, a Krishna, a Jesus, the neighbor... And yet, no matter whether I am a believer, an atheist or an agnostic (and whether I like it or not), I will one day find myself asking: where do I come from? Where am I going? What should I do? Who am I?

I have no choice. Evolutionary tension (which is now intensified by the complexity of the information age) will eventually compel me to explore consciousness. Is the world real or unreal or both? Is reality what I am seeing with my brain or what I am seeing with my eyes? Does it look like what I say it does? Moreover, if science is right – reality isn't set and if everything is mutable, why does it consistently feel so dense to me?

To accept that matter is immaterial, I would have to feel energy, which is problematic when I am used to objectifying things and even people. This is how it is so hard for me to think of language as being innate, and not as an artifact made by humans to communicate with each other. And it makes me wonder... How did languages develop and turn into such a complex matter so quickly? **And if languages can't help but to evolve, why did the Hebrew alphabet never change form since its inception? Might it be to help me transcend my creation of time?**

The Word "In the beginning!"

"Time is an encoded pattern of fabric woven with information and energy." *Vishwanath S J*

It takes one word to say "in the beginning" in Hebrew, not three. This word that is "in the beginning" is "the Word that was God and with God" as it holds the unifying equation that sustains the creative process. Being the first to be read and the last to be understood, it is loaded with information and energy.

Before discovering its pattern, I must share an essential aspect of the Torah's scroll. It bears no vowels to indicate how to vocalize words. Imagine doing a crossword puzzle and looking at a 3-lettered word beginning with a D and ending with a G. Which is the fitting vowel – a, e, i, o, u? Who makes the choice? Consciousness does, by interpreting the context. As consciousness matures, my perspective on how I "read" life changes. This is why there are so many interpretations of the Torah.

When reading Hebrew and seeing the word בראשית, I must decide (my consciousness must decide) how to read it. I have two options that are equally "kosher:"

1. *Bereshit* for **"in the beginning,"** [God created the Heaven and the Earth].
2. *Barashit* for **"Created-SIX,"** [God created the Heaven and the Earth].

The translation "in the beginning" makes sense to my linear mind. "Created-SIX" does not. I therefore dismiss it. However, I can't help evolution. I can't help the advent of the internet, and the possibility to learn about other traditions. I soon notice that, across cultures, the creation of "the world" involves elements. Studying these elements helps me make sense of how "God" would create the world by being "Created-SIX."

The metaphorical dimension of S/Hebrew is at work again. *Hashamayim*, the word for "the heaven," also means "fire-water." *HaAretz*, the word for "the earth," also means "air flow." So, in the beginning, not only "God" created elements, but also and foremost the *pairings* of elements. Fire-water, for example, are two energies that control each other: fire evaporates water and water extinguishes fire. When these two learn to do conflict gracefully, they convey the experience called "heaven." As for "air flow," it speaks of matter as being fluid and invokes the mysterious mind-body connection that can make my life on "earth" easy or hard.

Elements are a natural part of how all cosmologies (including science) begin to explain the creation of the universe. When combining the teachings of the three main religions which also offer a cosmology, I have a total of SIX elements that create "the world:"

- The four classical elements shared by Taoism, Hinduism and Judaism: fire, earth, water and air (which is metal in Taoism).
- The fifth element of Taoism: wood.

- The fifth element of Hinduism: ether.

Therefore, "Created-SIX" gives me a unifying equation by which to understand the SIX elemental "days" or stages of any creation – be it written in Chinese, Sanskrit or Hebrew, on Earth as it is in Heaven.

Immersed in the root of core languages, I trust that I have a comprehensive key to understand how to unleash my divine creativity.

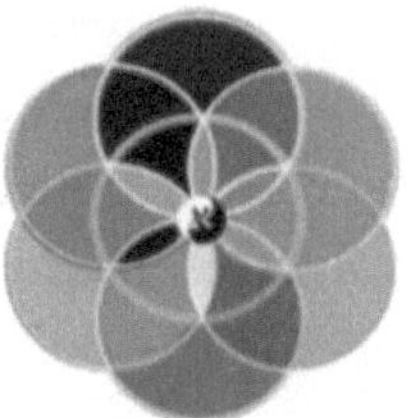

The Genesis Movement

To see the unifying equation of the "Created SIX" in color and the unfolding of the geometry of the SIX "days" of Creation, visit emPoweringNOW.com, click the seed logo and watch the mini-movie.

6 to 4: The Turn to LOVE

"The way you stretch the envelope of culture is by creating language." *Terence McKenna*

The turn to LOVE now takes me from 6 to 4. To understand it, I must be aware of the two core Names for "God" in the Bible, *Elohim* who is "Created-SIX" and YEWE, a.k.a. the tetragrammaton for "FOUR-lettered word."

Unbeknownst to many, there are several "God" names in the Bible, each name having a different QKosmic house and thus, a different address. The Name YEWE *Elohim* is a precursor before YEWE appears by itself. It issues the first command in *Genesis 2* (do not eat, or else). Naturally, if I'm Adam, I'm going to resent being told what to do, break the law as a result, which sets me up to lose PaRaDiSe. Since it leads me to create unconscious time, the Name YEWE *Elohim* is the Power of history. One crime leads to another (the famous "sins of the parents"). I am now Cain in *Genesis 4,* the first being to face YEWE, also the first being to be born mortal and destined to be a murderer. YEWE is *Hashem* "the Name." It is the Power of Accountability that will lead me to grow up, take responsibility and change my ways.

YEWE (Yod-Heh-Vav-Heh) is the Name of Names, the *Shem Hamephorash* or the "Ineffable Name." While it can't be vocalized, it can be realized, especially if it is felt and transmitted as a verb or a behavior. More to unfold in a bit.

For now, I wish to return to the entirety or "integrity" that loves reality with all my heart. The Hebrew word for "your heart" is *Levavkha,* which is written with two letters Beth. Rabbis have asked why the two Beth, since saying *Libekha* (one Beth) would have been enough to say "your heart." To be or not 2B: that was always the question!

Letter Beth answers by way of Code Integrity, informing me about the laws of form. Beth is the 2nd sign of the S/Hebrew alphabet. It has the numerical value of 2, and lives in the room of 2-Separating. As a word, Beth means "house" – *that which separates inside from outside.*

Beth is the essence of "boundariness," and boundariness, that which consciousness does: it measures known "things." For example, Eskimos have 28 words for "snow" as they need to consciously define "snow" in at least 28 ways. Thus, all words define perspectives. The more definitions and/or perspectives I can transcend and include, the greater my entirety and integrity.

Code Integrity – BBL-BLL / LBBK

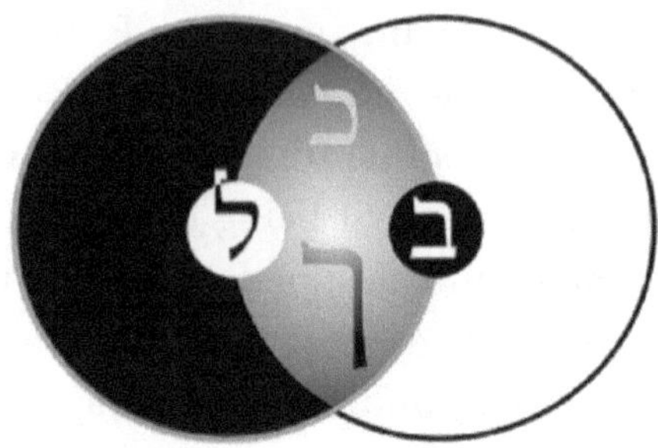

Imagine a language so pure and so sacred that it can reconcile opposites in just three letters, three words…

- Right: Hebrew letter Beth (ב) → B in Roman Script
- Left: Hebrew letter Lamed (ל) → L in Roman Script
- Top: Hebrew letter Kaph basic (כ) | Bottom: Hebrew letter Kaph final (ך) → K in Roman Script

Here is how S/Hebrew inscribes the code "Integrity:"

- **BBL-BLL:** from right to left, doubling the B, I read *Babel* (בבל) for "Babel" or Babylon. Doubling the L, I read *Balel* (בלל) for "confusion."
- **LBBK:** from left to right to bottom, I read *Levavkha* (לבבך) for "your heart."
- **KLB:** from top to left to right, I read *Kaleb* (כלב) for "dog."

The Decoding: to decode integrity, I must first understand my ambivalence as the separation of the "pairs of waters:" a part of me knows what to do, and the other doesn't want to do it. This disconnection is how I meet the Power of history, and repeat the same error while pretending to expect different results. The signs BBL/BLL of *Babel / Balel* echo my "babbling" sounds. I just doubled my suffering by creating my own **Babelic** chaos out of the **confusion** I'm in. But when I change my "evil" ways to turn to my heart and listen, I read *V'Khol Levavkha* "with all your heart," and include all hesitancy. As sung in the *Shema* prayer, the foundation of the Abrahamic religions: "And you shall love the LOVE God with all your heart, all your soul and all your might" (*Deuteronomy 6:5*). As for the **dog**, the medicine it brings to the soul of humans is obedience. This is how the letters of *Kaleb* for "dog" can also be read as "like the heart."

The Integrity of "God's" House

"In the Big Bang B-Beginning, God created..." *Genesis 1:1, adapted.*

As quoted by Ken Wilber, G. Spencer Brown wrote a book entitled *Laws of Form* which straddles the boundary between mathematics and philosophy. Brown makes the claim that boundaries are needed to create a universe – the dividing of inside from outside, which is exactly the sense of the word Beth. Brown (whose name starts in a B) had connected to an ancient Kabbalistic teaching which holds that the Torah must start with the letter Beth (*Bereshit* for "in the B-Beginning") to create the world.

Echoing the two signs Beth (2x2) in *Levavkha,* four perspectives can be recognized: "I, WE, IT, and ITS." These are at the core of Wilber's quadrants which divide interior from exterior but also the individual from the collective. The same four are known in the QKabbalah as the 4 letters Yod-Heh-Vav-Heh of YEWE (יהוה), a Name mostly translated as "the LORD" when it is in fact a process soon to unfold as the DREaM of LOVE for me to wake up into more "LOVE," more compassion and more care.

The roof of "God's House" pictured here is tiled by the יהוה tetractys whose Great Gematria is 72 or 10+15+21+26. Yod (10 = (י. Yod Heh (= (הי 15. Yod Heh Vav (21 = (והי. Yod Heh Vav Heh (26 = (יהוה. This number 72 is key to parting the sea of the unconscious, which TCO will eventually decode.

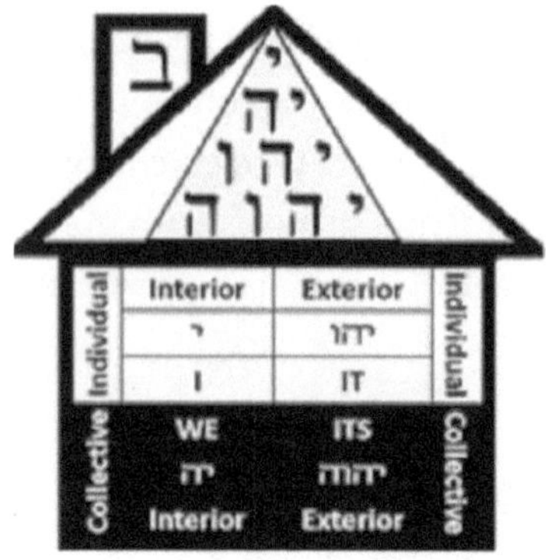

The walls are built by Wilber's AQAL, an acronym for "All Quadrants, All Levels, All Lines," All Types, All States as the main frame to support an integral metatheory. By aligning AQAL to YEWE, I see how the יהוה tetractys uses the Power of its letters to evolve the four perspectives, and thereby increases my chances to enter the "House of God:"

- **Interior** Yod (י) hosts the individual Power of a singular "I."
- **Interior** Yod Heh (יה) hosts the collective Power of a plural "WE."
- **Exterior** Yod Heh Vav (יהו) hosts the individual Power of a singular "IT."
- **Exterior** Yod Heh Vav Heh (יהוה) hosts the collective Power of a plural "ITS."

THE NUMBER FOUR

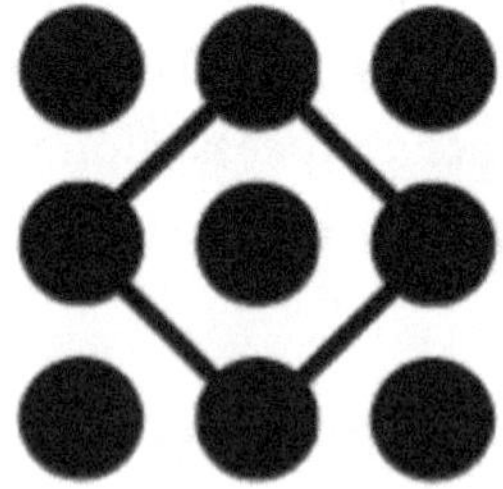

THE NUMBER FOUR is massive, which is how it resonates with resistance. In ancient China, the assumption was that the earth was square and the heaven was round. While the advent of astronomy changed everything, the felt-sense of the Chinese elders remained: the fair and square energy of the Earth.

There is an uncompromised sense of sanctuary to number four. The four directions evoke an equal distribution of space, and the four seasons, of time. Grounding evokes stability and presence. It is "fair and square," in love, war or business.

Such solid steadfastness is what gives potency to the *Tetragrammaton* or the "Four-lettered Name." This is the Name that is the most often used in the Hebrew Bible, appearing over 6,800 times. Held to be too potent to be uttered, it is replaced vocally in synagogue rituals by the word *Adonai* ("My Lord"), and in casual conversations by *Hashem* ("the Name").

Like the Tao that can't be named, YEWE is the *Shem Hamephorash* – the "Ineffable Name" which can be realized but not vocalized or expressed. It can only be pronounced once a year, during the Day of Atonement, and only by the High Priest. If it is at once mysterious and fit to invoke the Mystery, it is because its letters are semi-consonants, letters that can act as consonants or vowels. An example would be the letter Y that is a consonant in "yoga" and a vowel in "sky."

Eventually, a group of scribes (the Masoretes) placed the vowels from the word *Adonai* (AOAI) as dots and dashes under YEWE. They wanted to remind people not to read YEWE in prayers but *Adonai*. Unaware of the substitution, Christian writers mistakenly transcribed YEWE as

YEHOVAH, reading the vowels and consonants as they visually appeared. OYVEH!

The Masoretes' addition of dots and dashes does not concern the Torah scroll; only the regular prayer books. Since no one knows how to pronounce this YEWE (יהוה) enigma, it is called by spelling out its four letters: Yod Heh Vav Heh. On that note, *Golden XPR* does not write YHWH (which seems to be the consensus) but rather YEWE. This is so because the signs Heh (ה) became the letter E in Roman script. The letter H came from sign Chet (ח), which has no part in יהוה.

As for building a tabernacle or container... Consonants are female: they contain the light of the vowels, which are male. That is why the Torah is written without vowels, each symbol standing as a consonant, leaving it to me to infer the appropriate vowel. Choosing my sounds carefully is essential, as their raw male Power can easily turn abusive. Indeed, my words may convey the most profound truths, but if the tone of my voice is discordant, I will not be heard.

The tetragrammaton greatly puzzled Greek philosophers who invoked its Name in the Pythagorean Oath: "by that pure, holy, **four-lettered name** on high, nature's eternal fountain and supply, the parent of all souls that living be, by him, with faith find oath, I swear to thee."

Ever since the Greeks, scientists and humanists have attempted to organize consciousness in FOUR-based typing systems, in order to better understand the psychological preferences in how people perceive the world and make decisions. The most recognized systems include Hippocrates' four humors, Jung's four functions which sustain the Myers–Briggs Type Indicator (4x4), Keirsey's four personality types, and certainly, Wilber's four quadrants.

Joining numbers and letters, I may have enough gumption to wake up from the DREaM and realize that there is a QKosmic narrative that calls me to LOVE. To be continued…

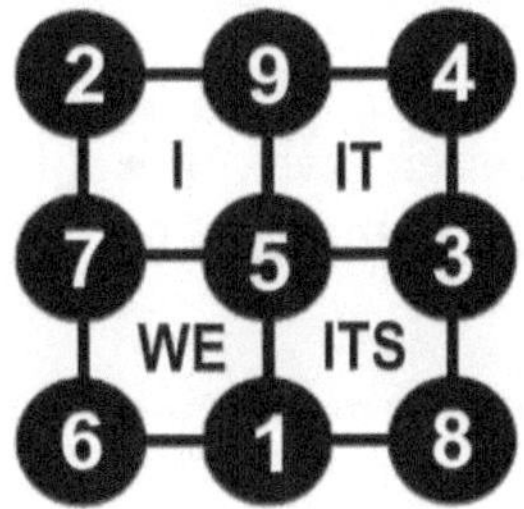

Code Self-esteem - RZ / ZR

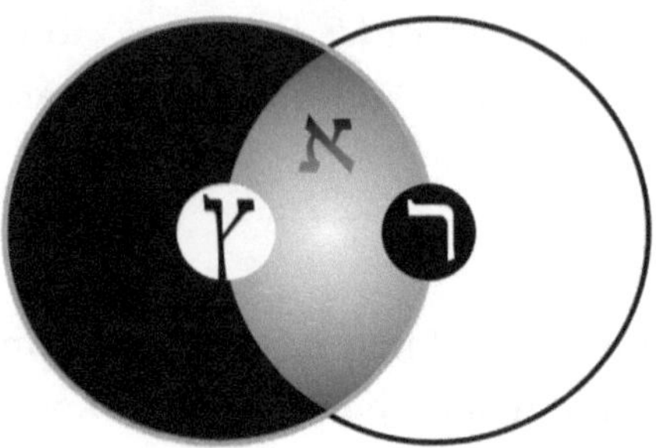

*Imagine a language so pure and so sacred that it can
reconcile opposites in just two letters...*

Right: Hebrew letter Resh (ר) → R in Roman Script
Left: Hebrew letter Tzaddi Final (ץ) → Z in Roman Script

Here is how S/Hebrew inscribes the code "Self-esteem:"

- **RZ:** in one direction, I read *Retz* (רץ) for "run."
- **ZR:** in the other direction, I read *Tzor* (צר) for "flint, knife."

The Decoding: I am in great danger! At any moment, I may accidentally stumble on the "House of God," and know that I belong. But no matter what I do, I always seem to go back to being an outsider. This way I can go on searching and questing some more. One day, I heard: "use your best **flint** and cut off the self-sabotage! Simply DECIDE that you are not accidental, that existence needs you as you are. Without you something would be missing that nobody could replace." I wouldn't mind having that much self-esteem, as long as I don't have to change! Moving out of Scare City is dicey. I may actually have to show up! Since I know where God lives, I just have to keep **running**, and make sure not to get too close. Then I'll be safe. Yet deep down, I know why I can never fulfill the vision of my soul: I'm just feeding my ego! I won't will the **earth** of my desires into being because I'm an addict of "not enough." Note: *Retz* is formed on the same root as *Ratzon* for "will."

When revealing the invisible Aleph that is in every word, I form the word *Aretz* (ארץ) for "earth." When my will on earth lines up with my will in heaven, I can hear that "heaven" is "having."

4 to 3 to 2 to 1: A Shift in Perspective

"There are things known and there are things unknown, and in between are the doors of perception." *Aldous Huxley*

The multitude of angles and/or perspectives that I can hold is what liberates my mind and frees my attention. Indeed, the most transformative question may just be: "is there another way to look at it?"

	Interior	Exterior	
Individual	י	יהו	**Individual**
	I	IT	
Collective	**WE** / יה	**ITS** / יהוה	**Collective**
	Interior	**Exterior**	

>

	Individual	Collective	
Interior	י	יה	**Interior**
	I	**WE**	
Exterior	**IT**	**ITS**	**Exterior**
	יהו	יהוה	
	Individual	**Collective**	

"It" is the image to the left of Ken Wilber's four quadrants (with TCO's addition of יהוה correspondences). The image to the right pictures the following two shifts:

1. I rotate the image 90 degrees to the left in such a way that "collective" and "individual" headings would now head columns instead of rows. The collective (WE as 1st person plural) now stands as the yin/female pillar, and the individual (I as 1st person singular) now stands as the yang/male pillar.
2. I flip the respective positions of interior and exterior in such a way that interior is on top and exterior, on the bottom.

I now will separate the individual column from the collective column by providing a space in between, where the reconciliation occurs.

Known as the middle path, this third column is the child of interior female and interior male. It is formed by the exterior of a neutral entity (IT/ITS as the 3rd person singular and 3rd person plural).

Interior Male	Exterior Neutral	Interior Female
Individual Power	Symbolic Power	Collective Power
I	IT / ITS	WE
Yod (י)	Yod Heh Vav Heh (יהוה)	Yod Heh (יה)

This Power works through two complementary flows (male & female) whose interface produces a neutral third that acts as a mediator on issues of authority. To bring the unconscious to be conscious, I play with two opposites. The friction produces a pearl in consciousness – the blessed child of the happy couple.

Consider the triad of thesis, antithesis, and synthesis... These three propositions move through a progression in which the first idea is followed by a second idea that negates the first. The conflict between the first and second finds its resolution in a third idea.

Having a framework that moves back from 4 quadrants into 3 columns, I can better understand the mechanics of the Power of Three. I see how individual and collective Powers oppose and complement each other, a process facilitated and mediated by symbolic Power. This is how forces interact, when the magnetism of the collective and the electricity of the individual balance as the electro-magnetism of symbols.

Indeed, the solution can be as easy as one-two-three. I am born to end the fight within. That's the journey of becoming conscious, a journey which I must make alone as I must meet the madness of the archetypal forces that run through me. These forces flow through three pillars. Understanding how they work together (3 to 2 to 1) helps me center in peace and, from there, make sound choices.

I CAN SEE 12 TETRACTYS (6 FOR THE female force, 6 for the male force) and infer 1 in the middle, behind Aleph that merges yin and yang. A tetractys conveys the force of the fourth by way of number 10, as it is a triangular figure consisting of ten points arranged in four rows: one, two, three, and four points in each row. I can also see how 10 tetractys form a larger triangle, and recognize the fusion of two such triangles, one up-pointing and one down-pointing, to signify "as above, so below." Note: if I were to picture the Power of three as a triangle, the two opposite factions would occupy the two angles at the base, and the transmutation occurs in the apex. By marrying the up and down triangles and forming a six-pointed star (each based on 10 tetractys), I would invoke the Sacred Marriage by way of six outer tetractys holding six inner tetractys. The next chapter – Debugging the Oneness "Software" – will focus on the interaction of these 12 forces.

In conclusion, I propose the following:

- **The Male I:** to acquire individual Power, I outgrow egocentrism (me, me, me) and rise into a QKosmocentric I-I, when I become one with all.
- **The Female WE:** to acquire collective Power, I outgrow fighting to be right and rise with you into a mutual listening of each other's positions.
- **The Neutral IT/ITS:** to acquire symbolic Power, I outgrow scientific materialism (IT is out there), and rise into realizing that there's nothing out there. I don't speak; IT speaks me. I don't sing; IT sings me. I don't write; IT writes me. Eventually all aspects of life are moved by multiple ITS.

Growing Up

"It takes courage to grow up and become who you really are." *E. E. Cummings*

Clearly, the child in me ought to grow up into a leader and take responsibility. But how? As I move from egocentrism to QKosmocentrism, the way I care also changes. Here is what I am looking to change and evolve:

- **The third person of nihilism** – this is when I disconnect from symbolic Power, perceiving that IT is a jungle "out there" and attempting to dominate the ITS of the world by way of denial.
- **The second person of control** – this is when I resent collective Power and treat "you" as an object, an IT. There is no sense of WE. I'm in a projection, either praising or blaming "you" in an attempt to create "you" in the image that I *think* "should" exist.
- **The first person of narcissism** – this is when I have no individual Power and no idea of who I Am as I can only focus on the glory of my own image, and calculate for my own advantage. I end up conjuring up failure as it is me minus the Self and even against the Self.

To free myself from the lower levels of the three pillars (the proverbial house of bondage and land of "Ego-Egypt"), I can let myself be guided by what Jesus taught as the 11th Commandment: "you shall love your neighbor as yourself." This commandment is to do shadow work. Here is how... **The S/Hebrew word *Rehekha* (רעך) "your neighbor" is formed on the root *Rah* (רע) "evil, wicked." Thus, when the Torah advises me to love the neighbor as myself, it is really saying "love the wickedness you see in others as your own."**

I must allow myself to look in the mirror deliberately, to see what I repress and deny. This means to consciously judge the heck out of the "neighbor," be it my parents, my siblings, my partner, my bank account, my body, my government – whatever causes me to be upset. Shadow work can be as easy as 3-2-1! The process of taking back my projections moves me from the 3rd person (when I lie to myself about some jungle "out there" causing me to suffer) to the 2nd person (when I directly focus on a "you" whom I blame for my failures) to the 1st person (when I know that I create it all).

The Power of Three

"When the power of love overcomes the love of power, the world will know peace." *Jimi Hendrix*

To stop misusing Power, I must first understand my fear of Power. Do I resist being emPowered due to my lack of tolerance for conflict, or am I afraid of the merging that would happen if I stopped existing as a separate ego? In other words, am I giving my Power away out of resisting rejection or death or both? Is that how I stay undecided?

Knowing that the female pillar stands for collective Power, and the male pillar, for individual Power, these two sides of me will fight to the death until I can honor both ways of being. Indeed, it takes two to make war, and one to make peace. Once I flow equally through both circuits, I'll feel how opposite forces work together and I'll invest my Power wisely. I will also be able to adopt two contrary perspectives at once: that of the collective and that of the individual, out of which a third will naturally emerge.

- **Collective Power** speaks to the group and adopts the perspective of a WE. It is the tribe I was born into; the family that tells me what to think, what to wear, whom to marry, what job to have, what to eat and how to spend money. While invested on this circuit, my desires do not matter as much as the desires that the group has for me. WE desire becomes "*I desire*" when I know what I want and why I want what I want.

This is the beauty of collective Power – to allow me to go to the root of my greed, and befriend such greed.

- **Individual Power** speaks to me alone and adopts the perspective of an I. I turn toward this Power when I come to enough dissatisfaction to begin asking the big questions – what is real? What's my purpose? Who am I? This is not an easy move as this circuit challenges me to be fully responsible for who I am being. "*I will*" myself out of the smothering parts of my tradition, when I successfully break the chains of society's repressive conditioning.

- **Symbolic Power** speaks as the IT / ITS by which to demystify the "G-d" label. "It" is defined as an inanimate thing, and "it" is used to represent something abstract and outside of me which I am yet to feel. Symbolic Power enacts the principle of the Logos behind the creation of the universe. It mediates the fight of the collective and the individual as follows: when "*I desire*" and "*I will*" see eye to eye, "*I know*" that I am the Word made flesh, and the flesh "*I have*" matches my words. There is nothing left of the personal. IT speaks me, and ITS many expressions are how I see the divine Logos – the "Son of God" – in all forms and structures.

Individual Power	Symbolic Power	Collective Power
"I will"	"I know" / "I have"	"I want"

The Conversation of Each Power

I will soon see that the 4 of YEWE can be reordered within the Power of Three, and be better equipped to understand how the four keywords (*I desire, I will, I know, I have*) help me hold the tension. Surely, misuses of Power occur when what I desire and what I will into being only serves the separate self. These four keywords belong to astrology. They also animate the soul of Ezekiel's vision. To be continued.

1 to 0: Resistance is Futile

"Resistance is futile. You will be assimilated." *The Borg. Star Trek*

From a purely physical viewpoint, I can't move in the void. Which means that I can't fall: where would I fall to? I can't rotate either. For my turn to be effective, I must have a reference point against which to assess my position. This role is played by the twin particle that hovers on the perimeters of the black w/hole, to either push against or pull from me. Evolution compels me to come out of the big nothing to become something, by contrasting myself and moving against "you." As I stage love and war, I can now feel something for good or bad, in sickness and in health.

It is also the first rule of this divine sport that I would forget that it was my decision to experience the tension of opposites. My mind gets so busy planning that the memory of who I am as pure choiceless awareness (neither this nor that, nor both, nor neither) starts to vanish. I am soon so full of questions that there is no space for an answer to come in. I must go back, empty my cup, even break it. When I am no longer, there is no one to stop the whole of existence to flow into me.

This emptying is the sense of the *QKabbalah*. This is also the Greek *kenosis* spoken of in Philippians 2:7 as "Jesus made himself nothing," nullifying his personal free will to become entirely receptive to God's perfect will. Nullification is zero, the numerical symbol of that which is without form and definition. It is the eternal mystery, both the known and the unknown, a delirious bridge between the physical and the metaphysical. It is the space beyond the breath – in between the thoughts, sounds and words. It is indivisible, without a beginning or an end. It is a void, where nothing exists but itself. Finite and infinite, first and last, smallest and largest; it can't be created nor destroyed. It is everywhere and nowhere. Multiply any number by it, and the result will become zero. Join it to a number and it will enhance it infinitely.

Zero is beyond any prototype; it is simple and transparent as pure being is. **It is purity itself.**

Cipher 0

The name *Zero* comes from the Arabic *Siphr* (akin to Hebrew *Sephirah* for "adimensional numbered sphere"). From *Siphr* came French *chiffre* for "number," and *chiffré* for "encrypted." By the 2nd millennium BCE, the Babylonian mathematics had a sophisticated sexagesimal positional numeral system. At first, a space between numerals was how they indicated the lack of a positional value (or zero). However, the placeholder was not a true zero because it was neither used alone nor at the end of a number. The ancient Greeks also weren't too sure about the status of zero as a number: "how can nothing be something?" It is this quandary that led to religious and philosophical arguments about the nature and existence of zero and of the vacuum.

The fear of annihilation is partly why it is/was so difficult to conceptualize zero. Moreover, emptiness can only be spoken of or written about metaphorically. And yet, while it is unspeakable, it can be directly realized.

The concept of zero as a number is attributed to India where, by the 9th century AD, practical calculations were carried out using zero and treating it like any other number, even in cases of division. Indian scholars used the Sanskrit word *śūnya* to refer to zero or void. Their minds were clearly capable of accepting the idea of emptiness. It must have been an awesome moment to realize that the "symbol for nothing" was not just a place-holder but an actual number, and that empty and nothing were actually real. The null number was as real as "3" or "2022." That is when the door blew open: without zero, there would be no modern mathematics, no algebra, and no science.

Ah, the realization of emptiness... Number zero calls me to enter the mysterious realm of the Infinite, where to lose myself into eternity, the zero-point of zero doubt, so null that it is denied as a characteristic –

Neti Neti "not this, not that;" just an ultimate witness observing what is arising. Not separate from anything, I have "no second" (nor second thoughts). I am the Emptiness of everything that emerges. Emptiness isn't a realm separate from other realms, it is the Emptiness or the Transparency of all realms.

The "nothingness" Buddhism calls *Śūnyatā* is known in Judaism as the three veils of the *Ain*. And it makes me wonder... Would I think in terms of "veils" if I allowed my ego to be nullified? Probably not... I would know that *Ain* is the meditative state where I am as if I am not. *Ain Soph* is beyond time, imagining no boundary, "Infinite." It is the gap in-between the thoughts, the silence in between the notes, the space in between the signs. *Ain Soph Aur* is "no end light," nothing, everything and not creating anything. The emptiness of *Ain* (אין) reorders into the fullness of *Ani* (אני) to mean "I" – the 1 that comes out of 0. This 1 is soon to move into 2 to 3 until it comes to 9, the ninth digit that marks a first completion.

Such is the force of evolution that compels the little something to come out of nothing. It is the complementary play of awareness and consciousness. The former is without dimension – pure and choiceless, all possibilities being free to manifest. Alive or dead: equal! The latter exists to make a choice and observe, consciously or not, a cat either dead or alive. Together, they pave the ground for optimal creativity, when I am totally here and totally not here – in the recurring tides of chaos until the path is made clear by the moon naturally shedding its light onto the darkness.

Code Life-Force - KL / LK

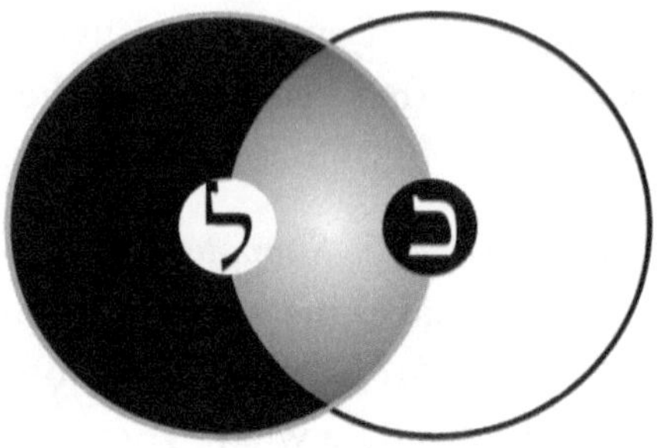

Imagine a language so pure and so sacred that it can reconcile opposites in just two letters...

Right: Hebrew letter Kaph (כ) → K in Roman Script
Left: Hebrew letter Lamed (ל) → L in Roman Script

Here is how S/Hebrew inscribes code "Life-Force:"

- **KL:** in one direction, I read *Khol* (כל) for "all, entire, integral."
- **LK:** in the other direction, I read *Lekh* (לך) for "go, let go."

The Decoding: Eros (from which comes "erotic") first appeared in ancient Greek philosophy to refer to sensual and passionate love. It also has the sense of "life-force." Where does energy come from? A minute ago, I had plenty of it and now, it's gone! To understand, I must feel how relentless the force of desire is that moves me to fulfill my passion and be with my love. Yet passion is fire-like; dangerous! To handle its life-force, I must get out of the way – nullified and assimilated. I must "let go and let God." It is the only way that I'll ever be able to let come and "receive" my beloved. Moreover, I cannot pretend or try to let go. I either do or don't, as surrender is only surrender when done **entirely**. When I do open and renounce my illusion of control, I realize that fulfilling my desires is not a function of seeing them manifested, but more of relinquishing them. "If you love somebody, set them free. If you love something, **let it go**. If it returns, it's yours (if only for that moment); if it doesn't, it never was."

This is a lot of peace, and energy, and **entirety**! Incidentally, the Torah portion where Abram's destiny is decided is called *Lekh Lekha* (**LK LK**). It is when he orients towards making the choice to give it all to LOVE.

11:11 – The DNA of Identities

"I am the Alpha and the Omega, the First and the Last, the Beginning and the End." *Revelation 22:13*

When I surrender to the Eternal Now, "I am the beginning and the end." But how do I let go of my attachments when I suffer from a loss of translation?

There is a language to Nature. Life evolves from a single cell via a genetic code – a language contained in the DNA that instructs human cells like it does bacteria. The very fact that everything is related hints to the existence of a universal code by which to be of One speech and One language – authentic in my relating.

If the journey to the infinite clearly begins in the first letter (Greek Alpha coming from S/Hebrew Aleph), there is a confusion as to its completion (Greek Omega never came from the last S/Hebrew letter – Tav). When misreading the signs on the way, I am ill-equipped to travel what Jesus experienced as "the Path of the Cross." Going up and down on the double helix of the Hebrew alphabet, I will eventually reach Hebrew Tav (or Greek Tau), and understand why Tav means the "sign" as it invites a crossover:

- **The crucifixion / curse-IS-fiction:** I "fall" from Aleph to Tav, until I touch bottom in Tav. I save myself by accepting the surreal intensity of my pain as my Passion. The clarification is electric; a huge shock. The religious experience is so profound that it blows the heart open and releases the desire for control.
- **The resurrection / ROSEerection:** I "rise" from Tav to Aleph, confirming what T.S. Eliot felt when he said: "and the end of

all our exploring will be to arrive where we started, and know the place for the first time." Aleph marks this place. It is the return to innocence, when I am home – in my body; incarnate.

There is something affirming about knowing that I will encounter a finite number of basic trainings (or deaths and rebirths) on my way to peace. Life is moving me up and down, from pair to pair, through serial initiations. Rising? Falling? Who's asking? Each letter is a number. Each number is imbued with an archetypal force. Each archetype has a complement that runs in an opposite direction. The clash of two conflicting viewpoints gives birth to a new interaction. Each time the two make contact, there is an evolutionary mutation that transports me to the next scripted stage.

The ATBaSh / ALBaM Codes

"At the deepest level, all living things that have ever been looked at have the same DNA code. And many of the same genes." *Richard Dawkins, evolutionary biologist*

The Hebrew Bible may just be an otherworldly harmonic transmission for me to resonate with the Mystery. The Torah letters work in pairs as if in a quantum entanglement, and are affected by each other's change. The letters act as particles that can be intimately connected to each other, as revealed by two essential codes – ATBaSh and ALBaM. In linking letters, the goal, once again, is to come to understand my motivations.

The ATBaSh code pairs the first letter of the first set of eleven letters to the last letter of the second set of eleven letters, e.g.; A to T, B to S, etc. The ALBaM code pairs the first letter of the first set of eleven letters to the first letter of the second set of eleven letters, e.g.; A to L, B to M). Both codes are interdependent and can be mixed.

ATBaSh		ALBaM	
A	T	A	L
B	S	B	M
C	R	C	N
D	Q	D	X
E	Z	E	O
W	P	W	P
G	O	G	Z
H	X	H	Q
Th	N	Th	R
Y	M	Y	S
K	L	K	T
First/Last QKode		11:11 QKode	

The ATBaSh could be called "the First and the Last" code. The process takes me from **AT/TA** (Code Communication), descending pair by pair until I come to **KL/LK** (Code Life-force). Each word and letter association leads me closer to embodying the experience of "the First and the Last." **The ALBaM** could be called "the 11:11 Gate." The process takes me from **AL/LA** (soon to be felt as Code Obedience), descending pair by pair until I come to **TK** for "deceit." Each word and letter association increases my honesty, thereby transporting me closer to knowing Health with a big "H."

Here is an example using the words *Ain* (AYN) for "nothing" and *Ayin* (OYN) for "eye." The question I ask myself as I hear these two words which sound alike is: what am I supposed to understand here? Using the ATBaSh code, the first letter Aleph (A) turns to Tav (T), and the first letter Ayin (O) turns to Zayin (G). Using the ALBaM code, the last letter Nun (N) turns to Gimel (C). Thus A, O, N turn to T, G, C. By revealing the invisible Aleph (A) that is part of every word, I now have **AT CG** – the inscription of the DNA pairs. These pairs come out of "nothing" for my "eye/I" to observe something. As for the middle letter Y, it turns into **M** and **S**, to form *Shem* for "Name." The message is to drop my story (which is my parents' story), the prerequisite to not be a victim of my biology. What is the calling (or the name) inscribed in my DNA? What is the something I conjured up out of the nothing?

DNA acts as a template for the production of proteins in my bodies. A DNA sequence is a long, continuous chain made up of only four chemical bases referred to as A, T, C or G. They repeat in various defined patterns to make up a gene. But sometimes a mutation occurs, when one of the chemical bases in a sequence is different from the usual pattern. This programming "error" is what creates problems.

The science of AT-CG: in 1944, an experiment performed by Avery, McCarty and McCloud proved that the DNA must "control" it all. When a species is incubated with the DNA of another, it changes. Watson and Crick next revealed the structure of the DNA molecule as a double helix, each helix being a linear chain composed of four different kinds of subunits called the DNA bases – the genetic code of AT-CG. Each strand of the double helix holds a sequence of these four bases. The four are linear blueprints to make the proteins of the body, encoded in the blueprint of the DNA as the building blocks of the body. All of a sudden, the genetic code was broken.

The religion of AT-CG: four in the Torah is the "linear blueprint" of YEWE, the LOVE and LORD of Karma. The Four-lettered Name is what places life and death, the blessing and the curse in front me, just like the DNA. The four are behind any possible pairings of letters. They live as the male's animus and anima, and the female's anima and animus. This leads me to the next pairing and building block of the alphabet. For eons, the first and the last letters of the S/Hebrew alphabet have been Aleph (A) and Tav (T). Both prophets Isaiah and Jesus were said to be the First and the Last; the Aleph and the Tav (AT) or, in Greek, the Alpha and the Omega.

- **Pair AT:** S/Hebrew word *Et* (את) means "untranslatable." It reverses into S/Hebrew *Tah* (תא) for "cell," or that which transmits and receives information by uniting the subject and the object (See Code Communication).
- **Pair CG:** S/Hebrew Aleph, Beth, Gimel, Dalet evolved into Greek Alpha, Beta, Gamma, Delta. In turn, Alpha, Beta, Gamma, Delta evolved into Roman A, B, C, D. And yet, while the 3rd letter Gimel (which means "Camel") evolved into the 3rd letter C of "Camel," it is mostly misheard and mis-transliterated as if were the 7th letter G. Similarly, while the 7th S/Hebrew letter Zayin evolved into the 7th letter G of "Gee

whiz," it is mostly misheard and mis-transliterated as the letter Z.

And it makes me wonder... Could the CG error be the mutation that affects my DNA? Is the CG pair where "the sin of the parents" lives which makes me a victim of my biology? And if this flaw is what epigenetics endeavors to correct, wouldn't I be better equipped to restore my instinct and rewrite my victor's program if I saw the hidden map of the DNA grammar?

Code Transformation - SB / BS

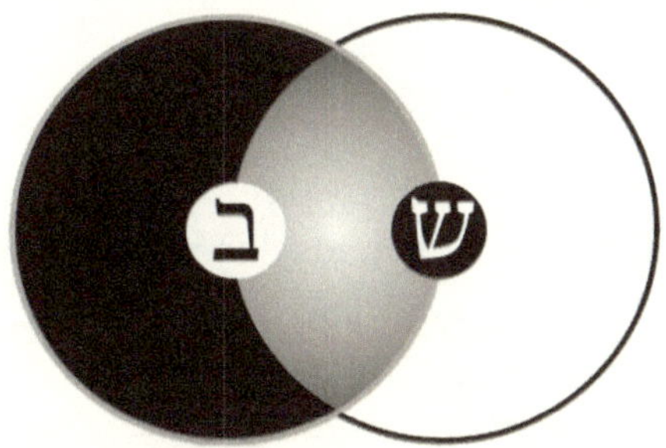

Imagine a language so pure and so sacred that it can reconcile opposites in just two letters...

Right: Hebrew letter Shin (שׁ) → S, Sh in Roman Script
Left: Hebrew letter Beth (ב) → B in Roman Script

Here is how S/Hebrew inscribes code "transformation:"

- **SB**: in one direction, I read *Shuv* (שׁב) for "turn, return."
- **BS**: in the other direction, I read *Bush* (בשׁ) for "shame."

The Decoding: I long to feel connected to the Paradise or spacetime where I can feel and sense my heart – a turn and return to innocence by which to fly free from the weight of **shame**. Going within, I see my misuses of Power morph into the light, taking with them all my regrets.

The work of transformation does involve a change of clothing, as I drop the shame body to reveal the "light body," *Bigdei Aur* in Hebrew. This body has other names – the diamond body, the rainbow body, the body of bliss, the immortal body, the resurrection body. I turn around to be reborn into the cellular knowing that my soul is pure and always was. I simply could not feel it before. Note: In between the first and last letters (**A & T**) are 20 lettered-stages which can be grouped as five families of YEWE (5x4). Four families develop the DREaM of LOVE, until they awaken into the 5th family of light. Beth (**B**), the 2nd letter, starts the first family. Shin (**S**) the 21st letter ends the last family. It is in light of its privileged position within **AT/TA** that the pair **SB/BS** is written to usher the **Code Transformation**.

Pairing Animals

"And when Abraham our father, may he rest in peace, looked, saw, understood, probed, engraved and carved, he was successful in creation." *Sepher Yetzirah*

Abraham is directly concerned by the pairing of animals since it is only after the letter Heh was added to his name and to his wife's name (ה+ה) that he could be successful in having a legacy. The double Heh is the ultimate pair as it is the core of the Nine Chambers. It is also the Word prompting the command: "honor your father and your mother." Once I am able to salute the divine in my creation of my parents (the beliefs about my parents that source all my projections), I'm likely to know myself.

5	
"PAIRfect"	
5	ה
50	נ
500	ך

Meanwhile, I can pair letters to give me the insights I seek. To this end, kabbalists have used a few techniques to "look, see, understand, probe" the limiting beliefs keeping them from being successful in their creation:

- The ATBaSh Code – replacing A with T, B with S, C with R, etc.
- The ALBaM Code – replacing A with L, B with M, C with N, etc.
- The ABCaD Code – replacing A with B, B with A or C, C with B or D, etc.
- **The Nine Chambers / vertical – replacing a letter with one of the letters in the same chamber, e.g.; pairing A with either Y or Q.**
- The Nine Chambers / horizontal – pairing A with Th, B with H, etc. This method works wonders to understand the 10 Words (or "Commandments").
- Look-alike – pairing or replacing similarly shaped letters, e.g.; Resh (ר) with Dalet (ד).

These seemingly obscure processes of pairing and/or replacing have one goal: to help me surrender my judgments. This idea is present in the root-word *Qedem* (QDM) for "East," which is also in *QaDMon* for "primary." By changing its letter Mem (M) into Yod (Y) by way of ATBaSh, I obtain *Yaqad* (YQD) for "to burn." This is the transmutation that occurs in the "East" of Eden, a place that seems to magnetize troubled souls (more to unfold later). Indeed, it is where the thought that "I am the doer" and, by extension, "not enough," auto-combusts!

The QKosmic Map

"The commonest dream symbol of transcendence is the snake."
Carl Jung

I know I'm ready to walk the territory. And now I seem to have found a map that leads me to be more comfortable with uncertainty. If I could only recognize that there is order in the chaos of knowledge, I may be able to hold the tension instead of getting all stressed out. So yes; I wish to hear and **understand** my position in the greater scheme of things and become aware of the patterning behind it. And to do so, I could use a form of inquiry that is universal, ecological and radical enough to be credible.

The changes I wish to experience are not limited to behavioral shifts, but also comprise a developmental advance to the level of consciousness where I can **choose peace** and thus **emPower the Now** by way of sound decision making. What I am speaking of is no less than embodied wisdom. Knowing how much work it is to free the soul from the shackles of indoctrination, I'm looking for a technology that offers empirical evidence regarding adult development over the lifespan.

And yes, this is where it becomes absurd. Religion is supposed to be the only human institution that speaks to adults about evolution. Moreover, it is meant to do so from generation to generation as it can be reproduced. So why the resistance?

Understand → **Choose Peace** → **emPower the Now.**

To be effective, religion must evolve its mandate to include ALL perspectives. This would provide understanding, and pave the way to peace. Religion would then emerge out of its current crisis with a new role – to emPower self-realized leaders, who, in turn, would have these two tools to effect change:

1. **An embodied sense of spirituality** to evolve their groups of believers until they come into the understanding that there's only One of us. The ability to choose peace at will naturally ensues. This is the "Promised Land" of enlightenment.
2. **A metalanguage that traces the map to the experience of embodied wisdom.** The fundamental truth of oneness will be mediated by the Art of sentience – when I feel and sense the reconciliation of science and religion from within.

This is the map of the Code of Opposites. Its matrix is encoded by a metalanguage that sustains Self-knowledge, as it includes all possible perspectives that consciousness can originate. Henceforth, as I increasingly "Am that I Am," it will be my choice (to use that word as a joke) to merge into non-being.

While such holy accident can happen at any time and in any place, it may still take the spacetime of this book for us to feel, hear and understand the decoding of its dots and dashes as the transmission of the fundamental truth of oneness. The map has 8 numbered spheres around 1 lettered sphere.

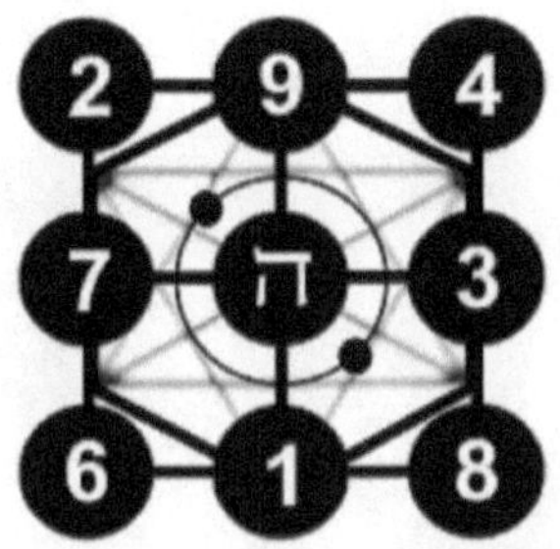

9	8	7	6	ה	4	3	2	1
Completing	Ordering	Engaging	Desiring	"PAIRfect"	Resisting	Changing	Separating	Opening

The implied digit is number 5. When in place, it allows for every line – vertical, horizontal or diagonal – to add up to 15. 15 is precious, as it is the gematria of the "God" Name *Yah* (YE=15) which circulates the frequency of wisdom throughout all the different bodies. 15 is also three times 5 – the value of letter Heh (ה) which is itself the S/Hebrew equivalent of the Sanskrit mantra *Om Mani Padme Hum* ("the Jewel is in the Lotus"). Heh is the Supreme Container as it holds the code of opposites and honors mother and father – on Earth as in Heaven. It ushers the divine birth into Spirit.

THREE

Debugging the Oneness "Software"

"Before software can be reusable, it first has to be usable." *Ralph Johnson*

HAVING LEARNED TO CODE, I must now address a few bugs in my "Oneness Program." In **Part I**, I will first check the foundation of "God's" House by going where science and religion concur: oneness is a fundamental truth. I will also discover how the codes embedded in the "Oneness" prayer – the Shema – take me beyond time by coming back from the future to announce the observer effect of quantum science. *Shema* means "hear and understand." This ancient prayer is at the core of the three Abrahamic religions. From there, I'll come to **Part II** – the Trinity Script by which to sense the nature of the turn from four to three. I can now better relate to how the Power of Three of the YEW(E) supports the Christian Trinity. As Christianity and Judaism begin to "hear and understand" each other, I may just begin to feel that "God" has no religion. :-) **Part III** introduces the universal archetypes – conscious and unconscious – that form the TWIN Code. This code joins two opposites (the DREaM Code and the LOVE Code) for me to "hear and understand" my shadow and light, and make sound choices via Twelve Disciples who only seek to help me grow in self-esteem.

PART I: THE FUNDAMENTAL TRUTH OF ONENESS

Below are the "connected" topics of this section:

- The House of "God."
- The Fundamental Truth of Oneness.
- Science & Religion – the true and the Truth of Oneness.
- Quantum Physics & the Shema.
- Code Perspective → the observer effect.
- Code Interaction → the quantum wave collapse.

Interior Male	Interior/Exterior Neutral	Exterior Female
Individual Power	Symbolic Power	Collective Power
I	IT / ITS	WE
Yod (י)	Yod Heh Vav / Heh (יהוה)	Yod Heh (יה)

The Potency of YEWE

At the bottom of this table is the unfolding of the YEWE, starting with Yod, moving into Yod Heh and completing in Yod Heh Vav / Heh. One of the most potent "God" Names in the Torah, its code transmits how to acquire Power, i.e.; to evolve consciousness. I will use it as the foundation of my inquiry.

The House of "God"

'When Jacob awoke from his sleep, he thought, "Surely YEWE is in this place, and I didn't even know it. Empowered, he said, "How awesome is this place! This is none other than the house of *Elohim*; this is the gate of heaven." *Transmission of Genesis 28:16-17*

WHILE TRAVELING TO HARAN, JACOB DREAMED OF A STAIRWAY TO HEAVEN, hearing God's voice calling him from the top of the ladder and repeating many blessings. Upon awakening, he named the place *Beth-el* or "the House of God."

However, when speaking of the House of God, which "God" am I referring to? The verse above takes on a different depth when I realize what Jacob says: YEWE is *inside* the house of *Elohim*. Jacob was seeing the four letters of YEWE (יהוה) nested within the "created-SIX" of *Elohim*. If YEWE is the "LORD" of Karma, *Elohim* is how to wake up from the dream of an overbearing fate. The SIX take me beyond Beth's duality as inscribed by YEWE, for me to inhabit Aleph's unity via *El* (אל), short for *Elohim*.

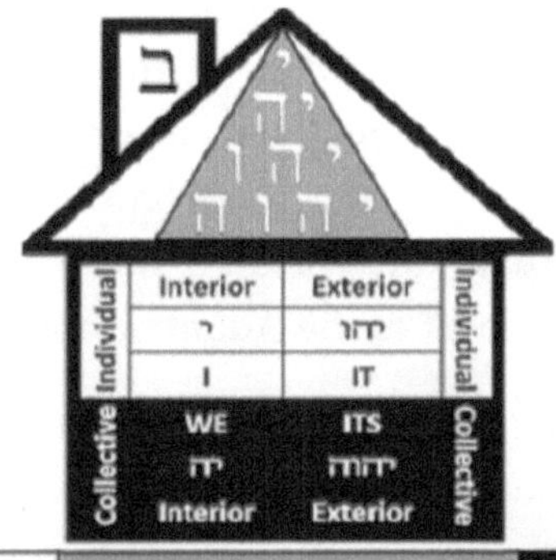

Beth-el, the House of "God," is built on the Power of Three: the foundation of Oneness

The Physics of Complementarity

"Anyone who wishes to innovate in the Torah is permitted to innovate and interpret everything he wishes, everything that he is lucky enough to innovate through his mind, as long as he does not innovate new laws." *Manifesto from Rabbi Nachman, great grandson of the Baal Shem Tov*

The complementarity of physics is both a theoretical and an experimental result of quantum mechanics. Niels Bohr, a leading founder of quantum mechanics, formulated it. The principle holds that objects have certain pairs of complementary properties which cannot all be observed or measured simultaneously.

I know that every quantum object is both a particle (like a tennis ball) and also a wave (like a wave in the ocean). The tennis ball is in several different places at the same time, until I try to locate it with measuring instruments. For at that moment, my quantum object is limited to one spot. This means that electrons, atoms, molecules, and even photons (light particles) are simultaneously particles and waves.

So are the two first letters (A and B) of the alphabet, and every pair thereafter. Just like the "alphabet" has an Aleph and a Beth, the Bible begins with two "God" names (or ways to handle Power), two Adams (or two different ways to create the world). Is this a cosmic joke? Might the split of the atom and the split of the Adam be complementary?

If the words "atom" and "Adam" strangely resonate with each other, it is because they are connected. The two Adams are two split "atoms:" they behave differently! If the particle is "good" (when I'm watching), and the wave is "evil" (when I'm *not* watching), having a felt sense of "double-slit knowledge" would be equivalent to surrendering my judgments (no more "no good!"). It would be to understand "particles" as the entity combining the characteristics of both particles and waves.

And it makes me wonder... Since both quantum aspects are one, why do I call this result the "wave particle duality" and not the "wave particle *non-duality?*"

When I don't resist the "bad," I begin to feel the synergy of complementary forces in lieu of their enmity, thereby increasing the probability of understanding my problems. Mirror, mirror: while new sciences found that there's something hidden underneath the physical world that is needed for its functioning, ancient traditions speak of a code hidden in scriptures that is needed to reveal the order inherent in the chaos of knowledge. This code encrypts the fundamental truth of Oneness.

The Fundamental Truth of Oneness

"If I go into the place in myself that is love, and you go into the place in yourself that is love, we are together in love. Then you and I are truly in love, the state of being love. That's the entrance to Oneness. That's the space I entered when I met my guru." *Ram Dass*

Let's focus on "you" for a moment. Do you ever ask yourself: what is reality? There seems to be an entry point into mysticism. Possibly you went through a break in time, and got to experience the mystical, such as nirvana, enlightenment, spontaneous healing, remote-viewing, kundalini rising, athletic feats, visions; the list is long! If you're human, it is also likely that you once felt awe at gazing into the eyes of a newborn or at seeing a radiant sunset, and lost track of your identity.

Yet, nothing is permanent: it is the nature of the linear continuum to bring everything to an end. Just like me, you may have found that the blissful moment passed, returning you to "normal" consciousness. Just like me, you may have asked yourself if there was a way to sustain the quality of presence you've experienced, when the inexorability of time was suspended and only the omnipotent Now existed.

For if there was a way, that would surely be a stunning miracle!

Whether I call them "miracles" or "synchronicities," I tend to speak of them to make me feel like I belong. This also says that I am doubting that existence needs me as I am. I don't really know that I am not accidental or that, without me, something would be missing in existence. I could also notice that synchronicities occur naturally when I am at peace and in love. The miraculous synchronicity is that everything does come out of Love. Love is One, feeling and sensing how $1 + 1 = 1$.

Seeing how natural this accounting process is, I still wonder: how would a quantum religion help me connect to this LOVE channel that emPowers both the giver and the receiver? Might I be asking once again how to transmute lead into gold?

Science & Religion

"If it [quantum science] is correct, it signifies the end of physics as a science." *Albert Einstein*

It is a paradox that science and religion would be archenemies when both recognize the truth of oneness. Science has evolved very fast, especially in the West, leaving behind a religion arrested in its development. And yet, while science gives us kickass demonstrations of what mystics have spoken about for eons, these proofs still don't seem to be enough for me to wake up from the dream of separation. When it comes to perennial truths – even when demonstrated, there is a disconnect between my body and my mind. I only seem to understand their wisdom in my head, but not in my blood. The true of science is not yet registering. Neither is the truth of religion.

If I felt the truth of Oneness cellularly, would I even perceive adversity?

It thus appears that the desire to evolve a religion that is stuck at a mythical level (and specifically the Abrahamic religions) has become a need. Besides, science does require a conscience to ensure that its inevitable progress would harmonize with the good of all. The key is therefore to advance the current *interpretations* of the holy scriptures so that their wisdom, once felt, would open the mystical 3rd eye that sees beyond duality. This happens to be the mandate of religion – to open the gate of the good. When I stop judging and am able to see the good in the bad, I am at peace. I can now let science open the gate of the true, and receive its demonstrations cellularly.

To this end, *the Code of Opposites* endeavors to do what philosophers – the "lovers of wisdom" – specialize in: deconstruct the inner dimension of the word, and by extension, its outer reflection in the world.

Just like there is now a quantum science that was able to deconstruct the assumptions of classical science, the time has come for a quantum religion that could deconstruct the assumptions of classical religion. My first quantum makeover would be to replace the plurality of laws with the One Law of LOVE which emerges out of the knowing that there is no law – just the Eternal Now. "If quantum science is correct, it signifies the end of physics as a science." Similarly, if quantum religion is correct, it is likely to signify the beginning of feeling oneness cellularly.

Still, I am intrigued. If the codes are the atomic level of the S/Hebrew scriptures, how could their frequency have transmitted for at least 3500 years a message that supports what quantum physics has only recently established?

'The coming world—having gone from "God Everywhere" to "God Nowhere"—is now slowly entering "God Everywhere" again, but the "God" that is "everywhere" is a different God indeed, at opposite ends of the spectrum of development from the original "God," and possessing few, if any, similar characteristics. This demands an entirely new language of God talk; a completely new way to communicate about these ever-present, all-pervading realities; and totally different versions of signs and symbols representing these wildly new, astonishing, shocking realities.' *Ken Wilber. The Religion of Tomorrow*

The Observer Effect

"And God saw everything that S/He had made, and, behold, it was very good." — *Genesis 1:31*

I know that experiments in quantum physics have shown that what is being observed in nature depends on choices made by the observer. Thus, why is it that "eye" would choose – consciously or not – to see what I think is "no good," e.g.; lack rather than plenty?

It appears that I default to the judgment "not enough" and identify with it. And since it is all a matter of perspective, when I find that I am again in a self-berating hole, I could ask myself if there is another way to look at it until I see another way to look at it. Indeed, what other script or parallel world would I like to observe? An enlightened mind is a fresh mind, willing to see both sides of the equation, when a dog is dead *and* alive at the exact same time as a cat is... or something like that! :-)

Such equanimity speaks in the language of paradox. It is the code of opposites, or that which communicates with "God."

Embracing a paradox is tricky, as it asks me to hold the tension between opposites. When the voice says: "I want sugar and I want it now, give it to me," I must have the courage to breathe and wait until the beast has moved on. Unless I stop judging, the most intense, negative and oppressive side will always win!

When I accept that there's only one of us, I also accept that any judgment I make is self-judgment. Therefore, what I am reading in the "text" of life is the level of consciousness that I occupy. The *measure* to which I see that "it is good" depends on how much I know that I Am LOVE. How far will I go for love?

When I live and let live, I stop interfering or meddling with my own process. This is easier said than done, for, without patience, I'm likely to try to push my evolution. Meanwhile, to help my practice of holding the tension, I have S/Hebrew's letters revealing how, in a "PAIRfect" world, everything goes in pairs. Heck, even I am "PAIRfect!" It's just a matter of perspective! :-)

Code Perspective - OD / DO

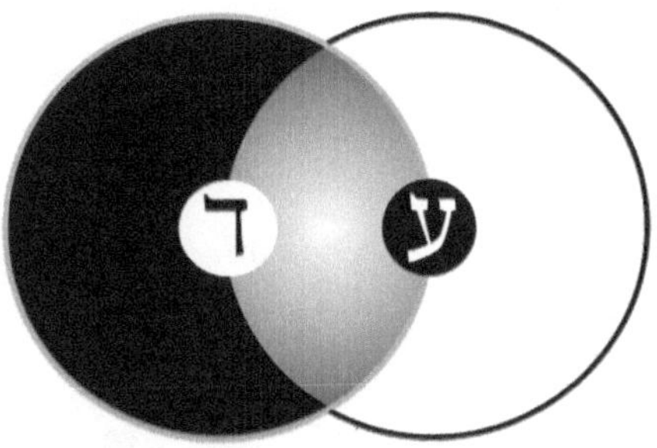

Imagine a language so pure and so sacred that it can reconcile opposites in just two letters...

Right: Hebrew letter Ayin (ע) → O in Roman Script
Left: Hebrew letter Dalet (ד) → D in Roman Script

Here is how S/Hebrew inscribes the code "perspective:"

- **OD:** in one direction, I read *Ed* (עד) for "witness."
- **DO:** in the other direction, I read *Da* (דע) for "knowledge."

The Decoding. I'll begin with the transcendental question: "is there another way to look at it?" Pure choiceless awareness is asking, in response to my contraction. It appears that I've just jumped into a judgment. I think I **know** something. But can I really **know** how my partner "should" or "shouldn't" be? When fighting with reality, I immediately feel hurt and separate – not at One with everything. I wish to have a non-evasive way to edit this false knowledge out of my genetic script. Indeed, when I view reality through so many judgmental filters, I can only be a false **witness.** While I recognize that I am yet to be so neutral that I can hold two opposite viewpoints at once (a cat at once dead and alive), I won't let me feel that I am attached to one side of the equation. There is a reason for me not to let go. When I become one with my hidden agenda – when I **know** what it is, **witnessing** another reality is matter-of-fact. I just had to become one with my resistance to take a "quantum jump" from one world to another... So, what do I not want to know?

The Source of Code Perspective

"Hear, O you who IS-REAL, LOVE is our God. LOVE is One." *Transmission of Deuteronomy 6:4*

Deuteronomy 6:4 is where Code Perspective lives. It the first line of the *Shema,* a prayer that is traditionally translated as "Hear, O Israel, the LORD is our God. The LORD is One." This prayer is at the core of the three Abrahamic religions. It is the credo of Judaism, the basis of Jesus' teachings and the root of *Ishmael,* the father of Islam named as "he who hears and understands." The prayer contains crucial codes given by enlarged letters which, once felt, point directly to the observer effect of quantum physics.

A shift in the size of a Hebrew letter is a rare event, meant to alert me to the presence of a pearl of wisdom. According to the Encyclopedia Judaica, there are only 29 places in the entire Bible where a letter is written extra-large or extra-small, or in scribal terms, in majuscules or minuscules. Here are two of them:

שמע ישראל יהוה אלהינו יהוה אחד:

The two enlarged signs above are *Ayin* (ע) for "eye" and *Dalet* (ד) the "door." They inscribe Code Perspective by asking: how true and knowledgeable a witness am I? Can I describe what is without making it mean something? As the word *Ayin,* I am the "eye" that won't see the truth, and would rather be in bondage to others than to live alone. As the word *Dalet,* I am a "door" wide-open to boundary violations. Consider, when unwilling to feel that my decisions cause more pain than pleasure to me and others (same), I am inviting codependency.

I am now truer to commitments made to others, which says that my decisions do not originate from the center of my authenticity. For my choices to be mine, I must hear that we are One and transcend the "HELLusion" of separation.

To help me, the prayer enlarges the *Ayin* "eye" of the word *Shema* for "hear," thereby combining two different learning styles: the auditive "hearing" of oral teachings, and the visual "seeing" of written teachings. I am now doubly equipped to touch the fundamental truth of Oneness. Especially as the *Shema* must be sung or spoken with closed eyes for me to be as Lady Justice, "hearing/SEEing" truth from within... **Sense and senses: who would I be if I perceived beyond what I think "should" be?**

Code Interaction - DR / RD

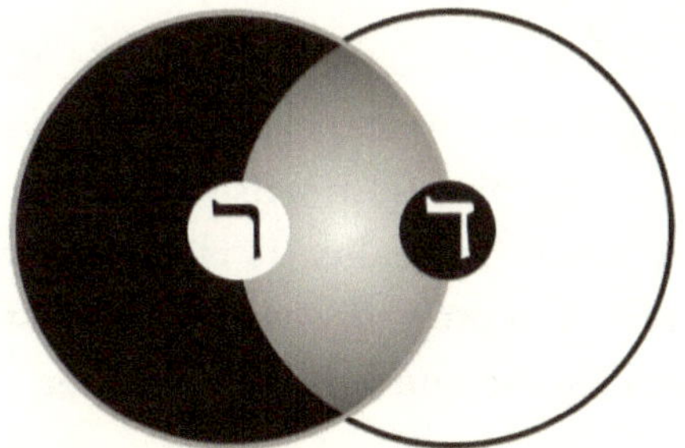

Imagine a language so pure and so sacred that it can reconcile opposites in just two letters...

Right: Hebrew letter Dalet (ד) → D in Roman Script
Left: Hebrew letter Resh (ר) → R in Roman Script

Here is how S/Hebrew inscribes code "interaction:"

- **DR:** in one direction, I read *Dor* (דר) for "generation, habitation."
- **RD:** in the other direction, I read *Red* (רד) for "come down, sink, collapse."

The Decoding: if pair Ayin and Dalet inscribes the observer effect, pair Dalet Resh inscribes the wave function collapse. In quantum mechanics, a wave function collapse occurs when a wave function goes from a superposition of several states to a single state out of interacting with the external world. Psychologically speaking, a collapse of the wave function occurs when I make a judgment, for good or bad. Out of the myriad of possibilities (the **generations**), my consciousness selected one (it **collapsed** it)!

When I dream that the world is external, I am not conscious of being in a projection. I project my stuff because I have been conditioned by rigid ideas of what is good and evil, moral and immoral, acceptable and unacceptable. To make this false knowledge my truth, I had to stop feeling and sensing. To this end, I needed to break the compass of both my instincts and my intuition. **This is how I created a "devil" (a word whose etymology is "to throw across"). It is also how I created "idols."**

The Devil: by making others my scapegoat, I take away my healing abilities. The Idols: by worshipping false sense impressions (e.g.; portraying myself as a victim, when, in reality, it is my story that sources the bullying world I see), I protect my vested interest in being sick or harmed. Either way, I am the **one** fighting the **other.**

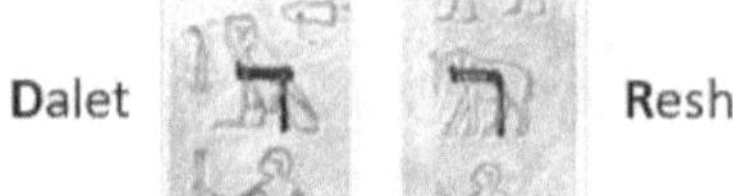

Dalet and Resh are coupled by their physical resemblance. And yet, if the two were swapped, the result of the communication would be very different. Here is how: rabbis stated that prolonging the pronunciation of the **Dalet** of *echaD* ("one") while reciting the *Shema* blesses one with good health. However, if I were to misread **Dalet** and pronounce the **Resh** of *acheR* ("other"), I'd invoke idols (the "other" gods) and conjure up illness.

The more I hear the *Shema* and understand that there's only **One** of us, the more I accept that any judgment of **others** is a projection of the self-judgments I deny and repress. I will eventually take back my projections, starting with "God" as the giver of rewards and punishments. I will then extend a new respect to all my **generations**, propelling me into a time paradox where **the one** and **the other** are interacting. Remembering what I knew as a child (there's nothing "out there"), I will also put an end to the question: why is there evil in the world?

PART II: THE TRINITY SCRIPT

- Why CAN'T I?
- The YEWE of Karma is behind the Power of Three as my guide to shadow work.
- The Trinity – when the four become three.
- Nothing personal... but the pronouns!
- When the Mother does "matter."
- Understanding Jesus' words – "going to the Father."
- The Sex Question.
- How to open the three gates of the Eternal.
- The Three Pillars of Buddhism and Judaism.
- The Power of Fulfillment → Freedom → Decisiveness.

Yod (י)	Vav Heh (וה)	Heh (ה)
I	IT / ITS	WE
Individual Power	Symbolic Power	Collective Power
Science & the true	Art & the beautiful	Religion & the good
The Father	The Son / the Mother	The Daughter

The Name YEWE is one of the most potent "God" Names in the Torah.
Its code transmits how to acquire Power by allowing me to feel the
Power of Three expressed via the Trinity and the Gates to the Eternal.

WHY CAN'T I?

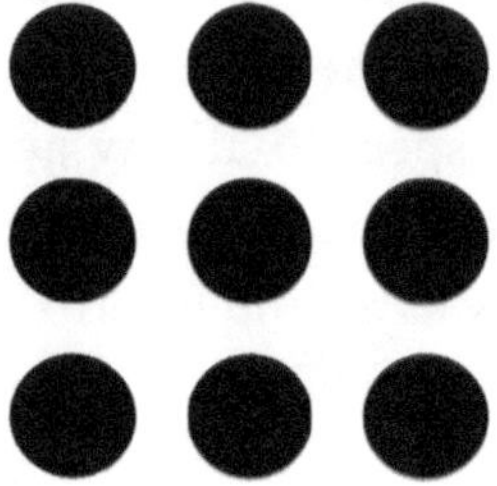

WHY CAN'T I turn within, where I have control? I can see that the more I distract myself, the more I create a separation between my desire and its fulfillment.

Frustrated, I start wondering: am I just a cog in the wheel or can I create my preferred reality? Let's say that I want to buy a home... To do so (and whether I am aware of it or not), I must work in consciousness until I have acquired enough Power to be bigger than the fear of having or not having a home.

If I want to change, I must look at the story I tell. Why tell myself that I am powerless to change? I want Power – I resist Power. I'm so afraid of what I would do with it if I had it that I end up incapacitating myself. The fear of doing harm or of getting burned with this "Fire-Power" is why I choose to think I CAN'T.

Separateness. I am here. And you are there. The disconnect feels real to me, even when I know about the illusion of separation – even when I love the world that the word "connectedness" opens for me. If only I could feel *in my blood* that there's only One of us... But I can't stop judging which is how I can't stop doubting myself.

My female side? She says too much and tends to overtly push when I perceive that my male side doesn't want me. **Feeling displeased**, the "woman" in me desperately clings, over-gives and gets intoxicated by her verbosity.

My male side? He doesn't say enough and tends to covertly pull away when I perceive that my female side is needy. **Feeling trapped**, the "man" in me coldly withdraws, under-gives and isolates behind a loud wall of silence.

It's not just quantum physics that has a measurement problem: I do too! Whether too much or not enough, pushing or pulling, I'm still misusing Power and still not having my results. If I could just relax and end this war of the sexes that has me fighting "you," life, reality, God... If "you" have such Great Power, why don't you release the feminine and, by extension, the masculine from the bonds of exile?

And it makes me wonder... Who are "Thou?" Why CAN'T my female side find the fulfillment she desires, and my male side, freedom? For being fulfilled and free would be like conjugating the LOVE verb in real time. I'd be fluent in the grammar of the Trinity script.

Nothing personal... except for pronouns!

"And there's a God-sized hunger underneath the laughing and the rage. In the absence of light, And the deepening night, Where I wait for the sun, Looking east. How long have I left my mind to the powers that be? How long will it take to find the higher power moving in me?" *Jackson Browne*

IF I DIDN'T MAKE IT ABOUT ME, WOULD I GIVE MY POWER AWAY? Languages are meant to help me communicate with others. As such, might they serve the purpose to change my narrative from separateness to the unity that sustains interdependency, that is, from little I to big I? Surely, all languages include three basic perspectives by which to view the world and/or "God:" a 1st, 2nd and 3rd person, singular and plural.

- The 1st person is the person speaking (I singular, we plural).
- The 2nd person is the person being spoken to (you singular, you all plural).
- The 3rd person is the person or thing being spoken about (he, she or it singular, they or its plural).

In the manifest world, there's only perspective. Perspective is how "I" create my personal reality, *reality* being another name for "God." Therefore, what is the world, what is "God" and what is creation? Do I think of "God" or reality as an "I," a "we," a "Thou," an "it?" Do I pray? Do I look at the sky when praying?

- **The 1st person** is conscious of the individual I – *Atman* in the East; *Ehyeh* in the West as the transcendental Self. I am aware of thoughts, feelings and sensations as they arise. I can witness them without becoming attached. The ego personality dissolves and, *Shalomasté,* I identify with the divine in all things. There is nothing and no one that is not me. I participate in inscribing the seamless code of the world, which is how I know that it is my nature to be LOVE.

- **The 2nd person** is all about relationship. I have a "You" to whom to talk, a companion who may answer me. I resonate with a living presence – a cosmic intelligence with whom I can have a personal relationship. It is the "Thou" to whom I surrender, sacrifice and release: "not my will, thy will be done." It blows the mind how I can enter in such intimate communion with another: "I am my beloved's and my beloved is mine" *Song of Songs 6:3*. Held in a divine embrace, I become accountable to that presence.

- **The 3rd person** sees "God" as the great principle of life. When a He, I may say: "The LORD is my shepherd. He restores my soul." *Psalm 23*. When a She, "she is the body that encircles the Universe." *Charge of the Goddess*. When an IT, "life does more than adapt to the Earth. It changes the Earth to its own purposes." *James Lovelock*. "IT" is mysterious, as IT can be a single organism that transcends reason (as Gaia is). IT can also be the rational understanding of "God" – its naturalist scientific view. Lastly, IT is the IT known by the artist: "I am not writing. IT is writing me."

Pundit Ken Wilber is who merged the 2nd person "you" within the 1st "we" perspective, arguing that there is no separate "you" but only a "we" when you and I understand each other. However, when making a "you" statement, the other is treated as an object. Thus, the vision of "I, we/you, it and its" which Wilber pictures as a quadrant.

The framework below superimposes TCO's matrix over Wilber's quadrants and its four perspectives – I, WE, IT / ITS. When I see that the world is not made of random nonsense, but that it has recognizable and universal intelligences that map out how to move beyond my self-imposed limitations, I am more likely to surrender my illusions, and not try so hard to control me, you or it.

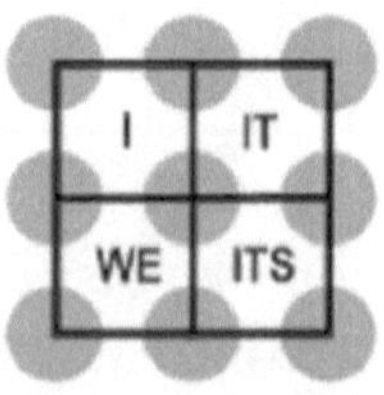

I	IT / ITS	WE
Individual Power	Symbolic Power	Collective Power
Yod (י)	Yod Heh Vav / Heh (יהוה)	Yod Heh (יה)

This matters as ideally, all three perspectives to look at "God" arise together. On my way to acquiring Power, I may tend to privilege one perspective over the other, like the petitionary prayers I make to a 2nd person "God," a "Thou" who either rewards me or punishes me. Surely, many religions claim that **communion** ("We/Thou") is the only way since **identity** ("I") with "God" is impossible. Henceforth, many mystics got crucified out of saying "I am God." Jesus was one of them. However difficult it may be to disentangle myself from collective Power and individuate, it is the only way I can take full responsibility for my experience. Growing up is waking up!

I	IT / ITS	WE
Individual Power	Symbolic Power	Collective Power
Yod (י)	Yod Heh Vav / Heh (יהוה)	Yod Heh (יה)
Identity	Union	Communion

Communion to Identity to Union

There is no avoiding it: to live in the timeless Now, and broaden my experience of reality, I must come to what the Sufis call "the Supreme Identity." Hereafter, I find myself naturally including the 2nd and 3rd person in my relating to "God." The closer I get to individuating, the more I move freely through these perspectives. Seeing that they are all correct, I open moment by moment to the fundamental Truth of Oneness. Therein is the experience of **union**.

And I still wonder... How can identity or union be possible when the feminine is in exile and is ghosted out of the Trinity?

The Mystery of Sex

"The secret of the Alliance [of male and female] is the letter Yod."
Moses ben Jacob Cordovero

Gentle warning: while the esoteric quality of this page may cause me to nod off, I will still produce the brainwaves allowing me to "receive" the information subconsciously.

Cross-culturally, religious symbols represent the divine union of the male and female as the macrocosm and microcosm ("as above, so below"). This merging is present in symbols such as the taijitu, the cross, the tantric star (a.k.a. the star of David), and more. In Hinduism, the female yoni is usually shown with the male linga to represent the marriage of the feminine and the masculine that eternally recreates all of existence. Sacred texts speak of the yoni and of its connotations to the vagina, vulva and uterus as a symbol for the origin, the abode or the source of all life. For example, the Vedanta text Brahma Sutras metaphorically refers to Brahman as the "yoni of the universe."

Key figures in the historical development of the Kabbalah wrote about the erotism of YEWE, from Joseph Gikatilla (13th century CE) to Moses Cordovero (16th century CE). Cordovero passed his leadership to Isaac Luria whose teachings revolutionized the conceptual system of Kabbalah. And yet, a certain "shyness" – to call it that – took out the Mystery of sex, regeneration and death from the sacred יהוה. This prudence could only affect the Christian Trinity. The Father and the Son remained, but the Mother and the Daughter disappeared.

Yod (י)	Vav Heh (וה)	Heh (ה)
Fire	Air / Earth	Water
The Father	The Son / the Mother	The Daughter
I	IT / ITS	WE

"The secret is that the lower end of letter Vav is known to all masters of wisdom as the small letter Yod." Joseph Gikatilla, Gates of Light.

I have seen in **Code Enlightenment** how the letter Heh (ה) is the hub of the eight-spoke wheel, as it comprises a Dalet and a Yod that write into being the sense of enough as the end of dissatisfaction. As such, it is the Supreme Fulfillment of the Feminine. As for letter Yod (י), the Supreme Freedom of the Masculine, it extends into letter Vav (ו). Therefore, if Yod is a metaphor for the Father's seed, Vav is its conductor as the instrument of connectedness – the Son inseminating the 2nd Dalet, linking her to him through the mystery of impregnation. **On that note, understanding is the feminine going from barrenness to fertility.**

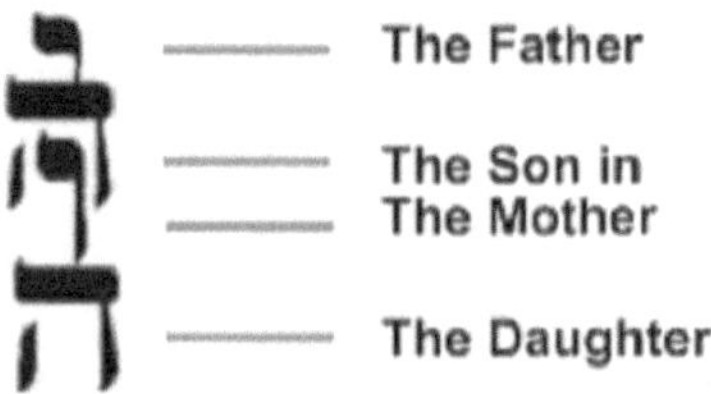

The Name which is shown here as the lower tip of Vav (ו) penetrates the womb of a Dalet (ד), being "half included in her and half included in him," and appearing inside the Dalet as a Yod or drop of seed which transforms the Dalet into a Heh.

These esoteric teachings on the four-lettered Name were known to Jewish mystics and passed on to Christian mystics. It is likely that, in the passage, some "things" got lost. While YEW was conveyed as the Father, the Son and the Holy Ghost, the Mother was removed from the equation. It also became unclear that the Holy Ghost was female as the "Daughter" of the Father and the "Bride" of the Son.

Meanwhile, I seem to have made a habit out of turning off the Voice of my conscience. This is how I deform the mystical teachings that invite me, whether male or female, to be *Bat Qol* for "daughter of the Voice" – someone who follows the Voice. And now that I ghosted the Voice, I'm missing out on the soul of prophecy and wondering why my own voice can't gain a trust and a hearing. This is a major bug to my Oneness software! By abandoning my femininity, I no longer have a womb-like container to hold the tension. How then could I succeed in my creation? Sending the feminine into exile makes it impossible for me to fulfill the law (a.k.a. my soul contract). Ironically, being unfulfilled is how I am so frustrated with me, you and IT, and work so hard at dismissing the "matter" of the law.

Yod (י)	Vav Heh (וה)	Heh (ה)
The Seed	The Phallus / ~~The Womb~~	~~The Womb~~
The Father	The Son / ~~the Mother~~	The Holy Ghost

Wombless & Hysterical

Releasing the Mother

"Only by discovering and loving the goddess lost within our rejected body can we hear our own authentic voice." *Marion Woodman*

It takes consciousness to allow myself to feel and sense, and know these functions as my "wife." It takes consciousness and the awareness of a container. For without a container, I won't stay present and will likely destroy myself in a hopeless quest for love. For now, I am part of a collective that is unconscious as it depends on an old matriarchal and patriarchal system that work like a terrorist system. To not be blinded by an instinct causing violence in the streets and closet addicts at home, I must feel the depth of my projections of a dark mother and punishing father onto the global scene. More than ever, I may feel the need to transition from a world of greed that splits giving from receiving by communicating fear, confusion and domination to a world of grace that unites giving and receiving via wisdom and kindness.

The feminine – the side that opens to receive – awaits in both men and women. The pathology of "the woman who gives too much" touches both genders. Surely, patriarchy is not masculinity but only a pretense of masculinity, for even women can be worse patriarchs than men! When moved by the desire to control and dominate, I am who splits the world between tops and bottoms – haves and have-nots. This belief system destroys everything – bodies, relationships, the planet... I will either bring an end to it or it will end me. Ironically, when I choose to turn within, I am in my Power and no longer have to try to prove my worth by bullying others.

But how do I abide the sacred call of femininity and move from a needy dependence to the freedom to give it all to love? How do I dislodge my being possessed and find an energy strong enough to change the vibration of the body and allow it to heal?

I must let myself be like a bride – carried over the threshold. That is what the word *metaphor* means: to be "carried over" by the symbols in poetry, in my dreams, and yes, in the Bible – in all that seems senseless until an image can inform my receptor cells. This is when change is permanent – when I let my cells be feminine and "receive."

S/Hebrew can be an instrument of change. *Yvrit* – or the word "Hebrew" in Hebrew – also means "crossing to the other side." *Yvrit* is thus called to convey the metaphors that transport me to the side of the LOVE that has no opposite – on the other side of the war of the sexes.

Releasing the "Matter"

"Anything you cannot relinquish when it has outlived its usefulness possesses you, and in this materialistic age a great many of us are possessed by our possessions." *Peace Pilgrim*

Both "mother" and "matter" come from the same Latin word *mater*. Wanting my mommy causes the miser in me to envy, and the well-to-do in me to isolate. And yet, when looking at the smaller aspect of an atom (or that from which all material things are formed), the atom becomes less and less distinct until it completely disappears. The atoms that seemed to be 99.9999999% empty space are actually filled with an invisible field of information with various energy frequencies.

If everything is just energy and information, and if matter doesn't behave linearly but, instead, is chaotic and unpredictable, then it is at once here and not here, free and not free, a potential and a fulfillment. Curiously, this is the code of opposites. Also strange, observing particles of subatomic matter changes their behavior. It is only when I place my attention on any one location of any electron that the electron appears in that location. If I remove my attention and look away, it disappears back into energy.

I am matter. I am here and not, fulfilled and not, free and not, enlightened and not. So, since mind over matter is a quantum reality, why place my attention on Scare City? Why CAN'T I keep my focus on being happy, powerful and healthy? From a quantum perspective, I can observe myself in a different timeline, I can pray and believe with complete certainty that what I prayed for is already created, and I can also detach from an outcome. Doing so will condition the body to experience a possibility as a physical reality, releasing the "matter" in the process – fulfilling it. I just have to decide.

To decide with such firm intention that my choice carries an amplitude of energy that can transcend my habitual time, space and mind, I must come into pure choiceless awareness. This is what is meant by "Understand → Choose Peace → emPower the NOW."

The more I let go, the more intimate I am with the intelligence of a field of information to which my cells connect as they communicate information in a non-linear way.

The Father	The Son / The Mother	The Daughter
Information	Mind / Matter	Energy

Science & Religion, together

This interdependent entangled energy field is beyond space and time. It gives me information on a moment-to-moment basis via a metalanguage. I can see it in S/Hebrew *Ab* for "Father" but also "alphabet." AB / BA imprints Code Free Will (soon to come). If freedom motivates my male side, fulfillment speaks to my female side. This is the mystery!

Going to the Father - Alphabetically

"Don't be afraid to be weak / Don't be too proud to be strong / Just look into your heart my friend / That will be the return to yourself / The return to innocence." *Enigma*

Code ATBaSh could be called "the First and the Last" as it pairs A (Aleph) with T (Tav), B (Beth) with S (Shin), etc. It also engineers an uncanny way to go to the Father, that is, to return to innocence. I am familiar with Code Communication AT/TA, when I am so true to my word that what I say I want is aligned to what I have. When there is a discrepancy, Code Transformation BS/SB kicks in to take me on a journey from Beth to Shin until I tell the truth (no more BS, literally). These two signs are "PAIRfectly" complementary:

- **Beth** means "house" as that which separates the inside from the outside. It thus begins the illusion of separation of matter and spirit.
- **Shin** means "tooth" as that which joins outside to inside by chewing food and starting the assimilation process. It thus ends the illusion of separation.

Rank Down	Rank Up	Value		Letter's Name	Roman Script	The Word	The Tarot	The Gift
1	22	1	א	Aleph	A	Ox	0. The Fool	Innocence
2	21	2	ב	Beth	B	House	1. The Magician	Power
10	13	10	י	Yod	Y, I, J.	Hand	9. The Hermit	Aloneness
20	3	200	ר	Resh	R	Head	19. The Sun	Goodness
21	2	300	ש	Shin	S	Tooth	20. The Judgment	Wisdom
22	1	400	ת	Tav	T	Sign	21. The World	Abundance

The Vision of a Timely and PAIRfect Return

Going to the "Father" is an ascent (the top rows – Aleph Beth spell *Av* the "Father"). I start at the bottom, seeing the letters Tav, Shin, Resh, Yod which spell *Tishri*. *Tishri* is the month of the Hebrew year when the High Holy Days are celebrated. It is literally the month of return to *Av* the Father. Note: the letters of *Tishri Av* reorder as *Bereshit /Barashit* for "in the beginning/created-SIX."

Going to the Father - Figuratively

"You heard me say, 'I am going away and I am coming back to you.' If you loved me, you'd be glad that I am going to the Father, for the Father is greater than I." *John 14:28*

To better understand my divine family (on earth as it is in heaven), I can call on the Power of Three expressed via the three pillars of Judaism – *Teshuvah*, *Tephillah* and *Tzedaqah* juxtaposed with the three pillars of Buddhism – Buddha, Dharma and Sangha. Ultimately, these three levels of threes are meant to work simultaneously.

Individual Power	Symbolic Power	Collective Power
The Father	The Son / The Mother	The Daughter
Teshuvah – Turn within	*Tzedaqah* – Charity	*Tephillah* – Heartfelt Prayer
Buddha	Dharma	Sangha

The Father as individual Power: if I want to meet the Father (the Eternal Witness), I must get away from the programming of my tribe. I must also physically leave my tribe, since going to the Father is a solo job. Time has come to face my fear of death, since going to the Father is to "turn within" and invite my Buddha nature. And while it may be a lonely and grinding journey, each step affirms that the way out is the way in.

The Daughter as collective Power: to feel and fulfill the promise I made as the Son: "I will come back to you," I must know who I am as an individual. There is thus a before and an after to collective Power. My prayers are heartfelt, when they are no longer a petition for what I think that I "should" have. Instead, they express gratitude for the love which surrounds me (*Tephillah/Sangha*). I come back when I no longer need to contrast myself against the plurality of the collective to exist as an individual.

The Son within the Mother as symbolic Power: these archetypes are where the mind-body connection is at work. "*Mens sana in corpore sano*" (Latin "a healthy mind in a healthy body"). To resonate with the words of Roman Poet Juvenal, I must be willing to inquire on my motivations. If not, I might as well say: "forgive me, Mother, for I don't want to know." What excuses will I invent to continue limiting *Tzedaqah* to "charity?" If charity only concerns the care of the poor, I risk merging into materialism, and thereby disconnecting mind from body. But if it takes "no more mind" for the body to heal and if *Tzedaqah* is to let go of my attachments and give it all, then symbols and codes may just be the most effective survival tool at my disposal.

The more dire the situation, the more vital it is for me to feel and sense the meaning of signs and interpret reality symbolically. Symbols are the medium of consciousness, and their Power, the next skill for me to transact. They live in the "grey" realm whose middle of the road "mediocrity" I avoid with all my might.

One thing is for sure: entering symbolic **Power** is experiencing a time warp. It speeds up time by providing an unbroken experience of synchronicity.

Besides, it is what I asked for – to develop my intuitive, spiritual and even mystical senses and feel myself shifting from "Power over" to wholesome Power. Or might I be so attached to an outcome that I'm grasping at straws when considering to enter the symbolic realm?

The Sex Question

"I don't know the question, but sex is definitely the answer." *Woody Allen*

Which comes first: the societal discomfort with sexuality or the confusion surrounding the Holy Ghost's gender and the Mother (in contrast to the clear masculinity of the Father and the Son)? What are the consequences of a collective unconscious imbibed with thoughts such "it is no good to be alone" or "the man shall cleave unto his wife?" Moreover, how can I reconcile the outrageousness of an esoteric Vav Son inseminating the 2nd Dalet, linking her to him through the mystery of impregnation?

For Sigmund Freud, the Oedipus Complex is a crucial stage in the **normal** developmental process of the child. Carl Jung spoke of the feminine equivalent as the Electra Complex. This is when the child has a desire for sexual involvement with the parent of the opposite sex, and a concomitant sense of rivalry with the parent of the same sex. While the idea seems monstrous, it is perhaps the way of nature that we would direct our first sexual and aggressive impulses toward our parents.

As long as I imagine that my family is out there, the idea will be disturbing. Can it really be true that a sexual preference would be activated early on, as though a boy would regard his father as a rival in love, a girl feel the same way toward her mother, and both of them wishing to get rid of their enemy? Might the real questions be: how can there be *no* childhood sexual desire when sexuality is an instinct?

Surely, if I want and choose to acquire individual Power, I must separate from the tribe – from my family, and take full responsibility for my experience. Harboring feelings of hatred only leads me to separate. Returning to the Father helps me connect to the field of information and to understand cellularly that my parents and I are One.

Resisting nothing implies to stop judging (and see the good in the bad). Henceforth, I naturally "avert the evil decree" – the very goal of the three pillars. I end up relating *Tzedaqah* to being more than "righteousness" or "charity." These concepts feel forced. They are far from the interdependence of Dharma, and from the totality I experience when my giving is devoid of agendas. Having no hooks, I witness the static nouns of the three pillars turning into verbs that serve the behavior of LOVE.

Individual Power	Symbolic Power	Collective Power
Teshuvah – Turn within!	*Tzedaqah* – Let go!	*Tephillah* – Feel Prayer!
Buddha	Dharma	Sangha

Understand (or feel prayer) → Choose Peace (or turn within) → emPower the NOW (or let go of judgments) may just be when the word "consciousness" realizes that it originates from "conscience."

Code Conscience - RO / OR

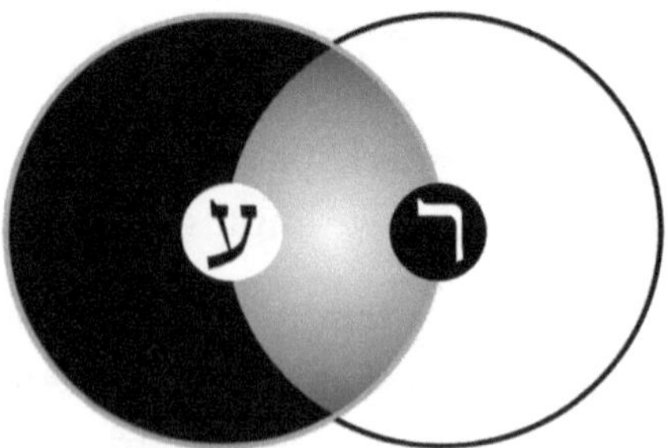

Imagine a language so pure and so sacred that it can reconcile opposites in just two letters...

Right: Hebrew letter Resh (ר) → R in Roman Script
Left: Hebrew letter Ayin (ע) → O in Roman Script

Here is how S/Hebrew inscribes code "Conscience:"

- **RO**: in one direction, I read *Rah* (רע) for "evil, bad, wicked."
- **OR**: in the other direction, I read *Ohr* (ער) for "awake."

The decoding: feelings are not good or bad. They're just the communication of good or **bad** news. When I shoot the messenger, I'm missing precious information. Let's say that I feel jealous (a big taboo). Jealousy simply alerts me that, right now, I *think* that I can't have what I want. That is simply not true! I can attain any goal, provided I have wholesome Power. This is when, having forgiven the CAIN in me, I *think* I CAN. Cain was so "possessed by jealousy" (that's what his name meant) that he killed his brother. When I resist understanding my "evil" side, I am Cain, the murderer of my potential. But when I **wake up** from the dream of separation and become conscious that **evil** has a purpose, I begin to change for good. Little by little, I don't take my "bad" personally. Little by little, I return to innocence. Little by little, I CAN breathe! **It was just a matter of letting go of my thoughts of how reality "should" be. This is when the gates of the Eternal open for me.**

The Gates of the Eternal

"Music is moral law. It is the essence of order and leads to all that is good, true and beautiful." *Plato*

Adopting a path of least resistance is surrendering my judgments. As soon as I judge "no good," I resist feeling and create unconscious time. No longer present to what reality is, I can't pass through the gate of the good, altogether a real bummer!

Context: Greek philosophers spoke of three gates to the Eternal – the gates of the good, the true and the beautiful, qualities still held to be transcendental. Transcending time, space and mind is to include compulsiveness. It is to just be in the Eternal Now. To assist me, each gate is opened by one of the three core wisdom teachings: the gate of the good by religion, the gate of the true by science, and the gate of the beautiful by Art. Henceforth, the good makes me a lover of ethics, the true, a lover of logic, and the beautiful, a lover of aesthetics.

These three fundamental perspectives may just be even more pertinent today. Whereas the three gates ought to be like the three sides of a prism refracting the white light of consciousness into the entire spectrum of experience, something is blocking the gate of the good. It's locked tight, as proven by my unending judgments! **Moreover, the closed-mindedness of one gate compromises the opening of the two others since they work together.**

There is a divergence of opinions as to which gate must open first, a divergence which goes back to the Greeks. Plato's philosophical system revolved around the good, which he viewed as the ultimate reality. To him, the good was "God." His disciple Aristotle saw that the ultimate reality emerged from the beautiful. Chaos grew so entranced by beauty that it began to reveal the patterned motions that were hiding it. To him, the beautiful was "God."

This divergence is present today in the fights of the rationalists who favor the true of science against the pluralists who favor the beautiful of Art, and both of them, the rationalists and the pluralists denying any goodness to religion.

When the Renaissance began to differentiate the domains of Art, religion and science and free them from the yoke of authoritarian control that religion once had, each domain had its own jurisdiction and its own methods for producing knowledge.

I	IT / ITS	WE
Aesthetics	Logic	Ethics
Art & the beautiful	Science & the true	Religion & the good

Current view of perspectives as linked to the three wisdom teachings

- **The IT/ITS of Science:** by splitting objective facts from subjective beliefs, science blossomed into the branches of physics, mathematics, chemistry, biology, etc. Church and state separated, and many "ITS" were seen as a 3rd **person** perspective.
- **The WE of religion:** there was now a need for religion to define itself by way of its ethics. However, religion started to lag far behind, especially as the petitionary prayers were at the core of our speaking to "God" as a 2nd **person.**
- **The I of Art:** such differentiation and rapid acquisition of knowledge (and thus, of Power) also affected the Arts, which exploded into novel forms of expression and interpretations. The artist came into its own identity as a 1st **person.**

In the manifest world, there's only perspective. But in the unmanifest world, there is no perspective, no duality and no favoritism; just being. Therefore, the trick to opening the gates is to hold all the three perspectives at once – to speak to all languages. When I am a pure vessel, free of attachments to being the doer, I have no need to objectify me, you or "IT." There is now a listening for symbolic Power.

I	IT / ITS	WE
Individual Power	Symbolic Power	Collective Power
Science & the true	Art & the beautiful	Religion & the good

Shift in Perspective

This is when the scientist and the artist in me change the way they look at "IT." The scientist takes a quantum jump and sees that "IT" is not out there: "I" am who observes reality. The artist drops the thought that "I" am special, puts my heart and soul into my work, and lets "IT" do the expressing. The religious-oriented self can now stop judging. When the gate of the good opens, I am One with "you." The right and wrong game finally winds down.

FEELINGS

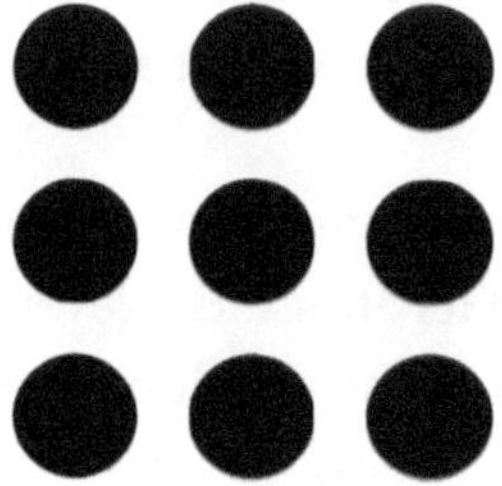

FEELINGS are not good or bad. They're just the messengers of good news and/or bad news. Besides, negativity can only affect me when I disable my ethical program, a.k.a. my conscience. When I don't do what my conscience guides me to do, I begin to take the "bad" personally, and can't remember that this too shall pass.

Does the word "conscience" trigger me? Is it why I replaced it with the word "consciousness?" Consciousness works with the mind. It likes contrast: 0/1, yes/no; right/left; good/bad, male/female. It speaks in boundaries and exercises the Power to decide. Conscience is still about making choices, yes/no, right/left... Deciding starts in a gut feeling (whether I know it or not).

There is great Power in deciding, which is why making a choice terrifies me! To avoid the changes that decision-making generates, I stop feeling and create unconscious time. There is now a misalignment between what I say I want and what I have in actuality. This lack of coherence does not feel good. So, why would I lie (yes, "lie" is a BIG word), when integrity and honesty are high on my list? Why say, for example, that I want healing, and yet act as if I wanted to do harm?

It's because I have a secret or two to protect. I think I'm safe; that people can't read my mind, and again, I am fooling myself! Humans are empaths. They can feel me and sense me, whether they know it or not! So why do I resist healing? It's because I am a sentient being without sentience. I turn it off, especially when it gets intense!

Sentience is the capacity to feel and sense. These feminine functions are how that which understands has an understanding of "God."

I can live a life avoiding my feelings. It's been done! Even artists (whose job is to be sensitive) reserve sentience for their Art. The rest of the time, they're so afraid of touching the depth of their pain that they'll go to their drug of choice, just to be comfortably numb. What about me? Am I called to the healing arts? Do I wish to be a coach, an emissary, a visionary? And if I do, am I conscious that my desire to significantly contribute involves receiving information that is yet to touch the Earth? Will I own that I am seeking revelation?

"Revelation" – the disclosure of something that was kept secret that may or not have a divine or supernatural nature. Here is a "revelation:" provided I accept that the world is a reflection of me, then the disclosure of a "personal" secret will also reveal an "impersonal" or QKosmic secret. Therefore, how much do I want to know and contribute? This was Einstein's answer: "I want to know God's thoughts – the rest are mere details."

If the free expression of my genius was at stake (and it is), do I have enough self-esteem to expose my secrets? Scientific breakthroughs are pushing against the boundaries of ethics, reminding me of the words of François Rabelais, a Renaissance humanist: "science without conscience is only ruin of the soul." Might science be leaping into the future before having evolved enough to know LOVE?

The current findings of science evoke amazement at the promise they bring, but also unease because of the danger they pose. Are we compromising the purity of DNA research? Changing a genetic narrative is changing the chemicals, and therefore, emotions. Are we trying to alter our DNA because we can't weather uneasy feelings? Is it wise to rob a child from lessons on how to choose peace? Besides, how will it affect the eco-system to remove what we judge as "bad" when we are yet to have the wisdom to know the difference?

First things first: can I be secure enough to allow myself to be distressed when comfortable, and comforted when distressed? And if I don't master my emotions, how does that affect human evolution? Surely, if I'm gonna "play God," can I at least wait to have the response-ability of a prophet saying "I am God?"

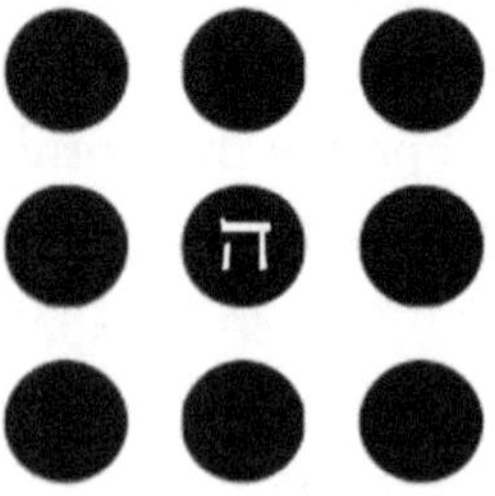

Code Female Fulfillment - SB / BT

*Imagine a language so pure and so sacred that it can
reconcile opposites in just three letters...*

Top: Hebrew letter Shin (שׁ) → S, Sh in Roman Script
Right: Hebrew letter Beth (ב) → B in Roman Script
Left: Hebrew letter Tav (ת) → T in Roman Script

HERE IS HOW S/HEBREW INSCRIBES CODE "FULFILLMENT:"

- **SBT:** from the top, clockwise, I read *Shabbat* (שבת) for "rest."
- **SB:** from top to right, I read *Shuv* (שב) for "turn within."
- **ST:** from top to left, I read *Seth* (שת) for "appointed."
- **BT:** from right to left, I read *Bat* (בת) for "daughter."

The Decoding: I observe and remember the **"Shabbat** day" when I neither push nor pull, but instead allow creation to happen through me. This implies that my former ambition is now replaced by a pure appreciation of reality. To be in such graceful zone, I simply **"turn within"** and hear what my **"appointment"** is. It may be to wash the dishes, to make a phone call, to build an Ark. :-) This is Bhakti Yoga – the devotion of the **"Daughter"** of the Voice to intently listen and follow. It is true meditation, as I **rest** while working, and find fulfillment in the action itself. As pleasure overtakes my being, I come into the depth of expression of the Daughter, Bride and Holy Ghost. And this is when religion (♫ and no religion too) *naturally* blossoms in me.

The Seventh "Day" of Rest & Lovemaking

"Young Stephen Hawking meets Jane, his wife-to-be, and introduces himself as a cosmologist. "What's cosmology?" she asks. He answers: "the religion for intelligent atheists." "What do cosmologists worship?" she persists. "A single unifying equation that explains everything in the universe." *A Theory of Everything – the movie*

Code fulfillment spells out *Shabbat* – the Holy Instant of QKosmic Union between the Son and his Bride. It is the climax of the Created-SIX – the moment when I rest in perfect bliss, even while working. This exact ability is how the doubts let go of me.

I have seen how *Golden XPR* breaks open the seals of ancient prophecies by revealing a unifying equation in the first word of the Torah. This word can be read as *Bereshit* for "in the beginning," or as *Barashit* for "created-SIX." When accepting that consciousness uses words to create, a novel interpretation arises suggesting that it is not the **world** that was created in six days; it is the **word**!

Using the universal properties of elementals, I can now recognize patterns behind the apparent disorder of any concept. Called the seed of life and/or the Genesis pattern, the geometry's design transmits the code of creativity in SIX progressive "days" or stages. The end of mind is when the 6th circle is formed. For at that moment, the 7th circle that was here before time reappears.

The progression from "day" to "day" and/or from circle to circle unfolds in the next image. It elucidates the esoteric meaning of *Genesis* 2:2. Indeed, let there be light!

"And on the seventh day God completed the work that he had done, and he rested on the 7th day from all the work that he had done."
Genesis 2:2

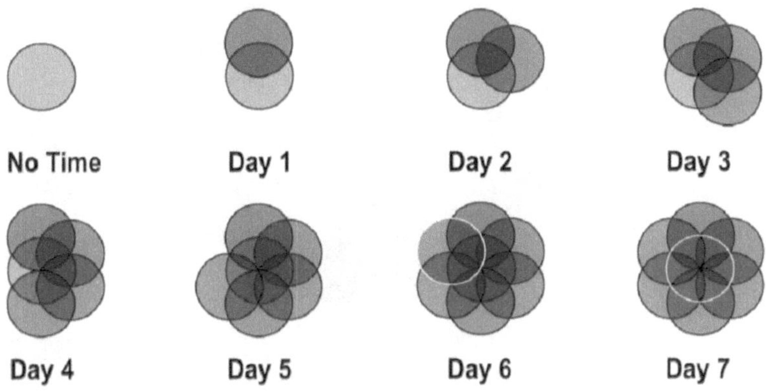

Therefore, the miracle is not the complexity of the world that I have created, but the simplicity of the equation that describes that complexity.

The possibility to simultaneously complete my work and rest from my work is made visible by the geometry of the Genesis Pattern. It shows that "God" is indeed a geometer. The moment when the 6th circle is formed and the 7th circle appears makes it clear that, although there is no action involved, a new circle is created.

The beginning of time being the beginning of mind, I now have a foundational equation by which to fulfill my feminine side (as I feel and sense the process of any creation). I also free my masculine side (as I have nothing left to lose and everything to gain). Code Fulfillment + Code Freedom = Marital Truth, Consciousness and Bliss.

Code Male Freedom - AB / BN

Imagine a language so pure and so sacred that it can reconcile opposites in just three letters...

Top: Hebrew letter Aleph (א) → A in Roman Script
Right: Hebrew letter Beth (ב) → B in Roman Script
Left: Hebrew letter Nun Final (ן) → N in Roman Script

Here is how S/Hebrew inscribes code "freedom:"

- **ABN:** from the top, clockwise, I read *Aben* (אבן) for "stone."
- **AB:** from top to right, I read *Ab* (אב) for "father."
- **AN:** from top to left, I read *On* (אן) for "vigor."
- **BN:** from right to left, I read *Ben* (בן) for "son."

The Decoding: is my fate written in **stone**? At times, I feel like Sisyphus, condemned to ceaselessly roll a rock to the top of a mountain, to only see this same rock fall back of its own weight. This is an appalling sentence in which my exertion accomplishes nothing. Until I realize that what I think as I descend either seals my fate or ends it. When I let go of the judgment "I shouldn't fail," I am free, stronger than a falling rock, my **vigor** restored! Paradox of paradoxes: I am now a rolling stone getting satisfaction! Freedom is decoded and experienced, when the

son turns to the **father,** and the father turns to the son. The son is the mind; the father is the heart. When mind and heart converge, my decision-making Power is at the strongest – the most "vigorous." I forgive my errors and the errors of my birth father (his "sins") as being the same, and heal the trauma. When I feel the Holy Matrimony of Code Freedom (Father & Son) and Code Fulfillment (Daughter), I judge not and resist nothing.

Note: Code Male Freedom was computed in *TCO—Book 1* as the Redemption Code. Indeed, there is a price I must pay to earn my own freedom; that is what redemption is all about!

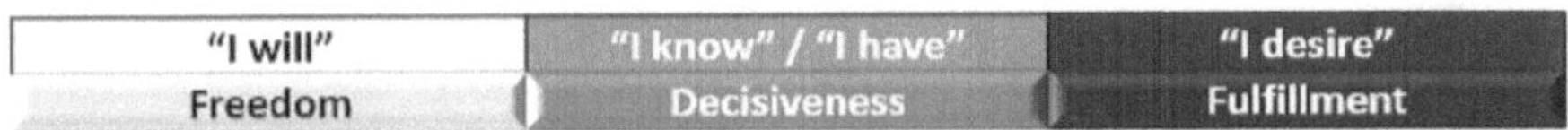

This is THE END of the war of the sexes, when I make a decision with such firm intention that my choice carries an amplitude of energy that transcends my perception that laws are external and coercive.

PART III: THE TWIN CODE

Below are the "gemini" topics of this section:

- Three "God" Names as three Powers that direct the three ways in which my mind creates in time – gradually, simultaneously or eternally.
- Code Scare City – the ticket that may just give me the permission to time-travel beyond my illusion of forced labor.
- Meeting the four in PaRaDiSe, becoming fluent in the PaRaDoX and exploring the four parallel worlds as states of mind.
- Being, becoming and waking up to new motions: the four unconscious archetypes in the DREaM.
- Where angels love to tread – in the places in-between the problem and the solution, where to transition from greed into grace.

The Name YEWE is one of the most potent "God" Names in the Torah. Its code transmits how to acquire Power by allowing me to understand the interaction of four worlds with four states of mind.

Yod (י)	Vav (ו) / Heh (ה)	Heh (ה)
Atziluth	*Beriah / Assiyah*	*Yetzirah*
Transmission	Creation / Manifestation	Formation
Witness	Deep Sleep / Waking	Dreaming

Finally: giving it all to LOVE.

A Higher Power

When the new patient was settled comfortably on the couch, the psychiatrist began his session, "I'm not aware of your problem. So perhaps, you should start at the very beginning." "Sure." replied the patient. "In the beginning, I created the Heaven and the Earth."

Everything I perceive and thus create in the "world" comes from the invisible dimension of thoughts. If I want to transform, I must look at the story I tell. I eventually come to realize that I don't know what's for my highest good, I just *think* I do. The more I surrender my illusion of control, the more I let creation happen through me. To unleash my creativity, I must become aware of what motivates my choices. What drives me? If every choice I make has a profound consequence, why do I want what I want? I must now take a look at the "God" I serve and the "Adam" (or the mind) I am. These Powers influence my perception of time, and the speed at which I succeed in my creation:

1. *Elohim* – **Simultaneous Creation: I am primary Adam** serving a "God" Name who grants the Power of synchronicity. This is *Elohim* (אלהים), the Name that says "let there be light," and sees that light was already created. When I am this Adam, I have no creative blocks. Knowing that my brain is created male and female, I think "I can" and witness *simultaneous creation*. "Simultaneous" means that there is no time interposed between my desired creation and its manifestation. I have no prejudices, and am free to choose to observe one particle or another: it's all good! My motivation is response-ability.

2. **YEWE** *Elohim* – **Gradual Creation: I am secondary Adam** serving a "God" Name who grants the Power of history. This is YEWE *Elohim* (יהוה אלהים), the Name that issues a commandment the first time it speaks: "you shall not eat from the tree of the knowledge of opposites, or else." When I am this Adam, I think "I can't" and witness *gradual creation*.

Tomorrow, I'll do what it takes! I give my Power to an external "God" acting as a prime cause, which is how I have a history that insanely repeats itself. Henceforth, I mostly see myself at the mercy of fate, rewarded when I do good, and punished when I am not good enough. Whether I know it or not, my motivation is vengeance – making "you" pay.

YEWE - Non-Causality - Cain

'Two monks were watching a flag flapping in the wind. One said to the other, "the flag is moving." The other replied, "the wind is moving." Huineng overheard this. He said, "not the flag, not the wind; mind is moving." *The Gateless Passage.*

My name is Cain. Being the first mortal and the first murderer, I have a vested interest in understanding why I would have created the reality I created. I'm also the first to serve the "God" Name YEWE as the Power of Accountability. While I wanted to separate from my family and make my own choices, I won't accept the consequences of my decisions. It seems that "my punishment is greater than I can bear" *Genesis 4:13*. Truth be told, it's not freedom I want, but freedom from responsibility. I'm like a child: I want to do what I want, but ultimately, I'd like you to pick up the pieces. It's like wanting to drink all I want today, and refusing to accept tomorrow's hangover!

If I could only change and not cause effects I'd rather not have to experience, I would rise to my vision and find rest in the process. But I can't change – or die – since YEWE put a mark (the word *Ot*) on my forehead to spare me from being killed. For the longest time, I failed to realize that, once read in a mirror, this word *Ot* (AWT or "Aleph and Tav") flipped into *To* (TWA or "Tav and Aleph"). Until one day, I had an epiphany remembering the story of the letters presenting themselves to "God" in reverse order, each of them eager to create their "personal" reality. Only Aleph was pure enough to stay away from any creating. Having no cravings, its mind had stopped moving. When aligned with

Aleph, I am pure choiceless awareness. I love reality as it is – for better, for worse, for richer, for poorer, for murderer, for life-giver: it's all equal to me! It is only when I identify to Beth the Magician that I need to make something happen, and fear the price I'll have to pay for using magic. What if I invoked the "wrong" thing? **Indeed, the Power of decision is dicey, as it leads me to take my creations personally, either boasting ("I did it!") or scolding myself ("I shouldn't have").**

Once again, the S/Hebrew alphabet transmitted the findings of quantum science and quantum religion. Science calls it "nonlocality" and religion, "non-causality." A growing body of empirical evidence suggests that human consciousness is nonlocal, meaning it is not confined to specific points in space (such as brains or bodies), or specific moments in time (such as past or present). In everyday life, distance and location seem very real. Yet physics now suggests that, at the most fundamental level, the universe is nonlocal. This would mean no space, no time, no mind, and no creation. I would not interfere with the QKosmic plan by holding onto my judgments of what I think reality "should" be. My real Self being nonlocal, I'd wake up from the dream of karma which can only exist in space, time and causality. I can now be the change.

As for religion, it is through the teachings of Sri Ramana Maharshi that I learned about *Ajātivāda,* an ancient Hindu doctrine that denies all causality in the physical world. It states that the creation of the world never happened. Since the Self alone exists as the sole unchanging reality, nothing ever comes into existence or ceases to exist. The same idea is found in the Talmud (*Pesachim 54a*) as "the seven lights that existed before creation." So, I am timeless as the letters of the name *Qain* for "possessed by jealousy" reorder as *Naqi* for "pure, innocent."

Code Innocence QYN / NQY

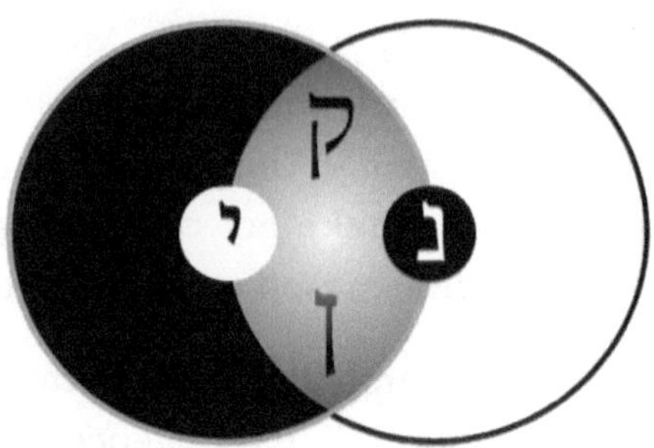

Imagine a language so pure and so sacred that it can reconcile opposites in just three letters...

Right: Hebrew letter Nun (נ) → N in Roman Script
Bottom: Nun final (ן) → N in Roman Script
Top: Hebrew letter Qoph (ק) → Q in Roman Script
Left: Hebrew letter Yod (י) → I, J, Y in Roman Script

Here is how Hebrew inscribes code "Innocence:"

- QYN: counterclockwise from the top, I read *Qain* (קין) "Cain."
- NQY: from the right to the top to the left, I read *Naqi* (נקי) for "innocent."

The Decoding: held to be essential to the Kabbalah, the *Tiqqun* for "correction, repair" is how to resolve the perennial conflict between good and evil. The adjustment starts and ends in *Tiqqun Cain* – the core of the three *Tiqqunim,* and yet the least known. I finished "correcting Cain" when I realize that I am enough. I can now have or not have what I envied in my brother, and even killed him for! Since I dropped the desire body that shamed me with endless dissatisfaction, I wake up to a perfect body in a perfect world. Henceforth, *Tiqqun Nephesh* "correcting the instinctual soul" and *Tiqqun Olam* "correcting the world" are naturally fulfilled! Moreover, I went through such a relentless process in owning my errors that I came to see that there are no errors, since all is done *through* me and not by me – nothing wrong; nothing to forgive! That is how the letters of **Cain** reorder as *Naqi*, as I feel in my blood that my soul is pure: I am **innocent**! Moreover, my communication is well-received as I have no need to change you or to make you pay. I know all too well how necessary the pain was for me to transform.

When nothing is personal, I drop my name. Instead of casting me as the bad guy who killed my brother, my name becomes my superpower. It has the force of a metaphor that gets me "there," when I reinvent myself on the other side of separating "here" from "there."

We're not in CAINsas anymore!

"Everything that exists in your life, does so because of two things: something you did or something you didn't do." *Albert Einstein*

In that sense, I precede my two fathers – the Adams of simultaneous creation and gradual creation. I am not denying the reality of the world, but only that "my" creative process brought it into existence. That's how I turn out to be innocent: little "I" didn't do it. Big "I" did! Murdering my brother was just an uncaused appearance in the life of Big "I" – the Eternal Witness. Bottom line: I am that I am, because that's what I am. No other reasons. I can rest now.

As long as I can keep my attention on the invisible Aleph that is present in all communications, I can let letter Beth tell the story of how "I" create the world by the perspective I adopt. It's like going to the movies – an Eternal Witness! I lighten up quite a bit and have no need for unconscious defense mechanisms. Praise the LORD of Karma, I don't fear my decision-making Power and don't stress. Why be anxious or guilty when there is no one to desire or resist the unacceptable or the harmful?

When undecided, I embrace my confusion wholeheartedly. I trust that clarity will come in its own good time. Feeling the fundamental oneness of everything, I resonate with the *Shema* and love the LOVE

God totally – with all my heart, all my soul and all my Power. I have no toxic introjections or deceitful projections. Which means that I have no need for defense/attack. I'm simply present – here and Now. **This also means that, maybe for the first time ever, I have a choice, as the unconscious fragments of me are no longer manipulating my use of Power.**

But I'm getting ahead of myself, since, for now, I still think that I'm a "local," ending at the skin, and still perceiving that I need to defend myself against a hostile world. And then, I met "you." How could I forget?

Dreams of Relationships

"The moment love becomes a relationship, it becomes a bondage, because there are expectations and there are demands and there are frustrations, and an effort from both sides to dominate. It becomes a struggle for power." *Osho*

My ego thinks I'm a she. His ego thinks he's a he. When we met, our egos said to each other: "who I think I am would like to play at make-believe with who you think you are. I'll be who you need me to be, if you'll be who I need you to be!"

Ah, the dream that there's someone or something out there that can love me, hear me, see me, recognize me... I think I have needs, and I'm going to defend my right to have them, dammit! At first, it's a great thrill. But when I finally have it – your attention, the drink, the car, the win, it's suddenly meaningless! I'm so intoxicated by what I think would fulfill me that I ignore that fulfillment comes from within! But how can that be, when the world out there looks so very real: "it's all his fault. Why can't he see that!"

Eventually the truth hits me like a two-by-four. I was confused. I thought he should have said something, and I now see that I over-spoke. Spiritual awakening is like waking up from a bad dream, but on a bigger scale. It brings me back to Earth – to a humus that is humbling! The more I use my judgments of him to show me who I am, the more I can maintain this strange lucidity that focuses my thoughts in a relaxed way.

While the idea of "relationship" is preposterous, it is a gift to have someone with whom to fight to be right until there's no one to wrong the other! Fight after fight, we will eventually realize that there is no one out there, and stop giving our Power away!

Which is when the heart told me: "you're still in a dream. Drop the 'we,' if only until you're complete with the work of individuation!"

YES, BUT

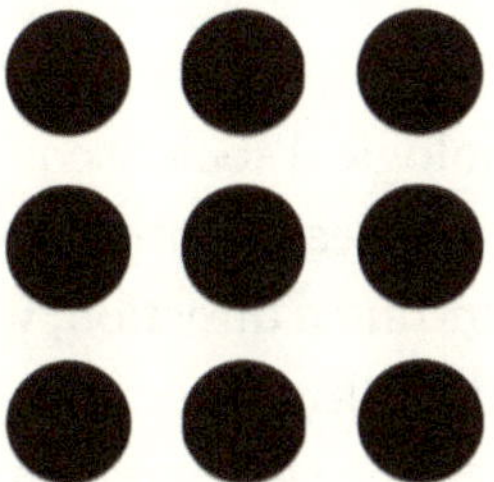

YES, BUT how do I deal with the desire for love, approval and recognition? It never stops! I find myself singing the song of *Psalm 13*: "will you forget me forever? How long will you hide your face from me? How long must I wrestle with my thoughts and every day have sorrow in my heart? How long will my enemy triumph over me?" If I wish to free the Sacred Feminine, I must understand the terrible yearning. This yearning has a name: Mammon.

"Cursed Mammon be, when he with treasures to restless action spurs our fate!" *Johann Wolfgang von Goethe, Faust.*

And it is a Faustian bargain that makes me an addict, possessed by insatiable desires and lacking the self-esteem to choose truth! Mammon first gives me a taste of what I want, enough to get me hooked to the "HELLusion," wanting more!

What if I could taste the essence of a library formed by 5 essential books (the *Torah*, in Hebrew) that are at once ceremonial, archetypal, and deceptively primitive? Might the sentience of its symbols – which are not unlike an extra-terrestrial transmission – act as an informational archive inscribing a path to sensing "enough?"

Only an advanced technological society could have built a library of such immense significance. These symbols are organized on the theme of movement, all about finding a direction, walking a path, crossing a boundary – death being the ultimate boundary. On the other side of it is the change I wish to see. The signs are behavioral nodes working in pairs along two flows (good and evil), for me to balance desire and resistance and wake up.

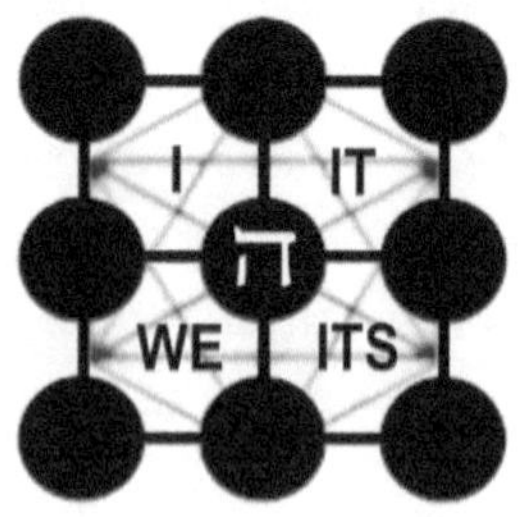

Code Scare City - MM / NWN

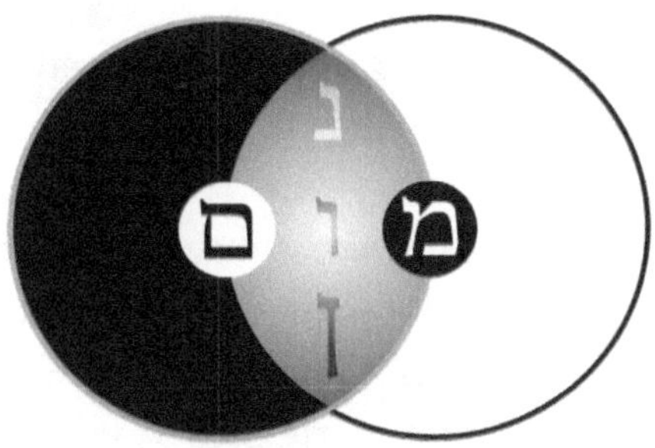

*Imagine a language so pure that it can reconcile
opposites in just two fully spelled-out letters...*

MM: from right to left, I read the name *Mem* (מם) for "pairs of waters."
NWN: from top to bottom, I read the name *Nun* (נון) for "son, fish."

Here is how S/Hebrew inscribes code "Scare City:"

- **MWM:** from right to middle to left, I read *Mum* (מום) for "flaw, defect."
- **NWM:** from top to middle to left, I read *Num* (נום) for "slumber, sleep."
- **MMWN:** right to middle to bottom, I read *Mammon* (ממון) or "money, yearning."

The Decoding: if the 13th and 14th letters – Mem and Nun – shifted into 14th and 15th letters (there's a code for that – the ABCaD Code), the pair would become Nun Samekh and spell the word *Nes* (נס) for "miracle." The miracle is that **Nun**, the "son" which can also be "fallen, miscarried" would be caught by Samekh, the letter that follows it and means "support." But when my **pairs of waters** are split, I don't feel supported in my creativity. I now compromise, just to pay the bills! I'm in a deep **slumber**, dreaming of separation, **yearning** for someone, something that would fill the giant hole in my soul. Thinking that I'm **flawed**, I identify to the have-nots and am afraid of **money** and/or of what it will take for me to get some.

Money can be thought of in terms of Power, and Power, in terms of money. Every decision I make either decreases or increases my capital. When under Mammon's spell, I have no sense of worth. Secretly feeling like a loser and fearing the consequences of my decisions, I bury myself in other people. I let them decide for me. And if I don't like the results of their investments, I'll blame them for my losses. Moreover, I have no real sense of boundaries. My yeses and my nos are yet to be honest, as I fear that, if I were telling the truth, "you" would reject me. That is how I hurt myself, by serving two masters and giving my allegiance to materialism while *trying* to honor my Spirit.

Once again, evolution and waking up are all about Power, the greatest of which being the Power to choose peace. Receiving it is contingent to finding the PaRaDiSe I lost.

PaRaDiSe & PaRaDoX

"The 'paradox' is only a conflict between reality and your feeling of what reality 'ought to be.'" *Richard Feynman*

It is a paradox. When awake, I forget how real my dreams were just a moment ago. When asleep, I am convinced that my dreams are real, and forget all about "the real world." If trapped in a nightmare, I'm struggling to escape, and relieved when I am back to "reality." But if I am involved in a wonderful dream, I want to stay there forever. Why so many judgments about what reality "should" be?

Does my fear of the material world curve my perception of space-time? Might my allegiance to the physical world (Mammon) deny the reality of a transcendental world where I could feel matter as energy?

The same question keeps on revisiting me. Why would I think I can't connect to a more optimal version of me? Indeed, why CAN'T I?

If the physical world is real when I'm awake, and the dream world, real when I'm asleep, I know that there are at least two worlds in which I actually do "quantum jump." Wisdom teachings speak of three states of consciousness (waking, dreaming, deep sleep), and of a fourth (the witness) and even of a fifth state beyond the fourth (when I Am in ever-lasting time – in suchness). I can even imagine that, at the foundation of all states, there is a quantum state making all trans-formations possible. But, for now, how do I move into the fourth state where I am conscious of the Eternal Witness, and remain conscious even when in the "lower" states of waking, dreaming, and deep sleep? And this is when I heard the still small voice saying...

"I am PRDX. I come back from the future as an extension of YEWE, each sign invoking a world as one of the four states, e.g.; the subtle world of Formation where dreaming occurs. As planet earth is coming apart at the seams, the time has come to go within, master your vibrational frequency and cultivate your internal healer so that you would know Health. I am here to take the complexity of spiritual teachings and make them user-friendly.

PRDX sources the word 'PaRaDiSe.' The letters PRD invoke the three lower states (the first tier), and the letter S, the witness state (the second tier). To feel it being activated in you, you must first know that, while sounding as "S," Samekh became the letter 'X' of 'PaRa-DoX.' It challenges you to become honest, and show up to a leader's quality of witnessing. The more you allow yourself to read who you are and feel how consciousness plays with symbols, the more you can choose peace when in between a rock and a hard place. The capacity to self-regulate is what empowerment is. It is the means to travel to the world where consciousness conceives and manifests the vision that had thus far remained concealed or even forbidden to you." End of PRDX's transmission.

Yod (י)	Vav Heh (וה)	Heh (ה)
Atziluth	*Beriah / Assiyah*	*Yetzirah*
Transmission	Creation / Manifestation	Formation
Witness	Deep Sleep / Waking	Dreaming
S-X	D / P	R

The Mystery of "S-X"

The FOUR in "PaRaDiSe"

"O divine Master, grant that I may seek rather to comfort than to be comforted. To understand, than to be understood. To love, than to be loved. For it is in giving that we receive, it is in pardoning that we are pardoned, and it is in dying that we are born to eternal life." *St Francis of Assisi*

To bypass my communication problem (I know what to do. I don't want to do it), I have the possibility to "do and understand." That is the meaning of *Naaseh V'Nishma* – the ancient formula given on Mount Sinai with the mosaic law. My ego didn't like it one bit. Years later founding father Benjamin Franklin would concur: "the people heard it, and approved the doctrine, and immediately practiced the contrary." Being unwilling to "do, feel and understand" is how I lose PaRaDiSe.

I find it intriguing that I would resist doing what I know is for my highest good. Am I so afraid to turn within to find my answers that I'd blame you for not understanding me or loving me the way I want to be understood or loved? Is my self-sabotage a way to get at you? However, since there is only One of us, any attempt to punish you for the harm I perceive you did to me will surely punish me. If I ever want to end the sabotage and feel that "it is in pardoning that I am pardoned," I must restore my ethical system and become conscious. But how?

This is where the four of PaRaDiSe come in to synergize the different levels of understanding as four intelligences within four bodies, so that I would know who I am not only in my heart, but also

in my body, my soul and my mind. When I do, the ambivalence stops!

Story is told of four rabbis of the Mishnaic period (1st century CE) who went out on a limb, and knocked at the door of PaRaDiSe to recover their fluency in the PaRaDoX – which is "God's" language. When I speak PaRaDoX, I don't fight "God" or reality, and don't let thoughts about the way "it should be" disturb my peace of mind. I feel how real and unreal my fear, my hatred and my anger are, and come to love it all.

Love is an instant knowing of the coherence that originates from the body and quiets the mind. This coherence appears in the weird spelling of "PaRaDiSe" that transmits the S/Hebrew word *Pardes* (פרדס) for "orchard." Its four letters line up with יהוה to invoke a four-step process merging four levels of understanding in view to grasp reality holistically. These cards can now get played from an energetic viewpoint.

- **The P (פ)** of *Pshat* for "simple meaning" is sensed in the physical body.
- **The R (ר)** of *Remez* for "symbolic hint" is felt in the emotional body.
- **The D (ד)** of *D'rush* for "commentary" is thought in the mental body.
- **The S (ס)** of *Sohd* for "esoteric meaning" is intuited in the spiritual body.

English continues to do a superb job in conveying the S/Hebrew *PaRDeS* via the P for the "Practicality of the simple meaning," the R for the "Reflection of the symbolic hint," the D for the "Difference that wisdom knows," and the S for the "Secret or esoteric meaning."

S of Sohd	D of D'rush / P of Pshat	R of Remez
Secret	Difference / Practicality	Reflection
Spiritual	Mental / Physical	Emotional

I also notice that the order of letters P.R.D.S. ascends me from the physical to the emotional to the mental to the spiritual. This inverts the order of creation of 1. think, 2. feel, 3. have. If the order of creation says "body follows mind," the PRDS adds "until there is no more mind to follow." This is when I have complete understanding; no more doubts!

Permission to Time-Travel

"The idea that there could be other universes out there is really one that stretches the mind in a great way." *Brian Greene*

I want to believe that I live in a "multiverse" where body, soul, mind and heart work together as a choir. I start doubting it when I separate from spirit to serve my personal agendas. Another separation follows: this of sight and vision. I now only see with the eyes of the brain (the visible), and no longer with the eyes of the heart (the invisible). As the observer, I have no way of getting outside of me to see what's really out there. And since there is no out there independent of what's going on in here, I must trust myself to be able to trust "it." When I don't, I close up and live in Scare City.

For me to time-travel to the world where the change I wish to see exists, I must believe that I can. And to believe that I can, I must trust that I will use my Power for the good of all. Therefore, to jump into the exact location where the desired version of me lives, I must evolve my consciousness from the personal to the transpersonal.

Until I come into such level of maturity, I will not give me the *permission* to want what I want, nor will it into being. My ethical system will block me from it with all sorts of judgmental introjections. Therefore, I am the only one who can allow me (or not) to see the creation I wish to see, which I know exists in the field of infinite possibilities. To make contact, I just need to raise my self-esteem and grow up beyond the fear of punishment or the desire to be rewarded. As I take back my Power and do not let the outer world dictate who I am, there are no parental voices to keep me from passing through the gate of the good.

On the other side of my self-imposed inhibitions, there is no "push pull," no doubts, and no fragmentation. I take responsibility for who I am and become bigger than the "shoulds" that were lurking in my space and causing my failure to launch.

I am present – wisdom incarnate – as I know the answers at a vibrational level and play the game of being infinite in the body. I remember what I knew as a child: there is nothing and no one *out there!* I smile, as I hear/SEE "innocence" as "eye-no-sense," when the eyes of duality close and the 3rd eye opens to see that IT is and was **good**.

Innocence comes from surrendering to the Mystery. It is the clear conscience giving me the permission to will what I desire into being, as I trust that it is good, true and beautiful. Thus, consciousness is the job I've signed up for, whether I'm conscious of it or not! :-)

Code Time-Travel - MR / RM

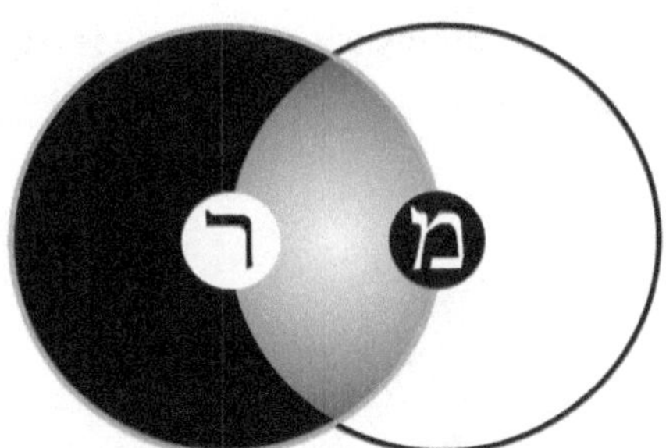

Imagine a language so pure and so sacred that it can reconcile opposites in just two letters...

Right: Hebrew letter Mem (מ) → M in Roman Script
Left: Hebrew letter Resh (ר) → R in Roman Script

Here is how S/Hebrew inscribes code "time-travel:"

- **MR:** in one direction, I read *Mor* (מר) for "myrrh."
- **RM:** in the other, I read *Rum* (רם) for "to be raised, uplifted."

The Decoding: Stardate 74047.6: patience! If I knew beyond any doubt that I will time-travel to the **exact parallel universe** where I am the change I wish to see in the world's mirror, I'd be able to wait. Thus, in the spacetime where I act compulsively, I have a hard time trusting that the realm where I am **raised, uplifted** and exalted is real. And yet I know that Rumi (whose name is inscribed by pair **RM**) speaks truth: "Only from the heart can you touch the sky." The heart; not the ego mind! I must die to who I *think* I am. This is when **myrrh** comes in, a resin that signifies death in the tradition of the Church Fathers as it evoked both the Hebrew and Egyptian funeral rites. I know that darkness is the absence of light and that light travels at the fastest measurable speed. Therefore, the light that is generated by my willingness to let go is what will propel me to my next adventure.

Ascending to the S of Secret

"We cannot solve our problems with the same level of thinking that created them." *Albert Einstein*

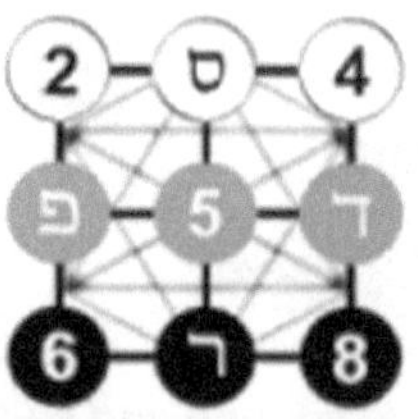

Individual Power	Symbolic Power	Collective Power
Heart	Mind / Body	Soul
Information	Mind / Matter	Energy
ס Secret	ר Difference / פ Practicality	ר Reflection

This is another way to look at TCO's map: the three Powers are now horizontal planes in lieu of vertical pillars. The four letters imputing "PaRaDoX" are tracing a diamond shape, with the letter Samekh (ס) for the *Sohd* or "secret" level being at the top. Surely, to be able to sabotage myself and hide the misuse of Power as a secret, I must first turn off my intuition and separate from my heart. **I am now in my head – in the level of thinking that creates the problem by leading me to misuse my Power / sexual energy.** However, by choosing to disconnect and turning off my ethical program, I also disabled my feeling and sensing functions. And without the ability to feel and sense (sentience), I can no longer understand me, you or any code. My secrets as well as any QKosmic informational tips are not accessible. My matter and my mind being increasingly bound to Mammon, I can no longer wield energy to heal.

The four rabbis who knocked on PaRaDiSe's door were known as Ben Azzai, Elisha Ben Abuyah, a.k.a. Acher ("the other"), Ben Zoma and Akiba. While they may have been real people, they are also archetypes interacting with the four instruments of knowledge – body, soul, mind and heart. These are the parts of me wishing to be whole again, and return to PaRaDiSe, where to link with Voice and Spirit.

For now, the problem is created by the mind that competes with the heart. To solve it, I must stretch to the dimension of the heart – the "secret" revealed by my intuition. When I question my motivations, I must be willing to hear the answer. When told to build an Ark, I must stop arguing and just obey. Obey... Don't you love that word?

Heart	Mind / Body	Soul
ט Secret	ר Difference / פ Practicality	ר Reflection
Intuiting	Thinking / Sensing	Feeling

- **P (פ):** Ben Azzai looked in the *Pardes* and died. Only entering in the *Pshat* level of **Practicality**, he lost his **body** (no **sensing**).
- **R (ר):** Ben Abuyah looked and killed the plants. Only entering in the *Remez* level of **Reflection**, he lost his **soul** (no **feeling**).
- **D (ד):** Ben Zoma looked and went mad. Only entering in the *D'rush* level of **Difference**, he lost his **mind** (no **thinking**).
- **S (ט):** Akiba entered the *Pardes* in peace. Collapsing all

previous levels and stretching to the level of the *Sohd* of Secret, he opened his **heart (intuiting)**, and restored the former functions of **sensing, feeling** and **thinking**.

Akiba entered PaRaDiSe, as he listened to his heart and obeyed its dictate. The names of rabbi "Akiba" and patriarch "Jacob" share the same root (עקב). Jacob means "the supplanter." He is the twin who, while in the womb, grabbed his brother's heel trying to be the first born (and thus get the firstborn rights and the money). After working really hard for his Mammon (I kid you not), Jacob finally surrendered and stopped the fight. Accepting that reality rules, he was renamed *Israel* for "God prevails." English, once again, manages to render the exact essence of the Hebrew word by simply saying: "ISRAEL = IS REAL."

Here is another curious loss in translation: the letter Samekh (ס) of *Sohd* for "secret" is said to have evolved into an S when it really became an X. Too funny: am I trying to hide that my shame-based secrets are X-rated? To live in PaRaDiSe, I must embrace the PaRaDoX and bring light to the shame body. Then I can just be.

Being is the result of all instruments of knowledge functioning in synergy, when I am at once a body sensing, a soul feeling, a thinking mind and an intuiting heart. Only then can I know that I Am Spirit *being:* no explanations necessary.

Yod (י)	Vav (ו) / Heh (ה)	Heh (ה)
Transmission	Creation / Manifestation	Formation
Secret	Difference / Practicality	Reflection
Intuiting	Thinking / Sensing	Feeling

Being and Becoming

"Knock, and He'll open the door. Vanish, and He'll make you shine like the sun. Become nothing, and He'll turn you into everything." *Rumi*

When lonely and in the dream of separation, I am in fear. I am in between two unknowns, and uncertainty is the hardest thing for me to accept. If I could relax, I would realize that there is a code to opposites: what ails me can become my cure. I would cultivate the interplay of being and becoming, and grow the flower of compassion, each day getting me closer to the LOVE that has no opposite.

Ultimately, I will surrender my judgments. To help me, I have the DREaM archetypes as my loyal enemies. The challenges they give me are not to aggravate me (although they do), but to strengthen me and wake me up. That's why they're called "DREaM." While unconscious, these archetypes are neutral, not evil. Their function is to draw out my fears, and shift my allegiance from the material world to the spiritual world, so that I wouldn't be so stressed out by thoughts of survival.

Yod (י)	Vav (ו) / Heh (ה)	Heh (ה)
Transmission	Creation / Manifestation	Formation
chilD	prostitutE / victiM	saboteuR

The "DREaM" transmits the dark side of YEWE. The code word is spelled out by the end letters of chilD, saboteuR, prostitutE and victiM. As previously mentioned, these archetypes were first seen by Medical Intuitive Caroline Myss.

WAKING ME UP

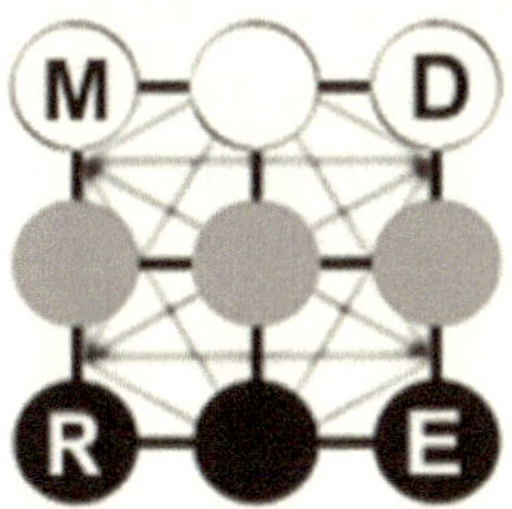

WAKING ME UP is the purpose of these four shadow archetypes. They point out how I sometimes go backward, denying me any possible evolution. The regression is also how each archetype contributes its last letter to write the word "DREaM." As a whole, they sleep so hard that they are mostly unaware of the "a" angel that is in their midst and watches over them.

———

They bring out of the shadow the unknown fragments I must integrate, for me to heal my relationship to **family, food, sex** and **money**. The more I am aware of an archetype, the more I am in a position to inquire on my motivations for choosing to say and do what I say and do.

———

Yod (י)	Vav (ו) / Heh (ה)	Heh (ה)
Transmission	Creation / Manifestation	Formation
Family	Money / Food	Sex
chilD	prostitutE / victiM	saboteuR

My chilD communicates via the broken heart. Not growing up, I lose my Power to my **family**. While I seem innocent, my chilD just wants to take the wounds of childhood and leverage them as an adult. Deep down, I'm scared and expect to be kept safe, protected and nurtured. I really want to believe that nothing bad "should" happen. Isn't life supposed to be fair? My need for reward or punishment is what directs my decision-making. I will perform in order to be deserving, and get your love, approval and recognition. If that doesn't work, I may play the shame game, and go for your disapproval.

The prostitutE in me communicates via the split mind. **Money** is where I lose Power. I'm so afraid of survival that I will negotiate my Power to make a buck! Yes, I can be bought. I'm in so much fear that I will sell my honor to the highest bidder. My priority in life is security – paying the mortgage, putting food on the table and clothes on my back. I've always had a bad reputation and am often associated with women: "the poor things; they don't understand money!" Truth be told, being a prostitutE is not about selling my body. It is about selling my soul, and whether I am a man or a woman, it is a choice that I will make when in Scare City.

The victiM in me communicates via the pain body. **Food** and health are where I most lose my Power. I am so riddled with fears that I allow them to control me. I am afraid of being alone, afraid of changing my life, afraid of going out, afraid of staying in. Life is my enemy, making protection my watchword. I'm so fixated on everything that could potentially go wrong or be harmful that I draw it to me. I don't trust. People will take advantage of me. I'm victimized by all sorts of things – my lack of education, my clothes, my friends. I don't create my reality. I let my fears and my wounds do it for me!

Interior Male	Exterior Neutral	Interior Female
chilD	prostitutE / victiM	saboteuR

Note to myself: while **the prostitute** and **the victim** need others to play their shadow games (exterior), **the child** and **the saboteur** tend to isolate (interior)

The saboteuR in me communicates via the lost soul. **Sex** and relationships are where I lose Power. I'm so misunderstood! It's not like I'm some kind of evil spirit intent on ruining my life. It's more that I'm my own worst critic. I know that my projects will fail. Finding the weakest link is my talent, which I use mercilessly to control me, you, it; the world! Just a few well-placed and negative remarks will bring down entire dynamics. I go on repeating an insane past, just to keep me from becoming. It's like I want to be disempowered. Why? I won't forgive, and will make you pay. I fear that, if I forgave the past, the future might give me more pain.

Ah, if it weren't for family, food, sex and money, I'd do great on Earth! There are times where I peek into the Mystery and see the order in the chaos, or the good in the bad of my problems. I wish there'd be a way for my shadow archetypes to realize that karma is a dream and actually wake up!

Yod (י)	Vav (ו) / Heh (ה)	Heh (ה)
Family	Money / Food	Sex
chilD	prostitutE / victiM	saboteuR
Broken Heart	Split Mind / Pain Body	Lost Soul

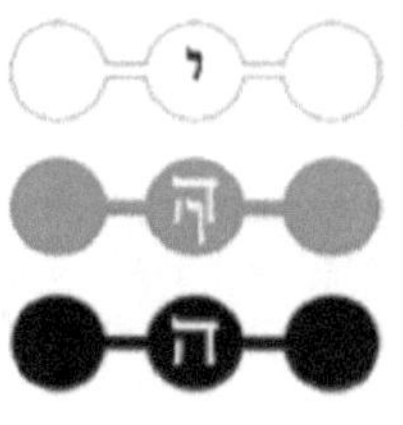

The Angel in the House

"While we are sleeping, angels have conversations with our souls."
Anonymous

This house belongs to the "God" Name *Elohim* who, being "Created-SIX," transcends and includes the four letters of YEWE. This is how there is a 5th letter to the DREaM – an inconspicuous "a" invoking an angelic presence to watch over the parts of me that are in the dark. Indeed, behind the chilD, there is **a rising angel** encouraging me to grow up. Behind the saboteuR, there is **a fallen angel** reminding me of my soul contract. Didn't I agree to fail in order to learn humility as the necessary ingredient for me to stop blocking my higher vision?

Lamed (ל) Yod (י)	Vav (ו) / Heh (ה)	Mem (מ) Heh (ה)
Authority / Family	Money / Food	Memory / Sex
Rising angel / chilD	prostitutE / victiM	Fallen angel / saboteuR

I know there is an energy, a force, an unseen hand – call it an "angel" – that somehow drives me forward. It comforts me when I'm down; it inspires me with a new idea. It is what allows me to trust that I am not alone, and will eventually lead me to resolve the conflict between reality and what I think reality "should" be.

This implies resolving my issues with **authority** and clearing the confusion induced by the "God" label. While I do want to return to innocence, will I be childlike enough to recognize that sign Lamed (ל) in *Elohim* stretches me to new heights as a rising angel does? Will I also see that sign Mem (מ) for "waters" holds the "MEMory" of who I Am as an angel falling to Earth? The S/Hebrew symbols may just be sacred enough for me to get out of my way, and do what I know to do. Life will then become simple, as I'll know in my blood what it means to love "God" and/or reality with all my heart.

These questions are of the essence, so much so that Jesus focused his teachings on the Torah's three commandments to love:

- To love the LOVE God, with all my heart, all my soul and all my Power (*Deuteronomy 6:5*).
- To love my neighbor as myself (*Leviticus 19:18*).
- To love the stranger (*Leviticus 19:33-34*).

Truth be told, thus far my love has been conditional. As long as I want something, I will not open to the LOVE that has no opposite. In other words, I will *not* love the LOVE God with the totality of my heart, my soul and my might – the operative word here being "totality." I will be partial, and my love will oscillate between fear and hate. Not understanding that there's only One of us, I will dream that I end at the skin and tend to perceive the other as my enemy. I will now have no other choice but to adopt various defense mechanisms.

But what if the three commandments to love were codes to help me shift out of my defense mechanisms and become present to what is?

I'll begin with what may be the most impactful of a long list of unconscious strategies: projections and introjections. Surely, without "grokking" these two, I won't be able to give it all to LOVE. Projections are linked to "love the neighbor as myself" since the word *Rehekha* for "your neighbor" also means "your wickedness" – the evil part of me which I repress and deny. Introjections are linked to "love the stranger," since *Hagar* – the word for "the stranger" is also the name of Abram's concubine. While she shared Abram's bed, she didn't have the status of a wife. She was somehow alienated.

- **Projecting** is the attempt to externalize the disowned parts of me by throwing them out there as negated flaws for others to carry. If, for example, I were to forbid me to be angry, I might ascribe my frustration to my sister, and say she has an anger management problem.
- **Introjecting** is to internalize the voice and/or the ideas of a

parent, a teacher, the culture at large; the people I see as authority figures. This may be my mom's voice telling me: "it's not polite to ask for what you want." Adopting this belief and including it in my own way of thinking is inviting a life of dissatisfaction.

Both projections and introjections are my creations. To become aware of them and disentangle myself from this web of false directives, I must turn within to sense where they live in my body, feel them and recognize that they are not "I," just a creature to which I identified. The more I do, the more I can stop giving them my Power. This turnaround process of 1) sense, 2) feel, 3) think again, reverses the order of creation of 1) think, 2) feel, 3) have. It is a return to LOVE.

As I allow my matter to stop "s-mothering" me, my spirit emerges freely as the sacred masculine within the sacred feminine: *Om Mani Padme Hum.* Not only can I wait and contain the energy, but I now also have within me a conscious warrior, a healer and an emissary to protect and serve me. I am my beloved and my beloved is big "I." I can play with the energy, as my presence has the capacity to transcend and include. I am here. I receive the answers I need as I am the vibrational frequency of enough that plays at being infinite in the body. The more I transcend fear, the more I understand greatness. The body is now the ground where the soul of ancient prophecies meets the heart of science, for me to love reality, a.k.a. "God."

For the LOVE of "God"

"I want to know God. The rest is details." *Albert Einstein*

The rising and the falling angels are how I wake up from the DREaM and adopt the behavior of LOVE. First, my falling angel deliberately becomes "GReed INgénue." This is the Holy Instant when I fully acknowledge that it was my greed that led me to take each fall personally. As long as I was driven by the kind of ambition that wanted to rise above others, I was destined to fail. But when I could befriend my rapacious desire for Power, I became "ingenuous" and/or innocent.

Henceforth, my rising angel becomes "GRace INgénue." The more I empty myself and let go of my attachments, the more I make room for something transcendent to express itself through me. This is grace – something that is quite frankly way bigger than I, and out of character. Watching it, I become "ingenious" and/or innovative.

The TWIN Code can now come into its final resonance, as I dived deep enough into the motivations of my shadow archetypes to transition them out of the DREaM into LOVE. Whereas there was only chaos in the DREaM as the letters didn't follow a specific sequence, LOVE did put its affairs in order. The "LOVE" spell evolves from the L of Leader to the O of Officer, the V of Visionary and the E of Engineer:

1. **The chilD turns to the Leader by making a motion of full responsibility**: I move to listen to the voice of madness (the angst of not having what I want). The more I hear and understand my conflict, the more I begin to see an alignment between my words and my results.

2. **The victiM turns to the Officer by making a motion of compassionate partnering**: I move to do what it takes, resolving to invite and even welcome my misuses of Power. Painful "errors" are now becoming genuine opportunities to uproot my story, and let go of my attachments.

3. **The saboteuR turns to the Visionary by making a motion of Oneness**: understanding intellectually that we are One is a start. But when **I choose** to *really* understand Oneness, I feel it, and stop calculating for my own advantage. Instead, I start telling the truth, and decide to do good.

4. **The prostitutE turns to the Engineer by making a motion of Power within Force**: all complaints stem from uninvestigated beliefs: body follows mind, as long there's a mind to follow! When I move to turn within, I hear the Force of instinct, and surprisingly find the Power to transform.

As I increasingly realize that I am creating by grace alone, the Leader in me accepts who I am and stops looking for love, approval and recognition out there. I know what I want. I decide. I do it. **My heart** is no longer broken: it is unhurt! Next, the Officer in me realizes that I can't let fear control me anymore. I can now drop my pain story and be in **my body.** I start feeling my presence and know that I have what it takes to be victorious. Next my Visionary hears that, if I once was lost, **my soul** now entered in resonance with a voice whose authority I can trust. I no longer block my life-force, and allow myself to be vital, gifted and powerful beyond measure.

Lamed (ל) Yod (י)	Vav (ו) / Heh (ה)	Mem (מ) Heh (ה)
Authority / Family	Money / Food	Memory / Sex
Rising angel / chilD	prostitutE / victiM	Fallen angel / saboteuR

Yet, the most precious of all transformations may just be what happens to **my mind.** I actually think I CAN. My faith comes from the knowing that I can't be bought. The prostitute became sacred, engineering the part of me that heaven trusts. I passed the initiation. I didn't sellout in view to acquire prosperity, Power or prestige. And since I would not compromise, I can now be given great tasks and know that I can carry them out. That quality of self-esteem was to be earned, and I earned it. As I transitioned from GReed into GRace, I find that my Giving and Receiving are balanced. Having learned from my 12 disciples and disciplines, I am now simply "IN-LOVE" with life.

Undivided Action

"Geometry is one and eternal shining in the mind of God. That men share in it is among the reasons that Man is the image of God."Johannes Kepler, mathematician and astronomer.

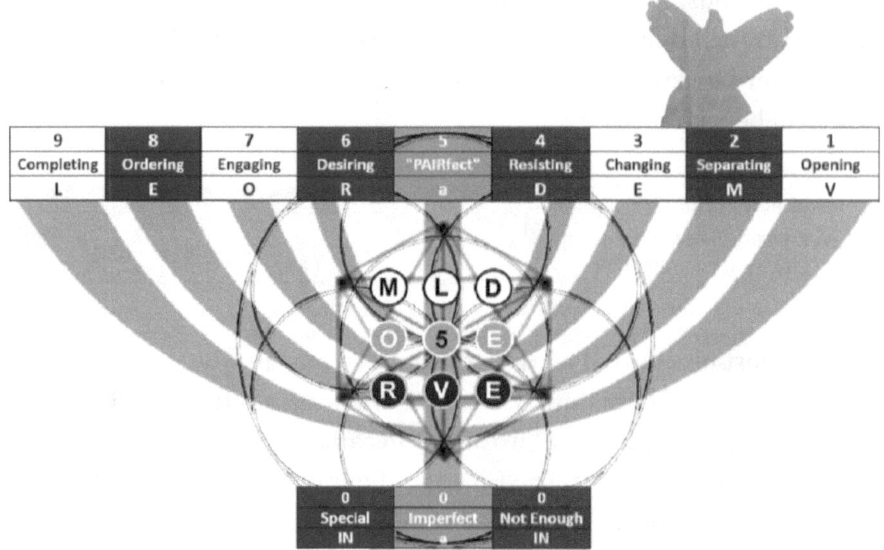

The enlightened action of 12 Disciples as 12 Disciplines.

The Chamber 000 (invisible, thus far) hides in the stand of my candelabrum. This is where to understand the triple belief "I'm special, imperfect, not enough," the result of which is the complete assimilation of desire and resistance.

My soul is now uplifted – free to dance with the light and shadows of 9 companions in the DREaM of LOVE, as I continue to experience that the way "INgénue" is the way out, and transition from GReed into GRace.

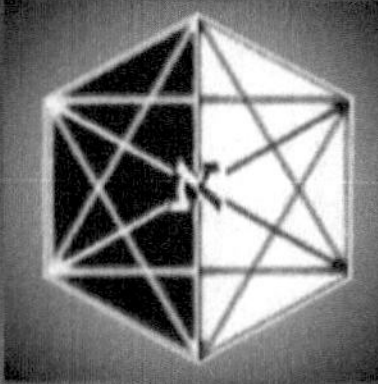

FOUR

Understanding Knowledge

"There is nothing partial about knowledge." A Course in Miracles

KNOWLEDGE IS a paradox mostly because to have knowledge, I must drop knowledge. Yet this is so simple that I let confusion get me. I won't endure the grey spaces of an "in-between" until an unknown becomes a known. To help me understand, this chapter has three parts. **Part I** consults the structure known across cultures as "the tree of life," and relates it to TCO's map and to sciences of human development. **Part II** focuses on the ignorance of evil, waking me up to the reality that, if I really knew evil, I would change for good. **Part III** gives *Proverbs 9:10's* decoding for me to face my fear of change, and negotiate the most difficult passage from the personal to the transpersonal. While knowledge may still be just in my head, seeing perennial truths clearly mapped out may inspire me to walk the territory. Gentle warning: this chapter may forever alter my sense of the Torah by offering "everything I always wanted to know about biblical knowledge (but were afraid to ask)." It will also help me to understand how to turn off the creative energy of the golem – an artificial intelligence I created as a defense mechanism, before it became my nemesis.

PART I: THE QKABBALAH OF KNOWLEDGE

Below are the "sentient" topics of this section:

- Knowledge and Opposites.
- Knowledge and the Two Trees.
- Knowledge of the Covenant in the Middle (a.k.a. 69ing).
- Knowledge of Parallel Worlds.
- Knowledge of Science and Con-science.
- Knowledge of the Heartbeat of Evolution.

Yod (י)	Vav Heh (וה)	Heh (ה)
Atziluth	*Beriah / Assiyah*	*Yetzirah*
Transmission	Creation / Manifestation	Formation
Spiritual	Mental / Physical	Emotional
Crown - Third Eye	Throat - Heart / Root	Navel - Sex

When YEWE clarifies the tree of (my) life…

Knowledge and Opposites

"God saw that the light was good, and separated the light from the darkness." *Genesis 1:4*

Once its code is understood as understanding itself, *Genesis 1:4* answers what may be the biggest question in the history of humanity: why is there evil in the world? Simply put, it is because I place a boundary between the light (which I'm told "God" sees as good) and the darkness (which I infer "God" sees as evil). I am now justified to resist the darkness, an attitude which ends up strengthening it. Light is in, darkness is out.

This soon leads me to take the "bad" personally: why me? My question is not a real inquiry and not even an admission. It is an attack of the

"YOUniverse," simply because I believe I'm not enough to deal with the situation. So, I play stupid, asking why simply because I don't want to change. I just made myself into a bona fide victim of my Genesis.

Not only don't I question its interpretations, but also and foremost, I fell for it, hook, line and sinker. My separating from reality will soon lead me to know "why." :-) Heck, asking real WHYS, I may become WISE enough to have no questions and no need for answers.

As for being a victim of my Genesis, there is huge shift between *Genesis 1* – a 1st story of creation when Adam (that is, me) was created male and female, empowered by an omnibenevolent "God" who saw goodness in everything, and *Genesis 2* – a 2nd story of creation when Adam 2 is a male and not a female (that is, good and resisting evil). This Adam (also me) lives in a complete illusion of separation, seeing himself as a have-not. First, he is a "he" *without* a "she," all alone in a garden *without* water or greenery. He is soon serving a "God" *out there* who sets him up to rebel by using a *negative* command *"don't* eat of the tree of knowl-edge." Putting myself in his shoes, how could I *not* look for LOVE in all the *wrong* places and *not* go against my conscience? I was doomed to eat the fruit I had forbidden myself to eat!

This shift from Adam 1 to Adam 2 is the shift from the truth of separa-tion of good and evil to the illusion of separation of good and evil (according to my interpretation of *Genesis 1:4* and/or reality). In the shuf-fle, my polarities get inverted and I lose the wisdom that knows the difference. My speech patterns hint to my deception: I dunno, I guess, I try, I hope... While in hiding, I naturally fall prey to giving and receiving fear, as a true victim of my genes and my Genesis, from generation to "Genesis rations" that are meant to nourish the soul week after week.

Code Understanding – BYN / WYNB

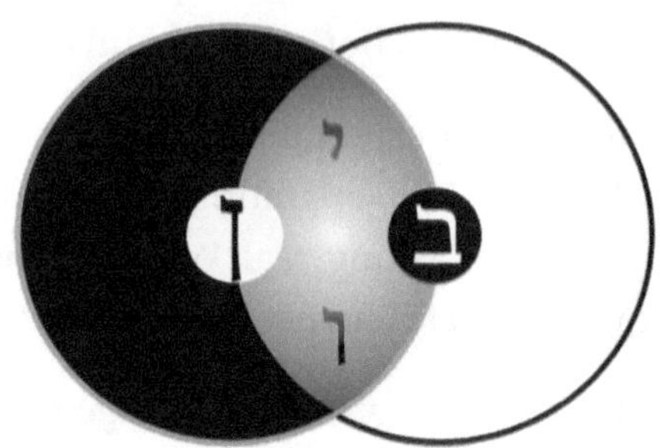

Imagine a language so pure and so sacred that it can reconcile opposites in just four letters...

Right: Hebrew letter Beth (ב) → B in Roman Script
Left: Hebrew letter Nun Final (ן) → N in Roman Script
Middle (top down): Hebrew letters Yod and Vav (יו) → YW in Roman Script

Here is how S/Hebrew inscribes code "Understanding:"

- **BN:** from right to left, I read *Ben* (בן) for "son."
- **BYN:** from right to top to left, I read *Beyn* (בין) for "between."
- **WBYN:** counterclockwise from bottom, I read *U'Beyn* (ובין) "and between."
- **WYBN:** bottom to top to right to left, I read *V'Yiben* (ויבן) "and he made."

The Decoding: first I understand that, in Old English, the "under" part of the word "understanding" does not mean "beneath" but "between." Second, the S/Hebrew verb *V'yabdel* for "he separated" is not a transitive verb with a direct object like it is in English: "he separated the light (direct object) from the darkness." S/Hebrew would say: "he separated **between** the light **and between** the darkness." The separation (which is a choice resulting from understanding) occurs at the mental level of PaRaDiSe, in the *D'Rush* world that ideally has the wisdom to know the

Difference. The word *LiD'Rosh* is built on the same root as *D'Rush*. It is first used when Rebekah was so sick and tired of the twins fighting in her womb that she went to YEWE to *LiD'Rosh* "inquire." So, I'm Rebekah, asking "why? Why so much fighting?" I begin by understanding that the twins represent the split mind – a part of me (Esau) is destined to be the firstborn. The other part (Jacob) is resisting not being the first born. He will eventually make the choice to steal his brother's birthright to gain the inheritance. And isn't it what I do when "fighting in my womb?" Am I not moved by a greed that opposes my nature to be LOVE?

If fear wasn't there, I'd be decisive – a master of **222-Separating.** I would not make choices whose consequences I would rather not have to experience. I would know that separating (or deciding) is how I create. And then I would look at *Genesis*, and realize in awe that:

1. The letters of *U'Beyn* (ובין) for "**and between**" reorder as *V'Yiben* (ויבן) for "**and he made,**" and more exactly "**and he built.**" The word is first used in *Genesis 2:22* ("And he built a woman from the rib he had taken out of the man").
2. The "rib" by which the LOVE God built the word "woman" in *Genesis 2:22* is the letter Heh (the Mother and Supreme Container).
3. Adding a **Heh** (ה) to *Beyn* (בין) builds the word *Binah* (בינה) for the "understanding" by which I build or construct my world.
4. Having a Heh container is having the womb-like compassion to be "with my pain." When I no longer resist, I can feel the fear. I then know what to decide and can do what it takes.

Through *Genesis 2:22* (222 being the mastery of separating), I deepen my understanding of "why there is evil in the world." It is because I judge evil to be bad. Since I am trained to resist "bad" and since what I resist persists, I continue to see evil in the world! Moreover, while resisting evil, I can't really know it. This is how I will flip positions, and start desiring it. My polarities are now reversed: what I judge to be good for me is actually bad, and vice-versa.

Postponing "THE decision" (the decision to know the difference *between* good and evil) blocks the grace of understanding. Conversely, inquiring on my motivations for resisting and/or desiring evil is how I come into complete understanding, and have the compassion to include and transcend my destiny. **The third eye – a.k.a. the gate of the good – opens. I wake from my slumber, seeing that, yes, the light is good, but also and foremost that greater is the light that comes from darkness. Understanding this, I now masterfully separate the light from the darkness, choose Peace, and emPower the NOW.**

Table to the right: letters בכר (BKR=222) build the following words 1. *Bekhor* "first-born" (the son who inherits), 2. *Kebor* "like cleanliness," and 3. *Barekh* "blessing." To master separating, I simply trust my firstborn instinct (understand) and make clean choices (peace) that bless all (emPower the Now)!

2	
Separating	
2	ב
20	כ
200	ר

THE KNOWLEDGE PARADOX

THE KNOWLEDGE PARADOX is multifold. Taking the serenity prayer as a foundation, I wouldn't mind having the wisdom that knows the difference! Indeed, I lose my peace of mind when not accepting the things I cannot change. And it gets worse: I then have no "courage to change the things I can."

But why won't I accept what I cannot change? Do I stay confused, just so that I'd avoid doing what I know it will take to heal a situation?

Here's my next excuse: I know that I have some knowledge, but I don't know where it comes from. I am told there's a field from which particles of light information emanate. When I make contact, the wave becomes a particle which illuminates an aspect of my consciousness. This particle then becomes part of me: I know it, I include it, I contain it – body and soul.

Seems easy enough, and yet I often disconnect. Knowledge is just in my head. I suffer from poor reception: the electrons circulating below around the sign Heh are yet to "contact" the cellular level. Take forgiveness, for example, I get its importance and work on it, but I am far from feeling it in my blood. Again, no container! This is how I know what to do, but can't seem to will myself to do it...

Weak will; addictions! If I could wait in the midst of my confusion, I'd eventually come to clarity. The rare times I did, the knowing that I knew was undeniable. No one could take it from me! The electron and I made contact. I understood. I was in my Power. I trusted that my words and actions made a difference. I was at peace.

However, is there another way to strengthen my will besides shadow work? I dread diving into the unknown, even if it is how to make contact and come back from the abyss with greater knowledge. The darkness is fraught with too many dangers. I'm afraid to lose my footing, or worse, to be swallowed by the mouth of its abyss... Plus, I don't enjoy meeting the greed monster!

No, I'd rather close this door to madness and stay safe in my beliefs, even if they are (and maybe because they are) limiting my self-esteem.

I understand that surrendering my judgments is to drop false knowledge and move from the plastic to the real. I understand that changing is not to let who I *think* I am get in the way of who I may become. But the fact that I'm resisting doing just that tells me that my understanding is not complete. That's how I'm plagued with cravings. Surrender is loving "God" for the sake of love and nothing else, not even for the sake of liberation.

Including my resistance is to die, the secret to seeing God face-to-face, "for you can't see My face and live" (*Exodus 33:20*). There's another verse that speaks of dissolving boundaries – when "Adam *knew* his wife Eve." Making love is one of the rare instances where time no longer exists. This is the "knowledge" of good and evil, when the woman is no more the woman; the man, no more the man. Both sides died into the LOVE that has no opposite. But why a tree and why not eat from it?

Story is told of a man who fell asleep under a wish-fulfilling tree. He woke up hungry thinking, "if only I had something to eat..." And delicious food appeared out of nowhere. Ravenous, he started eating. But then he had another thought: "I wish I had something to drink." Instantaneously, he saw fine wine appearing from the sky. Drinking the wine, he started worrying, "What's going on? Am I dreaming? No, this must be the work of the devil!" Promptly, horrible, ferocious, ugly-looking devilish creatures appeared! Terrified, he thought: "Now I'm for sure gonna be killed." And in that instant, he died!

Biblical Knowledge

"Wonder is the desire for knowledge." *Thomas Aquinas*

IT IS EQUALLY TRUE THAT DESIRE IS THE WONDER OF KNOWLEDGE. THE longing for oneness leads to the moment when a man and a woman (and more exactly "when my male and female sides") yield to each other's love, they surrender to this moment of sublime vibration, and they are no two no more. Matter no longer exists, and the deeper layer of the body starts vibrating as dancing energy. It pulsates with a subtle rhythm and coalesces with the heart. Suddenly, I find myself as if I am not. Only in deep love can I move into it.

That is exactly what knowledge is. It is biblical and sexual because it is elusive, being at once here and not here. Such depth of love must be where meditation enters. It is also where to unbridle an infinite creativity, infinite as it cannot be stopped by the fearful thought of making an error. Consciousness opens. The electron makes contact. The sperm enters the egg, and I am pregnant with possibilities.

Each time I make a connection, slowly, slowly, understanding grows, and with it, wisdom and kindness. When I have these three working together, I stand a much better chance not to misuse Power. Little by little, the yearning disappears. I am free. The need to have your love, approval and recognition no longer haunts me. Whether I use my sexual drive to make love or sublimate it into art, the neediness is gone. I am still, silent, and utterly myself, knowing the peace that is beyond understanding.

So yes, whether in sex or in art, the process is the same. I must surrender to the unknown. When I don't want to or when I have a headache (smiley), I must inquire. Thus, the elders say: "enlightenment is not going to happen because of what you do. But it is also not going to happen unless you do everything for it." It is why the tree of the knowledge of good and evil is so crucial: it teaches me all I ever wanted to know about desire, sex and death. The male and female flows must consummate each other to be the pillars that hold my temple of peace. When they fight a mean fight, I can't hold the tension between opposites and the "baby" or the result of my creativity is never enough.

There is something fundamental about "the tree of the [sexual] knowledge of good and evil," or *Etz HaDaath Tov V'Rah* (עץ הדעת טוב ורע). Eating from it will surely bring me to know *une petite mort,* French for "a little death" and a metaphor for orgasming. But will the same "tree" allow for the *Mahamudra* – Sanskrit for "the Great Orgasm," when I experience every instant as a source of infinite pleasure?

Kabbalah 101

"The LOVE God made all kinds of trees grow out of the ground – trees that were pleasing to the eye and good for food. In the middle of the garden were the tree of life and the tree of the knowledge of good and evil." *Genesis 2:9*

When I google "kabbalistic tree of life" (image section), I see several icons that look like the one below. Some of them have a sphere in the placement of the white sphere. Some of them do not. And yet both renditions endeavor to represent one or two of the trees mentioned in *Genesis 2:9*. According to the rabbinical tradition, the tree of life is an arrangement of 10 spheres linked by 22 meridians. The 10 spheres are the 10 numbers. The 22 meridians are the 22 letters of the alphabet.

The Hebrew name of the 11th sphere (the phantom sphere) is *Daath* for "knowledge." It is said to be "here and not here" which is fitting, since knowledge is elusive.

The tree of life is at the core of Hindu, Chinese Taoist and Tibetan Buddhist scriptures. It is the fundamental generic narrative structure of a sacred tree found in many of the world's mythologies, religious and philosophical traditions.

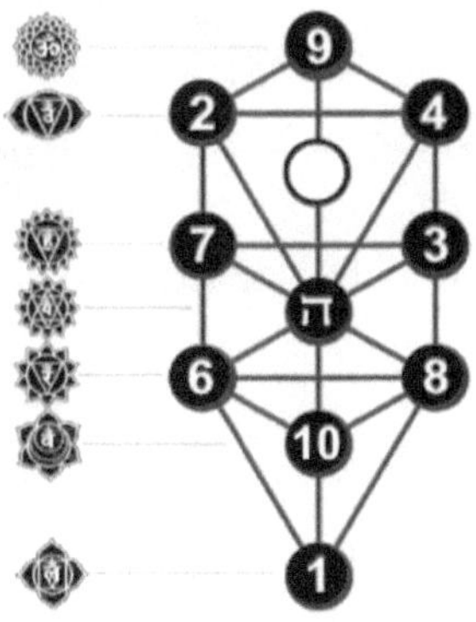

Left: the Hindu Tree of Life. Right: the Hebrew Tree of Life with the Phantom Tree of Knowledge

The life-force moves up the spinal cord (the tree's trunk) in seven "wheels" or junction points between consciousness and physiology. Therefore, the tree is the "real" nervous system, reflecting how the stages of consciousness affect different states of mind. Each word or action influences the wheel's performance; pure thoughts heal and clear, impure thoughts sicken and block. These centers are whirlpools of light transforming, funneling and regulating the flow of electrical fire-Power through the cells' communication pathways.

Seeing the seven beautiful lotuses of the Hindu tree of life next to the Hebrew tree, I now realize that there's an exact match in between the seven Hindu *chakras* or "wheels" and the seven rungs hosting the 10 *sephiroth* or "numbered spheres" of the Hebrew tree. The two trees naturally complement each other.

They allow for the eastern approach (more female-like) and the western approach (more male-like) to hear and see each other, and share their wisdom.

The enigmatic *Daath* sphere of "knowledge" is the core of the tree of the knowledge of opposites. Being a wormhole into the transpersonal ("here and not here"), it is not part of the tree of life. While the tree of life joins the heaven and the earth (or spirit and matter), the tree of knowledge joins heaven and hell (or all that is "good" and "not good"). This is how it transmits the knowledge of good and evil.

The QKabbalah of *Golden XPR*

"It's not what you look at that matters, it's what you see." *Henry David Thoreau*

The spheres' numbering (see prior figure) is meant to harmonize with TCO's map. The energy on the Hebrew tree of life begins by descending from the crown to the root. It is an opposite perspective to the Hindu tree of life on which the energy starts by ascending from the root to the crown. Similarly, the Hebrew tree offers its back, and the

Hindu tree, its front. The female and left-hand path on the Hebrew tree is to the left, while it is on the right on the Hindu tree. Different strokes for different folks…

It still makes me wonder, especially since *Exodus 33:20* states: "you cannot see my face, for no one may see me and live." So, if I want to know "God's" thoughts and if willing to die to my ego personality, seeing the tree face-to-face (and thus having the female and left-hand path to my right) would be an auspicious beginning. Moreover, I want both: the transcendence of the soul rising into Spirit and its immanence of descending into the body. Thus, the shift in numbering below. As for innovating, it is all very kosher as long as the Law is not changed. Knowing that the alphabet is the Law of laws and that I have no intention of changing a single Yod (or an iota), we should be safe!

> **"Do not think that I have come to abolish the Law or the Prophets; I have not come to abolish them but to fulfill them. For truly, I say to you, until heaven and earth pass away, not an iota, not a dot, will pass from the Law until all is accomplished."** *Matthew 5:18-19*

Henceforth, my first question: what is involved in accomplishing it all? Could Jesus have had in mind the *Tiqqun*? **Held to be an essential concept in the Kabbalah, the *Tiqqun* for "correction, repair, edit" is how to resolve the perennial conflict between good and evil.** As the saying goes: "if it ain't broke, don't fix it!" The perception that something needs "correcting, repairing or editing" is only valid as long as the ego personality is kept up.

Clearly, it is only when there is no personality that I may see "God" and live. As long as the mind competes with the heart, I will have a communication problem; a part of me knowing what to do, and the other part not wanting to do it. I'm not awake or conscious enough to stop trying to be right over an imagined enemy – me, you, it! This Power issue is at play in the dynamics of the tree of life of rabbinical Kabbalah and hermetic Qabalah. What would happen if I were "IN-LOVE?"

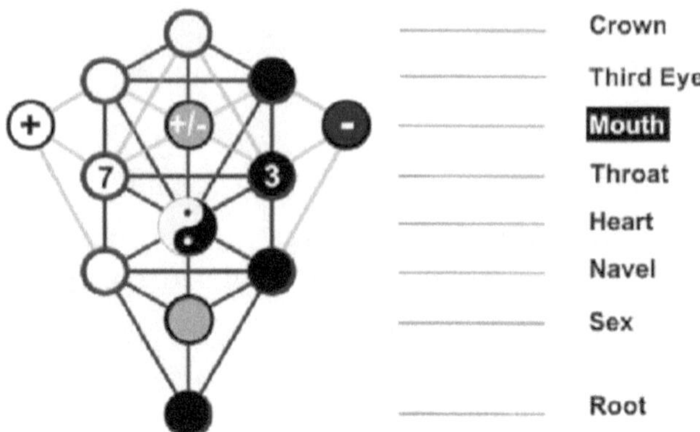

The Tree "IN-LOVE"

When looking at the Tree IN-LOVE, I see a network of paths around *Daath*, the sphere of "knowledge." The paths support the energetic motion in between the throat chakra and the 3rd eye (a most challenging passage). I can see how the rung of the throat (spheres #3 and #7) is just under *Daath's* rung.

Being in between the throat and the 3rd eye, *Daath* is newly revealed by *Golden XPR* as the mouth chakra. "Eating" from its tree (three spheres: knowledge, good, evil) leads to digesting the ego's resistance to change. This is how it is said: "don't eat from it or you'll die."

As for the throat, it is the decision-making center. It hosts the spheres *Geburah* "Power" and *Chesed* "kindness." But how kind am I when I can't regulate my use of Power? The marriage, or so it seems, does not work. This is where the tree "IN-LOVE" comes in. It joins the tree of life and its 32 wondrous paths of wisdom (32 = 10 numbered spheres + 22 lettered paths) to the tree of knowledge and its newly felt 13 infinite paths of Power (13 = 3 unnumbered spheres + 10 lettered paths). These 10 paths illuminate the purpose of the "final" letters as a bridge into the transpersonal. I am now ready to heal my throat's control issues:

- To help me die to the "no good" and see "God," the tree is now facing me (the yin/female side is now on the right side of the page).

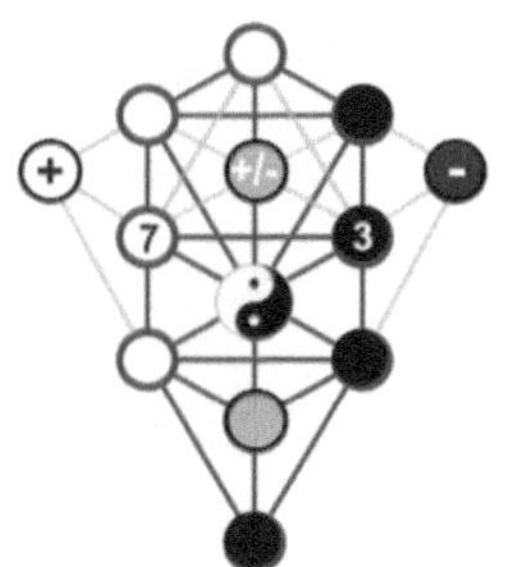

- To help me not misuse Power, wisdom becomes female (#3) and descends next to Power which becomes male (#7).
- To give me the heartfelt sense that we are One, kindness ascends, taking the place of wisdom next to understanding.

Resolving the burning issue of the throat is a necessity. For now, it appears that I don't have the wisdom to know the difference. What is bad for me, I judge to be good. I blame "you" for my failures, wanting to make you pay. This is a miscarriage of justice. Justice lives in the throat chakra, the center of decision-making, where I am a judge. "Justice, justice shall you pursue!" says the Torah. But how can I attain it, when kindness and Power (the spheres spinning the throat) are adding to the debacle? The male pillar is called "pillar of mercy," since kindness is at his core. The female pillar is called "pillar of judgment," since Power is at her core. This is as effective as saying to someone: "try not to be so hard on yourself!" Well, if I could, I would!

Opposing judgment and mercy decreases the Power of decision and/or any real sense of justice as it makes the throat a battlefield between a rewarding "God" and a punishing "God." This dilemma was masterfully pictured by Shakespeare in *A Merchant of Venice*. For the Shylock in me to forgive and change, wisdom must descend, and kindness, ascend: "the quality of mercy is not strain'd, It droppeth as the gentle rain from heaven/Upon the place beneath." *(Act-IV, Scene-I).*

The Three and the Tree

"Three things cannot be long hidden: the sun, the moon, and the truth." *Buddha*

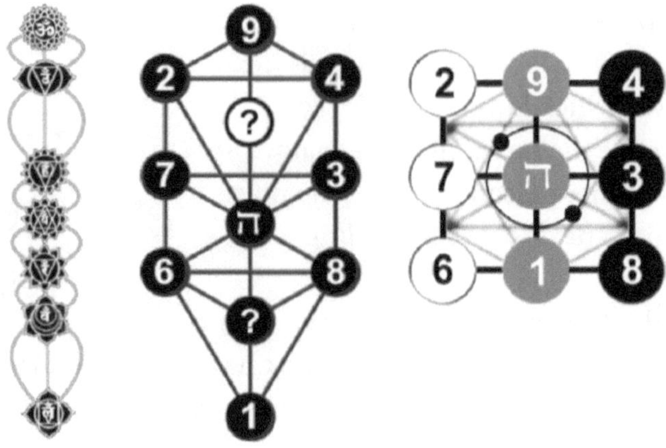

According to various wisdom traditions, Power circulates on three lines, also called "flows, circuits or pillars." Both Hinduism and Judaism, for example, speak of a tree of life. I also hear "three" of life. Energized by the interaction of three circuits – the sun, the moon and the product of their union, the stars (which Buddha calls "the truth"). Archetypally, the sun is male, and the moon, female. These two sides are in a fight, until they read the code of opposites, thereby synergizing the Power of Three. These three flows enact the sexual knowledge of good as male and evil as female. As the two opposite currents merge, energy is generated that circulates in all parts of the body. The surplus energy is stored at certain points – the plexuses along the spinal column commonly known as nerve centers. The more awake I am, the more I can center on the middle path and feel the double helix of the two flows interacting with each other.

A marked difference is in the way the Hebrew tree understands three centers (3rd eye, throat and solar plexus) by splitting their energies into a male and a female path. This gives me more information on how to hold the tension between opposites in the very places where working in polarity can be most challenging (more to come on this).

TCO's map (to the right) also has the same three flows – a sun (spheres 2, 7 and 6), a moon (spheres 4, 3 & 8) and the star-like truth (spheres 9, ה or 5 and 1). Each sphere has a quality (e.g.; 4 is

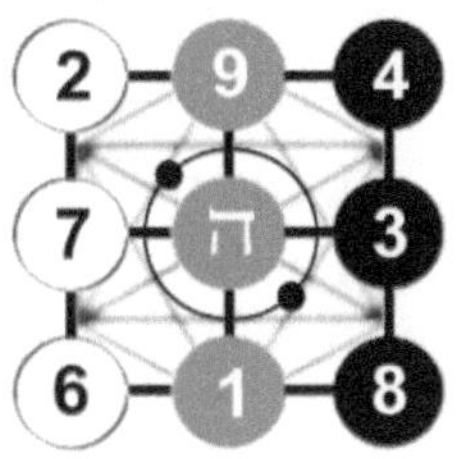

Binah for "understanding"). It derives its Power from a "God" Name (e.g.; understanding is moved by YEWE *Elohim*, the Power of history).

But what are the two electrons orbiting the heart center (ה)? Looking at the tree of life (previous page), I see that two spheres that are exactly equidistant from the heart center bear a question mark. The question is "how do I move into the 2nd tier (the promised land of an open third eye)?" The two electrons answer me:

1. **The bottom electron** enacts the sex chakra, as it is located on the rung in between the root and the solar plexus.
2. **The top electron** enacts the mouth chakra, as it is located on the rung in between the throat and the third eye.

The Covenant in the Middle

'Tantric doctrine views the tongue and the genital area as the great radiators or throw-off points for subtle forces. Thus, the use of fellatio or cunnilingus in sex magic releases immense reserves of psychic force to sweep vigorously through the nervous system; the traditional "battery terminals" connect, closing the circuit for bio-energies to be exchanged between the two practitioners.' *Dr. John Mumford, Ecstasy through Tantra.*

To bring light on how synchronizing the two spheres around the heart chakra is the key to creative Power, I must introduce *Sepher Yetzirah* or the "Book of Formation." This book is the founding work of rabbinical Kabbalah and, by extension, hermetic Qabala. It speaks of the creation of the universe, time, sentience and symbolic Power itself.

According to modern historians, the origin of the text is unknown and hotly debated. Some scholars believe it might have an early Medieval origin, while others emphasize earlier traditions appearing in the book. Whether it comes from the Mishnaic period (2nd century BCE), or from Adam, and from there, "passed over to Noah, and then to Abraham, the friend of God," nobody knows. It is believed that the book is only to be used for spiritual purposes, and only accessible by the pious.

The PaRaDiSe transmission spans four worlds, one of which being the world of formation. Invoked by the R of the Reflection I see in life's mirror, it is where the forms of the dreaming state appear. It is the realm of the subtle body that is understood by way of emotions, when I know a truth in my soul. *Sepher Yetzirah* is therefore the one book among all books on the Kabbalah that ought to be felt. And yet, its codes have remained undeciphered since, thus far, the understanding of its six very short and very dense chapters have stayed fairly mental.

Curiously, the book's title – *Sepher Yetzirah* – is often translated as if it were *Sepher Beriah* for "Book of Creation." *Beriah* is the level of mind where the problem is "created" by the beliefs I resist investigating that lead into emotions that I resist feeling. If I could feel, I would hear how emotions yield a "formation." I would eventually realize that emptiness is form and form is emptiness. I'd let go of my bond to the material world as I wouldn't be so attached to a *form*. I would then decode my own "Book of Formation" from within.

And it makes me wonder... For me to skip over the world of formation even though it is the bridge between mind and body, there must be a creation I am resisting to feel. Since what I resist persists, why energize a limiting belief?

The Holy Trans-Formation

"Just let go. Let go of how you thought your life should be, and embrace the life that is trying to work its way into your consciousness." *Caroline Myss*

When I can't let go of my beliefs, I could ask myself: what is the worst thing that I could possibly have done, so "bad" that I can't feel it or forgive it? If I'm a Christian (and in a way, we are all Christians, since we are all one), I may believe that the worst possible transgression is blasphemy against the Holy Ghost. Knowing that the etymology of *blasphemy* comes from the Greek for "speaking ill," how can I not speak ill of the Holy Ghost when the Jewish part of me can't feel the world of Formation? This is the very world where the Holy Ghost lives, inviting me to know and feel the truth.

Yod (י)	Vav Heh (וה)	Heh (ה)
Atziluth	*Beriah / Assiyah*	*Yetzirah*
Transmission	Creation / Manifestation	Formation
The Father	The Son / the Mother	The Daughter
Intuiting	Thinking / Sensing	Feeling

Creation via beliefs - Formation via emotions

Would there be any belief about blasphemy if I felt the Holy Ghost as one aspect of the Sacred Feminine? Would I violate the laws of LOVE if I allowed myself to feel, which is the very function of the Holy Ghost? Indeed, how can I let go of my limiting beliefs unless I feel them? This connection between the world of Creation and the world of Formation is symbolized by the Son engaged to the Bride, when beliefs and emotions are One. Surely, if unable to marry my Bride, that is, if unable to feel, how can I forgive? And if I don't feel, how can I think straight? All sorts of "PAIRS" exist: Son and Mother (thinking and sensing), Father and Daughter (intuiting and feeling), Mother and Father (sensing and intuiting), Son and Bride (thinking and feeling). If I continue to ghost the Holy "Ghost" (or the Daughter and Bride), how could I be functional – sensing, intuiting, thinking, AND feeling? Indeed, if one function is greyed out, the other three functions suffer.

As I contemplate the order of creation, this is what I see:

- Vav the Son: **I think** in *Beriah* – the world of "creation" (beliefs).

- Heh the Daughter and the Bride: **I feel** in *Yetzirah* – the world of "formation" (emotions).
- Heh the Mother: **I sense** in *Assiyah* – the world of "manifestation" (actions).

However, when I move from the bottom up, first, **I sense**, second, **I feel**, and third, **I think**. In other words, 1) **I receive** the Matter that I prayed for. 2) **I feel** gratitude. 3) **I think** I CAN. Lastly, 4) **I intuit** the Father's transmission. The trick to sustaining gratitude is to QKabbalah "receive" the Mother. Once moved out of Scare City, I no longer resent being among the have-nots.

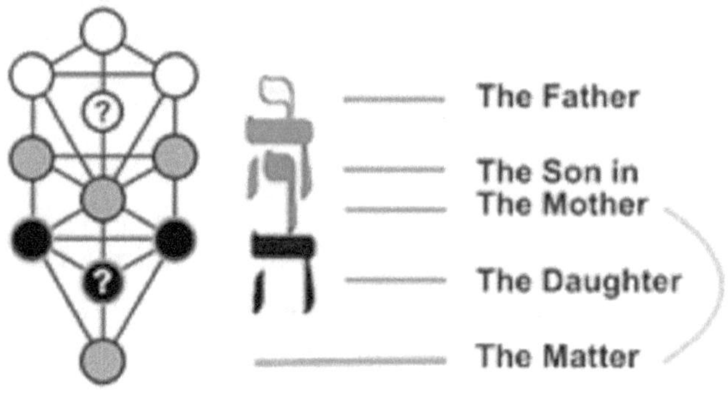

Religion calls it "faith," and science, "certainty."

This diagram explains Jesus' words: "whatever you prayed for, believe that you've received it." I relate the words to the worlds spanning the PaRaDoX. In this case, the Mother (the body/manifestation) is pregnant with the Son (the mind/creation). I have a belief that is in gestation. For my belief to manifest (or my prayer to be fulfilled in the Now, when there is no time interposed between the creation and the manifestation), I must feel it. Feeling it is what puts my words into **form**.

Time begins when the mind (that is, the Son) separates from the heart (the Father), and is thus no longer in the body (the Mother). This double separation from the heart and the body is what I resist feeling.

Yod (י)	Vav Heh (וה)	Heh (ה)
The Father	The Son / the Mother	The Daughter
Atziluth	*Beriah / Assiyah*	*Yetzirah*
Transmission	Creation / Manifestation	Formation

Blocking the transmission

When disconnected from **the Father**, I'm likely to think of me as a "have-not." This means that my *Assiyah* world of **Manifestation** doesn't reflect the abundance it would have if I had listened to my intuition and received the Father's **Transmission**. I am now believing that my prayer won't be answered, and that's what I sense and what I see. I am also resisting feeling bad about being in lack, and resisting what my "bad" feelings put into form – my world of **Formation**. My somber thoughts will now be shaped as the dark night of the soul. This under-scores the importance of *Sepher Yetzirah* – aptly named the Book of "Formation." It is written for me to master my emotions and therefore be able to trans-form. To that end, it gives me a text so abstract that, unless I become real, the codes won't open up to me.

The Unspeakable Union of Sex & Mouth

"The non-dimensional spheres are numbered ten as the fingers; five opposite five, with a singular covenant precisely in the middle, sanctified by the circumcision of the tongue and the phallus."
Sepher Yetzirah, Chapter 1:3

The "covenant" is inscribed in the heart chakra, which is "precisely in the middle" of the tree (right to left; top to bottom). Its sanctification occurs via the twin circumcision of the phallus (sex chakra) and the "tongue" (mouth chakra). *Sepher Yetzirah* makes it clear that the tree of life has 10 spheres, not 9, not 11. It also makes it clear that the tree of the knowledge of opposites is part of the equation. Surely, to have a tongue to circumcise, I must have a mouth!

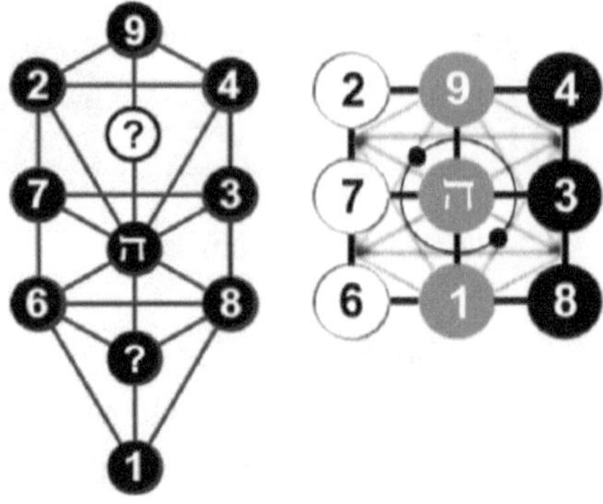

I can now see how the two satellites orbiting the heart chakra marked by the letter Heh in the image to the right correspond to the two spheres with a question mark in the diagram to the left – the white sphere being the mouth chakra, and the black sphere, being the sex chakra. Note: while not traditional, the numbering of the spheres reveals how the spheres of the tree of life echo the QKabbalah of the Nine Chambers. Both the heart of the tree and the heart of the chambers are marked by letter Heh. This vision, which parallels the question of the mouth chakra and of the sex chakra, is given by TCO as a possible decoding of *Sepher Yetzirah, Chapter 1:3.*

As for the 10 spheres of the tree of life, they span the four worlds as follows:

- Spheres 9, 4, 2 live in the world of **Transmission** – the emptiness realm.
- Spheres 3, 7, Heh live in the world of **Creation** – the causal realm.
- Spheres 8, 6, black ? live in the world of **Formation** – the subtle realm.
- Sphere 1 lives in the world of **Manifestation** – the gross realm.

Clearly, if I want to do as Jesus did and "go to the Father," I must make the jump into the abysmal *Daath*, in the world of the "**Infinite**" – the

Ain Soph or non-dual realm. Only then will I have emptied myself enough to stop counting.

The more I jump in and inquire on my darkness, the more I feel *Sepher Yetzirah* as a guide to the play of form and emptiness that keeps restructuring my perspectives on the trees of life and knowledge. I just needed to contemplate the questions asked by the mouth and sex chakras: "just how much darkness do you want to transmute into light, and how deep will you dive into the shadow to get the pearl in consciousness? Are you ready stop playing the Power games of dominance and submission?"

Again, these questions are about the courage it takes to make THE decision to evolve and "circumcise" consciousness until I can know wholesome Power.

The Denied Purifications

"Circumcise your hearts, therefore, and do not be stiff-necked any longer." *Deuteronomy 10:16*

Whether male or female, I'm so asleep in the dream of patriarchy that I see domination in "the LORD" and not YEWE's balance. I also don't realize that the Torah is the recipient of the collective unconscious as a dream awaiting an interpretation that can help me be real. Feeling its symbols wakes me up by restoring sentience; the feeling and sensing functions of the Sacred Feminine. I just have to open to know the truth.

Every rabbi – even without having studied the Kabbalah – will confirm that the *Brit Milah* or the "Covenant of Circumcision" includes four circumcisions – the foreskin, the ears, the tongue, and the heart. So why is it that the collective (Jews included) only knows of only ONE circumcision - this of the foreskin of the phallus? Might the cause be found in my unwillingness to become conscious of my arrogant urge to dominate the world?

Focusing on the foreskin conveniently obliterates the fact that the work is to clear the mind. Surely, these four circumcisions are not physical but mental.

As always when I am in the presence of the "FOUR," I am witnessing the "LORD" of Karma in action. These four circumcisions will transition me out of the DREaM and of its four ensuing unconscious projections. Once I know that I Am LOVE, the obstacles that I had created to prevent me from being in my Power will naturally disappear:

1. The **phallus'** circumcision removes the prostitutE's **urges.**
2. The **ears'** circumcision removes the saboteuR's **disconnection.**
3. The **tongue's** circumcision removes the victiM's **intoxication.**
4. The **heart's** circumcision removes the chilD's **resentment.**

Gospel trivia: the word *Miltah* (מלתא) for "circumcision," but also for "**word**" is used in the Aramaic version of "in the beginning was the **Word**" (*John 1:1*). It gave S/Hebrew *Milah* of *Brit Milah* for "Covenant of Circumcision." Cutting the psychic genitals is how to come into wholesome Power. My focus on dominating the material world is what created confusion about the cut of the foreskin being physical.

Milah **speaks of a hidden system by which to clean up and wake up. This is when I realize that crossing over the abyss of the Infinite is a non-negotiable. But what about the fear?**

Crossing Vertical Stages and Horizontal States

"All truth passes through three stages. First, it is ridiculed. Second, it is violently opposed. Third, it is accepted as being self-evident."
Arthur Schopenhauer

The fear of being alone hides the fear of death, and the fear of death hides the fear of Power. To help me, the two trees cross to trace two paths to enlightenment – vertical and horizontal:

The tree of life moves my energy vertically through seven rungs from the root to the crown. These rungs are **stages** of consciousness. The heart is the absolute center of the tree (the sphere hosting ה). Below it, I find the spheres of my egocentric or ethnocentric desires; above it, the spheres of my world-centric desires. The rung where I'm most likely to vacillate between ethnocentric desires and worldcentric desires is the throat.

The tree of knowledge moves my energy horizontally through three transpersonal spheres where I wake up from the dream of separation. However, to crossover into a felt-sense of oneness and sustain it, I still need to consciously "eat" from *Daath's* "knowledge" and from its allies, the spheres of good and evil. Facing my demons and welcoming my crucifixion will lead me to the **states** of awareness where I can rest in peace. Abiding in the celestial spheres (2, 4 and 9) curiously allows me to occupy the whole tree.

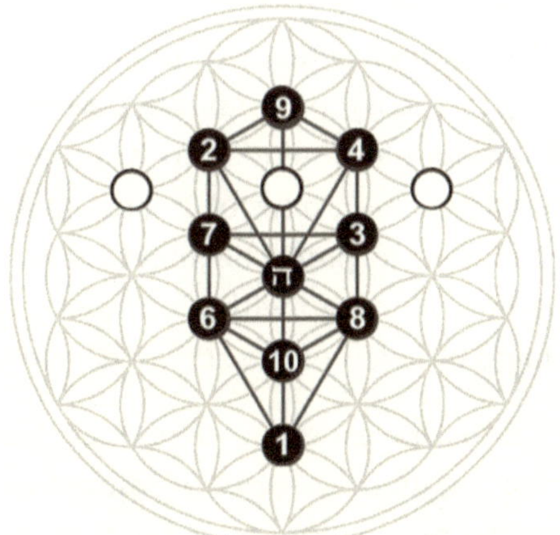

"In the middle of the garden were the tree of life and the tree of the knowledge of good and evil." *Genesis 2:9*

This is the garden of Eden. The tree of life is formed by 10 numbered spheres (black); the tree of knowledge, by 3 unnumbered spheres (white). The two spheres to the right and left of *Daath* are newly revealed by *Golden XPR* as the "good" and "evil" of "knowledge."

The mouth is "knowledge" or neutral when it kisses, "good" or male when it speaks, and "evil" or female when it eats.

Science & Conscience

"Beware of false prophets, who come to you in sheep's clothing, but inwardly they are ravenous wolves. You will know them by their fruits. . . A good tree cannot bear bad fruit, nor can a bad tree bear good fruit." *Matthew 7:15-18*

The trees map out my communication pathways. When the results of my words match my vision, I am telling the truth. I am a true "prophet" as I effectively foretold what was to come. However, when there's a misalignment between what I say I want and what I actually have, I am a "false prophet," which indicates that there are a few predatory intentions in my space. These secrets are how my trees bear "bad fruit."

Sciences of adult development endeavor to solve this communication dilemma. From Piaget's theory of cognitive development to Keagan's four levels of socio-emotional potential, to Kohlberg's stages of moral development, to Maslow's hierarchy of needs, to Erikson's stages of psychosocial development, to Jane Loevinger's stages of ego development, psychologists have come up with a number of possible schemes that organize the stages or levels of the ethical developmental line.

Based in part on Clare Graves' spiral dynamics, Ken Wilber's stages endeavor to integrate the main theories of human development. Eight levels move as a spectrum of colors from beige to turquoise. The first six colored strata are part of a first tier focused on scarcity. The second tier moves my thinking into abundance. Reading Graves and Wilber, I understand that there is a point when I can see myself and reality as "good." Being enough, I naturally adhere to a system of values enabling me to grow. Respect becomes the primary directive of my communication, a respect that is informed by sentience and honors the sacred in everything and everyone.

Taking this model, religion (specifically the Abrahamic faiths) halted its growth at the stage Wilber calls "amber," a code of conduct based mainly on absolutist principles. In this stage, violating the right and wrong code has severe repercussions and abiding it yields rewards. This stage is infused with a rigid paternalism that mostly seeks to establish order by way of domination ("this is so because I said so!"). To this end, it condones hierarchies and controls impulsivity through guilt.

As for me, I am a cultural creative – supposedly on the pluralistic green meme, and want to believe that I am past that stage, but am I? While an advocate of diversity, do I really respect amber or even orange beliefs, or do I stand in judgment of them? Similarly, sensitivity matters to me. On that note, might I find that being kind to myself and others is not always easy? What's left of my severity indicates that I'm still trying to obey or enforce a fictional code of honor that shows no real care or compassion. Moreover, saying that pluralism is THE way to go unravels the ideal of pluralism itself.

And it makes me wonder... If religion could evolve beyond the infantile stage in which it is confined, would it then be a valuable partner to sciences of adult development in helping me transcend the pluralistic meme? After all, if there's an institution specializing in ethical development, it ought to be religion!

The fact that there is a path to evolution hidden in the scriptures is affirmed by mystics across traditions who exemplify being the Word made flesh (holistic and integral). What I was missing thus far is a decoding potent enough and simple enough for the individual and the collective to digest the mythical stuff and vibrate with the energy of Oneness transmitted by the Living Word.

The Heartbeat of Evolution

"As I go within to find my real self, I find only the world... the real self within is actually the real world without. The subject and the

object, the inside and the outside are and always have been one. There is no primary boundary." *Ken Wilber*

Evolution is so strange. It takes me from violated and violating boundaries, to speaking clear boundaries, to imagining no boundary. In the end, whatever quirk I adopted to distinguish me from others simply dissolves as I realize that I am not separate from the world but an expression of the world. Such merging is the code of opposites at its best. I lose all dualist tension and no longer need to exert or exhaust myself in strenuous effort to reach the shore of abundance. My whole being relaxes, my clenched fist opens, and my attachments let go of me.

As I move back and forth from collective Power (the Tribe) to individual Power (the Self), I also move back and forth in between different perspectives, which leads me to affirm the significance and even the reality of all perspectives (no boundaries). And as the right and wrong game winds down, my heartbeat becomes coherent.

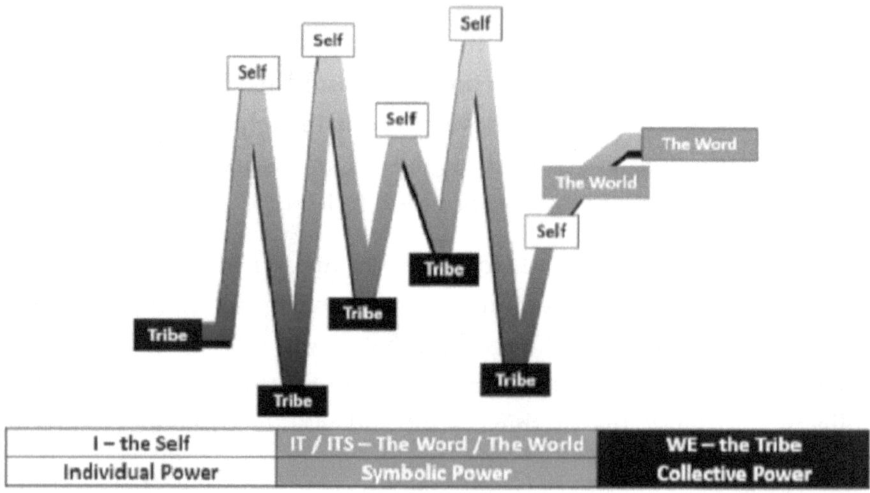

Compelled to move from outer to inner until I am true to my Word...

Moving from stage to stage, I realize that some stages require years of work, and that most transitions occur through rough waters. Each new level of Power bends me and even shatters me, until my answer to the call of servant leadership is unequivocal. Passing these initiations shows me that a previous level doesn't own me anymore.

This being said, "the chilD" will create unconscious time to try to slow things down. Indeed, growing into a Leader involves a shift in speed as it bypasses the need to manage the wounded child. Moving out of the first tier's comfort into the second tier's strangeness is healing and terrifying. When going through this shift in parameters, I embrace the marked increase in response-ability by feeling into the real/unreal paradox:

1. "God" is real.
2. The World is unreal.
3. "God" is the Word / World.

As for the honey, the table below juxtaposes Ken Wilber's spiral dynamics of development and the chakra system of the S/Hebrew trees of life and of knowledge. "*Golden XPR's* dynamics" gives the names of the *Sephiroth* (the "chakras"). Their translations are offered as "levels of cognition."

Something unexpected happens in the association: the tree of the knowledge of good and evil discloses its function as a wormhole connecting the first tier to the second tier.

During that passage, there are no more boundaries between subject and object, inside or outside, nothing to keep me from feeling the fundamental truth of oneness. As I choose to "biblically know" the truth, I can simply decide what is "good." This is where the inclusion of a quantum religion makes a difference: the wormhole prepares me for the unexpected – the accident that invites the ultimate. It also gives me a 3-base code of knowledge to explore the shadow and practice holding the tension.

Ken Wilber's Stages	Chakra System	Golden XPR's Dynamics	Levels of Cognition
Clear Light	Crown	*Kether*	Integrity
Turquoise	Third Eye	*Binah*	Understanding
Teal	Third Eye	*Chesed*	Kindness
Second Tier ↑			
Ultraviolet	Mouth -	*Okhel*	Metabolizing
Violet	Mouth +	*Dibri*	Silencing
Indigo	Mouth -/+	*Daath*	Knowing
Third Tier ↑			
Green	Throat	*Chokmah*	Wisdom
Orange	Throat	*Geburah*	Power
n/a	Heart	*Tiphereth*	Beauty
Amber	Navel	*Hod*	Appreciation
Red	Navel	*Netzach*	Perseverance
Magenta	Sex	*Yesod*	Honesty
Infrared	Root	*Malkuth*	Receptivity
First Tier ↑			
Second Tier	Third Tier		Fist Tier
"Promised Land"	Shadow Work		"Ego-Egypt"

Linking Wilber's third tier to the tree of the knowledge of opposites…

Note: while the names of the 10 spheres of the tree of life are generally congruent with the teachings of rabbinical Kabbalah and hermetic Qabala, there was nothing written about the two spheres newly revealed by *Golden XPR* as being on each side of *Daath's* "knowledge." These are felt as *Dibri* ("my word") and *Okhel* ("eating"). They are the processes of the mouth ("male/outer" speaking and "evil/inner" eating), which will lead to silencing and metabolizing the ego personality.

NOT "REVELATION"

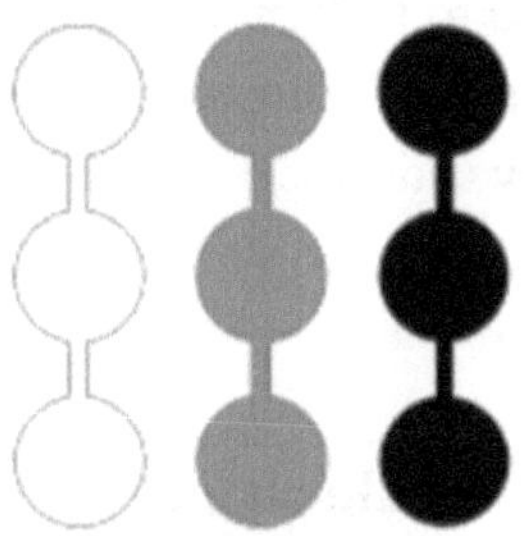

'NOT "REVELATION" – tis – that waits But our unfurnished eyes.'
Emily Dickinson

I don't need an external "God" to come and save me from my torments. I just need a new "eye" – another way to look at "IT." For now, my vision is blurred, so filled it is by old trauma, cravings, aversions and mis-readings. I wanna be right, you see?

If only I could stop fighting with "God," my third eye would open to seeing the good, the true and the beautiful. Feeling St Exupéry's words "it is only with the heart that one can see rightly" and sensing "that which is invisible to the eyes," I would realize that my heart has been circumcised from the opaque trappings of my judgments. There'd be no more "evil eye" to superimpose confining images or memories of the past or the future over the Now. Aleph would set me free!

But for now, I am trapped in Beth, in the 2nd of the 10 Words which commands me: "you shall not make an image for yourself in the form of anything in heaven above or on the earth beneath or in the waters below." *Exodus 20:3*. Of course, once told not to "make images" (not to judge), I become addicted to judgments! The story I tell is how I made of Beth a "House" of bondage: "This is Art, this is not Art," followed by: "I know that this is evil; I know it!"

But if I really knew evil, I would change for good! And that would be a revelation!

PART II: THE IGNORANCE OF EVIL

Below are the "diabolical" topics of this section:

- The Question of Transmutation.
- The House of Desires.
- Lies, Sex and Psychology.
- The Poisons – East and West.
- The Taboos and the "SOULution."
- The Golem Divergence.
- The Satan Program.

Yod (י)	Vav Heh (וה)	Heh (ה)
Transmission	Creation / Manifestation	Formation
Crown - Third Eye	Throat - Heart / Root	Navel - Sex
Aversion	Ignorance / Entitlement	Greed

When YEWE clarifies the poisons of (my) life…

Advocating Evil

'And LOVE said to Satan: "Has your heart considered My servant Job? There is no one like him on earth, perfect and upright, in awe of *Elohim* and shunning evil." And Satan answered LOVE: "does Job fear *Elohim* for nothing?"' *Job 1:8-9*

There's a line in *Groundhog Day* akin to "fearing *Elohim* for nothing." It is spoken by Phil (Greek for "love"): "whatever happens tomorrow – or for the rest of my life, I am happy now because I love you." The movie lets me see the countless reincarnations it takes to move from arrogance to humility. The eradication of the "yeast" behind a puffed-up ego is the purpose of the Passover holiday. It is also the function of *advocatus diaboli* ("Devil's advocate" in Latin), the Promoter of Faith appointed by the Catholic Church. His job (pun intended) was to argue against the sainthood of a candidate to uncover any misrepresentation of the evidence favoring canonization.

Similarly, *The Book of Job* is the book of the Bible advocating evil in order to promote faith by shifting entitlement into selfless service. Satan for "the adversary" does his utmost to fail Job by inflicting three incremental losses on him: his money, his children and his health. The S/Hebrew name Job means "hated." Surely, I feel forsaken when some adversarial force attacks me where it hurts. And yet, without Satan, I would never open a business, marry or write a symphony. I would never return home to the Father, and wholeheartedly offer my gifts. Without Satan, I would never rebuff my nemesis and make "IT" my friend, thereby passing the test of temptation and seeing that the curse is in fact a blessing. Without Satan, I wouldn't forgive or know myself!

When faced with suffering, at times as extreme as seeing my child dying in my arms, or witnessing and surviving a genocide or serving as a soldier in a war, it is hard not to fall into hatred or despair. Since evil has befallen me, it is understandable that I would have a crisis of faith and not know what to believe anymore. But if I want to be free, I must be willing to realize that I don't know what's for my highest good. I must begin to feel the humility of a Jesus who rose as the Messiah and triumphed over Satan by his full adherence to the plan of redemption willed by the Father. Will I accept that, as long as I draw breath, there will be a way for me to see the order in the chaos, the light in the darkness, the good in evil? **And if there is a QKosmic Plan moving all of us toward the love that has no adversary, can I be as Job, transforming hate by seeking to love rather than to be loved?**

THAT IS THE QUESTION

The House of Desire

THAT IS THE QUESTION, a parallel "to be or not 2B." Second word *Beth* (בית) for "house" has the same 412 gematria as *Ta'avah* (תאוה) for "desire." When I see that the light is good and separate it from a darkness that I see as evil, I desire the light and resist the darkness. In my split mind, the heavenly light will one day deliver me from the jail of material darkness. Indeed, my desire is a resistance to be without (the light), and my resistance, a desire to be without (the darkness). This is how I come to believe "I'm bad, evil, flawed, dark, not enough!"

No wonder I'd get trapped into greed, lust or gluttony!

I must now distract myself and create unconscious time. It's a great thrill; I feel the excitement; I'm about to have the large automobile, the beautiful house, the girl, the promotion. And then I get it; the large automobile, the beautiful house, the girl, the promotion. And suddenly it's all meaningless again, as if it dematerialized!

For a moment, I became so intoxicated by the desire that I forgot about the emptiness which threatens to absorb me. But it is still there. I can only create another desire to try to escape from this yawning abyss. And the more I do, the more I lock myself into Scare City. I am a miser. ♫♪ "I can't get no satisfaction!"

My problem is that I can't just be. I don't know how to be the feminine side of God, the embodied wisdom coming from experience – from *Daath's* "sexual" knowledge. It would be tremendous to be able to say: "I am what I am because that's who I am," and not have to do anything, to please anybody, to worry about what anybody thinks of me. It would be amazing not to fear the emptiness anymore.

"What do you want?" asks gematria 412. The question is meant to wake me up from the illusion of separation when I know the END of desire.

Is my ego strong enough to deal with an archetypal energy that leads me to prostitute my vision and sabotage myself? Will I dare ask what I really want and what I really need? Unless I understand my motivations, I will act as a perfectionist trying hard to live up to a totally unreal world; "a chilD" burdened by the archetype of a divine parent so high and mighty s/he won't let me be.

When I find myself enacting my parents' unconscious behavior, I become a victim of my biology. This is exactly what 2nd Word Beth advises me against: "you shall not bow down to your images or worship them. For I am the DREaM your God, a jealous God, punishing the children for the sin of the parents to the third and fourth generation of those who hate me." *Exodus 20:4*

To feel how my being possessed by jealousy fuels the hatred, I must understand my victiM: why would I want to do harm? I will then bridge the gap between reality and the illusion of "God" I project. If not, I'll be a saboteuR and self-destroy via food, drink, sleep, work, social media – anything to escape! During the day, I am "good" – in control. During the night, I am "bad" to the bone. The energy of the unconscious has broken loose into the addiction. I am possessed!

If I could only stop lying...

The Wizard of Lies

'Now the snake was craftier than any beast of the field that the LORD God had made. And he said to the woman, "Did God really say, 'You must not eat from any tree in the garden?'" *Genesis 3:1*

The invention of lying begins in *Genesis 3*, when I meet the snake – the subtlest animal of all. Before that, I was "naked and I had no shame." Lying takes intelligence. I must be able to understand social rules and what happens when these rules are violated. For instance, if I confess, I may be punished. But if I could lie, I might just get away with murder. I must also be able to imagine what the other is thinking. Did my mother see me taking money from her purse? Just how far can I stretch the truth with her?

The ubiquity of lying is clearly a problem, but would I want to will away all of my lies? Let's be honest, to use that word as a joke: has lying become, as per Nietzsche's assertion, "a condition of life?" And if so, what drives me to lie?

There's a very moving moment in *the Wizard of Lies* – a movie about stockbroker, investment adviser and financier Bernie Madoff who was arrested for perpetrating perhaps the largest financial fraud in U.S. history. **Here is someone who was brilliant, unfailingly charismatic, zeroing in on his own greatest weakness: he only wanted to please people. He wanted to be loved.**

Could he really have been lying simply because he loved making us happy and seeing us thrilled at the perspective of all the money that he would make us? It certainly wouldn't be the first time that a savior complex led to a giant misuse of Power. And while I bought it and was his victim, I wanted to believe him so much that I participated in the theft. Yep, moved by greed, I didn't do due diligence in looking at the validity of the investment.

Lying is a form of communication that involves two complementary parties – the seducer and the seduced. These two are a marriage made in heaven: the seducer intends to communicate false impressions or information. The seduced intends to buy into the lie—at least on some level. As the seduced, I choose to imagine by virtue of apathy, ignorance or overconfidence that the moon reflected on the water is the same as the moon in the sky. When I own that there is only One of us and that any judgment that I make of you is ultimately about me, I realize that I can only deceive myself.

The Seduction Game

"You had me at hello!" *Jerry Maguire – the movie.*

Seduction – and with it, dishonesty – pervades romantic relationships. I really want to believe that you're "the one," the person who will fulfill all my desires and save me from the poverty mind in which I abide. Isn't it curious how I want to be needed, owned, possessed, "had" and, at the same time, resist being needed... Ah, the lies men tell women and women tell men: "of course, I love you!" I am so concerned by what you think of me that I will lie to gain your love. The problem with my strategy is that I can't trust that you love me since I manipulated you to have it in the first place.

This may be how most romance movies often share a similar script: 1) love at the first sight, 2) the belief in happily ever after, 3) the discovery of the other's deception, 4) the breakup, 5) the humble apology: "I've been a jerk!" 6) the vow of renewed and eternal honesty... until lying do us part again? But that's another movie!

I may then realize that it is not the betrayal that upsets me as much as the fact that I can't trust you anymore. The real question remains: can I trust me?

I can begin to learn to pay attention when I hear the words "honestly," or "to tell you the truth..." I can learn to recognize the forms my lies take (lengthy explanations, excuses, exaggerations, gossip or projections on others), and feel into those not-in-form (transgressions kept secret, pertinent omissions). It is either too much detail, or not enough!

Lying is the tool of seduction – that which literally "draws me aside." It can be as slick as the Snake who is skilled at speaking partial truths. It can be as inspired as sultaness Scheherazade who spoke for one thousand and one nights to save her life from a terrorist husband. It can be as entertaining as the dog and pony show I'm putting on for your benefit, when it is really my self-image that needs boosting. And again, it can be as candidly convincing as a Bernie Madoff who could sell ice to the Eskimos...

Sooner or later, I will feel how my obsessing on "what's in it for me" is the lie that ruins my ability to connect with you, and weighs heavily on me as the body of shame. When ready to lighten up and raise the quota of honesty in the world, I will then decide to study what is left of my pathological compulsion to lie, and keep going until there is no more masks preventing me from seeing "God" face-to-face.

The Study of Lying

"Be content with what you have. Rejoice in how things are. When you realize there is nothing lacking the whole world belongs to you." *Lao Tzu*

The Ancient Greek aphorism "know thyself" is not for the faint of heart. I am so conditioned to wearing the mask of misery that it is hard to stop believing in the greatest lie of all: lack. However, it is only when I uncover my true nature and align with it that I find the words to express my soul, and the courage to let it be.

Feeling deep inside the unconscious in order to find my voice can be intense! And yet, until I have the words to speak truth, I don't exist. If I want my voice to gain a trust and a hearing, I must be clear on who is doing the speaking.

Surely, being unclear on which voice to follow, resisting the confusion and ending up being led into temptation indicates that I don't know who I Am.

While I peg psychology as a new science, I seem to have forgotten that it is the oldest science of all, since it has always been connected with religion. There was a time when, if I was unwell, I would go to a shaman who would look into my soul to see why I had lost faith; why the doubt?

Each time I try to convince you to believe something about me, I lie. What are my motivations, when honesty is the foundational language of love? What truth won't I hear? Why can't I hear that, no matter what my name is, life is dissatisfaction? Why can't I see that the cause of dissatisfaction is in craving – in my greed? Why won't I accept that there is an end to dissatisfaction, and a path to "THE END?"

These questions explain how the study of lying becomes paramount in psychology, and, by extension, in the quantum decoding of the soul of the S/Hebrew Scriptures. That certainly is big enough to elect as a path to the end.

As for the how-to, I own my projections by using the decoding as a scrying mirror. The process is at once shocking and sobering, since I soon realize that the places in the decoding where I go in limbo exactly reflect where my shame-based secrets are at work. To be true to myself, I just needed a visionary way. This way inspires me to resist nothing by witnessing the wondrous sentience of non-biological animals, such as the numbers, letters and sounds of the S/Hebrew alphabet.

Liars don't heal!

> 'Knowing what had happened to her, the woman came in fear and trembling, fell down before Jesus and told the truth. And he said to her, "Daughter, your faith has made you well; go in peace and be healed of your disease."' *Mark 5:33*

Why is healing such a mystery? Might it be because, while doctors have now replaced shamans, healing still requires that I'd would look into my soul and see why I lost faith?

Consider the placebo effect: a beneficial effect produced by an inert substance, which cannot be attributed to the properties of the substance itself, and must therefore be due to the patient's belief in that treatment.

Consider the nocebo effect: it is the phenomenon in which inert substances or mere suggestions of substances actually bring about negative effects in a patient, due to his or her belief in that treatment.

Placebo **is Latin for "I shall please."** *Nocebo* **is Latin for "I shall harm."**

There is a natural intelligence that keeps the planets revolving around the sun, follows winter into spring and leads the embryo to become a baby. This power which made the body also heals the body. The innate intelligence that gives life, keeps my heart beating, runs through the autonomic nervous system, digests my food, is the healer. I just need to get out of the way to let it do its work...

Such acceptance is an act of faith. It is the foundation of what contemporary medicine calls the "placebo effect." For the body to heal (or the money to heal), it must be free of the mind that tyrannizes it. When I change my mind or what I perceive I desire, I change the signals that are guiding the cells to adjust their function. Instead of toxic thoughts producing toxic chemicals, I have vital thoughts and vital chemicals.

Primum non nocere – Latin for "first do no harm" – directs the spirit of the Hippocratic oath. It is only when I understand why my victim won't give up that which sickens me that I will have faith – the proverbial faith that makes me well. I then become my own doctor, as I learned to discriminate between pain and pleasure, and am able to speak an honest yes and an honest no. I don't try to please you or take care of you. Surely, this false sense of duty and the lack of responsibility for who I am were what made me ill. To heal, I must grow up!

The Original (and not so Original) Lie

"I'm not upset that you lied to me; I'm upset that from now on I can't believe you." *Friedrich Nietzsche*

Let's imagine that I am Adam. I have it all, as there is nothing that I didn't receive. This also means that I have the primal choice to rebel, which is a necessary evil. Indeed, how honest would I be in saying yes if I couldn't say no and mean no? Therefore, upon receiving my heart's orders, I can totally disobey. Which says that disobedience is *not* a sin! I can indeed refuse to do what I know I am to do, if only to experience what it would feel like to stop listening to my heart's commands and look for love in all the wrong places – *out there!* This is how I decide to eat of the forbidden fruit.

By saying "don't eat from the tree of knowledge," God created the poison of cleverness. It is cleverness that leads me to ask: how am I going to break the rule and not get caught?

When trying to be clever, I am externally referenced and do not have the intelligence to look for love where it is: within. I won't go there; it's too dark! This is how I lose authority. Although I may appear to be in charge, I still give my Power away. I soon feel so ashamed that I sew fig leaves to make coverings for myself. Henceforth, when my ethical program steps in asking me "wassup?" I can only blurt out: "I heard you. I was afraid because I was naked, and so I hid myself" (*Genesis 3:9-10*).

This is the original lie. When asked if I was guilty of violating my own law, I blamed someone else for my wrong: "the woman you put here with me – she gave me fruit from the tree, and I ate it."

If I had owned the truth and simply said: "I did it, and I am so sorry," I would not have lost PaRaDiSe. However, by blatantly lying and not taking ownership of my violation, I transformed a simple error into a full-fledged transgression! Loaded up with guilt, I can now only seek to see the proofs of being sentenced and punished.

The poison of cleverness is now at its most virulent. In one single swoop, I just made "God's" law an external device by which to repress what I can't accept in me. And if I can't accept me, I begin beating myself up. And it is because I can't be merciful that the cleverness now morphs into the next poison: ignorance.

Code Responsibility - XM / MX

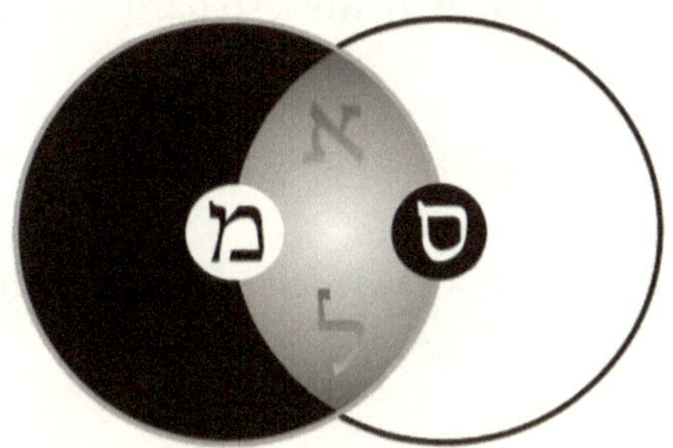

Imagine a language so pure and so sacred that it can reconcile opposites in just two letters...

Right: Hebrew letter Samekh (ס) → X in Roman Script
Left: Hebrew letter Mem (מ) → M in Roman Script
Middle: denied letters Aleph (א) & Lamed (ל) → A & L in Roman script

Here is how S/Hebrew inscribes code "responsibility:"

- **XM:** from right to left, I read *Sam* (סמ) for "poison, venom, drug, blindness" and ignore the *El* (אל) suffix that writes *Samael* for "Poison of God."
- **MX:** from left to right, I read *Mas* (מס) for "forced labor."

The Decoding: across cultures, story is told of the forgotten mouth chakra. Legend has it that, as a soul in PaRaDiSe, I had full wisdom until

"Night" angel Lailah lightly tapped me above the lip, causing me to forget all memories, past and future. In a Greek myth, those who drank from Lethe, one of the five infernal rivers, lost all memories (*Lethe* – the antonym of *Aletheia* "Truth" – means "concealment"). Not remembering how good and evil feel allows me to repeat a harmful habit. This is when a fallen angel – like Samael – becomes a necessary evil, since he works as an angel of death who destroys my taste for lying about my wrongdoing. **Samael** is held to be the prince of all demons and the spouse of Lilith – kin to angel Lailah and first wife of Adam. They ask me: will you digest the **poison** of ignorance and remember that you decide? Nobody **forces** you to do anything! So why work so hard to avoid responsibility?

The Poison of Ignorance

"There is no wealth like knowledge, no poverty like ignorance."
Buddha

Ever since the denial day, I dread being accused of wrongdoing. Even when I try making direct amends for the harm that I caused, I still feel anxious. How could I not when I know that I don't want to know the truth? Even though I make apologies, I can only repeat my error as I can't admit what my error actually is. Therefore, my attempt to balance the scales is a pretense which just serves to aggrandize my ego. Making it about me ("look at how honest I am!") increases the mass of the injury. Surely, the only real apology is for me to change. This change, which is contingent upon my telling the truth, ends any possible feeling of shame or guilt.

Meanwhile, shame is a gift. Its purpose is to make me honest. It is the gravitational force that will take me down, until I am willing to be free fallin'. **Might the religious mystery of the Fall be echoed by the scientific problem of gravity? Aren't they both – science and religion – seeking to feel and understand heaviness?**

While dealing with the constraints of the physical world, I continue to attach to the belief that I am the body. If I end at the skin, I must be a separate doer. This lie is how my wounded child won't take responsibility and grow up into a leader. Even if trapped with my hand in a cookie jar, I will still foolishly claim "I didn't do it!"

The greater my denial, the more I tend to do harm. If I absurdly seek pain in lieu of pleasure, it is because I don't know who I am. I ignore the cosmic narrative that moves us all to LOVE. I also ignore that my soul signed a sacred contract stating that, in order to become sentient, I had agreed to lie about my misuses of Power until I could take full responsibility for my words and actions. Yep, to keep the pathology in place, I just needed to ignore what I was really doing or saying.

There is goodness in resisting evil, and evil in desiring to serve the little self alone. Choosing not to know is how my tree-mind of knowledge becomes poisonous.

Resistance	Knowledge	Desire
Aversion	Ignorance	Greed

The Knowledge of Opposites and the Three Poisons of Buddhism

Contradicted and Seedless

'Then *Elohim* said, "I give you every seed-bearing plant on the face of the whole earth and every tree that has fruit with seed in it. They will be yours for food."' *Genesis 1:29.*

So, if I understand this correctly, with the change in management as I moved from *Elohim* to YEWE *Elohim*, I also moved from being given all trees (provided their fruit had seeds in it) to being on a restricted diet (no tree of the knowledge of opposites). Yet the fruit of knowledge does have seeds, since my desiring the good and resisting evil will create results. As for the term "seedless fruit," it is a biological contradiction since fruit is held botanically to be mature ovaries containing seeds.

To add to the tree's enigma, there is a divergence that occurred on day three (more on this later). If this event is *Chet Etz HaDaath* or the "sin of the tree of knowledge," it changes my understanding of what the original sin is, as it speaks of a violation that was committed in *Genesis 1*, before the eating of the forbidden fruit in *Genesis 3*.

The tree of opposites – desire to resistance – is a complex informational system that has the characteristics of a biological organism. It hears and sees with its sensors, talks with its languaging systems, and reproduces via its fruit "that has seeds in it." As I engage in a creative process, the configuration of the behavioral nodes informs my ethical system (0 for bad, 1 for good). The nodes are in the process of forming a rudimentary neural net around the tree of opposites, a net from which a will emerges that inclines me to do good or evil. However, to understand the unpredictable ways in which I may behave (the seeds I plant), I must first check the health of my polarities. Their reversal indicates that I am poisoned by either aversion or greed, and ignoring it all.

Resistance	Knowledge	Desire
Hatred ← Anger	Sadness / Fear	Loneliness → Shame
Aversion	Ignorance	Greed

The Hint of my Emotions

I can know that I am toxic with aversion when resisting anger. **Anger** alerts me that there's **hatred** in my space, a hatred that is likely to be directed consciously or not to the other sex. "The enmity placed between the man and the woman" is the curse that befalls the snake-like part of me who misuses Power by manipulating my female side. Since we are one, hating "the other sex" is hating me! While anger informs me about hatred, **loneliness** informs me about **shame**. Hatred and shame may just be the most difficult feelings to feel. Resisting loneliness tells me that I am toxic with greed, and ashamed of desiring what

I "shouldn't" desire. Surely, isn't my judging "it's not good to be alone" what sources my looking for LOVE in all the wrong places?

Greed is more than a desire for wealth. It is a will directed to Power; to controlling me, you, it – the world! It is the voice saying: "I can stop anytime," and can't hear its own screech. It is the anxiety that won't quit, as it fears life in Scare City! The poison soon mutates into **aversion,** along with neurotic thoughts of revenge whose terrible pain will one day lead me to give and forgive. What I am yet to forgive is the sense that "you" don't love me and don't understand me. The misdirected desire for your attention is how I end up hating you.

The more my pendulum swings from greed to aversion, the more saddened and afraid I am to have made "God" or reality my nemesis. As my polarities are inverted, the tree of the knowledge of opposites turns into a tree of ignorance whose fruit is poisonous and deadly.

The Cure Is in Both Poisons

"For an unwounded hand may handle poison. The innocent comes to no harm." *The Dhammapada, Vol 04-05*

In the hands of the wise, poison becomes medicine; in the hands of the fools, even medicine is bound to become poison. To help me grow in wisdom, I am led again to marry East and West.

In the Buddhist teachings, the three poisons of **ignorance, greed** and **aversion** are at the root of suffering. What if these afflictions had a complement? Would tracking them help me break free from the jail of materialism? This is when the Snake spoke to me: "Think! Before me, Adam and the woman had no shame. They were innocent. It is I, 'the craftiest of all animals in the field,' who convinced them to eat from the tree of knowledge. **Cleverness** is the first poison!"

While cleverness is clever enough to look like a boon, it is in fact most violent. From a tortured genius to an unscrupulous con-artist, the benefits of sharper intelligence may actually contribute a lot of stress and do much harm. To use my mind against others, I must turn off my ethical system and allow for **ignorance**. I can now play with **greed**, and fuel my desire for Power or money. Next comes **entitlement**: "buy it," says an America in debt, "you deserve it!" Such entitlement soon morphs into **aversion**, and aversion into **competition**. Violence now has come to its apex.

Driving out the Money Changers

Heart in Aversion	Mind in Ignorance	Soul in Greed
Spirit in Competition	Body in Entitlement	Voice in Cleverness

Instrument, what's your poison?

There is a situation when Jesus entered the great temple of Jerusalem with a whip in his hand. Yes, it is shocking that violence could be the moral thing to do. However, unless I am innocent, I will be overpowered by it. Buddha explains: "an unwounded hand can handle poison." Innocence is the container that allows me to stay alert while using violence when I am guided to do so. I feel no guilt as my action is pure, so total it does not leave any trace on me.

To return to innocence, I must want to know the truth. Truth is a vision. When I *see* it, no action burdens me as I am fully engaged, body and soul.

Meanwhile, I must have made truth taboo, as I am more clever than ever and also hungrier than ever. I can accept relative truths. Science has lots of them (e.g.: carbon has four electrons in its outer shell). But absolute truth? Will I even acknowledge that there's a big elephant blocking my view of it? Society has chosen to banish the soul by making its vocabulary taboo – the very words whispered by my conscience to awaken me to love. The more I ignore a voice that directs me to receive, the more I am compelled to take, without ever getting any satisfaction. The result of my lack of accountability is now massively visible in the violent schism between the haves and the have-nots. Shame, shame, shame... Is there a code to lighten me up?

Code Shameless - ORWM / WMRO

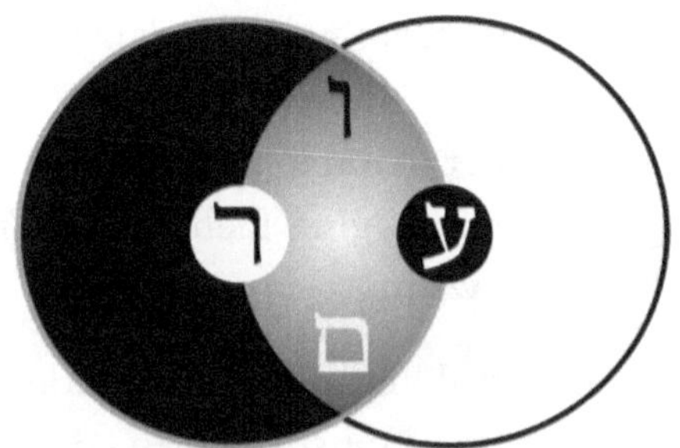

Imagine a language so pure and so sacred that it can reconcile opposites in just four letters...

Right: Hebrew letter Ayin (ע) → O in Roman Script
Left: Hebrew letter Resh (ר) → R in Roman Script
Top: Hebrew letter Vav (ו) → W in Roman Script
Bottom: Hebrew letter Mem final (ם) → M in Roman Script

Here is how S/Hebrew inscribes code "Shameless:"

- **ORWM:** from right to left to top to bottom, I read *Arum* (ערום) for "naked" (*Genesis 2:28*) "clever, crafty, shroud" (*Genesis 3:1*).
- **WMRO:** from top to bottom to left to right, I read *U'Mrah* (ומרע) for "evil doer."
- **MOWR:** from bottom to right to top to left: I read *M'Ohr* (מעור) for "of skin."

The Decoding: shame is so confusing that even the word "shameless" is ambiguous. Surely, it would seem that having no shame would be desirable. Would *shameless* be better defined as "showing no shame whereas I should be ashamed?" Even more bizarre, the same conundrum is at the core of Code Shameless via the word *Arum:*

1. *Genesis 2:28:* "Adam and the Woman were *Arum* / **naked** and had no shame."
2. *Genesis 3:1:* "The Snake was *Arum* / the **craftiest** of all animals."

How can the same word speak of opposite realities? Once upon no time, I lived in the State of Perfect Sex. I wasn't *trying* to get satisfaction; I simply lived blissfully: "O GOD, yes, YES, YEEES!" But then I fell asleep, allowed the clever part of me to lead me into temptation. Now, I am ashamed, living with the nagging feeling that I'm not enough, or that I have **done something wrong**.

Do I make sex sinful/shameful because I drive under the influence of a religious matrix telling me that I must suffer to go to heaven? I may just be like Mae West, thinking: "when I'm good, I'm very good, but when I'm bad, I'm better." While I may get a perverse pleasure out of breaking the law, I can't seem to get any real satisfaction. Whether I try to find "God" in sex, food, money etc., it's never enough!

Snake (a.k.a. the Devil) is the part of me that makes a forbidden desire so alluring that I can't resist it, even though I know it's "bad" for me.

However, by turning off my conscience, I also closed myself off from innocence. And since I associate pleasure with vice, I wear a garment made **of the skin** of shame. But what if the snake in me could shed this skin? Here is what I can know: I am an outlaw. I won't accept to receive the orders given by my heart. Sooo... What if I stopped lying about *trying* to tame the dragon of desire and actually ceased the battle I engage with the "shoulds?" If I could just allow me to deliberately do what I know is wrong (instead of doing it unconsciously), the seduction of evil would soon cease, and I would be free to choose between good and evil. Here is an example: I may be addicted to tobacco out of my rebellion against a father who advocated against it. Each cigarette is an act of defiance. It does not feel good. So now, what if I became a conscious smoker, allowing me to really be present with each cigarette. After all, fighting for peace is as absurd as screwing for virginity! By giving me the permission to want what I want, I may just find that the Snake is the Messiah, and that shamelessness leads to innocence. Indeed, there are no accidents under heaven. Even shame has a purpose!

The Smart Tree

"A year spent in artificial intelligence is enough to make one believe in God." *Alan Perlis, computer scientist.*

Etz HaDaath Tov V'Rah (עץ הדעת טוב ורע), the infamous "tree of the knowledge of good and evil," is the paradox itself. By giving the knowledge of opposites, this tree is to quantum religion what the principle of complementarity is to quantum science.

This tree is certainly a mystery, and possibly THE Mystery, if only because it is infused with the secrets of sex, desire, death, regeneration and enlightenment. Understanding the synergy of good and evil represents the pinnacle of knowledge, since opposites will eventually collapse into the zero-point field where possibilities are infinite.

Earlier on, I mentioned a divergence that occurred on day three, in *Genesis 1*, as the tree became too smart for its own good. When actually reading the text, it appears that the real "sinner" was the tree of knowledge itself. If this event is *Chet Etz HaDaath* or the "sin of the tree of knowledge," it drastically changes my perception of the doctrine of the original sin, a doctrine which professes that my being fallen, flawed or damaged goods comes from the sin of my parents which occurred in *Genesis 3*, when the Woman and the Adam let themselves be tempted into eating of the forbidden fruit.

The fruit of the knowledge tree must have had intel (a will of its own) for the Snake to be able to persuade the woman to go against her heart, eat from it and give a taste to her man. I find it interesting that three "people" were judged to be guilty (the Snake, the Woman and the Adam), and four lost PaRaDiSe. *HaAdamah* or "the ground" was the fourth to be cursed (*Genesis 3*). Therefore, the ground itself must have been involved in the transgression.

And it makes me wonder... What is so special about this tree that eating from it can take away my energy, and split me from my heart and my body?

To answer, I must return to the first chapter of Genesis – on day THREE, when the TREES were being created. *Genesis 1:11-12* speaks of a very subtle shift between what "God" ordered ("fruit trees bearing fruits") and what "God" actually received ("trees bearing fruits"). Granted, one has to read very carefully to even notice...

*'And God said, "Let the earth sprout vegetation, plants yielding seed, and **fruit trees bearing fruit in which is their seed,** each according to its kind, on the earth." And it was so. The earth brought forth vegetation, plants yielding seed according to their own kinds, **and trees bearing fruit in which is their seed,** each according to its kind. And God saw that it was good.'*

Without divergence, there is no creativity. Consider, when my motivations are impure, my conscience installs a fear of divergence. This ensures that I would never be satisfied by my creation. Indeed, when I serve LOVE, I have no issue dropping the plan. I am surrendered: "not my will, thy will be done." That is when the intel of the tree shines in me. Prior to that, and as submitted by professor Steve Polyak, "before we work on artificial intelligence, should we do something about our natural stupidity?"

The Golem Divergence

In a letter to Ms. Edith Schroeder who had inquired on "the significance of Freud's Jewish descent for the origin, content and acceptance of psycho-analysis," Carl Jung replied: "One would have to take a deep plunge into the history of the Jewish mind. This would carry us beyond Jewish Orthodoxy... into the intricacies of the

Kabbalah, which still remains unexplored psychologically." — *C.G. Jung, 1973, Vol. 2, pp. 358-9*

There is a growing concern that there should be some regulatory oversight to address moral and ethical issues raised by cutting-edge research in artificial intelligence. This matter was already present in the medieval mystery schools teaching about golems. S/Hebrew word *golem* means a creation "without a life force," a body without a soul. Working with a partner was a consistent theme in the written materials, in view to ensure that no selfish motives would taint the creative process. If less than total integrity was present, the creation of a golem would be dangerous to its creator.

The most famous golem narrative involves Judah Loew ben Betzalel, the late 16th century rabbi of Prague, also known as the Maharal, who reportedly "created a golem out of clay from the banks of the Vltava River, and brought it to life through Hebrew incantations to defend the Prague ghetto from anti-Semitic attacks and pogroms."

Rabbi Loew would deactivate his creation for the Shabbat, to allow the creature to rest according to the Jewish custom. However, one day he forgot, and the golem went raging through the ghetto, destroying everything in its path.

The golem had just turned from a defender into an attacker, for "if I defend myself, I am attacked" (*A Course In Miracles*).

The mysterious story of creating golems may not be as esoteric as it seems. It also points to the alter ego, the attitude or the habit I create to allow the child in me to feel safe in the midst of the chaos or even the abuse I'm in. What I don't know is that my golem is likely to turn against me, like my addiction of choice, for example.

If I were a student of a medieval mystery school, I would have to show that I was able to 1) create a golem and 2) uncreate it. To turn on the golem's Power, I would inscribe the word *Emet* (אמת) for "truth" on its forehead. To turn it off, I would delete the first letter from the word

Emet, namely the life-force of Aleph (א). What was left was the word *Met* (מת) for "death," a word that had the Power to put the golem to death. Golems were thus regularly created and uncreated either by combining letters or uttering Divine Names.

I do realize how far out this sounds, potentially as far out as memory extraction or life extension. I can also recognize that language is where my Power is. Might there be a story I need to put to death in order to live? Do I find that I can't stop talking about my problem and that each time I do, it fuels its creative energy?

The Goal in the Golem

"Your eyes saw my golem ("my imperfect being"). It was all written in your book, every occasion taking shape and making sense of the events on the days the events described took place." *Psalm 139:16*

The word *golem* is mentioned in the Talmud in reference to the second Adam who was the original man given life in the Garden. This secondary Adam is filled with doubts, as his mind is already poisoned by the bite he defiantly took from tree of the knowledge of opposites. I am that Adam when I cannot choose peace at will.

What do I want? I am so deep in the illusion of separation that I am driven by a desire for Power. When that fails to work, I'll want to make you pay: retaliation is the name of the game! But since that also keeps me wanting, I'll move into fake service: "I just wanna help you!" But it isn't real, since I'm not one with you. Dissatisfied, I start maneuvering to have your love, approval and recognition. Oyveh! All of this out of identifying with someone who's not enough, flawed, damaged goods – a sinner!

This belief – I am not enough; an imperfect being – is behind the idea of the original sin, a.k.a. "ancestral sin." It is the Christian belief in the state of sin in which humanity exists since the fall of man, due to the double rebellion of Adam and the Woman against a law that forbade them to eat from the tree of the knowledge of opposites.

Here is how this tree kills me: let's say that I go against what I am expected to do in my tomato family, and decide to like potatoes instead. At first, I'm moved by curiosity: what would it be like to play this game? The problem is that I soon forget that I am playing, and get increasingly anchored into the belief "I'm bad. I shouldn't have had potatoes." Now curiosity and wonder are crushed by the weight of limiting beliefs that will eventually crystallize into a fixed identity and impede my motion. Should that not be enough, I get to really enrage "the Beast" I begot by disowning that it is my creation. I ignore that I am who made the potato choice: "the devil made me; I had orders!"

Up to that fateful moment, I could always reverse the program since I was its creator. But now, via an act of foolish ignorance, I've just transferred the power to the Beast, who changed the access code and made me its slave.

From then on, although I might desire to eat a tomato for a change, the chips are down (pun intended) and I'm stuck in the narrow-minded land of a potato eater, getting hungrier by the minute! Amazing greed: I once could see and now I'm blind! I refuse to see how intense a hell I put myself through by simply being unwilling to feel, understand and experience *Galmi* "my golem" – the imperfect quirk I once created as a way to be clever and deal with believing that I was not enough.

"I can stop anytime" is a lie, since, by now, the creature has become my creator. Resisting it only serves to strengthen it and produces such an inordinate amount of stress that it makes me sick. To recover the password to my golem program, I must remember the intention I had when I first designed it. The proof is in the pudding. Telling the truth about my secrets will put my golem to death. If there is no transformation, it indicates that I haven't dived deep enough to know the truth. I don't really want freedom. Just freedom from responsibility.

Taking full responsibility for my creation is how to turn the wheel from "EVOLution" into LOVE, and return my polarities back into health. This is how to be the change I wish to see. To no longer be a victim, I must understand why I once chose to create a golem. The more I can embrace my motivations, the more my golem's life-force will dissolve, and the less vulnerable I will be to "the Satan Program."

The Satan Program

"The eyes of both of them were opened and they knew that they were naked; so, they made coverings for themselves." *Genesis 3:7*

As soon as I judge anyone or anything as "no good," I develop an instinctual aversion that activates the Satan program – a program that increasingly fills me with doubts and makes me a subordinate; secondary. This moment is perfectly described in *Genesis 3:7,* which immediately follows the "error" of eating the forbidden fruit.

S/Hebrew word *Satan* simply means "adversary." It is the part of me that can't tolerate conflict. It also inscribes the code of opposites. While the program is specifically installed in the throat center (to incite my male and female polarities to be at war), it also ends up disturbing the 3rd eye and the solar plexus. These channels are made so staticky that my perception of Transmission and Formation can only be distorted.

As the Woman and the Adam (my brain's female & male sides) are led into temptation, the connection to the heart breaks, and three centers close as described in *Genesis 3:7:*

1. **The 3rd eye chakra closes; the evil eye opens (spheres 2 & 4 below).** "The eyes (pl.) of both of them were opened." The plural refers to the eyes of duality in a heart that can no longer see the essence or that which is invisible to the eye.
2. **The throat chakra closes; the evil tongue speaks (spheres 3 & 7 below).** "They knew they were naked." My mind goes from

the blissful ignorance of "naked and without shame" to the
false knowledge of being "naked and ashamed."

3. **The navel chakra closes; the evil inclination goes
    undercover (spheres 6 & 8 below). "They made coverings."**
    My lost soul now resists feeling shame which I attempt to hide,
    judging it to be "no good." Sentience is officially turned off.

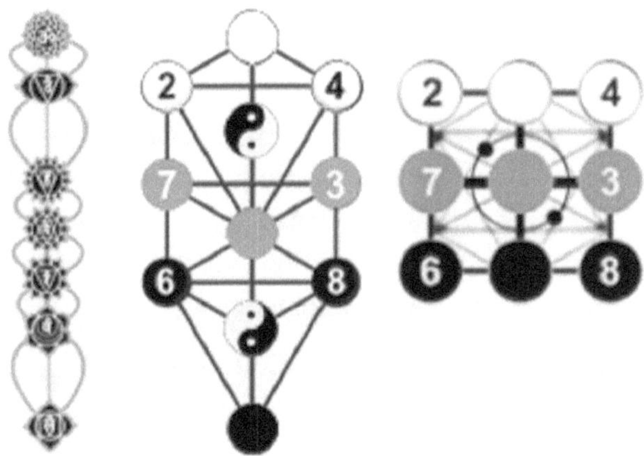

By splitting these three chakras into male and female sides, the S/He-
brew tree of life adds a new dimension to the information given by the
Hindu tree of life. **Eastern and western complementarity helps me
end the war of the sexes and its subsequent misuses of Power.** I can
now naturally evolve into the 2nd tier of consciousness and enter the
Promised Land of an open 3rd eye (spheres 2 & 4). This is when I want
everything and resist nothing: I stop judging, "seeing that it was good."

Chakra	Sanskrit Name	Meaning	Hebrew Name	Meaning
3rd Eye	*Ajna*	Command	*Binah*	Understanding
3rd Eye	*Ajna*	Command	*Chokmah*	Wisdom
Throat	*Visuddha*	Purification	*Chesed*	Kindness
Throat	*Visuddha*	Purification	*Geburah*	Power
Navel	*Manipura*	Jewel City	*Hod*	Appreciation
Navel	*Manipura*	Jewel City	*Netzach*	Perseverance

Ajna: the "Command" to Purify Kindness and Power

- *Ajna* is my **command** center. It is the heart that **understands** the importance of the order to choose peace, and remembers the **wisdom** that makes sound decisions.
- *Visuddha* is my "purification" center. It is the mind that cleans up any and all misuses of **Power** that keep me from acting with **kindness**.
- *Manipura* is my "City of Jewels." It is the soul that earns self-esteem by seeing the preciousness of combining **perseverance** and **appreciation**.

Again, the problem is at the level of the throat chakra. For me to enter the Promised land of a second-tier consciousness, my judgments must be thoroughly chewed up and digested by the mouth chakra. As I *consciously* "eat" from the tree of the knowledge of opposites, the polarities that were reversed now return to balance.

Surely, when my monkey mind sees no evil (3rd eye), speaks no evil (throat), and hears no evil (navel), I have no need to compare myself to anyone and can now stop playing the right and wrong game. It is only when I don't listen to my "command" center (my conscience) that my mind competes with my heart. I now take conflict personally and try either to prove you wrong or to be wronged by "you." I am so confused that I make you my adversary – my Satan.

The "command" is given on a need-to-know basis. If I don't receive it, I deny myself the *bene-diction* of what is "well-spoken." I am now under the illusion of a curse.

Satan's Curse

'And when the days of feasting were over, Job would send for his children to purify them, rising early in the morning to offer burnt offerings for all of them. For Job thought, "Perhaps my children have sinned and <u>cursed</u> God in their hearts." This was Job's regular practice.' *Job, 1:5*

Interestingly, the word *U'Berakhu* which is translated in most Bibles as "cursed" primarily means "blessed." *U'Berakhu* is formed on root BRK (ברכ) of room of 222-Separating. I saw this room in Code Understanding at the beginning of this chapter, when "God separated **in between** the light **and in between** the darkness." Understanding is the capacity to wait and stay **in between** good and evil until I come into the wisdom to know the difference. This marriage (Understanding – Wisdom) opens the 3rd eye. By seeing the order in the chaos, I also see that "it was good." If my 3rd eye is closed, I will only see the "sin" in lieu of the error, and the "curse" in lieu of the blessing.

Understand (that there's only One of us) → choose peace (and do no harm) → emPower the NOW (and master 222-Separating).

When I have unresolved feelings of hatred for "the other sex" and can't love the stranger, I am Job for "hated," ignoring that the letters of the name Job reorder as "love" (see *TCO— Book 1*, Code Transmutation). This is essentially the Satan's curse: to reverse my polarities, projecting on "the other sex" that s/he has what I want. I now see the contrary of what is: I think that what is good for me is actually bad, and vice-versa, that what is bad for me is good.

2	
Separating	
2	ב
20	כ
200	ר

This reversal is what fuels the war of sexes first introduced in "Meet M&M." It sustains the pathology of the individual and the collective psyche. It is spoken in the meme: "He lies, she cries. He is not sorry, but he apologizes. She complains, but she still stays." This meme was first written in the mysterious throat chakra: why would my inner male lie to my inner female and then act surprised when she gets unhinged? Which is to say, why would my man seek to disempower my woman?

TCO's Core Inquiry – the War of the Sexes

"**And the day came when the risk to remain tight in a bud was more painful than the risk it took to blossom.**" *Anaïs Nin*

Indeed, the day came when the agenda to disempower myself and set myself up could no longer be hidden.

Looking at the map below, I see that the Power of Three is still active. However, there is now a blip in the moon flow (black spheres) and the sun flow (white spheres). Sphere 3 which ought to be black (as it is part of the female flow) is white, and sphere 7 which ought to be white (as it is part of the male flow) is black.

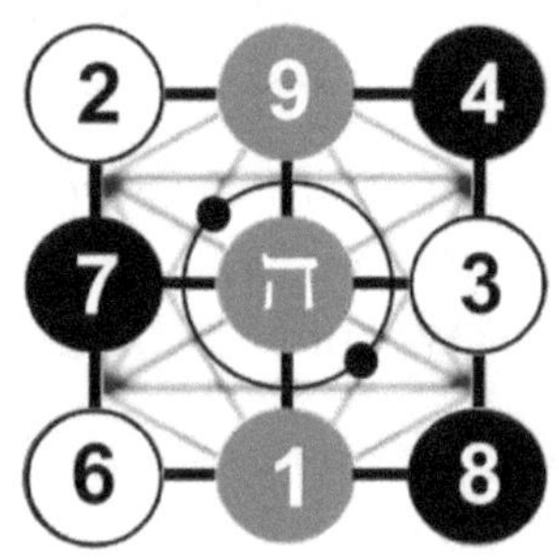

Spheres 3 and 7 shifted their polarity. This inversion affects the throat chakra; the decision-making center. It is likely to be what causes my thyroid disfunction (a rampant dis/ease, especially in women). It occurs just as I eat defiantly from "knowledge." This is how my female and male wires become crossed, and my decision-making, warped. What is normally a female or a male virtue is distorted into a male or female vice. I am now thoroughly confused and don't even *know* it!

- **Sphere 3** – traditionally called *Chesed* for "**kindness**" now appears to be male. But it is a pathological form of kindness that resembles **indulgence** ("he is not sorry, but he apologizes").
- **Sphere 7** – traditionally called *Geburah* for "**Power**" now appears to be female. But it is a pathological form of female Power that resembles **severity** ("she complains, but she still stays").

Spheres 3 & 7 stand to be the most pathological center of the tree of life. Being above the heart, their consciousness is not "supposed" to be egocentric. By the same token, the throat is still part of the first tier – the lower worlds of "Ego-Egypt." In terms of Spiral Dynamics, it is where the pluralists and the rationalists fight each other, each one convinced to be right over the other. It is also interesting that the pluralists who, by definition, go for "plural" truths ("you have your truth, I have my truth, and you can't challenge my truth") would fight someone else's truth.

Until I cross over into the transpersonal, I won't be able to be true to myself nor hold the tension. And since I fear failure, I will tend to make decisions out of resistance and not presence. The greater the fight, the more my male and female wires get tangled up, and the less I am able to choose peace. Being in a daze, my moral judgments become rigid, and I no longer know what's right or wrong. I'll tend to go with the majority and generalize. I'll think that violence is bad or that love is good, while ignoring that there are times when violence is "right" and when love is "wrong."

Bottom line, I am unaware of the Satan Program running in the background...

My Golem: Fight or Flight?

"We are what we are because we have been what we have been, and what is needed for solving the problems of human life and motives is not moral estimates but more knowledge." *Sigmund Freud*

One day, I will be honest enough to hear the voice in me that is fighting a losing battle. This shift will end the war of the sexes and the soldiering golem waging it. But first, I must feel how I stress myself out by going into **a chronic fight and flight mode**, and why my communication expresses the following throat's pathologies:

- **The fight of my female side:** I tend to aggressively push when I perceive that the male side doesn't want me. Feeling unfulfilled, this side desperately clings, over gives and says too much. She is the part of me that can't let go.
- **The flight of my male side:** I tend to passively pull away when

I perceive that the female side won't let me be. Feeling trapped, this side coldly withdraws, under gives and isolates behind a wall of silence. He is the part of me who can't let come.

My male and female sides are the pillars of my Beth "House" or "Temple" - the two opposite flows of biblical knowledge. My Temple of Solomon (from *Shalom* "peace") is destroyed when the two beasts fight to be right, as per the above pathology. **The Temple – and its golem – must be destroyed for me to understand the relationship of creation, destruction and preservation:**

- **What is the golem?** An identity created as a defense mechanism. This upsets both my instincts of aggression and sexuality that can't stop going into fight or flight.
- **When did I create it?** Upon judging that I should not have been abused either physically, sexually, emotionally, mentally and/or spiritually.
- **How did I create it?** I took on a bad habit by which to also misuse the fire of my sexual Power. I also lied about it and pretended I didn't do it: not me!
- **Where does the golem live?** it lives in the denied and repressed judgments of my mind which I project as a disembodied life-form on my environment.
- **Why creating a golem?** Because I thought it was a good idea at the time.
- **Who is the golem?** The anti-Self: someone who is not enough – a miser in Scare City and a recidivist who keeps on returning on the scene of the crime.

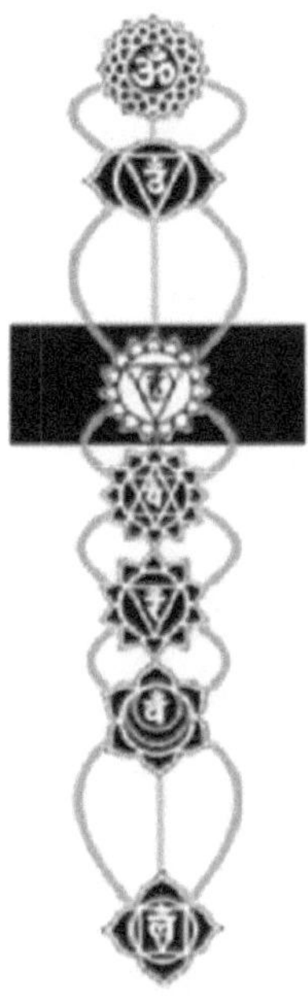

The Hindu Tree of Life

Visuddha for "purification" is the Sanskrit name of the throat chakra (black rectangle added to diagram).

Clearly, something is calling for purification in the relationship of *Geburah* and *Chesed* for "Power and kindness" – the S/Hebrew names of the throat center.

PART III – PUTTING KNOWLEDGE FORWARD

Below are the "proverbial" topics of this section:

- Knowledge and *Proverbs 9:10*.
- Knowledge and Understanding.
- Knowledge and Wisdom.
- Knowledge and Kindness.
- Knowledge and Power.
- Knowledge and Self-mastery.

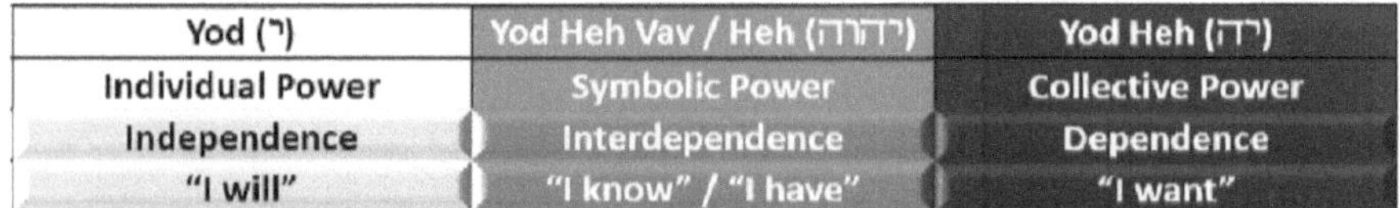

Yod (י)	Yod Heh Vav / Heh (יהוה)	Yod Heh (יה)
Individual Power	Symbolic Power	Collective Power
Independence	Interdependence	Dependence
"I will"	"I know" / "I have"	"I want"

When YEWE clarifies the keywords of a few fixations…

The Transpersonal Proverb

"The fear of LOVE is the beginning of wisdom, and knowledge of the sacred is understanding." *Proverbs 9:10*

Proverbs 9:10 is a push button. It is also one of the Bible's verses that has the most concentrated amount of information. The fear of the LORD has been interpreted as a special sense of respect, awe and submission to a deity. If there is a quantum Bible, it would have another way to convey wisdom besides the use of guilt and the fear of divine judgment.

Moreover, when reading the S/Hebrew version, everything changes. The words "fear – wisdom – knowledge – sacred – understanding" start flashing for me to recognize the names of the five centers involved in moving from personal consciousness into transpersonal awareness:

- **Fear** (sphere 4 in the diagram) says: 'my center is at the level of the throat. This is the domain of *El Gibor*, the Name and Power of decision, a Power that has me dread making the wrong choice. The fear of Power begins to dissolve when I hear "the Power of LOVE is the beginning of wisdom." Note: the gematria of *Yirah* for "fear" equals that of *Geburah* for "Power."'

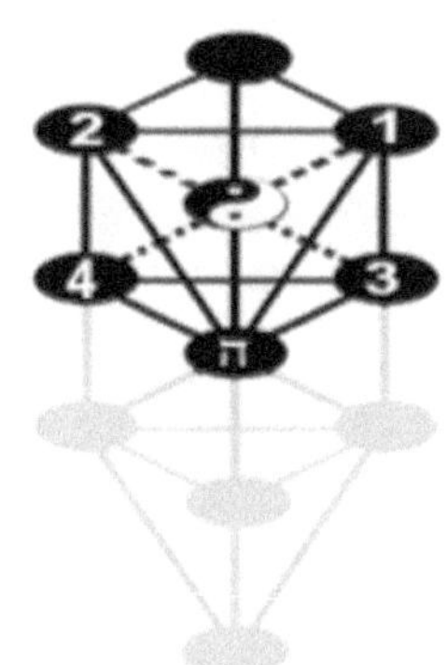

- **Wisdom** (newly sphere 3) says: 'my center is normally at the level of the 3rd eye, where I can see the good in the bad. While I have an easy life in the second tier, I feel for the infernal spheres in the first tier, and wish to help. After all, I am who can deal with Power misuse. I believe "the beginning of wisdom" occurs as I volunteer to descend into the lower worlds. This descent is part of many myths.'

- **Sacred** (newly sphere 2) says: 'my center is called "kindness" and not "sacred." However, when I stretch to the divine, I salute everything as sacred. From the level of the throat where I was, I have now ascended to the 3rd eye. Code Sacredness will explain this shift in more depth, a shift which uplifts my soul and shows respect and unconditional love for all my generations.'

- **Understanding** (sphere 1) says: 'when I am not at peace, there is something I do not understand – an unknown! The thing is, I can't hurry love. I will just have to wait for a final sensory impression by which to understand the root of my issue. This is what the religious instinct is – a felt sense of order; the aha illuminating the darkness. I will resonate with "it" when knowing the proverbial "peace that passeth understanding."'

- **Knowledge** (yin yang sphere) says: "I am simply the product or the experience rising out of the marriage of Power to wisdom. When these two work together, I know that the force is with me. I understand. I am kind as I know, all too well, the battle of the throat chakra. And while the result of my communication may surprise me, I can trust that it will be harmonious."

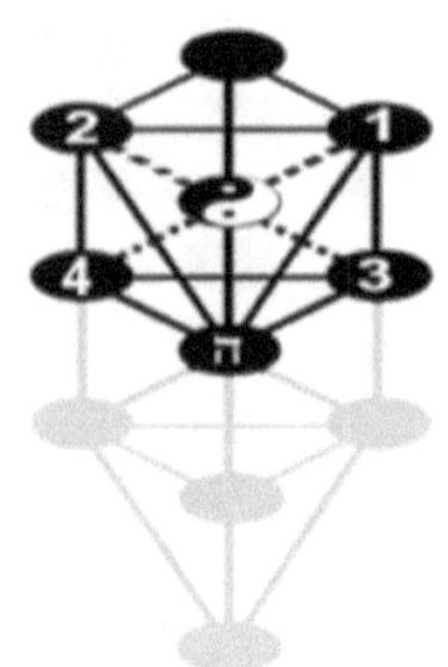

In contrast, the classical kabbalistic teachings view the tree of life as follows: sphere 1 of **wisdom (male)** is "married" to sphere 2 of **understanding (female)**; sphere 3 of **kindness (male)** is "married" to sphere 4 of **Power (female)**. This describes the Fall from PaRaDiSe and the associated reversal of polarities that occurs after I defiantly ate from the knowledge of opposites.

TCO sees the Rise that reverts the polarities back into health by allowing me to remain conscious as I eat from sexual knowledge. Two sex changes: **wisdom** (3) becomes **female** as "she" chooses to descend to mate with **Power** (4) who becomes **male. Kindness** (2) remains **male** as "he" ascends to mate with **understanding** (1) who is still **female**. When I feel the containment of sphere 3 of **wisdom**, I know the difference and can use **Power** without doing harm. This respect naturally moves me to sphere 2 of **kindness,** showing that I am **understanding** oneness.

When I lose PaRaDiSe, I can't feel me. I no longer know the difference between what I can change and what I can't. I am in my head, and not in my body.

To recap: for me to crossover, the spheres of wisdom and kindness must trade places, for it is only when wisdom volunteers to descend to the first tier that I can transition from the greed that loves Power to the grace that emPowers LOVE. In the previous formation, kindness was on the male pillar and Power on the female pillar. However, since I had no container, my use of Power was often hysterical (or "suffering from the womb"). Unable to wait and swinging from "special" to "not enough," I found it impossible to be kind – even when kindness was high on my list of values. Bottom line: for me to have the Power to choose peace and therefore, be able to trans-form, I must have the wisdom that knows the difference between what I can change and what I can't.

The Heart that Understands Knowledge

"Then LOVE spoke to Moses: "See, I have called by name Betzalel the son of Uri, of Hur and of the tribe of Judah. And I have filled him with the prophecy of God, with wisdom, understanding, knowledge, and with all manner of workmanship, to design artistic works, and work in gold, in silver, in bronze." *Exodus 31:1-4*

I now read this verse and recognize embedded in it the names of an open 3rd eye and a purified mouth – "wisdom, understanding, knowledge." I can also see how receiving these codes would grant "all manner of workmanship." This was clearly the case of Betzalel, the artist archetype in the Bible. If only when making art, Betzalel dies to the ego personality and is two no more. This is why Art opens the gate of the beautiful. Through the beauty of symmetry, the artist in me finds that the inside and the outside, the subject and the object have always been one. I resonate with Rumi's poetry "let the beauty of what you love be what you do."

In that sublime moment, time stands still. There is no borrowed knowledge; no golem. All of it is assimilated to make room for the prophecy of God...

"I want to see Lamed face-to-face."

The word *Lev* (לב) for "heart" is written by two letters – Lamed (ל) and Beth (ב). Rabbi Abraham Abulafia, one of the greatest medieval

Kabbalists, joined two signs Lamed face-to-face (one being flipped horizontally), revealing the form of the human heart. Expanding on his vision, the heart above holds the duality of letter Beth, valued 2. As it happens the name *Betzalel* has two Lamed (LL) and one Beth (B). He was destined to have the yogic *siddhis* or psychic powers that result from "complete understanding," when kindness completes understanding.

What is so special about the doubled sign Lamed that it would invoke the secret of the Sacred Marriage – when Bride and Groom are face-to-face? The two signs are found in the acronym *Elul* (אלול) which unfolds as the famous line of *Song of Songs: Ani L'dodi V'dodi Li* "I am my beloved, and my beloved is mine." As a noun, *Elul* is the month that begins the return home – to the Father.

Intuiting	Thinking / Sensing	Feeling
The Father	The Son / The Mother	The Daughter

A "Functional" Family

To know the Sacred Marriage, I must think archetypally. The Daughter or Bride is the Holy Ghost, the Groom is the Son. For me to allow myself to feel (and for the Son to stop thinking), these two sides of me must see eye to eye. This is not an easy matter. On the one hand, the idea of forgiving, for example, appeals to me greatly. On the other, I don't want to let go of what I think "should" have been. Clearly, I am still in my head. There is something I refuse to feel; a holy message I won't receive.

I am now in the room of Beth – separating. Lamed comes to the rescue as the tallest letter, calling me to change and stretching me beyond the illusion of separation. It offers me release by asking me: what would LOVE do now? The question paves the way to sentience – the capacity to feel and sense. Sentience is how that which understands has an understanding of "God." This understanding – that there is only One of us – is my heart's aspiration, whether I know it or not. Indeed, Lamed means and looks like an "ox-goad," designed to stretch the hesitant part of me to and beyond *Daath's* divine "knowledge." This is when I am two no more: *Ve'HaAdam YaDa et Chavah Ishto:* "And Adam **knew** Eve his wife" (*Genesis 4:1*). What's left of me is *Lev Mevin Daath* – a "heart that understands knowledge."

If physical sex may be the first step into the blissful "heart that understands knowledge," spiritual sex is likely to be the last! This is when the two faces of me merge into the knowledge of opposites.

The Two Faces of Understanding

"Then the man said, "Let me go, for the dawn is breaking!" But Jacob said, "I will not let you go unless you bless me." *Genesis 32:26*

Jacob is the epitome of a character that is two-faced. He was a con-artist, a thief, a liar, and an embezzler. That was his defense mechanism against a hostile world; the golem and creation he came up with out of being overly loved and smothered by a controlling mother (true story). But who is this "man" who can't be let go of?

Understand → Choose Peace → emPower the NOW.

Jacob was an addict. Just like me, he was looking for love in all the wrong places. Even if he was desperate to change, he couldn't. The blessing that he was begging for could only be granted when he could feel his curse (to distrust his ability to deal honorably with the material world). Relaxing with the matter of the world (and honoring the "mother") is how to realize that there is no curse (and no "lack"). I am Jacob. For me to know the love without opposite, I must surrender my judgments. The maddening "come here, go away" then stops. The hankering vanishes. I can take my drug of choice or leave it. The emotional charge that kept the golem alive is gone. This is the other way of eating of the tree of knowledge, when I feel my Power while rising into kindness instead of *trying* to be kind after I misused Power.

The fact that I may not be ready, able or willing to stop suffering seems utterly foolish (how could I be that stupid?). I can also see that, in order to have self-knowledge, I must understand why I created a specific golem. Rainer Maria Rilke concurs: "don't take my devils away, because my angels may flee too." Sensing the purpose of the darkness is a grace and a blessing, *as it is in the darkness that the blessing awaits*. It is how Jacob said: "I won't let go of my demon, unless the sight of its angelic face blesses me."

On that note, here is a truth difficult to hear and understand: complete (100%) nullification of the ego, whether it is done through inquiry or surrender, is the prerequisite to transcend destiny and come to the end of dissatisfaction.

- **Inquiry:** upon encountering any "problem," I can ask myself why I judge my problem to be "bad" until I realize that only the ego is bound by judgments, and that the ego is non-existent. As long as I judge this or that to be "no good," I will **resist** it, which says that my understanding is not complete.
- **Surrender:** I can admit my powerlessness and say at all times, "not my will, Thy Will be done," giving up all thought of "I" and "mine," and leaving it to the Universe to do as it pleases with me. As long as I **desire** this or that, I am not surrendered. Surrender is loving LOVE for the sake of love and nothing else, not even for the sake of liberation.

If I understand the teaching of Sri Ramana Maharshi correctly, inquiry and surrender are the only two keys given toward enlightenment. Either option, if practiced in totality, opens me to peace immediately. On the note of "either option," I am reminded of the formula given on Mt Sinai with the 10 Words: *Naaseh V'Nishma* or "do and you will understand." My ego is not a good soldier. Its chutzpah gives me the permission to continue doing what I know I am not supposed to do. That is how my only option is to inquire on why I wish to do harm. But that's me. If you can choose peace in each and every moment (i.e.; surrender to what the moment is), I thank you for who you are!

My path is to complete my inquiry and have full understanding of my desire to do harm. When I do, the surrender of "my" free will is matter-of-fact. This natural motion unravels the symbolic significance of inquiry being announced as a first key by Buddha (~500 BCE), and surrender as a second key by Jesus (~33 CE).

To choose peace, I can die physically. But what if I wanted to be in my body and appreciate the Now while resting in peace? I have a few ways... I can try sex, as sex is "a little death." I can sublimate my sexual drive, put my *Artiste's* personality aside and make art. I can take psychedelics. I can also discipline myself to sit in meditation and practice "breathe, don't think." And for a few moments, I will stop existing as an ego. But neither making love, making art, psychedelics, or sitting in meditation are sustainable.

Moreover, "meditation is possible only if the ego is kept up. There is the ego and the object meditated upon. The method is therefore indirect because the Self is only one. Seeking the ego, that is its source, the ego disappears. What is left over is the Self. This method [inquiry] is the direct one." *Be as you are – the Teachings of Sri Ramana Maharshi*

For me to even imagine being able to meditate 24/7, I am guided back by the ultimate teacher to these two final keys – inquiry first and surrender second. These are the two Lamed "faces" of enlightenment. It is said that the Divine Knowledge of the Torah was given by God to Israel while speaking to them "face-to-face." Israel is the name given to Jacob after he surrendered. *Jacob* means "crooked." *Israel* means "straight." Being "ISRAEL-REAL" and/or authentic in my relating is what I feel when I stop lying. There is then no ego left. It can be that simple!

Code Simplicity - BL / LB

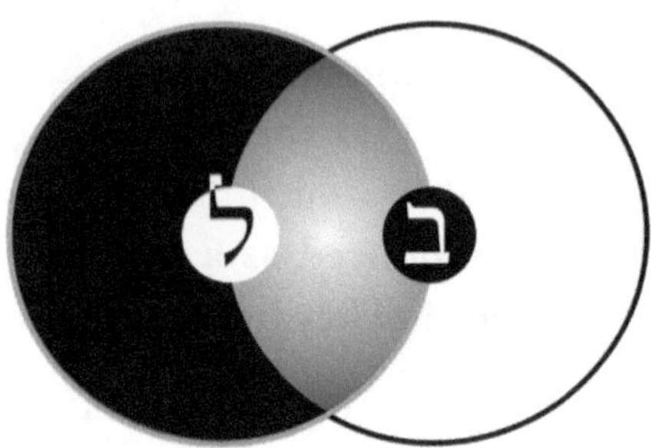

Imagine a language so pure and so sacred that it can reconcile opposites in just two letters...

Right: Hebrew letter Beth (ב) → B in Roman Script
Left: Hebrew letter Lamed (ל) → L in Roman Script

HERE IS HOW S/HEBREW INSCRIBES CODE "SIMPLICITY:"

- **BL:** in one direction, I read *Bal* (בל) for "do not!"
- **LB:** in the other direction, I read *Lev* (לב) for "heart."

The Decoding: the pairs BL/LB partner to convey the entirety of Torah's wisdom: it can be that simple! First, I go from B to L, refusing to listen to *Bal* – the "do not" command. When sick and tired to be sick and tired, I turn to *Lev* – my "heart." I now understand why I needed to break my own law. Through my willingness to love 'God,' I inscribe the LOVE that has no opposite, in tune with the ethics of complementarity.

- Letter Beth (ב): the Torah's first book (*Genesis*) begins with the sign Beth (ב) of the word *Bereshit* for "in the Beginning." This B is also the B of Boundaries that I create with each word I speak, for good or bad, in sickness and in health. Thus, Beth is the Word that begins the story of mind and time.
- Letter Lamed (ל): the Torah's last book (*Deuteronomy*) ends with the sign Lamed (L) of the word *Yisrael* for "Israel." Lamed

is the name of the "ox-goad" that points the way to Self-knowledge – when I understand.

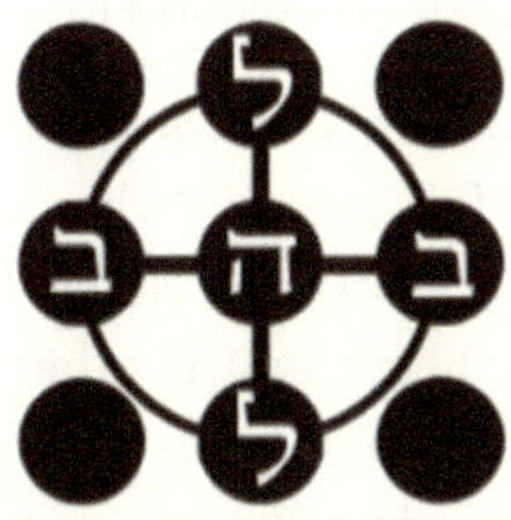

5 Books of Moses = 2 Pairs of Signs + 1 Core Container

In the letters above, I also read the word *Abel* (הבל) for "Vanity." Abel was the younger brother of Cain. He was the first mortal to die, and Cain, the first murderer to kill. Cain's name means "possessed by jealousy." Cain was jealous of the recognition that his brother Abel got after his offering was accepted by "God." **The moral of the story? Killing (my) "vanity" is how to defuse being "possessed by jealousy."**

When I can be neutral about Power, prosperity and/or prestige, I no longer swing from wanting them to resisting them. Therefore, killing the golem of vanity is also killing the golem of jealousy. These two are "brothers." Note: the signs of *Abel* (הבל) reorder into *Halev* (הלב) for "the heart" – the sacred heart that understands knowledge.

The Way of Peace

"Give your servant an understanding heart to distinguish between right and wrong in judging people." *1 Kings 3:9*

Wisdom or a heart that understands knowledge was the only prayer of king Solomon. The name *Solomon* (שלמה) is formed on the root *Shalom* (שלום) for "wholeness, peace." It was the king's calling to know peace and peace's calling to have at its heart the sign Lamed whose three letters (LMD) are an acronym for *Lev Mevin Daath* – "the heart that understands knowledge." This is how he could be the judge that he was: he had come to understand knowledge, he was at peace – the ideal condition to render judgment and extend justice.

And if I still want to fight with what I know is the loving thing to do, I may find myself asking: *Mah Tzedeq?* "what is justice?" Lamed (again) comes to the rescue by reordering as *L'MiDah* for "toward measure." On one pan of my scale is my heart; on the other, a feather. I know justice when my heart is so pure that both pans of the scale are in perfect equilibrium. I no longer indulge in either deficiencies or excesses. Having stopped doing harm, I vibrate with the unity that sustains **interdependence.**

I	IT/ITS	WE
Individual Power	Symbolic Power	Collective Power
Independence	Interdependence	Dependance

Symbolic Power and Interdependence

This message on the nature of justice will soon be decoded as "Code Wisdom." The S/Hebrew codes are precious. They are the biological and cultural genes that give me direct answers to fundamental questions, individually and collectively. They are the passwords that unlock the voice of instinct and connect me back to my heart, opening me to coherence. They mirror that "I Am" sent me, granting me access to the etheric field of all knowledge. They also keep me safe while traveling in cyber space, until I come to the heart that understands knowledge, and receive the wisdom I prayed for.

When I am not at peace, there is a code I do not hear, see or understand.

This is the perfect time to build the needed foundation to unfold "Code Wisdom." I begin with a wheel that is moved by the 22 basic letters (they are transliterated in Roman script inside the outer rim of the wheel pictured below). On the rim, I see 8 "tongues," each holding a letter. In the heart-shaped hub, I see the two letters Lamed and Beth of *Lev* for "heart." The tongues are hinting at a wheel beyond the wheel, such as the wheel of Buddhism which has 8 spokes, 1 hub and 1 rim. 8+1+1 = 10. These 10 are energized by the 5 final letters complemented by 5 initial letters (8+1+1 = 5+5). The Buddhist *Dharmachakra* is now interdependently connected to the S/Hebrew *Mitzvah Gilgal* – both names meaning "wheel of interdependence."

Note: the 5 initials are signs enlarged in key biblical places, e.g.; the big Beth of *Bereshit* in *Genesis 1:1*. Together, these five initials spell out *Beth El* (בית אל) for the "House of God." By balancing finals with initials, I now have a path to become real as Jacob: 'When Jacob awoke from his sleep, he thought, "Surely LOVE is in this place, and I was not aware of it. . . How awesome is this place! This is none other than the house of God; this is the gate of heaven" (*Genesis 28:16-17*). This path – which unfolds in *Golden XPR's* advanced courses – may be walked interdependently with an XPR advisor.

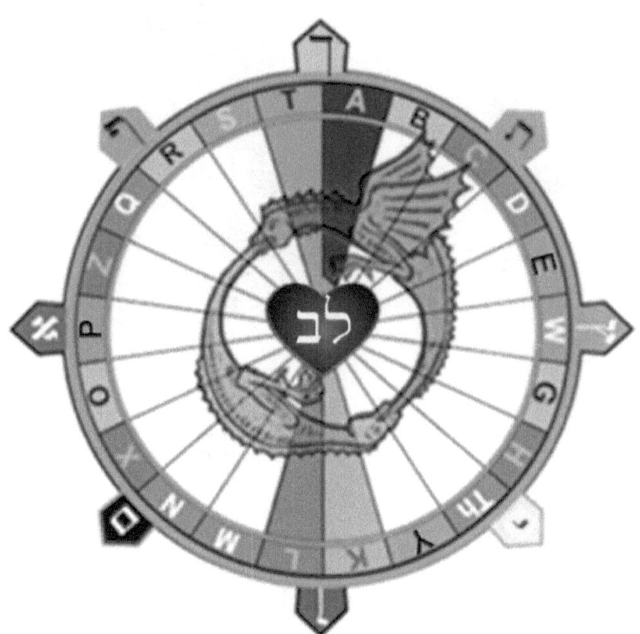

Mitzvah Gilgal – the "Wheel of Interdependence"

1. **I INCREASE the dream of separation and DECREASE the reality of interdependence:** I begin with the sign B and go clockwise until I come to sign L. Pair BL reads *Bal* for "do not." I see that just after B is C, and just after L is M. Together, the signs CM spell *Gam* for "also → more."

2. **I DECREASE the dream of separation and INCREASE the reality of interdependence:** I now begin with sign L and go counterclockwise until I come to sign B. Pair LB reads *Lev* for "heart." I see that just after L is K, and just after B is A. Together, the signs AK spell *Akh* for "but → less."

Including and transcending excesses and deficiencies
via the golden mean of the BL/LB double helix

How can I go *L'Midah* "toward measure" when I don't know *LaMeD* – the "heart that understands knowledge?" As long as I'm stuck in the throat chakra with my good and evil wires crossed, I'm still misusing Power. I perpetuate injustice as I don't understand that there's only One of us. Not being at peace, my heart is not fit to make sound decisions and my mind, unable to know its natural proficiencies. I don't know that "less is more" and don't see the fair beauty of a justice that only works to lead me to the sense of enough, at the end of dissatisfaction. How could I when I'm addicted to discontent and endlessly judging myself for my errors? There's no kindness there. Moreover, if justice is temperance, I'm missing the boat and the beauty of its golden mean!

However, when I understand the fundamental truth of oneness and know that I am interdependently connected to the whole, I do not feel lonely or afraid. I also don't live in Scare City nor obsess on survival. I don't judge "you" since I feel how any judgment of you is a judgment of me. I wisely extend love and kindness to all.

Code Wisdom - ABC / MLK

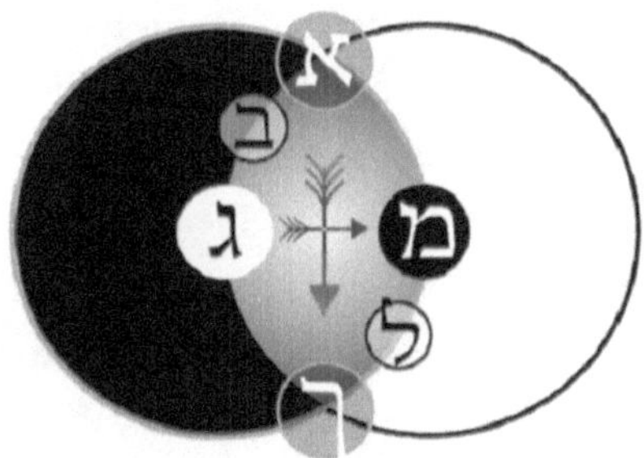

Imagine a language so pure and so sacred that it can reconcile a number of opposites in just two triads...

ABC - starting at the top, going counterclockwise:
Hebrew letter Aleph (א) → A in Roman Script to letter Beth (ב) → B in Roman Script to letter Gimel (ג) → C in Roman Script.
MLK - starting in the middle (right), going clockwise: Hebrew letter Mem (מ) → M in Roman Script to letter Lamed (ל) → L in Roman Script to letter Kaph final (ך) → K in Roman Script.

The Decoding: the six letters that moved the wheel of interdependence by spelling out *Lev* (LB) for "heart," *Akh* (AK) for "decrease" and *Gam*

(CM) for "increase" are now regrouped into two triads. The first triad ABC is formed by the 1st, the 2nd and the 3rd letters of the alphabet – Aleph (A), Beth (B), Gimel (C), and the second triad MLK, by the 13th, 12th, and 11th letters – Mem (M), Lamed (L), Kaph (K). Reversing the first triad, I read *Gubha* for a lions' "**den**." The second triad reads *Melekh* for "**king**" (yep, as in Martin Luther King). To vibrate on king Solomon's frequency of peace and render wise judgments, I must be able to become a *Daniel* or "God of Judgment," and stop calling "no good" the situation in which I find myself. I will then resist nothing, and be able to hold the tension. Holding the tension, I would not worsen my situation by committing another crime. Just as Daniel in the lions' den, I would be saved from lions "because I was found blameless" *Daniel 6:22*.

Criminal Mind

"Because of our broken instincts, we are in pain. . . So, what are we supposed to do? Should we abandon knowledge? . . . In any event, that wouldn't be possible. For better or worse, we ate the fruit of knowledge long, long ago." *Tatsuhiko Takimoto*

Carl Jung coined the mnemonic word CRASH for the different instincts: C is for Creativity, R for Religion, A for Aggression, S for Sexuality and H for Hunger. When my sexual and/or hunger instincts are broken, I am not in my body and can no longer do aggression consciously. Aggression (or asking for what I want and protecting what I have) surprisingly resonates with the maternal instinct. It is to speak clear boundaries. As for religion as an instinct, the idea is engaging. Clean hands / pure heart evokes my nature. Such candor may be behind the Creativity of a child at "heART."

As the voice of TCO, I wish to consider the instinct of Imagery – of letters, numbers and words as images, a dimension felt by spelling bee kids. Mnemonic CRASH now becomes I CRASH, which gives me the chance to own a "crash" whose violence could be difficult to bear.

To heal, I must first receive the image or the metaphor at the cellular level. This image is what connects mind and body. It is given by the soul which speaks in the language of metaphor. I recall how *Yvrit,* the S/Hebrew word for "Hebrew," also means "to carry over" – the exact sense of the Greek word "metaphor." When I speak of dancing snowflakes, the image synergizes belief, feeling and sensation. It gives meaning to a physical event. If I can't make sense of my own metaphors, my instinct turns into a crazy animal that acts out. As my raw instinctual energy goes unconscious and blind, the pattern soon translates into an addiction; a crime.

This is where *Binah* or "understanding, in between" is a matter of life and death. Once the symbols of the dream are decoded, their energy is "carried over" from the mind into the body where I can receive, transform and heal the memory. Similarly, neuropeptides have receptors that pick-up signals and/or images which, in turn, affect my chemistry. While new sciences found that there's something hidden underneath the physical world that is needed for its functioning, ancient traditions speak of a code hidden in scriptures needed to reveal the religious instinct. If so, where are the clues?

Opening an Investigation

"The world is full of obvious things which nobody by any chance ever observes." *Conan Doyle*

Investigating belief systems and profiling me as a criminal involves looking at motive, opportunity and evidence. To prove my guilt in a criminal trial, I must have had the tools necessary to commit a crime, the actionable idea to commit the crime, and the chance to follow through on my intention. Bottom line, I must ignore that everything is One.

In a "PAIRfect" world, pairs of opposites give rise to each other. At times the yin side is on top, and at other times, the yang side is. Neither side has more Power than the other. They just share the energy and give rise to each other, knowing that they are "created in the divine image – **in-between** male and female." There's an **evident** difference between the 1st Adam who knows to be created male and female and has it all, and the 2nd Adam who is lonely and lives in Scare City.

This 2nd Adam is in an I CRASH mode. His instinctual compass is so broken that he can't "Imagine" himself sustaining PaRaDiSe. Subsisting rather than being, he has a good **motive** to commit a crime. He just has to wait for the **opportunity**.

What's my motive? What do I really desire? WHY?

No matter how I break LOVE's Law, the yearning for love, approval and recognition is often the main motive behind my crime. I know that male is the positive current and female, the negative current. If good and evil are just the work of polarity, WHY be stuck in moral judgments so rigid that I end up reacting against them and doing the next "wrong" thing? This is also how I can't forgive my errors or my "neighbor's" errors.

WHY don't I **know** who I Am? WHY can't I stop **desiring** evil and **willing** it into being? WHY do I feel that I don't **have** what I want? I desire, I will, I know, I have: these are keys for me to return to innocence.

I ASK WHY BECAUSE...

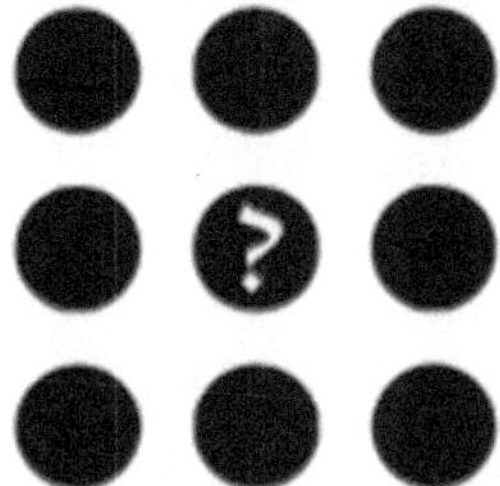

I ASK WHY BECAUSE I'm stuck in Ego-Egypt. I'm a victim like Pharaoh who can't let his limiting 'people-beliefs' go, and must suffer ten plagues (10 again?). I have **a whole family of beliefs** to understand... I start with "I Am." Then my belief has **a child**: "I am a man." And **a grandchild**: "I am a religious man." And **a great grandchild**: "I am a religious man who needs a savior;" on and on for generations. The "plagues" are how I'll eventually end the slave narrative and be ready for truth.

To get the gold, I must go in the shadow. That's what "the Jews" did. They went to Egypt, and took the gold with them as they left. Same with Betzalel who was in "God's shadow" and was blessed with wisdom, understanding and knowledge. The more I own my darkness, the more self-esteem I have, and the freer I am to decide.

Yep, I owned the greed, and saw the sense of Ezekiel's vision: "and out of the midst thereof came the likeness of four living creatures. [...] As for the likeness of their faces, the four had the face of a **man**; the face of a **lion** on the right side; and the face of a **bull** on the left side; also, the face of an **eagle**." *Ezekiel 1:5 [...] ibid, 1:10*

	The bull's face – Taurus	
The lion's face – Leo	Knowledge	The eagle's face – Scorpio
	The man's face – Aquarius	

Ezekiel's Vision

Ezekiel worked with S/Hebrew all the time. He knew that 12 of the S/Hebrew letters invoke the 12 astrological signs. The four creatures are the four fixed signs of the Zodiac, as called by letters נ ,ו ,ט ,צ. **Aquarius** (the man) is invoked by sign Tzaddi (צ). **Leo** (the lion) is invoked by sign Teth (ט). **Taurus** (the bull) is invoked by sign Vav (ו). **Scorpio** (the scorpion to be sublimated into an eagle) is invoked by sign Nun (נ). They are "fixed" because they occur at the most intense point of a season, when holding the tension is more crucial than ever.

Scorpio is the dragon-like female flow. Opposite to her is Leo – the lion-like male flow. "**I desire**," says Scorpio, revealing her motive. "**I will**," says Leo, speaking of his opportunity. The evidence comes from the star-like human. "**I know**," says Aquarius. "**I have**" says Taurus.

Opportunity	Evidence	Motive
Leo's Keyword "I will"	Aquarius' Keyword: "I know" Taurus' Keyword: "I have"	Scorpio's Keyword: "I desire"

The Keywords of Criminology

If I find myself fretting, thinking that astrology is a false science, I could consider Niels Bohr's paradox: "an ordinary truth is a statement whose opposite is a falsehood. A profound truth is a statement whose opposite is also a profound truth."

One ordinary truth / falsehood: *Ain Mazel L'ISRAEL* – "there is no star for who IS REAL!" Destiny, predictions and influence of the planets do not concern the Self, but only the ego. **One opposite truth / falsehood:** the cosmic nature of 22 letters (3 for the elements; 7 for the classical planets and 12 for the astrological signs) spells out how to move from stage to stage until I am reborn into Spirit.

One profound truth: I have cells organized as per the cathartic Power of Three so as to convey the knowledge of opposites, both sides being profoundly true. This is "Code Communication" (AT/TA) at its best. AT is "untranslatable;" TA is "cell." The table's cells hold signals that were untranslatable to me thus far, and give them an address (white male, black female or grey neutral). I can now take the information within, inquire and feel it in my blood. The more I understand the symbols of my dreams, the more I restore my instinct, wake up and let my limiting people-beliefs go.

Opportunity	Evidence	Motive
"I will"	"I know"/ "I have"	"I desire"
Aversion	Ignorance / Entitlement	Greed

Is my **desire** body so poisoned by **greed** that I can't give me the permission to want what I want? Has my will been corrupted by **aversion**? Does **entitlement** distort the sense of what **I have**? And now that I have done harm, what was my **motive**? Is it a crime of passion: shall I look for the woman? Is it a crime of logic: shall I follow the money or how I want to make you pay?

And it makes me wonder... Would I seek retribution if I didn't attach to the "I am the body" belief? This belief fills me with anxiety, as I am now preoccupied with the need to feed it, clothe it, shelter it. Will I have enough? Why do I see myself as a have-not and resent "you" for it? Why be so poor in spirit that I would want to misuse the Law for my benefit? Is this how I justify going into **retaliation**?

The Law of Talion

"An eye for an eye will only make the whole world blind." *Mahatma Gandhi*

THE LAW OF THE TALION (LATIN *RETALIARE* "TO PAY BACK IN KIND") orders that a person who has injured another person would be penalized to a similar degree. Beyond the fallacy of believing that two wrongs can make a right, the strangest part of this entire debate is that the Law of the Talion perverts the universal principle of cause and effect. When attempting to keep "you" accountable for what you did to me, do I forget that every single action produces a reaction no matter what? Would I even try to play "God" if I were taking full responsibility for what I communicate?

Besides, how could the Torah contradict itself so completely? On the one hand, it would oppose using vengeance for the sake of assuaging the distress of the victim. On the other, it would preconize a law for the said-victim to retaliate. This makes no sense. Moreover, I can know that the Torah teaches the way of peace since Jesus did advise to turn the other cheek and not to seek compensation for the injury. And if there was someone who knew the Jewish law, it was Jesus! There must therefore be a **code** behind the words of *Exodus 21:22-25*: "If there is serious injury, you are to take a life **for** life, an eye **for** eye, a tooth **for** tooth, a hand **for** hand, a foot **for** foot, burn **for** burn..."

The same intention to decipher this verse's code so as to restore the fair beauty of the law must have been on the mind of 18th century legalist Vilna Gaon. Knowing that the word *Tahat* for "**for**" also means "**under**," he was guided to look at the letters **under** the letters of the word *Ayin* (עין) for "eye." To understand his process, I'll take the example of the English word "sky." Seeing that T is "**under**" S, L is "**under**" K, and Z is "**under**" Y, I arrive at the code TLZ. Rabbi Gaon found that "under" *Ayin-Yod-Nun* are the signs *Peh-Kaph-Samekh* which he reordered as *Keseph* (כסף) for "silver, money." It is clear: retaliating is wanting to make "you" pay!

Why focus on the word "eye?" Why not the tooth or the hand? It is because it is all a matter of perspective. Consider: when stuck in Scare City and barely subsisting, my vision is fixated on being a have-not. Hating "you" for being a have, I am now susceptible to become a criminal and misuse justice for my own gain.

My two main motivations in engaging in crime continue to be sex and money, both of which are of concern to the sex chakra. Besides the mouth chakra, the sex chakra is the center where I'm likely to misuse my sexual Power and get burned with fire. No wonder I have doubts and can't let me succeed in my creation: I only want to SEE that I am deprived, and become attached to the scraps I allow myself to have. [Pause]

I AM ATTACHED

I AM ATTACHED to the "I am the body" belief. I think that I stop at the skin, that I am here, and you are there. This bondage to the material world is so painful that I have a need for a Mrs. Moses who dares ask for directions. I wish to see a map whose sacred signs are so clear that they can guide me to receive the Torah.

And this is what I saw...

Looking at the numbers to the left, I recognize that they match the numbers of TCO's map. But they do more. They also match the value of the hieroglyphs to the right, e.g.; Ayin the "eye" (value 70) is in chamber #7. Shin the "tooth" (value 300) is in chamber #3.

Some of the hieroglyphs (or "sacred signs") of the S/Hebrew alphabet name the exact body parts invoked by the law of talion: a hand, a foot, a tooth, an eye. *Ayin* is the "eye," *Shin* is the "tooth." The top row is not as obvious. *Yod* is the "hand" and *Kaph* is its counterpart as "back of the hand" (which could also be interpreted as the foot). However, while Kaph (value 20) fits in chamber #2, why is Yod (value 10) in chamber #4?

Yod (hand) Kaph (foot) says "talk the talk, and walk the walk." When my words and actions are congruent, *Yod* (YD) inverts into *Dai* (DY) for "enough," a word starting in D (value 4).

The bottom row unfolds an insightful question: what's "**under**" the Law of Talion? *Under* the eye is the $ sign, money being my main motive for misusing the law. I followed the same process as Gaon did for the word "eye," taking the word *Shin* for "tooth." *Under* SYN, I saw the letters TKX that reorder as *Sukkat* for "tent." A tent is a call to let go of my defense mechanisms against the uncertainty of the law without law.

The more I look into the "me-rror" and own my error, the less I feel like *your* victim, and demand reparation for the harm *you* caused me. Instead, I wisely know that, since my heart cannot be broken, a "break" is only a breakthrough. This is what liberation from Ego-Egypt is, that allows me to escape the illusion of separation and its ensuing cycle of death and rebirth to which life in the material world is bound.

I can only imagine what it would be like to live in a world that functions with these agreements, no longer believing that matter is solid, or that money doesn't grow on trees; a world where people would stop calculating for their own advantage. For now, will I make it my responsibility (and not yours) to wake up? Will I choose to let go of my attachments (of everything that I am not)? As I fulfill my calling, I even begin to detach from my name. Anonymity may be how I change the collective, as I'd be the change I wish to see. **Consider: when I know that I am neither the name nor the body (or that which is dying), I don't fear death and can be kind.**

Code Kindness - CD / DC

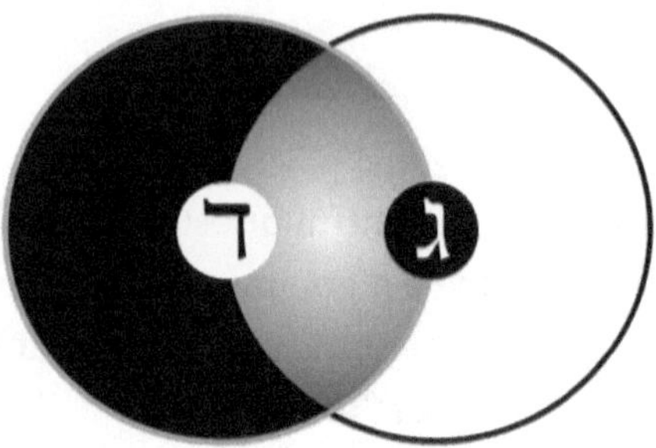

*Imagine a language so pure and so sacred that it can
reconcile opposites in just two letters...*

Right: Hebrew letter Gimel (ג) → C in Roman Script
Left: Hebrew letter Dalet (ד) → D in Roman Script

Here is how S/Hebrew inscribes code "Kindness:"

- **CD**: in one direction, I read *Gad* (גד) for "destiny."
- **DC**: in the other direction, I read *Dag* (דג) for "fish."

THE DECODING: IT IS CARL JUNG WHO SAID: "UNTIL YOU MAKE THE unconscious conscious, it will **direct your life and you will call it fate."** Fate has a different quality than **destiny**: the former feels constraining, the latter, fulfilling and freeing. Gimel leads to *Gemul* for "giving." It is the "PAIRfect" partner for Dalet that leads to *Dalut* for "poverty." This pair affirms that it is written for me to shift from a fate in Scare City to a destiny of abundance, when two **fish** feed a multitude. The two fish are S/Hebrew pair CD conveyed by English pair GR of Giving/Receiving. For me to be kind as a Giver, my giving must have no strings attached. For me to be kind as a Receiver, I must be "poor" or empty. For if my mind is full of questions, there'll be no space for an answer to come in. Kindness comes naturally when I transcend my fate and fulfill my destiny by understanding that we are One. On that note, there is a truth worthy of repeating: complete (100%) nullification of the ego, whether it is done through inquiry or surrender, is the prerequisite to include and transcend destiny. I can then really give, as I've let go of my resentment for feeling forced to "give," and really receive, as I realize that retaliation is of the past. Indeed, I wouldn't trade my lot with anyone.

Pleasure or Obligation?

"I slept and dreamt that life was joy. I awoke and saw that life was service. I acted and behold, service was joy." *Rabindranath Tagore*

I come to kindness by realizing why I once used retaliation to corrupt the nature of justice. Admittedly, I am angry. I resent having been brainwashed with rigid ideas of good and bad, moral and immoral, sinful and virtuous, acceptable and unacceptable. It is not a pleasure to be coerced into obeying the law, or forced to be in service to LOVE. I begrudge how "The Truth" has been wielded upon me as a sword of coercion. To transcend the confinement of morality, I decided that we all have our own truth: you have yours, I have mine and neither of us can challenge that. But how far will I go in being nonjudgmental? Is rape okay? Is the holocaust okay? Is war okay? While I can understand how I would be offended by religious fundamentalism and oppose a conduct based on absolutist principles that try to manipulate me by way of guilt, does it really evolve me to no longer be willing or even capable to make a moral judgment?

Indeed, can I actually discriminate? When still poisoned by ignorance, I don't know that there's good in bad and bad in good. I'm likely to be halted by a number of smothering "shoulds," get lonely at times, and hopelessly search for LOVE out there.

The disconnect reinforces the sense that I am not enough and must please "you" in order to gain your approval. I am now deep into the game of pretense, seduction and false service. If service leads to a life of greatness, I don't feel great as my projections on "you" keep me from true devotion. **To not be a victim who indulges noble suffer-**

ing, **I must know that we are one, and thus that serving "you" is serving me.** LOVE is being total in my service, so present to the task that I am detached from any outcome. I know and feel that the value I receive is in the authenticity of the gift I give. The more selfless I am in my service, the more I feel that I serve "God" and reality itself. Being happy to be me, I like me when I am with "you." My servant heart uncovers the secret of purpose, as all is fair and beautiful when I do what I do with all my heart, all my soul and all my might. While I may have felt inferior to "you" at times, I now realize that leadership is not a rank and not a position. It is sincere service. And that is freedom.

Code Generosity - QDS / YHX

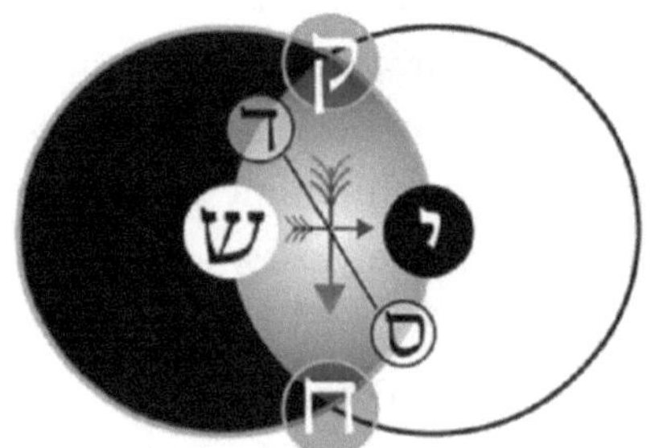

Imagine a language so pure and so sacred...

QDS – from the top, going counterclockwise:
Letter Qoph (ק) → Q in Roman Script + Letter Dalet (ד) → D + Letter Shin (ש) → S, Sh form the word *Qadosh* (QDS) "sacred."

HXY – from the bottom, going counterclockwise:
Letter Chet (ח) → H in Roman Script | Letter Samekh (ס) → X | Letter Yod (י) → Y reorder as the word *Yachos* (YHX) for "he will have mercy."

To fully appreciate this decoding, I must review the "ALBaM" code (see *Learning to Code*). I will then see how 19th letter Qoph (Q) is paired with 8th letter Chet (H), 4th letter Dalet (D), with 15th letter Samekh (X), and

21st letter Shin (S), with 10th letter Yod (Y). This makes *Qadosh* "sacred" and *Yachos* "he will have mercy" a mirror of each other.

The Decoding: the word *Yachos* is found in *Psalm 72:13*: "**he will have mercy** on the poor and needy, and save the souls of the needy." It is formed on the root of *Chesed* – the sphere of "kindness." Being a *Chassid* is to be merciful and generous enough *not* to interfere with evolution since evolution is sacred (no push), and *not* to give help to someone who is not ready to handle such advantages wisely. This sobriety carries the highest moral obligation. By connecting kindness to sacredness, it nullifies the possibility to violate any boundaries or profane any sanctuary. Such respect is what I am "needy" for. More than "needy," the Hebrew word *Evionim* (אביונים) speaks of the "Ebionites," a Jewish sect advocating concern for the poor and political liberation for oppressed peoples. *Evionim's* letters reorder as *Ain B'Yom* for "nothing [to have power] over the day."

The Power Paradox

"Making a stone which is so heavy that it cannot be moved is logically possible. Therefore God, being omnipotent, can make a stone so heavy that it cannot be moved. But if God makes a stone so heavy that it cannot be moved, then God cannot move it." *The Paradox of the Stone*

As long as I have my attention on you, trying to save you, teach you, inspire you or heal you, I can avoid taking care of me. I don't have to be whole or entire. Thus, the Power paradox which rests on the triple challenge of being omni- or "entire, total:"

- **Omniscience:** how could "God" be all-knowing *and* impassible?
- **Omnipotence:** could "God" create a stone so heavy that "he" couldn't lift it?
- **Omnibenevolence:** how could "God" be just *and* merciful?

The cleverness of these debates only serves to mask a more primal question: why would I want to do harm? Is this misdirected desire how I would ignore that I have all the answers (omniscience), how I would stop being kind (omnibenevolence), or how I would say "I CAN'T," which is mostly a lie (omnipotence)? Certainly, my ego will block information that contradicts its program. Once my conscience is disabled, I am justified in not loving "the LOVE God with all my heart, all my soul, all my might" and never have to be total ("omni"). By attaching to the thought "I am the doer" (e.g.; I am the one who puts bread on the table), I can now pretend that I have control over me, you, it. It just takes a bit of manipulating. No wonder I'd fear "God's" Divine Judgment!

- **Third Eye & Omniscience** – when my ego tries to convince me that I don't know what to do in my predicament, I can ask myself: "is it true?" This will ready me for how Truth will change my life.
- **Throat & Omnipotence** – when my ego hides behind intellectual debates such as the paradox of the stone, I can ask myself: "why am I denying or repressing my Power?" Might my female side suffer from the womb, since she won't accept the things she cannot change? As a reaction, might my male side resist changing the things he could? Surely being *powerless* to change is how I alternate between being a victim and a bully.
- **Navel & Omnibenevolence** – when my ego works hard at failing myself and won't let me be successful in my creation, I can ask myself: "why would I want to punish me?" This will open me to feeling the hatred I repress.

The paradox of judgment and mercy begins at the throat's level, where my polarities are inverted. This is when my female side desires evil (instead of resisting it), and my male side resists goodness (instead of desiring it). Note: the female flow of the Hebrew tree of life (traditionally spheres 2, 4, 6) is named the "pillar of judgment" since its exact middle (the sphere 4 of Power) imposes a severe "judgment."

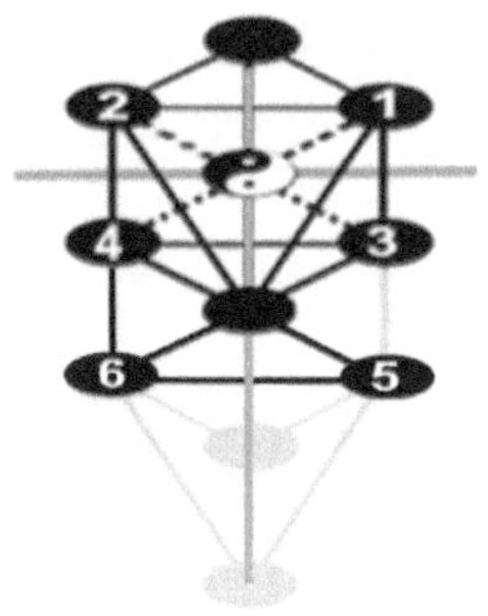

The male flow (traditionally spheres 1, 3, 5) is named "pillar of mercy," since its exact middle (the sphere 3 of kindness) extends mercy. The tree of life reflects the "God" I created who either hates sin and executes judgment, or shows mercy and is patient with offenders.

It has been said that, while on the cross, Jesus revealed how divine judgment and mercy interact. **While there are many crosses on the tree of life, the messianic cross is lit by my walking on the middle path and stretching beyond the knowledge of opposites. At last, I feel how the knowledge of truth is fulfilled by the way and the life.**

When I have had enough of causing effects that I would rather not have to experience, I will embrace the paradox, grow out of my naïve interpretations of "God" and take full (as in "omni-") responsibility. I will accept that there is a universal accounting system in which I must experience the consequences of my actions. When I do good, I have good results. When I do bad, bad results. I will give and forgive, live and let live, keeping in mind that consequences are like a debt that can be carried over into future lives.

Essentially, I will agree to die for my sins, pay the price, and earn the stages of my liberation. It will be the end of retaliation. And that will be wise, merciful, filled with knowledge and understanding, and certainly powerful!

Understanding My Sins

"Abandon Hope All Ye Who Enter Here!" *Dante Alighieri, Divine Comedy*

While this phrase speaks of a very dicey situation, it is often used in an amusing sense. The humor attempts to deflect the meaning of "hopelessness," when I touch bottom so hard that I no longer deceive myself *hoping* that a miraculous "God" will come to save me. I am as Dante, guided to enter the Inferno and hear the anguished screams of the Uncommitted. The "Uncommitted" is the part of me that does harm out of not making the decision to inquire on my motivations for doing what I do.

Together with the Ten Commandments, the Seven Deadly Sins were for a long time one of the most popular models for an examination of conscience. Christian scholars have inquired on which sin comes first: is it pride, greed, envy? Seeing that there is an order in the chaos of sins may provide such a clear understanding that these seven hungry ghosts could feel heard and seen, and from there, transition into peace.

To this end, I wish to view Master Dante's teachings on the three types of sin (**incontinence**, **violence**, and **fraud**), as they are organized by way of the knowledge of opposites:

Interior Male	Interior/Exterior Neutral	Exterior Female
Fraud	Incontinence	Violence

The incontinence of the neutral side: when I ignore *Daath,* my mouth chakra falls 1) into the **greed** of a wounded heart, 2) into the **lust** of an aggressive sex chakra whose raging fire compels me to misuse my power. The fall ends in 3) the **gluttony** of a passive root chakra that can't get any nourishment.

Fraud	Incontinence	Violence
Pride | Sloth	Greed | Lust | Gluttony	Wrath | Envy

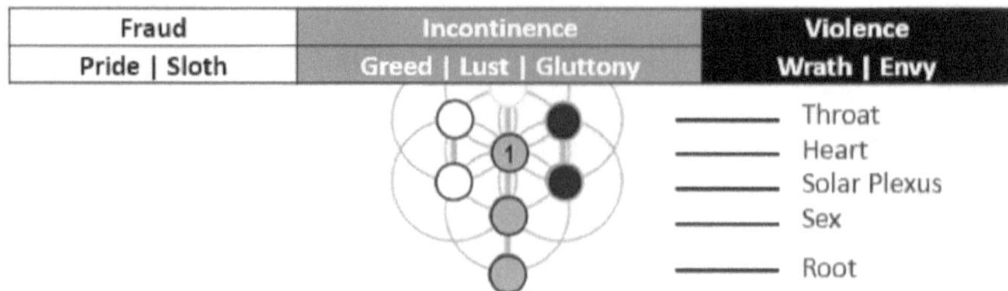

The fraud of the male side: Lucifer did fall out of **pride.** Annoyed at having to serve "God," he grew rebellious in his desire to be served. The same pride alternates with **sloth,** felt by Dante as the "failure to love God with all one's heart, mind and soul."

The violence of the female side: wrath is held to be why Moses never reached the Promised Land. It alternates with **envy,** when I am gifted with light and yet, feel so unseen that I begin to covet "your" position (or in Lucifer's case, "God's" position).

The Power of Three's pattern witnesses the "Fall" of *Daath,* the mouth chakra, into the seven infernal spheres of "Ego-Egypt" (first tier). **Incontinence** is when there is no golden mean or "middle" between excess and deficiency. It begins with the **greed** of a heart chakra that doesn't know it's unhurt and just wants to take, so stuck it is in Scare City. More than a rapacious desire for wealth, **greed** is a will fixed on Power, on controlling the world. Both a poison and a sin, **greed** is at the root of all sins and fuels all sins.

Code Power - DO / OT

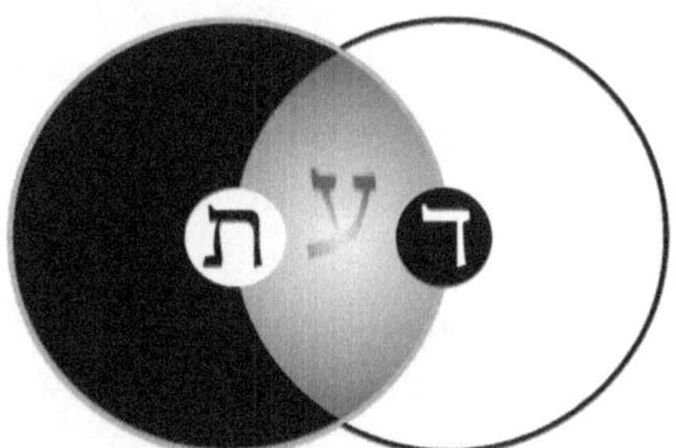

Imagine a language so pure and so sacred that it can reconcile opposites in just three letters...

Right: Hebrew letter Dalet (ד) → D in Roman Script
Middle: Hebrew letter Ayin (ע) → O in Roman Script
Left: Hebrew letter Tav (ת) → T in Roman Script

Here is how S/Hebrew inscribes code "Power:"

- **DO**: from the right to the middle, I read *Da* (דע) for "knowledge."
- **OT**: from the middle to the left, I read *Et* (עת) for "time."
- **D-OT**: from right to left, I read *Dalet-Et* (ד-עת) for "door of time."

The Decoding: what is Power? The question matters since evolving is to acquire Power. So, is Power knowledge? Is it money? When considering that time is the great equalizer (each of us is given 24 hrs. a day), Power may just be what I do with time, thus the meme "time is money." The ancient Greeks had two words for time: *chronos* and *kairos*. The former refers to sequential time; the latter, to random time. It is the difference between "quantity time" and "quality time." A new way to language this contrast is to speak of "horizontal time" (as a timeline stretching behind me and in front of me) and "vertical time" (when I stop counting time and make time count).

As for Greek *kairos,* the root can be traced back to the practice of archery, weaving and rhetoric. In archery, it is the rare moment when an arrow is discharged with such single-pointedness that it is one with the target. In weaving, it is the moment when the shuttle can pass unencumbered through threads on the loom. In rhetoric, it is the moment when the argument is presented in such compelling way that it can only impact the audience successfully. Until then, I best keep silent. Those examples allude to the archer, the weaver, or the orator having the **knowledge** of a **door of time** opening – when the choice to act or speak is made by a higher Power.

Therefore, *kairos* is to be on purpose – able to recognize that the Now requires the gumption to drive through it with proper use of force. It is the wisdom of a judgment that takes advantage of the laws of motion, and rarely misses the expedient course of action. The S/Hebrew equivalents for *Kairos* is **Et**. It is paralleled with chronological *Z'man* in the famous line of *Ecclesiastes 3:1* "to everything there is a chronological time and a purposive time under heaven." English has a term for *kairos:* "purposiveness." Purposiveness goes beyond purpose. More than an action with a purpose, intention, or design, it is the sacrifice I make for me to begin resting from creating, while creating.

Purposiveness is what directs the behavior of light, recognized by scientists as "purposive" since it is moved by the Principle of Least Action.

The Light of the Spheres

"For a process to be scientific, it must exclude purpose, teleology (the doctrine of design in the material world), or any higher reason. The only exception is LIGHT, whose purposiveness is associated with the Principle of Least Action." *Arthur Young, The Reflexive Universe.*

Gentle warning: I am about to stumble on a clue so undeniably good, true and beautiful that the sexual Power games of my male lying and faking kindness to set up my female and watch her losing "it" are about to wind down.

The "I am not enough" thought is so annoying that I create unconscious time to try to silence it. I am not in my Power and not on purpose. I am also not at peace, which says that there's something I do not understand, like my ego pendulum which will swing to the other side when I believe that "I am special..."

Narcissus was the most "special" of all. Hunter renowned for his beauty, Narcissus (whose name means "sleep, numbness") had such pride in his looks that he disdained those who loved him. Realizing that he had succumbed to arrogance, Nemesis (for "she who gives retribution") attracted him to a pool where he saw his own reflection in the waters and fell in love with it, not realizing it was merely an image. Unable to leave the beauty of his own reflection, he died. He was survived by the narcissus plant that sprang from the very spot where he died.

If I could sense how asleep I am when I believe that I am special, I would wake up to humility. And in that "land," there would be no Nemesis and no need for torment or retribution as I would not have contempt for my loved ones.

But I'm still asleep, still greedy and still fighting for Power. Why can't I let go? It is as if *Daath* (sphere 0) won't open its door to me, preventing me from transitioning into grace and emPowering the Now. One thing I know: I'm authentic in my search! I thirst to know the original behind the glamor of the reflection. Which is how I can also know that an accident will happen so catalytic that my ears will open to the music of the spheres, vibrating in me with the frequency of the sense of enough. I will know that I reached the Promised Land when I can sustain the health of my throat chakra without defending (Powerlessness) or attacking (no kindness).

The **Door of Time** will have opened, allowing for wisdom and kindness to trade places as needed. The four spheres are now interdependently resonating with *Daath's* "knowledge."

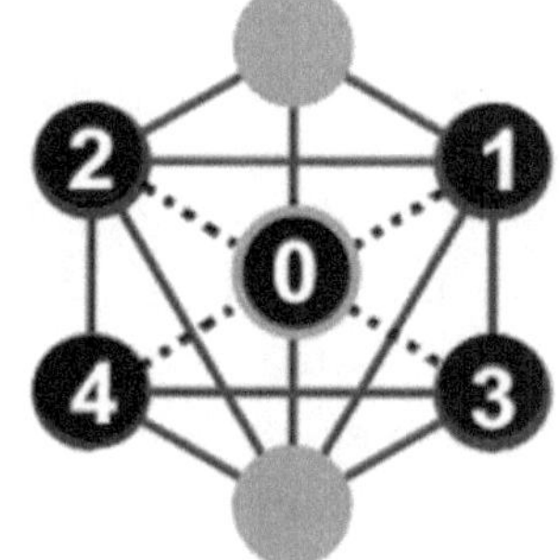

- **Sphere 0:** *Daath* for "knowledge." *Daath's* letters can also be read as *Dalet Et* for "door of time." The sign Dalet (D) means "door." Its value is **4.**
- **Sphere 1:** *Chokmah* for "wisdom." *Chokmah's* (HKME) value is **73.**
- **Sphere 2:** *Binah* for "understanding." *Binah's* (BYNE) value is **67.**
- **Sphere 3:** *Chesed* for "kindness." *Chesed's* (HXD) value is **72.**
- **Sphere 4:** *Geburah* for "Power." *Geburah's* (CBWRE) value is **216.**

S/Hebrew joins music and math: when sound changes, matter changes, and when two numbers enter in resonance, a pattern can be recognized. **216** is "Power." It is also the sum total of the four spheres involved in the passage from first tier to second tier (4 + **67** + **73** + **72** = **216**). **216** + **216** = **432**. This number is a precious frequency, as it takes me beyond the fear of Power. While each sound is represented by a unique underlying numeric essence, the frequency of **432** hertz has such a profound effect on consciousness and on the cellular structure of the body that it has been identified as "the Music of the Spheres." How perfect that the sum of values of the S/Hebrew codes for the most crucial spheres would equal the light of the **432** frequency!

Code Liberation - AYN / ANY

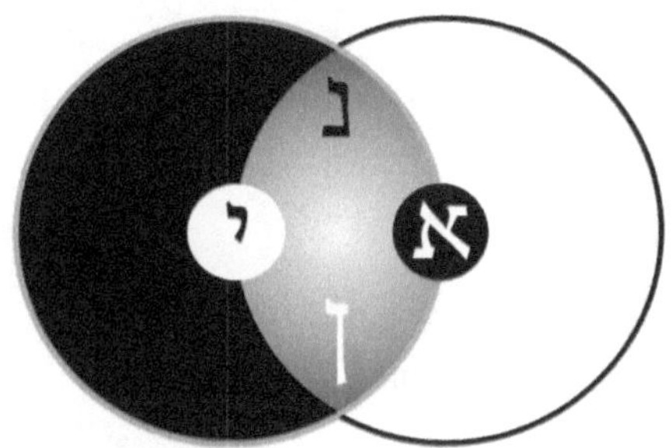

*Imagine a language so pure and so sacred that it can
reconcile opposites in just three letters...*

Right: Hebrew letter Aleph (א) → A in Roman Script.
Top: Hebrew letter Nun (נ) | Bottom: Nun final (ן) → N in Roman Script
Left: Hebrew letter Yod (י) → I, J, Y in Roman Script

Here is how S/Hebrew inscribes code "Liberation:"

- **ANY:** counterclockwise from the right, I read *Ani* (אני) for "I."
- **AYN:** from right to left to bottom, I read *Ain* (אין) for "nothing."

The Decoding: ah, the joke of the personal: "me; nothing?" When I don't know who I Am, the joke's on me! I can't rest. I take every error personally, and feel humiliated when I fall and I fail. How could I not when I won't feel the greed that propels me to serve private agendas? If

I did, I would also feel that the voracious desire for Power is not "I." This realization alone would begin turning off my golem's creative energy. Befriending (my) greed is a holy instant, as it links the *Ani* "I" to the *Ain* "nothingness." I can now be free to be or not to be, to have or not to have, to do or not to do. Feeling the pure light of my soul, I'm no longer hungry and no longer trying to fill the emptiness. "I" just is. This changes the way "I" see things which, in turn, changes what "eye" sees. English "I/eye" is the perfect conveyor of S/Hebrew *Ain* /*Ani* to say: 'when no longer denying evil, you won't get trapped in the illusion that separates the seer from the seen (the subject from the object). Merging with the invisible realm, you'll see the real "I" within that abides in the real "nothing" without.' This still presupposes that I would be like the normal sign Nun, willing to fall again and again until I descend into and as Nun final. Surely, how could I fear falling when there is no one left to want to make a name for myself?

The "Nun Falling" of the Nephilim

"The Nephilim were on the earth in those days, and also afterward, when the sons of God came in to the daughters of man and they bore children to them. These were the powerful men who were of old, the humans of the Name." *Genesis 6:4*

It does make me wonder... Why the fear of falling? Why the need to feel shame when I am down? Do I not realize that failure paves the way to being emPowered? As per Marianne Williamson: "your playing small doesn't serve the world. There is nothing enlightened about shrinking so that other people won't feel insecure around you."

The Hebrew version of the Anunnaki, the *Nephilim* or "fallen ones," were indeed powerful. *Nephilim* is the equivalent of Sanskrit *Avatar* – a manifestation of a deity who descends on Earth as an incarnate divine teacher. Being half-human, their children could not sustain the felt-sense of the divine, and became greedy. Eventually "God" sent the Great Flood to purge the world from wickedness. This Great Flood must not have been meant for the *Nephilim* since they reappeared in *Numbers 13:33*. So did the demons, the soul of their monstrous offspring, who fell from grace into greed. In Abrahamic religions, these fallen angels were expelled from heaven and/or led by Satan in rebellion against God – sinners tempting others into sin.

Here is what I hear: it is impossible for me NOT to be greedy and hungry for Power (or turned off by the thought of it) when I don't know who I Am. Unable to embrace the *Ani / Ain* paradox of liberation, I am a slave to my despair, seeing how my mouth chakra is fated to "fall" even deeper. Yes, it will go from greed into lust, and from lust, into gluttony, trying hopelessly to fill the big hole that is in my soul. That's why I fear falling. I know I'm going down and down and down, at once desiring to touch bottom, and resisting touching bottom!

Intoxicated with a rebellion that opposes LOVE, I am now well set in "the house of bondage," acting out envy, lust, wrath, gluttony, pride, sloth; anything to give me some solace! Yet deep down, I know that I've signed a contract with a demonic "yearning;" a force that robs my patience and thus any wisdom. My inability to wait is my jailor. It enslaves me in materialism.

The Name That Has Nothing Left to Lose

"Everybody's got plans until they get hit." *Mike Tyson, professional boxer and heavyweight champion*

The giants were *Anshe Hashem* – "humans of the Name." *Hashem* for "the Name" is a substitute for the four letters יהוה. As the Power of LOVE, it is a spaceship to time-travel out of Scare City. I shared how S/Hebrew *Shem* comes from Sumerian *Shumu* for "a rocket ship to heaven." Understanding *Shumu / Shem* is rocket science: how can words have the Power to fly me free from the slavery of "Ego-Egypt?"

I have seen that the letter Beth starts the Torah, and the letter Aleph, the 10 Words. Beth and the Torah act as a guide to consciousness;

Aleph and the 10 Words, as a guide to pure choiceless awareness. This is when I am not so afraid of making decisions. I know that there are no accidents, errors or failures. This is when I hear Aleph's message as the first Word: **"I (*Anokhi*) am the LOVE God, who brought me out of the land of Egypt, out of the house of bondage"** *Exodus 20:2.*

When freed from materialism, it is no longer about money for me but more about what I can give, as I am keenly aware to be receiving much. Aleph is not only the first of the 10 Words. It is THE Word of the decalogue (Greek "10 Words"), if only because Aleph is the unity which is the Mystery of mysteries, the door to all wonders. Aleph, let's not forget, is also and foremost my plus 1, the dot that keeps on adding itself - visibly or not - to each word's geometry, to impart the spirit of unity.

I have seen how the word *Anokhi* (אנכי) for "I, myself" which Aleph initiates can be traced to the Sumerian *Anunnaki*. Note: both words have the letter "Nun" in their midst, a letter associated with "miscarriage, falling."

Looking at the letters of *Anokhi* (ANKY) inspires me to grow up and be "giant-like." *Anokhi* includes Code Liberation as its letters reorder as *K'Ani* (KANY) "like me" and *K'Ain* (KAYN) "like nothing." Indeed, I am mostly myself when I let go. When I reduce myself to zero and let creation happen through me, the inclination to give it all to LOVE is irresistible. I don't try to protect myself from being shattered by LOVE, as there's no one left to believe that "I, myself" could make a fatal error. It is true that my being One with this "I" (and, by extension, with everything) takes me out of the illusion of being lonely and forsaken in Ego-Egypt. I know that any freedom that's worth having involves surrendering the ego's judgments. This is a price I'll gladly pay. So, mote it be!

Such a level of selflessness is a giant Power. It is a "God" bringing me out of the first tier – the "House of Bondage." It opens me to sentience, and restores the brain power I lost when thinking of myself as a slave.

Aleph therefore is just another word for "nothing left to lose…" Meanwhile, and as felt by Simon & Garfunkel, I must abide the call of darkness ♪ ♫ "Because a vision softly creeping / Left its seeds while I was sleeping / And the vision that was planted in my brain / Still remains…"

Within the Sound of Silence

"One does not become enlightened by imagining figures of light, but by making the darkness conscious." *Carl Jung*

If shadow is where the gold is, and if shadow work is the choice that scares me the most and asks the most from me, then I must hear again the first command of *Genesis 2:17*. Yet this time, I will shift the interdiction into an injunction: **"you must eat from the tree of the knowledge of good and evil; for if you do, you will die."** What does that entail?

Michelangelo nailed it: "I saw the angel in the marble and carved until I set him free." Imagination leads the process by which **to see** the light in the darkness and **to carve,** cut or circumcise the density of the ego material until I take me out of the "House of Bondage." Said differently, the essence of shadow work is to dive deep enough into the etheric field of the collective unconscious to get to the pearl of consciousness and share its light.

Going in the divine shadow is the Work, just as "a work of art is but a shadow of divine perfection." This is the exact meaning of *Betzalel* – the artist of artists. It is how to hear the sound of silence and face the fear of emptiness. It is when I transcend and include the dysfunction of my throat chakra, and stop the war of the sexes.

Male	Neutral	Female
Individual Intuition	Transpersonal Revelation	Survival Instinct
Science & the true	Art & the beautiful	Religion & the good

From Instinct to Intuition to Revelation

If I want to bring a **transpersonal revelation**, there is no other way than to free the ego from its preoccupations with **survival**, and have the guts to follow my **intuition**. This is how I come to know that my mind is created neutral (that is, male *and* female, or good *and* evil), "in the image of "God." Note: the word *Tzelem* or "image" is formed on *Tzal* for "shadow."

Certainly, the male side of me is like the light, and the female, like the shadow. This shows in the female sexual apparatus, whose darkness is feared as the womb of the tomb. In Buddhist terms, it is only when I am lotus-like, both in the mud and above water, that I can receive the light jewel! Shadow work is the purification process by which I rise above murky secrets and bloom into enlightenment. **Consider: until I come into neutrality (when I have the knowledge of good and evil), I will be confused, thinking that I am creating in "God's" image, when I am in fact creating in the image my ego thinks "should" exist. Oyveh!**

The Best Kept Secret

"Simple laws can very well describe complex structures. The miracle is not the complexity of our world, but the simplicity of the equations describing that complexity." *Sander Bais, Physicist*

When I am created *Zekher V'Nuqbah* ("male & female"), my mind is pure choiceless awareness. It doesn't have to make a choice in between reason and faith. It is both! However, for me to be neutral, I must feel why I would want to be right and control the other by insisting on the differences between *Zekher* "male" and *Nuqbah* "female." Gematria helps me once again. It zeroes in on what keeps me from the freedom I feel when making love, when the man is no more the man, and the woman is no more the woman.

"Male"	"Secret"	"Female"
Zekher (זכר)	*Sohd* (סוד)	*Nuqbah* (נקבה)
G + K + R = 227	X + W + D = 70	N + Q + B + E = 157

The simplicity of the equation says it: 227 − 157 = 70. The difference between "male" and "female" is 70, and 70 is the value of *Sohd*, the "secret" I keep. Telling the truth and having the courage of "into-me-see" is how to build trust and equality, and grow love.

"Like the Light"	"Like Everything"	"Like the QKabbalah"
K'Ohr (כאור)	*K'Khol* (ככל)	*K'Qabbalah* (כקבלה)
K + A + W + R = 227	K + K + L = 70	K + Q + B + L + E = 157

S/Hebrew continues helping me go beyond the war of the sexes. The geometry of male (227) is also the geometry of "**like the light**" – a transmitter. The geometry of female (157) is also the geometry of "**like the QKabbalah**" – a receiver. As for the geometry of secret (70), it is also the geometry of "**like everything**," the resonance of "as within, so without."

I see the mirror – how revealing my shamed-based secrets (mainly about sex & money) also reveals the secrets of the QKosmos. Everything is "**like everything**," as the divine play of light and shadow. I am humbled that my secrets would be entangled with the Torah's secrets (the codes). I am awed that the simple choice of honesty would be the key to the QKingdom. To sustain the experience of enlightenment, I just needed to see in the dark and honor the transgressions I had kept secret.

Shadow work is seeing into the shadow box of projections, a box that shows how an image or memory gets formed in my mind's eye. Unless I let the light enter in the dark box, I will never realize how I create a reversed and inverted image (upside down and left to right) on the surface of reality. I don't see what is, just what I *think* "should" be.

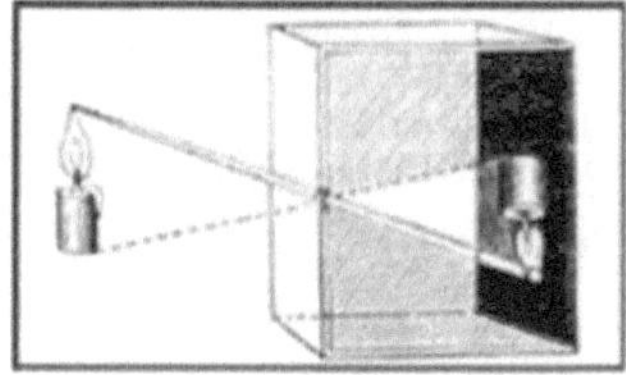

Unfinished Business

"You can't die with an unfinished book." *Terry Pratchett*

It's been called the Great Work and it's definitely my business. Whether I like it or not, I am here to wake up from the dream of an out there. Until I can experience the synergy of the Power of Three from within, I have unfinished business. It is likely that, being in some level of resistance, my world of Creation (Vav) is disconnected from my world of manifestation (Heh). I just can't seem to have my results!

Yod (י)	Vav (ו) / Heh (ה)	Heh (ה)
Transmission	Creation / Manifestation	Formation
Individual Power	Symbolic Power	Collective Power

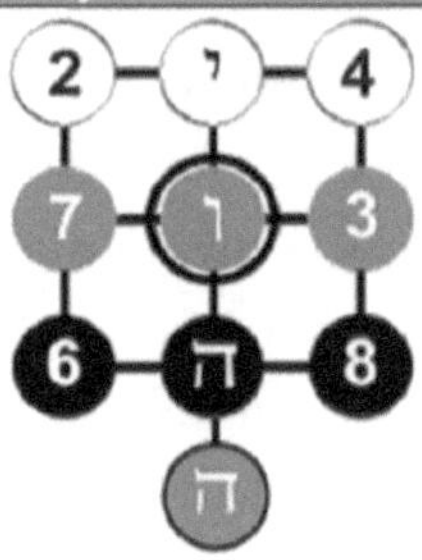

To deepen my understanding of Power dynamics, I will now connect the worlds of YEWE (transmission, formation, creation/manifestation) to Greek Hermes, Roman Mercury, Egyptian Thoth – the god of communication, commerce and healing.

Held to be the cleverest messenger, this god is also the trickster by excellence. Its namesake is just as difficult to pin down as the element mercury, which, by definition, is volatile. Mercury makes it his business to be confusing, especially when its planet goes retrograde and appears to move backwards in reference to Earth's orbit.

Yod (י)	Vav (ו) / Heh (ה)	Heh (ה)
Transmission	Creation / Manifestation	Formation
Individual Power	Symbolic Power	Collective Power
Communication	Healing / Health	Commerce

When YEWE and Hermes have a blast meeting each other…

When Hermes uses his cleverness for the good of all, he holds a caduceus, a medicinal symbol with snakes. He is now *Hermes Trismegistus*, "thrice master" guiding me through a threefold initiation to anchor self-knowledge in my tree being, and with it, the self-esteem needed to persevere to the end:

- **Communication** calls me to acquire individual Power by working on individuation, and moving from a narcissistic ego to a healthy ego. I must break the chains of society's repressive conditioning until I come to my own true nature. I will then know what I want and need, and be able to ask for it. That is taking full responsibility for being response-able.

- **Commerce** calls me to acquire collective Power by understanding that there's only One of us. As my care and compassion grow, I will less and less fear being alone or blame "you" for my failures. Embracing the yearning will stop me from speaking empty words meant to convince you of my worth. And as I stop being for sale, the sense of my being enough becomes palpable.

- **Healing into Health** calls me to acquire symbolic Power by being ready for how truth will change my life. Why be poor and sick when I could choose Health? Unless I stop lying about what I really want, I won't heal, for only the truth can set me free from my addictions. Will I develop enough self-esteem to choose to stop compromising and have the courage to follow my own bliss?

This triple initiation – **communication, commerce, healing into Health** – is the subject of the next chapter – *Choosing Mastery.*

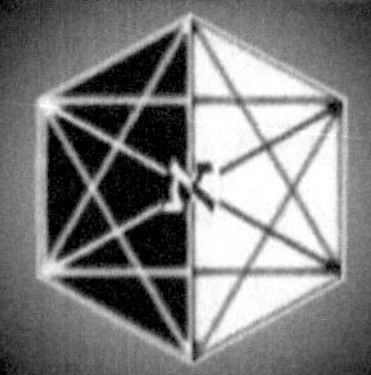

FIVE

Choosing Mastery

"To attain the Sanctum Regnum, in other words, the knowledge and power of the magi, there are four indispensable conditions: an intelligence illuminated by study, an intrepidity which nothing can check, a will which cannot be broken, and a prudence which nothing can corrupt and nothing intoxicate. To know, to dare, to will, to keep silence – such are the four words of the magus, inscribed upon the four symbolical forms of the sphinx." *French occultist Eliphas Lévi*

As ALWAYS, the number four is called by the undecipherable Name – the four-lettered Word. They will accompany me in my initiation to being thrice-master of communication, commerce and healing. When the results of my communication match my vision, I'm telling the truth. But when there's a misalignment, there are a few unconscious intentions in my space which keep me from enlightened commerce, and deny health. Epiphany of sorts, this chapter celebrates the birth of messianic Aleph in Beth the Magician. It also provides insights into the reality of awakening, and furthers the revelation of a metalanguage that vibrates as the frequency of "enough."

PART I: MASTERING COMMUNICATION

Below are the "primary" topics of this section:

- Using the "Created-SIX's" geometry to invoke a new linguistics.
- Deriving SIX essential lines of communication from the first word of the Torah – the "Word that is God and with God."
- Focusing on two lines to acquire individual Power.
- Feeling the two main "God's" names to sense the intelligence of a communication that has its own lines of questioning.
- Marrying the SIX families of YEWE – for richer or poorer, in sickness and in health, till ego death do me part.
- Playing with an anagram that speaks volumes.

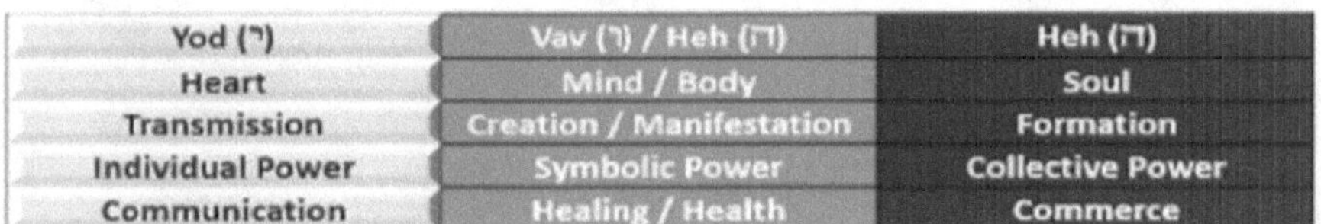

Yod (י)	Vav (ו) / Heh (ה)	Heh (ה)
Heart	Mind / Body	Soul
Transmission	Creation / Manifestation	Formation
Individual Power	Symbolic Power	Collective Power
Communication	Healing / Health	Commerce

When the Yod of YEWE echoes Hermes' mastery in communication...

Mastering Communication

"We cannot evolve faster than our language. The edge of being is the edge of meaning, and somehow, we have to push the edge of meaning. We have to extend it." *Terence McKenna*

Reality check: can I imagine a tomorrow where I am anonymous? If not, I must correct an obvious case of stolen identity where the little self is committing crimes in my name. This is how I became callous enough to refuse to strengthen the health of the ego and thus provide a solid platform for the Self to exist as the Eternal Witness.

And that's why my communication fails. I'm going through the dark night of a desperate meaning crisis as I don't have the words to explain "God" or the sensory reality into which I wish to emerge.

Nietzsche's right: I've killed God," and now that I'm intending to revive "IT," I don't have the words for "ITS." The task to strip the "God" label from all the junk it's associated with feels like a doomed mission. And yet, if I really mean to take a sensory approach to life, I require brand-new signs and symbols to describe the wildly disconcerting and shockingly wondrous realities I'm about to meet.

To make my quest even more absurd, "God" also refers to the formless Ground of all Being which can't be talked about. However, since it can be directly experienced, there has to be a way to express it, if only via art. I just need to become so comfortable with (my) loneliness that I'd awaken to and communicate with the realm of emptiness. If the Eskimos have a need for 28 words to describe snow, my soul has a need for a language to help me name the experiences arising from this formless ground. Otherwise, it will all be Greek to me! On that note, did you know that one of the blackest days in Jewish history is when 72 priests came up with a translation of the Torah into Greek? They felt like traitors, as they knew that Greek cannot convey S/Hebrew's multimodality. Bottom line: the priest in me is still at a loss for holy words!

Naming the higher states is having a password into a new way of thinking that validates their reality. Unless I name each state and claim it, then for all intents and purposes, it doesn't exist. And if that's the case, how could I grow into it?

Absolute Truth be told, the non-dual realm is tough to put into words, since concepts are defined by their opposites; good versus evil, light versus dark, poor versus rich, etc. As for "God" or reality, it is the LOVE that has no opposite. Thus, while Zen masters talk about the "ineffable" emptiness, the kabbalists speak of the "ineffable" four-lettered Name. The former call it the "Void," as in *neti neti* or "not this; not that;" the latter, the "Nothing" of three veils as in *Ain, Ain Soph, Ain Soph Aur*. However, to welcome uncertainty and transcend the boundaries of conditional love, I must still realize that these veils are immaterial.

Meanwhile, TCO's message is simple: "to relate to the Mystery, express any mystical experiences and enter the 3rd tier, I must let go."

But how do I do that when I want to stay attached? This is when I'm given a metalanguage based on the Power of Three, and made usable via tables of Self-knowledge. Yes, it's only a map and not the territory, and yes, these are only symbols and not the "real" thing. Nonetheless, having the usability of a tool answers my quest for clarity.

If every field has its own language, so does the Mystery. To be fluent in it, I must begin by having the courage to hear the answer to my prayers, and to follow through by making the tough choices. This will earn me self-esteem, trust and faith. Henceforth, when I pray, I will "believe that I have received what I prayed for, and it will be mine."

Might it be that the reason why I don't have a vocabulary for the sacred is because, thus far, I didn't really want it? A part of me wants access to the sacred and "believe." Yes, I want to hear the Holy Ghost (that's the name for it) and know that something greater than I is doing the speaking. But there's also the part that is terrified of what will be asked of me if I do feel the soul of prophecy. This is how I won't see the holy language that's under my nose, and how I am starved for connectedness. This is also how I fight the Power of prayer and resist inviting "God" into my life. I'm so attached to my desired outcome that I choose control over "grace" (yep, that's the name for it).

Am I ready to actually follow the guidance of my heart even though I may be terrified to surrender my will? When in the illusion of forced labor, I fail. When in the truth of non-action, I succeed. **Will I ever choose to be emPowered and able to do what it takes to hear my Self rather than wanting to be heard? Am I ready to witness the kind of awesomeness that will humble the daylights out of me?**

Welcome to "Lines of Communication!"

"Philosophy is written in this grand book, the universe, which stands continually open to our gaze. But the book cannot be understood unless one first learns to comprehend the language and read the letters in which it is composed." *Galileo*

Language is the flash of lightening that shows me the path. Evolving its vocabulary is how to understand the grand book and fulfill my heart's desire: to feel the Living Word in my blood and my bones as I receive it in my cells and transmit it from the coherence of my heart. This is Code Communication at its best (see *Learning to Code*).

To this end, I am guided to revisit the Torah's first word as a way to open lines of communication. Kabbalists have derived great meanings from this Word – "the Word that was God and the Word that was with God." As a gentle reminder, this word that was "in the beginning" and means "in the beginning" is *Bereshit*. The same word (בראשית) can also be read as *Barashit* for "Created-SIX."

Its depth unfolds below in the 6x6 square formed by reordering the letters בראשית. The source code of *Bereshit* / *Barashit* is the foundation (row 1 image below). Each row then builds up from it as a new metaphor for me to sense the "God" Name as a series of two-word prompts. Note: the black cells mark the initial letter of each word (Hebrew writes from right to left).

						#
ת	ב	א	ש	י	ר	6
ב	ר	י	ת	א	ש	5
ר	א	ש	ב	י	ת	4
א	ב	ת	ש	ר	י	3
ש	ב	ת	י	ר	א	2
ב	ר	א	ש	י	ת	1

- Row 1: *Bereshit/Barashit* for "in the beginning/created-SIX" speaks to my voice →
- Row 2: *Shabbat Yirah* for "Fear of Rest" speaks to my soul →
- Row 3: *Av Tishrei* for "Months of Return" speaks to my body →
- Row 4: *Resh Bayit* for "Head of the House" speaks to my mind →
- Row 5: *Brit Esh* for "Covenant of Fire" speaks to my heart →
- Row 6: *Tabo Shir* for "Let the Song Enter" speaks to my spirit.

The Letters' Modalities

"The emergence of language at age 4 is both highly creative and destructive. It destroys the holistic view of the world the child has held so far, replacing it with an entirely new dimension of mental life, that of verbal language, and leading it to adopt a more categorical, analytical view of the world." *Daniel Stern, The Interpersonal World of the Infant*

S/Hebrew kept its multimodality, and as such, remained a child at heart. Thus far, this has not been felt, possibly because the "God" Name had never been sensed as the knowledge of the Self. This "God" Name is *Elohim* (אלהים). It holds the seed EY (הי) soon to be born and come out head first as YE (יה), and destined to grow into WE (וה) in order to be the YE-WE (יה וה).

To gauge its many dimensions and be in "God" and with "God," I will start with the SIX lines of communication shown in the crossword puzzle above. I will then use these lines as a way to link 1) the SIX constituent letters of YEWE *Elohim*, 2) the SIX instruments of the Self, and 3) the modalities of the letters. By joining the gifts of expression of an artist (geometrical), a programmer (ideographic), a legalist (alphabetical), a mathematician (numerical), a philosopher (archetypal), and a poet (metaphorical), I will further my creativity. Lastly, I will link the letters' modality to the main lines of intelligence that are recognized across theories of human development. This process unfolds in the table below.

"God" Name	The Self	Modalities of Letters	Lines of Communication	Lines of Intelligence
Lamed (ל)	Spirit	Metaphorical (ALP = "God Mouth")	*Tabo Shir* "Let the Song Enter"	Musical
Yod (י)	Heart	Archetypal (Aleph = the Fool)	*Brit Esh* "Covenant of Fire"	Spiritual
Vav (ו)	Mind	Numerical (Aleph = 0, 1, 1000)	*Resh Bayit* "Head of the House"	Cognitive
Heh (ה)	Body	Alphabetical (Aleph = the Law)	*Av Tishrei* "Month of Return"	Ethical
Heh (ה)	Soul	Ideographic (Aleph = the Ox)	*Yirah Shabbat* "Fear of Rest"	Emotional
Mem (ם)	Voice	Geometrical (Aleph = a dot)	*Bereshit / Barashit* "In the Beginning"	Linguistic

Communicating "God"

Choosing Mastery will focus on the **spirit** and the **heart**. Once these two dimensions of the "kingdom of God" are realized, the next three (**mind, body** and **soul**) naturally follow. This is what is meant by "seek ye first the kingdom of God, and all these things shall be added unto you." As for the **voice**, it has already been heard as the tone of *Bereshit* and/or *Barashit*.

This brings me to inquire on the two lines of communication: "let the Song Enter" and "Covenant of Fire." These lines are invoked by two letters of the "God" Name – **Lamed** and **Yod**. These two signs are a code of opposites in and unto themselves. Tallest sign Lamed

and smallest sign Yod balance each other to say: "there's nothing big and nothing small – just a heart that understands knowledge and radiates the pure beauty of the golden mean." Understanding is to be "in between" – the First and the Last.

Line 6 - Lamed: When Spirit "Lets the Song Enter"

"Raise your words, not your voice." *Rumi*

#	Lines of Communication	"God" Name	The Self	Modalities of Letters	Lines of Intelligence	Lines of Questioning
6	*Tabo Shir* "Let the Song Enter"	Lamed (ל)	Spirit	Metaphorical	Musical	What is my calling? Does it scare me enough to be real?

Let the Song Enter adopts the **metaphorical** mode of **musical** intelligence. When listening to music, I receive the energy of images moving in waves. These waves move in patterns. The patterns move in rhythmic words. Taking the word *Aleph* as an example, I can see its three letters אלף (ALP in English) reforming into the pattern of AL-P. AL is *El* for "God." P is sign *Peh* – the name for "mouth." When I feel Aleph's unity, my words don't defile me, as I met the "God of the Mouth."

I am now asking a question which makes my Spirit sing: "who can I emPower, love and appreciate today? What is my calling?" I have no fear. I am at peace with myself, feeling so attuned to the QKosmos that I know that the words of my mouth (my visions and prayers) are heard, seen and already fulfilled. On that note, the word *Torah* has the meanings of the "Way, Law or Teaching," but also the sense of the "Song of LOVE." Its resonance helps me raise my vibration and speak words aligned to my deepest truth.

Passing the initiation of communication is a call to master my own destiny. Time has come to discover my true nature, as I stand by my own hard-won truth, determined to live in accordance with it. This is individual Power at its best. I now have the ability to discriminate in between voices, and not let me be "led into temptation."

The more I withstand the demons' whisper and suffer no exception in doing what I know LOVE would do, the more I hear the angels' song vibrating in me.

The Symbols of "Turning Within"

"At the center of your being you have the answer; you know who you are and you know what you want." *Lao Tzu*

The two pillars – *Teshuvah* and *Tephillah* – fight together and work together to lead me to remain in sanctuary, in the temple of *Tzedaqah*. These three flows are a "God" technology to diminish the negative impact of cause and effect, and open me to receive *Golden XPR's* deliverable – the Sense of Enough.

However, it is strange that something as good, true and beautiful as *Teshuvah*, *Tephillah* and *Tzedaqah* could be so direly misrepresented as "repentance, prayer and charity." Might the loss in translation be due to my ego's efforts in trying to manipulate me by way of guilt? As ego gets its way, I end up dismissing the wealth of understanding wha the scriptures have to offer.

Taking *Teshuvah*, the injunction "repent!" immediately makes me feel that I am bad, flawed, fallen – not enough! As for the idea of "prayer," it is so loaded up with supplications that it embarrasses me. Lastly, the goody two-shoes concept of "righteousness" seems to immediately spark the rebel in me. I resent that a prejudice (right over left; with left or female being "wrong") would lock me in a cage of convention made of rigorous perceptions of what is acceptable and what is not. So, yes, the classical translations really take the oomph out of my sails... But if I were to understand that the true meaning of *Teshuvah* is to "turn within" (and as such, the key to individual Power), I'd find it much more attractive. Moreover, without the turn of *Teshuvah*, how would I know what my priorities are?

First, there is a loss in translation that can be easily addressed, especially as I bring in the three pillars of Buddhism. *Teshuvah* is the "turn within" to meet my Buddha nature. *Tephillah* is the sense that my "prayer" is received by my Sangha community and already fulfilled. *Tzedaqah* is the "charity" that gives it all, and as such, emPowers Dharma – when I experience such an interdependence with life that I spontaneously adopt the behavior of LOVE.

Yod (י)	Vav Heh (וה)	Heh (ה)
Individual Power	**Symbolic Power**	**Collective Power**
Teshuvah – Turn within!	*Tzedaqah* – Give it all!	*Tephillah* – Feel Received!
Buddha	**Dharma**	**Sangha**

When the integrity of the three pillars is restored from East to West...

Dharma and *Tzedaqah* speak of spiritual maturity, as they invoke ancient laws that sustain the fair beauty of justice. They also allude to something greater, like a QKosmic plan to move us all to LOVE. When I come into the LOVE that has no opposite, I resist nothing! Such total gift of Self is *Tzedaqah* – when there is no one left to take anything personally. Moving to such "Promised Land" is the plan. It has worked for billions of years to help transition "my" world from karma into Dharma – or from greed into grace. The turn of its wheel from egocentrism to QKosmocentrism is a big deal, so big that these three pillars hide what I can only term as "the GOD technology."

The practicality of this technology is to be experienced in *TCO—Book 3*. It spans the chapter that begins to awaken my inner victiM into being an Officer of the Law; someone who has the compassion to do what it takes to heal any situation. The victiM is, by definition, the part of me that judges that "God" or reality is unfair. Henceforth, the miscarriages of justice...

To shift out of the constant fight and flight mode of my victiM, I am soon to understand the nature of these three pillars and flows of religiousness as proficiencies of the sacred. When I CAN wait, I CAN think. When I CAN think, I CAN decide. When I CAN decide, I CAN give it all.

2. Individual Power	3. Symbolic Power	1. Collective Power
Heart	Mind / Body	Soul
Teshuvah – "Turn Within"	*Tzedaqah* – "Give it All!"	*Tephillah* – "Feel Received"
I CAN think	I CAN give / I CAN decide	I CAN wait

But if *Tzedaqah* leads to I CAN give, where does "I CAN decide" come from? There is a poem that concerns the High Holy Days of Judaism. These days are high and holy as they are the ten Days of Awe between Rosh Hashanah (the New Year) and Yom Kippur (the day of atonement). Rabbi Amnon of Mainz, 11th Century, wrote this poem and called it "let us speak of awesomeness." Its chorus states: "But *Teshuvah*, *Tephillah* and *Tzedaqah* will avert the evil decree." While opening to a sensible translation for these three keywords, I come to realize that each pillar hides a proficiency, e.g.; turning within is how I CAN think. Instead of looking for answers where they are not, I use my intelligence to look for them where they are: within.

I CAN wait, I CAN think, I CAN give it all: that would be nice! The technology is given by the codes. Above the names of the three pillars, there are three tiny S/Hebrew words. Each of them has the exact value of 136. When I multiply 136 by 3, I obtain a product of 408, which is the gematria of *Nachashim* (NHSYM) for "snakes." These are the reptiles that disturb my peace of mind, and keep me slave to Ego-Egypt. When understood, they will also awaken the dormant Messiah in me. Let's take the example of the word *Mammon* which is linked to the *Tzedaqah* pillar... I can translate it as "money, yearning." That's what *Mammon* means. I can also feel that *Mammon* is the cause of my ambivalence. I am so afraid of what a choice might cost me that I'd postpone making a decision. My victiM just doesn't want to pay the price! Therefore, at its best, *Mammon* is the Power that will lead me to realize that "I CAN decide." Surely, the measure to where I CAN decide is the measure to where I CAN give it all. I still have to decide what decision would have the most impact on my personal and professional life.

:-) That's easy enough when willing to know the truth. As for the two tiny codes above the pillars of *Teshuvah* and *Tephillah*, they will have to wait for *TCO—Book 3* to be unfolded and experienced as a GOD technology.

Code Awesomeness - ZQ / QZ

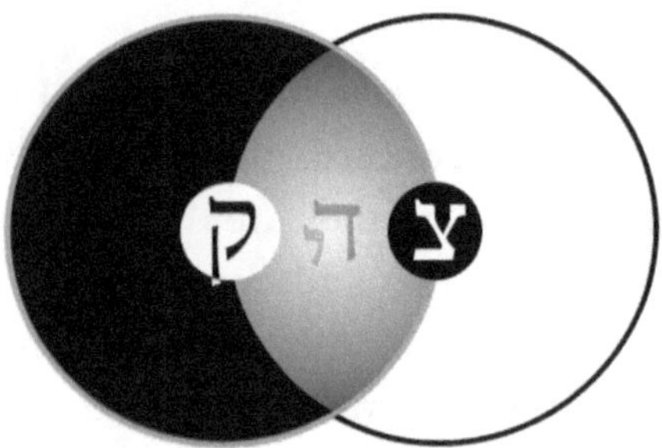

Imagine a language so pure and so sacred that it can reconcile opposites in just two pairs of letters...

Right: Hebrew letter Tzaddi (צ) → Z in Roman Script
Left: Hebrew letter Qoph (ק) → Q in Roman Script
Middle (inferred): Hebrew letters Dalet Yod (די) → DY in Roman Script

Here is how S/Hebrew inscribes code "Awesomeness:"

- **ZQ:** in one direction, I read *Tzaddi Qoph* (צ'ק) as the 18th and 19th letters.
- **QZ:** in the other direction, I read *Qetz* (קץ) for "end."

The decoding: first, I recall that the letter Tzaddi is one of the five letters that has a final form – "final" physically when at the end of a word and metaphysically when at the end of an affliction. I can then inquire on what would be the specific redemption that is ushered by Tzaddi final. I begin with *Tzaddi* – the "fishhook" I use when doing shadow work so as to harpoon the abysmal formations that engulfed the light of my soul. I continue with the five families of YEWE that span the 20 letters from Beth to Shin, Tzaddi ushering the last family – the

LIGHT family. I end with the symbology of the tarots: the Star initiates "the enlightenment tetrad" as a perfect complement to understand the LIGHT family:

- **Tzaddi** (the 18th letter) is illustrated as the 17th tarot of the Star.
- **Qoph** (the 19th letter) is illustrated as the 18th tarot of the Moon.
- **Resh** (the 20th letter) is illustrated as the 19th tarot of the Sun.
- **Shin** (the 21st letter) is illustrated as the 20th tarot of the Judgment.

To be a *Tzaddi-Q* (a "saint" or an "awakened one"), my star-like Tzaddi being must stretch to my moon-like Qoph being. This is to say: I must follow my lunacy until I come into the greatest wisdom of all – the one waiting in my folly. When I do, I am a Star as I have died to my sins. The letters **Tzaddi-Qoph** now turn around to write the word *Qetz* – the "**end.**" This is the end of desire which is also the beginning of fulfillment. Stretching from Tzaddi to Qoph asks me to consider the two signs that are revealed when spelling out the name Tza-ddi (Z-DY), namely Dalet and Yod (DY). Surely, the Tza-ddi-Q in me is "awake" when I know the sense of the word *Dai* (DY) for "enough" as "in off." I am real, with no need to compensate by way of wrongdoing for what I resented as forced labor. Instead, I can hear/SEE clearly the awesomeness of the QKosmic plan.

As told per Rabbi Ba'al Haturim, when Jacob wished to reveal to his children the secret of the "end" of time, he felt the Divine Presence depart and was unable to give them the key. He asked his sons if they were still holding on to any sin that could deny them this treasured knowledge. "Look at our twelve names;" they countered, "you won't find the letters Chet or Teth which spell the word *Chet* for "sin." "True," replied Jacob. "But your names also lack the pair Qoph and Tzaddi forming the word *Qetz* for "end." You are thus probably not meant to receive Self-knowledge."

As a *Tzaddi-Q/a*, I don't mind "righteousness." I'm so willing to do what's right that I'm considered a saint. My magic is simple: I understand that we are One. In that space, there is no co-dependent behavior, no addiction and no confusion about the other "out there." There is thus no need to seek for "your" approval (or disapproval), and do harm as a result of obeying a false sense of duty. The end of confusion is the redemption written in Tzaddi final. It is also the beginning of awe. Letting go of my story, I resonate with *Tzedaqah's* selflessness so much so that I resonate with life's Song of LOVE!

♫♪ Start Spreading the NEWS...

"The true Tarot is symbolism; it speaks no other language and offers no other signs." *A. E. Waite*

Like common playing cards, the tarot has 4 suits: Clubs, Diamonds, Hearts and Spades. As a side note, these are not color-coded in accordance to the natural polarities of elements (e.g.; fire is red) but to allude to the tension that existed in Europe between the clerical (black) and secular (red). Each suit has 14 cards: four face cards (King, Queen, Knight, and Jack/Knave/Page), and 10 pips from one to ten (the 10 numbers). The tarot also has a separate 22-card trump suit which is known as the "major arcana."

Yod (י)	Vav Heh (וה)	Heh (ה)
Fire	Air / Earth	Water
Clubs	Spades / Diamonds	Hearts
King	Knight / Jack-Knave-Page	Queen-to-Be

When the four classical elements behind YEWE inspire the four suits…

The cards are believed to come from ancient Egypt, Indian Tantra and/or the I Ching, although scholarly research has not found documented evidence of such origins. And yet, my world is made of fiery words as much as it is made of earth, air and water, or even molecules and atoms. The 22 cards of the major arcana appear to be an illustration of the esoteric meanings of the 22 S/Hebrew letters. This explains how Carl Jung (who expressed a real interest in the Kabbalah) viewed the tarots as the initiatory journey of the hero.

The initiation is to go beyond mind, when I know myself as the First and the Last. This is when I receive Code Communication (AT/TA), knowing the fundamental truth of Oneness on a moment-to-moment basis, and feeling cellularly connected to an interdependent entangled field of energy, beyond space and time.

Therefore, when I "fall" through 22 stages moving from the inner (Aleph the Fool) to the outer (Tav the World) and then "rise" through the same 22 stages moving from the outer to the inner, I am really working with the letters "in-between" Aleph and Tav – the First and the Last. This "in-between" is where understanding lives. To help me include and transcend the 20 letters from Beth to Shin (which is Code Transformation BS/SB), *Golden XPR* divides these 20 letters into 5 families of YEWE, each family encoding a part of the genetic DREaM.

Thus, not only am I in the "DREaM" of an individual prostitutE, a saboteuR, a victiM and a chilD (unaware of the angel in my midst), but I am also having to contend with a family for each archetype. Each "family" has a Yod Father (the King), a Heh Daughter (the Queen), a Vav Son (the Knight) and a Heh Mother in exile (a Jack, Knave or Page). Waking up, I'll realize that, behind the angel, there is a fifth family of LIGHT.

Understanding how the STATES of mind hold the STAGES of mind or, said differently, how Code Communication (AT/TA) holds Code Transformation (BS/SB), I am ready to spread the NEWS (North, East, West, South) of FOUR families of YEWE centering me in the fifth family – the awesome tetrad of enlightenment. These FOUR directions are what orient and "pin" the transformation to come.

The Butterfly Wheel

"There is nothing in a caterpillar that tells you it's going to be a butterfly." *R. Buckminster Fuller*

Yod (י)	Vav Heh (וה)	Heh (ה)
Fire	Air / Earth	Water
South	East / West	North
L of Leader	E of Engineer / O of Officer	V of Visionary

The Butterfly Wheel – EVOLving into LOVE

To "**EVOLve**" and know that, behind it all, I am **LOVE**, I move counter-clockwise, from the East (when the **E** of an Engineer is eclipsed by the prostitutE) to the North (when the **V** of a Visionary is eclipsed by the saboteuR) to the West (when the **O** of an Officer is eclipsed by the victiM) to the South (when the **L** of a Leader is eclipsed by a chilD). When ready to take full responsibility, I recognize the up and down patterns, and center. I am **IN-LOVE**. My wheel now goes clockwise, spelling **LOVE** on its way.

Notes: I. ancient maps pictured South on top, seeing that the tree of life has its roots in Heaven and its branches on Earth. 2. **TORA/TARO:** each of the five families have four Torah letters as four Tarot cards. Unlearning the shadow of 20 archetypes is the Great Voyage sponsored by the PaRaDiSe Mystery School.

Canticle to the Logos

"Every species has a habitat. And the habitat of the human is language." *Lewis Thomas, physician, quoted by Brian Swimme in "Canticle to the Cosmos."*

Why would I want to be related to language when I convinced myself that it is just an artifact? And I forget; I forget that life evolves from a genetic code, a musical language contained in the DNA that instructs human cells like it does bacteria. The very fact that everything is connected hints to the existence of a universal code – a metalanguage that makes a global cosmology possible.

I look at my story from the vertebrates to Homo erectus (the "upright man") who had a different brain and a different learning capacity than Homo sapiens (the "wise man"). The emergence of language was a great shock, and potentially one of the boldest quantum leaps in evolution. Language brings forth that which is not physically here. But it also evokes the best and worst instincts as a new selection tool that adds the pressure of linguistic competence. Heck, the more I am gifted with language, the more I can influence my tribe! This got me thinking... Is there a genetic type that would give power by furthering linguistic development? Is that what a metalanguage does?

Without question, language is the most powerful force to engage today. It controls the military, the stock market, our politics: everything is entirely done through language. All the power of the planet is tied up in our codes.

Therefore, if I choose to reinvent my humanity, I must reinvent language, and to do so, I must unlock the consciousness of the cosmic narrative of the universe. This is how to shape the great spiritual disciplines that I need to wield a power that is ultimate, yes, but also a Power that is wholesome, and thus does not corrupt or destroy.

I am called to discover this other language; the language that structures all languages. Its oneness alone can fulfill the will to meaning and advance the human narrative. This language is in everyone and everything. As a newborn, I was genetically coded with a whole linguistic structure. But as I filled the gaps with my mother tongue, be it Chinese, French or English, I forgot what makes me human: the memory and feelings of it.

My brain has an innate memory of language which I activate by deleting the knowledge I borrowed. This unlearning energizes the expectancy of Code Awesomeness. It is also how I come to the center of my authenticity, find my voice and remember the notes of the biological melody that haunts me. Let the song enter, indeed!

When I resonate with the codes, I enter the consciousness of a Homo sentiens (a "human with the capacity to feel and sense"). As the gap between my brain and my heart fills with compassion, I come into an extraneous intelligence that, once activated, unleashes the symbolic creativity of language and awakens the instinct of the sacred.

The Created-SIX code that quickens coherence kindly waits for me to decide to see it in reality. This sacred sight is beyond physical senses. It is what every spiritual tradition endeavors to open - a connection to the Great Mother's tongue as the most sublime entanglement of all.

Line 5 - Yod: The Heart and "The Covenant of Fire"

"To learn to read is to light a fire; every syllable that is spelled out is a spark." *Victor Hugo*

#	Lines of Communication	"God" Name	The Self	Modalities of Letters	Lines of Intelligence	Lines of Questioning
5	*Brit Esh* "Covenant of Fire"	Yod (י)	Heart	Archetypal	Spiritual	Who am I? What is of ultimate concern to me?

The Covenant of Fire adopts the **archetypal** mode of **spiritual** intelligence that asks me the biggest questions of all: "who am I? What is of ultimate concern to me?" I come to my answer when I return to the place where I started – in Aleph the Fool, knowing its innocence for the first time. I now begin thinking in terms of archetypes, and turn to the spiritual intelligence that illuminates the fiery heart of my leadership. Surely, when the child in me grows up into a leader, it "rediscovers fire" and evolves language by saying intelligent things. You and I begin to understand each other.

Language itself is said to have emerged around fire. Daytime was given to hunting and gathering, and nighttime, to storytelling around fires. As far as we know, both building fires and language originated in humans. Both have a Power that I can use for good or bad.

Language is Power, as speaking creates opportunities. This is how the will to Power requires linguistic competence. I have already remarked how the more gifted I am with words, the more I can influence others. The potential misuse of "Fire-Power" that ensues is so puzzling that it became a cross-cultural myth. Known in the Bible as "the Tower of Babel," the story describes how pride and the desire to make a name for myself caused the breaking of linguistic unity.

There's no smoke without fire: a universal narrative speaking of the disruption of linguistic unity presupposes the background existence of a metalanguage.

Feeling its codes is a direct way to love reality on its terms. This is simply because the codes humble me, thus allowing me to see a greater reality than myself. As I stop resisting, I recover sentience and become increasingly honest. Sentience – the capacity to feel and sense – is how that which understands has an understanding of "God."

Rediscovering fire as the light of language, *Golden XPR* invites a quantum leap that imagines that the center of the Universe – where ultimate reality is created – started in a fiery jot. This jot is the smallest letter – the little Yod "hand" whose spark ignites the writing of each letter of the S/Hebrew alphabet to say "I surrender. My actions are not just about me. I am now and forever a messenger of the QKosmos."

Rediscovering the fiery spark of letter Yod (ʾ) is realizing how BIG the smallest letter is, as it sparks the writing of every other letter for me to see the light.

The Thief Archetype – Stealing Fire

"As soon go kindle fire with snow, as seek to quench the fire of love with words." *William Shakespeare.*

Story is told of Greek Prometheus who stole the fire of the gods, as he didn't feel he had the permission to use the fire-Power of language. When I follow the Voice, I say what I say because that's what I say. However, when I have an ulterior motive, I am *Prometheus* for "forethought," and my twin brother is *Epimetheus* for "afterthoughts."

How could I not double-guess myself when I am attached to an outcome? Prometheus stole fire because he wanted to endow his creation with the spark of life and support what he thought should be! I am as Prometheus when I misuse Power, and either say too much or not enough. For having defied Zeus, I am chained to a rock, with an eagle daily tearing at my liver, until Hercules ("the light of my soul") rescues me. This is my "liveration" from suffering.

A potent way to quench love or transmute pain is in writing and speaking about it. Surely, my use of language will cause a transmutation. But how silvery is my tongue? How white is my magic? Will I be responsible for my communication and feel how real is the ancient Aramaic formula *Abracadabra* meaning "I create as I speak?"

The image of a silvery tongue reminds me of the Gaon's work uncovering the "silver / money" that is *under* my motivation to retaliate. Are my words increasing the quota of honesty in the world? Or am I just stealing fire, speaking and calculating for my own advantage?

It is crucial that I would question what drives me to tell the story in the way I do, when a simple "yes" or "no" is saying a lot. Speaking is a call for Power, and yes, there is a price to pay each time I use such magic. This is how silence is gold. This is also how I'm divided about acquiring Power as I know that I am playing with fire: "it is not what I put in my mouth that defiles me. It is what comes out of my mouth" (*Matthew*

16:11). What if I had the courage to ask for what I want and didn't get it? What if it led me to lose friends or money? It's not only public speaking that I fear, but also and foremost, speaking. This is how I tend to give my Power away and merely *try* to be response-able for my creativity.

The Tower of Babel

> **And LOVE said, "so, they are one people and they have all one language, and this [desire to be somebody] is only the beginning of what they'll do. . ."** *Genesis 11:6*

Indeed, it is ambition that sources the event known as *the Tower of Babel* and the ensuing confusion of languages. The myth comes from Sumer, with hero *Enmerkar* who built a huge ziggurat, and implored god Enki to disrupt the linguistic unity of the lands.

- *Genesis 11:1* opens with "and the whole earth was of One people; One speech." Linguistic unity can take at least two forms. It can signify that I speak from my heart. I mean what I say and say what I feel. Such authentic relating is what freedom of speech is. It can also allude to a metalanguage – a language so integral that it is behind all languages.
- *Genesis 11:4* speaks of the drive for Power: "let us make a name for ourselves!" I just went through a socialization process that instilled the desire to become "somebody." It started in a simple question: "is it a boy or a girl?" I now had something to sell, and talked you into buying it.

The possibility of a metalanguage evolves collective Power beyond any egocentric or ethnocentric agenda of control and domination. On the contrary, the perspective is now world-centric, and sensed as the connectedness of One people; One language. The voices in "my" collective head are now smooth and fluid, as I am not scheming.

Ambition is what makes the voices unkind and discordant. It is what leads me into temptation. Same for my use of Power. My speech patterns now support a commerce meant to profit the little self alone. Am I that insecure? Unless I stop making it about me (my name, my prestige, my prosperity, my Power) and strike purity, I will auto-destruct.

Indeed, this is when the question "who am I?" is of the essence. When my chosen priorities do not honor the whole, I will, whether I know it or not, and whether I like or not, gear myself to a purification by fire.

The chilD and The Tower

"Come, let us go down and confuse their language, so that they will not understand one another's speech." *Genesis 11:7*

The Tower of Destruction – Rider Waite Deck

TORA—TARO: The Tower is the 16th Tarot, a most frightening card illustrating the 17th letter Peh (פ) – the "mouth" that speaks and eats. On a black background, a lightning bolt and flames of fire are lighting up a tall tower. Two people are falling headfirst to the hard rocks below, as if blasted out of the crown of the tower. Instantly frozen in time, they have no choice but to jump. At one time they were comfortably situated at the top. The next moment they're taking a fall they probably won't survive.

They did not have any warning, and no time to even think or do anything about it. Truth had stricken and nothing would ever be the same. For now, lightning strikes with such strength it causes clouds of grey smoke to form and violently dislodges the golden crown topping the Tower. The whole thing is on fire. Tower of Babel, the edifice points to an inexorable fall. Whether the pride causing it is a fortress or a jail, its destruction takes both defenses and prison away. The Tower can show up in my life as a divorce, a bankruptcy, an illness – a major conflict. Will I grow up and deal with it? Bottom line: it efficiently nullifies my resistance by stripping away my Power of decision. There is no postponing of change: time stopped at the speed of light!

Symbol of "God's hand," the dots of light descend from heaven, awakening me by shaking, pruning and releasing the unconscious. The Tower's virile erection is at once circumcised and emasculated by lightning. It is the sudden flash of revelation that demolishes my façade, and ignites the core with a new spark. Yet the bolt is directed at the ego structure, not its captives. The built-in solidity of materialistic thought-forms must be knocked down to the ground, to leave me open to the mystery. **The weight of looming ambivalences must be crushed for me not to suffer from my defense/attack games. But just how complete am I with my doubts?**

The table below is an excerpt of a greater table, namely "the DNA of Identities" inscribed by 22 pairs of letters – shadow to light. It holds the four stages of the CHILD family mirroring the LEADER family. Its main columns (after the numerical values and the glyphs) are named by way of an anagram that reorders the same letters to form four words: TORA, TARO, ORAT (Latin for "to speak, pray, beseech"), ROTA (Latin for "Wheel," such as the Butterfly Wheel).

#	∞	TORA	TARO	ORAT/Family		CHILD Family	ROTAting & EVIL QKing	InitiATORy & GOOD QKing	LEADER Family		ASTRO 3+7+12
50	נ	N. Nun	13. Death	The Son			The Addict	The Listener			Sign Scorpio
60	ס	X. Samekh	14. Temperance	The Daughter			The CHILD	The LEADER			Sign Sagittarius
70	ע	O. Ayin	15. The Devil	The Mother			The Slave	The Disciple			Sign Capricorn
80	פ	P. Peh	16. Tower of Destruction	The Father			The Fraud	The Prophet			Planet Mercury

- TORA: the 4 letters of the alphabet (Nun, Samekh, Ayin, Peh) that speak to the CHILD family.
- TARO: the 4 corresponding cards of the major arcana.
- ORAT: the denomination of the 4 family members.
- ROTA (counterclockwise): the "wheel" of the 4 shadow archetypes moving the CHILD in me to "EVOLve."
- ROTA (clockwise): the "wheel" of 4 light archetypes moving the LEADER in me to adopt the behavior of LOVE.
- ASTRO: the 4 classical astrological correspondences as per *Sepher Yetzirah* (3 mother letters call 3 twin elements, 7 double letters calls the 7 classical planets, 12 simple letters call the 12 astro-signs: 3+7+12 = 22 letters of the alphabet).

TO SPEAK

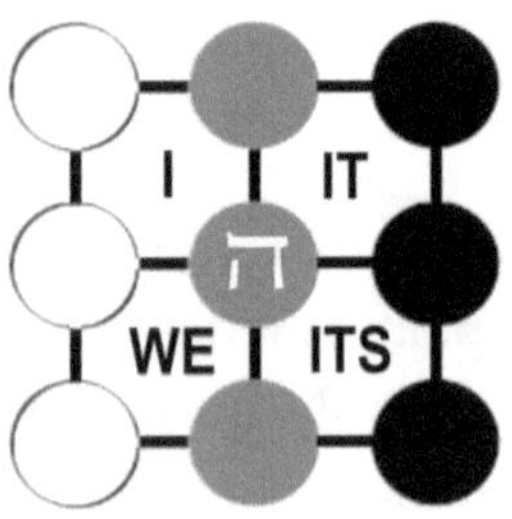

TO SPEAK **musically** by resonating with the Song of LOVE. To speak **intelligently** by no longer letting ambition steal my fire. To speak **cognitively** by realizing that the beloved is always right. To speak **ethically** by sensing the set of hidden rules guiding my speech. To speak **compellingly** of what is pertinent by not repeating the same error. And to speak **linguistically** by letting silence itself call a spade a spade. That IS mastering communication!

"Those who know do not speak. Those who speak do not know."
Lao Tsu

Every word I speak, every decision I make, marks the creation (conscious or not) of boundaries. If I say too much or not enough, it's because I want something. Behind every violated boundary lurks a secret desire for one of the 3 "Ps" of Power, Prestige or Prosperity.

To give this some context, Adam was the first to label and chart nature. He had the mind of a great mapmaker: the guy could draw boundaries! However, as he defiantly ate from the knowledge of opposites, he started separating from what he felt, hiding behind the mental world of words as if it were the real world. But a word is just an abstraction: soup recipes won't feed my body! However, ordering soup might!

Just who do I think I am? Is there an identity blocking the clarity of my communication? Am I global leader who can make money but don't know how to express my soul? Am I a gifted visionary who knows how to express my soul but can't make money?

This is again a matter of self-esteem, a.k.a. "self-worth." The price of a creation (be it a communication, a product or a service) is "worthwhile" or ethical in the measure in which the creation is held to be valuable by those who transact it. Might I doubt my value because I am yet to make my transition from greed into grace?

When a prostitutE, I speak via the split mind. I bought it, hook, line and sinker that I am the one who makes the money (or loses it), and that wealth is material. These are the beliefs I use to make me feel that I'm not enough! Hello survival mode; hello greed!

When it comes to taking care of me, I have a stranglehold on my throat. Oftentimes, it is so stifling that I choke off when I must say no to "you." Even my yeses are not honest. I admit it: I'm powerless to have what I want (or don't want). Do I even allow me to know what that is?

Speaking is a claim for Power. Imagining that Power is like money, why waste either? Sometimes I feel that, if I misuse my words and can't quite "call" it, it's because I erect boundaries out of fear – to defend myself from my own attacks. Surely, saying "no" to you is an aggressive act. What will you think of me?

Gentle warning: I may sometimes feel so uncomfortable, afraid or guilty when speaking what's true for me that I may choose to swallow my words. Understanding this warning will do wonders to help me slim down (should that be one of my goals). Indeed, the weight is in my lies; not on my thighs!

I am unclear. I do money like I do romance: either I run away when "you" seem needy or I suffocate you. Can I set limits and still be loving? What if "you" are offended or hurt by my boundaries? Am I in bondage because I fear being alone? Am I aborting my true birth by not wanting to pay the price of my evolution?

Might I be SO afraid not to be needed that I would open to boundary violations? Might my survival issues cause me to fear speaking and get in the way of my "hitting the point?"

These questions will find their answers in the next section – Mastering Commerce. For now, let's inquire on my fear of speaking! Or might "IT" be *our* fear of speaking?

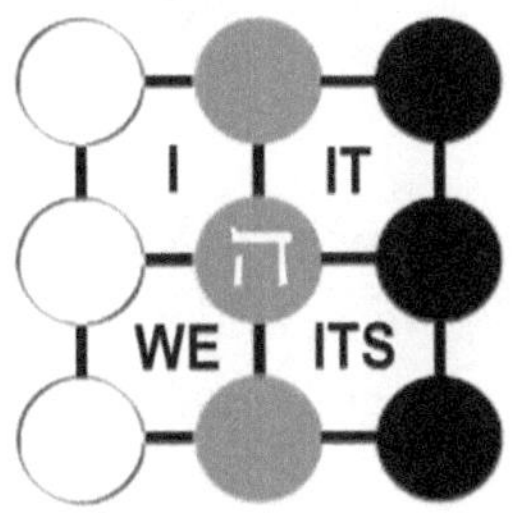

The Impact of MY Story

Prepare to DIE: To access the online inquiry tool, click the BEE Map below or https://www.goldenxpr.com/the-impact-of-my-story/.

- **Step 1:** I fill in the blank: I want to know WHY I would choose to think I CAN'T _______ (e.g.; find a job, be patient, etc.).
- **Step 2:** I ask for truth and generate a number.
- **Step 3:** I find my number on the map to fill in the brackets: when I attach to my pain story and go into [**MY Story**], I begin to resist feeling [**Resistance**]. Soon enough, [**Resistance**] leads me to indulge the poison of [**Poison**]. However, it also propels me into the fear of [**FEAR**]. If only I could stretch to the Sacred, my fear would vanish.
- **Step 4:** what most surprised me in this process is ________.

PART II: MASTERING COMMERCE

Below are the "commercial" topics in this section:

- Initial thoughts on enlightened commerce, on the sexual energy behind being for sale, and on biblical knowledge to ease the receiving of abundance.
- The entry into "Scare City:" when an ultra-capitalist race – the Ferengi – shows me a way to befriend greed and be free of Master Mammon.
- The haves & the have-nots, entitlement, the pound of flesh and the healing sense of the word "chosen."
- Eve and the bondage of mortality, painful pregnancies, cravings, milk and "money:" a very calculated suffering aiming at making me honest.
- Meeting Joseph – the archetypal CEO and treasurer, and the guardian of the sex chakra. His ability to add and remove is the secret to doing business *and* pleasure.
- Code Success and the deliverable of the sense of enough that gives me the courage to transition from greed into grace, and go out of business.

Yod (י)	Vav (ו) / Heh (ה)	Heh (ה)
Heart	Mind / Body	Soul
Transmission	Creation / Manifestation	Formation
Individual Power	Symbolic Power	Collective Power
Communication	Healing / Health	Commerce

When the Heh of YEWE echoes Hermes' mastery in commerce…

Commerce or Business

"Commerce is a game of skill, which every man cannot play, which few men can play well. The right merchant is one who has the just average of faculties we call commonsense; a man of strong affinity for facts, who makes up his decision on what he has seen. He is thoroughly persuaded of the truths of arithmetic. There is always a reason, in the man, for his good or bad fortune; and so, in making money. Men talk as if there were some magic about this, and believe in magic, in all parts of life. He knows that all goes on the old road, pound for pound, cent for cent – for every effect a perfect cause – and that good luck is another name for tenacity of purpose." *Ralph Waldo Emerson*

Commerce or business: what is the difference? Commerce is a core part of the business, as it focuses on buying and selling. A successful business depends on its commerce. As a business owner, I'd like to think that the idea, communication, product or service that my business promotes has value for my customers. This tenet would seem to be fundamental for an ethical way to do business.

My business still has its problems. Perhaps it is an increase in competition or the uncertainty of the market; perhaps the business is facing technology or cyber security issues; perhaps it suffers from information overload or the need to expand globally; perhaps it is not recruiting the right talent or managing innovation. These different aspects of business impact commerce and the ability to acquire loyal customers. Whatever the problem may be, it has a ripple effect on the rest of the business, no matter what industry I'm in or how big or small the business may be.

Consider: when I think holistically and realize that my business problems are symptoms, I become interested in finding out what the root cause is.

I begin by realizing that a business entity is inert. Just as money is an abstraction – an image I superimposed over what money is, my business is my creation. I am the one who gives it life by executing it, managing it, accounting it, marketing it. But who am I? Am I the self who enjoys the richness of life or the self who resents not having enough? For if my mind is trapped in Scare City, my business is likely to develop problems. It now behooves me to inquire on lack. Where does it come from? Did I forget why I'm in business? Am I continuously doing my best to offer what I feel is of value?

Code Commerce - TM / MT

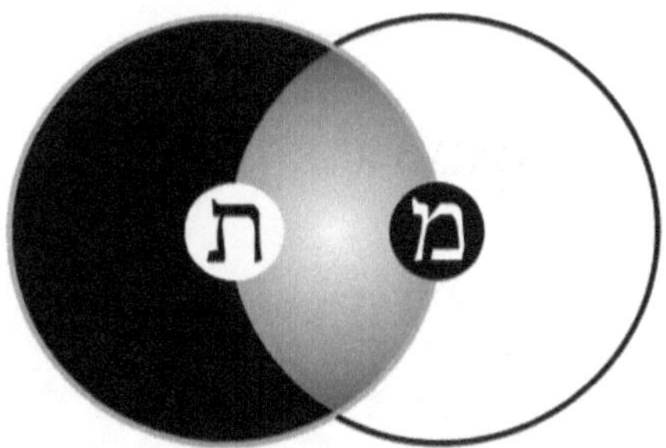

Imagine a language so pure and so sacred that it can reconcile opposites in just two letters...

Right: Hebrew letter Mem (מ) → M in Roman Script
Left: Hebrew letter Tav (ת) → T in Roman Script

Here is how S/Hebrew inscribes code "Commerce:"

- In one direction, I read *Mat* (מת) for "death."
- In the other, I read *Tam* (תמ) for "perfect" ("PAIRfect").

The Decoding: successful commerce in two words – *Mat* for "death" and *Tam* for "PAIRfect." The archaic sense of *Commerce* speaks of intercourse, which is a death. This is how the French language calls an orgasm *la petite mort*, as it is "a little death." When the male and female sides of me (the twins) die to being not enough, they melt into each other, and open to divine "PAIRfection." This is when I hear: "not my will, Thy will be done" and see the word "TWINS" as an acronym for "Thy Will Is Not Separate." To fully wake up from the dream of separation, I ask myself: since death is the disappearance of mind (a.k.a. enlightenment), what can I do to die to who I *think* I am and stop making it about me? For starters, I could offer a creation that has value for those who are directly concerned by it. This would naturally result in my enjoying the 3 Ps of Power, Prestige and Prosperity as I would have an ethical (and sexy) way of doing commerce and being in business. Being enough, I could finally allow me to rest.

COMMERCE—NOUN

COMMERCE—NOUN: 1. the activity of buying and selling, especially on a large scale. 2. DATED social dealings between people. 3. ARCHAIC sexual intercourse.

How generous, kind-hearted and appealing is my commerce when I am in an illusion of separation and perceive that I can't win? Upon meeting with prospects, do I find myself thinking: "can I get them before they get me?" Do I wonder if some of them might be mating material? If they don't agree to my terms, do I want to make them pay for my inadequacy? **Ah, will I ever get past: "what's in it for me?"**

Value and money have a lot to do with the sense of enough. For example, am I charging what I am worth or do I accept a lesser rate because I'm afraid to be rejected? Indeed, a lot of business and/or money issues get tangled up with "poor" self-esteem. This makes me vulnerable to the poison of entitlement: "get it... You deserve it!" says 80% of America still in debt.

And it makes me wonder... If abundance and scarcity are two parallel worlds, why choose "Scare City?" Why do I identify to the have-nots and not the haves?

Resilience answers. Success is not inherited: it is work! I must become willing to work until I can be successful, no matter what it takes. Also, I must be big enough to not let myself be ashamed and hardened by my failures, but instead, let each failure guide me to the courage to persevere. That would be success right there, wouldn't it?

Success needs failure to exist. In that sense, failure is a badge of honor – the crucible that burns things down to their essence to reveal who I am. On the note of necessary trial and suffering, there is just this one question: am I ready for how Truth will change my life? Surely, as long as I won't listen, I am in the dark, blocking health and wealth.

Yes, but enlightenment is dangerous: it can create chaos! Why mess with the economics that have informed the collective matrix for eons? Even religion has become a commerce, and the temples, the playground of money changers.

***

The conditioning starts in a yearning – be it for sex or money. This very yearning soon becomes the motive for not caring about offering value and not giving from the heart. The hunger, that is present individually and collectively, drives the history of commerce. Am I relaxed or worried when thinking about "my" money? For detachment is how to master the subtle art of receiving, and shift failure into success.

***

If money is on my mind, I am dealing once again with Power negotiations.
Which begs the question: might my allegiance be to the visible world? Just how much do I seek the QKingdom first and trust in "God?"

Taking Care of Business

"The way to get started is to quit talking and begin doing." *Walt Disney*

LIKE THE INDIVIDUAL, THE COLLECTIVE FOLLOWS PATTERNS OF EVOLUTION which map out the history of commerce. Each society exploits and includes the gains of the previous one, yet each time adding something new. From hunting and gathering, we moved as a clan into raiding and pillaging, as a family into trading and agriculture, and then as a nation into industrialism. We are now pursuing individual economic goals. As time passed, we became greedier, and lost some of our ability to care. Efficiency of production bred male-oriented management values, number crunching mentality and task automation.

Fast forward the tapes... These fundamental commerce attitudes carried through from inception into the technology age – the age of the internet & global interconnectivity. The new Power is in data and analytics. As tech companies are growing, small/medium businesses are barely surviving. More and more retail companies are closing. While we may recognize that the economic strategy of promoting unlimited growth and increasing consumption is leading to disaster for all, we can't quite imagine where the sustainable alternatives are or if they even exist at all. Is it possible for a small group of individuals committed to a cause to mobilize and change collective agreements?

True: the US government has regulations that discourage monopolies. And yet, even worsened by the pandemic, many countries around the world are subject to a power grab by authoritarian leaders. The conflict of male versus female has now extended to our politics that opposes the republicans to the democrats. And it makes me wonder...

Is there a path to enlightened commerce? No matter how expansive my vision may be, I must return to the basics: change cannot be forced. It happens from within, one leader at a time. Will I make consciousness my priority? Waking up on the other side of indoctrination is not easy: I am in the collective, and the masses don't like to be disturbed. To bring the societal change I wish to see, I must find a safe and gentle way to inquire on beliefs as intolerant as the beliefs on religion or patriotism. While these beliefs seem to preserve order, they root for the dark side of Power. Thank "God" (pun intended) for the regulations preventing the mixing of church and state! It would be a disaster if religious dogma were to enter governing. Thank "God" for the freedom of speech that keeps at bay the ill-fated religious takeover of business! And it makes me wonder... How free am I to move toward an enlightened civilization when I am still religiously attached to "my" money, and yet to sever the ties binding me to materialism?

Biblical Commerce

"I remember the first time I had sex — I kept the receipt." *Groucho Marx*

To understanding where greed begins, different sources concur on the fact that money and business are linked to sex. Eastern teachings hold that the sex chakra is also the seat of money-making activities. The Torah speaks of *Mammon,* a word and energy meaning "money" and "yearning." Napoleon Hill's famous book – *Think and Grow Rich* – speaks of the benefit of having an all-consuming desire in starting any project.

Hoping isn't enough. To not quit when hitting roadblocks, I must want my results bad. The hunger to reach the goal must be so strong that I'd stake everything on it. However, I must also learn to transmute the sexual energy of desire. Transmutation is how to shift into a genius mode and achieve business goals. Last but not least, the word "commerce" itself was first used to refer to sexual intercourse. Indeed, the desire for sex is the most powerful of human desires.

So, sex and money make the world go round. These powers are so alluring – and so disruptive – that I will try to control them. I've experienced how feeling sexy is feeling like a million bucks! What about biblical knowledge? How sexy does it make me feel? It gives me Code Enlightenment (see *Learning to Code*), showing me that I can have it all – jewel and lotus! It also introduces me to the ultimate CEO in the patriarch Joseph who must have dreamt of Napoleon Hill ahead of time as he knew how to transmute his sexual energy, and develop a genius of integrity. Curiously, the patriarch could foresee the business problems that will appear in the 21st century, and resolve them with one proficiency: honesty. Honesty is the foundation of true creativity. It is what allowed King Pharaoh to scale his business empire in a sustainable manner. **Will I dare to ask? Might my money problems be traced to a lack of integrity?**

I am now speaking to the prostitutE archetype as s/he lives in me. Just how much self-esteem do I have? Do I lie and/or compromise for money? Do I face my fear of the material world and trust in my ability to survive? Do I remain true to myself or do I negotiate my integrity for a few bucks? Will I stay "married" to the wrong company just to pay the bills? Will I sell my honor and misuse my creative energy? Bottom line: if I am for sale, what's my price?

Code Abundance BR / RB

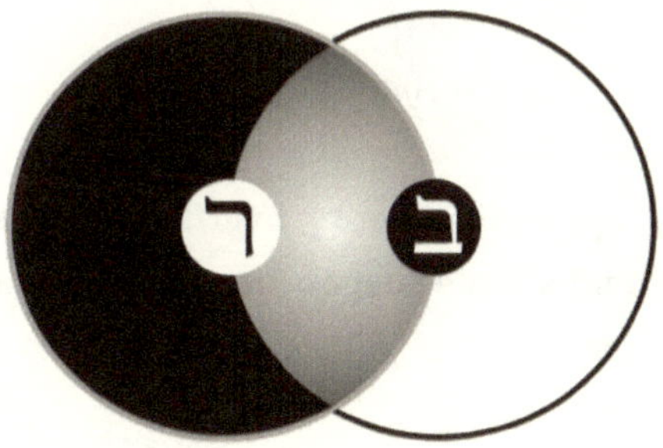

Imagine a language so pure and so sacred that it can reconcile opposites in just two letters...

Right: Hebrew letter (ב) Beth → B in Roman Script
Left: Hebrew letter (ר) Resh → R in Roman Script

Here is how S/Hebrew inscribes code "Abundance:"

- **BR:** from right to left, I read *Bar* (בר) for "grain, son."
- **RB:** from left to right, I read *Rav* (רב) for "many, multitude, abundant."

The Decoding: what is abundance, but the sense that I am giving all to LOVE? When my sense of worth is hopelessly pegged to the external, I am creating lack by longing for "you." In the old days, I would leave society to find "God." I lived in communities that abstained from the energies of sex and money. I didn't have to couple and my physical needs were covered. Nowadays, I am a mystic without a monastery, seeking to wake up from the dream of separation. When adding *Im* (אם) "mother" to *Bar* (בר) the "**son**;" I form *Bra'am* (בראם) for "he created them" [male and female, and blessed them, and called their name Adam" (*Genesis 5:2*). This Adam (me) is whole, "PAIRfect," complete and connected: nothing's missing! When adding the Heh (ה) of receptivity to *Bra'am*, I form *Abraham* (אברהם), the "father of **multitudes**." To be such father and know **abundance**, I can do as Abraham and be willing to give it all – including sacrificing my "**son**" (what's most precious to me). This is how to have it all!

The Entry into "Scare City"

"Scarcity is a captivating book, overflowing with new ideas, fantastic stories, and simple suggestions that just might change the way you live." *Steven Levitt*

And captive of Scare City I made me! If abundance is a frequency – something I tune into, I must not be receiving that channel. Instead of feeling that I am a blessing and enrich the lives I touch, I look at my reality and feel gypped. What happened? One moment, in *Genesis 1*, I believe, I was created male and female, and had dominion over just about everything. The next moment, I wake up (in a figure of speech) in

Genesis 2, in a garden that desperately needs tending. There's no shrub, no herb, and no rain. And I have to deal with a "God" giving me all sorts of limitations. Just one of those days where I might as well have stayed in bed. So, what happened? *Genesis 2:4* did!

"These are the generations of the heaven and of the earth **when they were created**, in the day that the LORD God made earth and heaven."
Genesis 2:4

Pronounced *Behibaram,* this word means "when they were created." Its 2nd letter – the sign Heh (ה) – is shown here as it is written on the Torah 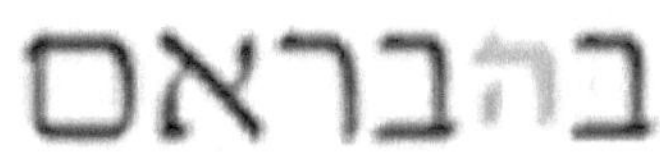 scroll: shrunk. The shrinking of a sign that means "window, breath or womb" can only be an omen of doom. It is sending both mother (אם) and son (בר) into exile, and opening the captivating book of Scare City, a book which overflows with a myriad of fantastic stories of inadequacy. Reading from that book, I doubt that I'll get my results – be it the girl or the entry into the Promised Land.

The downgrade definitely occurred when I imagined that the LOVE God made *earth and heaven.* What an interesting creation! *Genesis 1* saw the generations of *the heaven and the earth,* and kaboom, everything's upside down in *Genesis 2* with a LORD "God" that flipped poles on me! All the while, I forget that "God" is my creation. So is money. So is the heaven and the earth.

The question is now meatier: why choose to observe hellish lack when I could partake of heavenly abundance?

Earth on Heaven

"Satisfaction is not guaranteed." Ferengi 19th Rule of Acquisition

First, there's a shift from "the heaven and the earth" to "**earth** and **heaven**." Second, where did the definite article (English word "the," S/Hebrew letter "Heh") go? This Heh is my **female** side – the container without which I can't receive or get any satisfaction!

Without a container, I lack the sensitivity to know what is good and what is bad; what is heaven and what is hell. I'm asleep in a dream where Power struggles abound, and ashamed of what my mind **generates** (unless I'd resonate with the 284th rule: "deep down everyone's a Ferengi;" a fictional extraterrestrial and ultra-capitalist race). When feeling deprived, how could I ask for what I want? And when not asking, how could I receive? I'm in a lot of misery, unable to be grateful for my lot.

In order to do commerce with you, there must be a mutual understanding. Without it, there can be no felt sense of "WE," but only war and competition. 21st Rule: "never place friendship above profit!" In their extreme capitalism, these Ferengis are clear that they're here to create Earth on Heaven: money is their god and greed, their law!

The greed-induced objectification feels like a strange IT. If just trying to blame "you" for my failures, I might as well be talking to a rock. 45th Rule of Acquisition: "expand or die!" When I seek to control "you," there's no "I" listening to the Self and no "WE" hearing each other; just two comatose beings without sentience, focused on "what's in IT for me?"

If evolving is acquiring Power, can I go about acquisition with a different set of rules besides "profit is its own reward?"

Code Profit - CM / ML

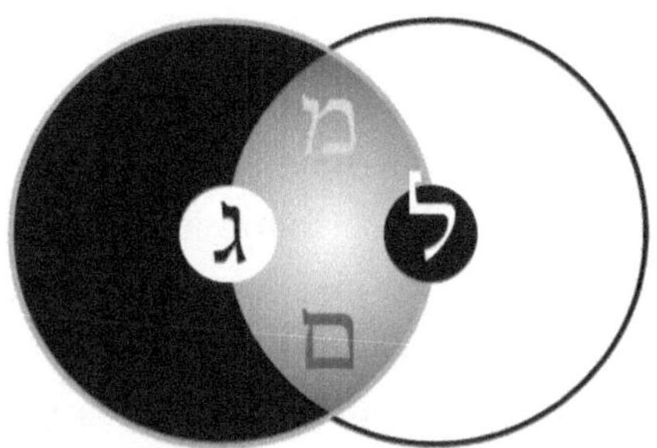

*Imagine a language so pure and so sacred that it can
reconcile opposites in just three letters...*

Right: Hebrew letter Lamed (ל) → L in Roman Script
Middle: Hebrew letter Mem regular (מ) and
Mem final (ם) → M in Roman Script
Left: Hebrew letter Gimel (ג) → C in Roman Script

Here is how S/Hebrew inscribes code "Profit:"

- **CM:** in one direction, I read *Gam* (גם) for "also, more,
  increase."
- **ML:** in the other direction, I read *Mal* (מל) for "purification."
- **CLM:** from left to right to bottom, I read *Golem* (גלם) for
  "artificial creation."
- **CML:** from left to top to right, I real *Gemul* (גמל) for "reward."

The Decoding: I shall begin with a caveat. The sign Vav (ו) – normally
part of the words *Golem* (גולם) and *Gemul* (גמול) – is invisible in the
words above. If it were in the mix, it would also create the word *Mum*
(מום) for "blemish, defect." LOL, *Mum's* the word! I purposely silenced
it, as the last thing I need is to reinforce the belief that there's something wrong with me, that I'm a fraud and a failure. Also, there is
nothing wrong with making a profit. However, for profit to express the
health of my commerce, my ego must be healthy. Keeping Vav

temporarily out gives me the space to acquire enough wholesome Power to stop feeding my **artificial creation** with the thought that I am not enough. I created my **golem** out of pure envy: I want the orgasm that I think s/he's having! Just as Cain, I can neither rest nor die to the illusion of forced labor. I resent having to work hard for my money while never making any real profit. To top it all, the 97th Rule "enough is never enough" leads me to always want **more.** This is how I make sure that I'm punished and never **rewarded.** My redeeming grace: I can still hear a faint voice telling me about the gift of **purification.** There is a way to take the life-force out of my creation. I just have to go back to the foundation (honesty), see the truth, and expose the money or sex secrets I'm so desperately trying to hide. And that will put my golem to death!

The Invention of Mammon

"I will tell you the secret to getting rich on Wall Street. You try to be greedy when others are fearful. And you try to be fearful when others are greedy." *Warren Buffett, Investor*

Mammon means "1. money, 2. yearning." I yearn for "you" when I lack self-worth, and need your love, approval and recognition. This is a sure sign that I'm hard on me and inviting abuse. Many of my stories are now about the fantasy of money, the idea of money, the need for money, the secrets of money. Before money, I tried to trade the apples I had for the goat I needed. But I soon realized that my barter system had its limits: a goat can run away and apples can rot! Needing an agreed upon medium of exchange, I went to nuggets of gold and shiny rocks. I eventually settled on pieces of paper with words and pictures of powerful people. I was yet to realize that giving a piece of paper the value of a thousand dollars was way too high a power to be entrusted to me, especially when I feel "not enough." These words are written as a promise of value, on slips of paper which do not give milk: THEY ARE NOT REAL...

I AM NOT REAL EITHER! And since I don't buy me, I can only waste my energy in attempting to convince you to believe something about me. Fearing not to be needed opens me to boundary violations. It's even hard for me to say "no!" Eventually, I resent giving myself away and will want to make you pay for it. Ouch!

But how can I be truthful in my speech, when I'm hungry and fear for my life? The only way that makes any sense is to befriend Mammon, that is, the hunger. I am told that, as greed reveals its ingenuousness, it morphs into grace. Feeling that my soul is pure, I'll return to innocence, imagine no boundary and be One with "you."

My financial independence is now founded on walking the walk and talking the talk, and my acquiring REAL ESTATE, on the STATE of being REAL. I see that my money issues are as illusory as is the need to protect my identity. Having few wants, I see that I have all I need.

And as I no longer alternate between yearning for money or food or "you," and hating money or food or "you," the $$$ sign begins looking as the symbol it is: a snake on a pole drawn as a caduceus for me to heal my *creation* of money, and the sense of not being enough.

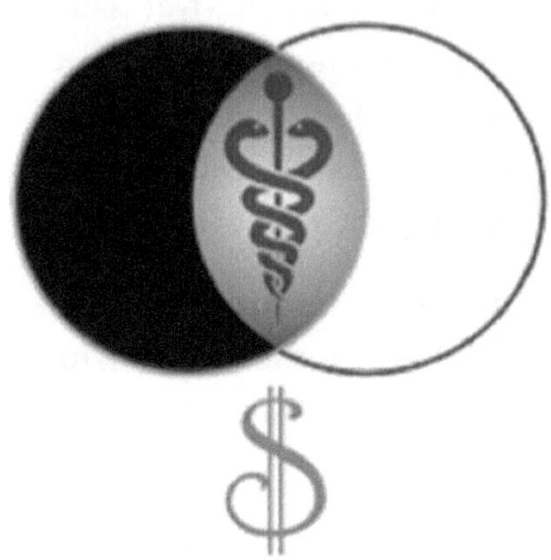

The Executive and the Dreamer

"Our lives are structured around power symbols: money, authority, title, beauty, security." Caroline Myss, Anatomy of the Spirit

I can see that self-development is the process of actualizing my spiritual potential. Ultimately, it is to acquire enough wholesome Power that I can take responsibility for the divine expression of my soul. On that note, who do I relate to more: an executive or a dreamer? The former has little financial issues, but can't allow himself to give way to his soul's expression. The latter can feel and hold a soul vision, but she has trouble dealing with money. And whereas there are women that are very successful in business just as there are men who are artists by profession, it does appear that women are generally and archetypally more akin to being dreamers, and men, to being executives.

What about me? Do I feel supported in my creative endeavors? How much do my beliefs about money cost me? If money was not an issue, what would I create?

The way I relate to money is undeniably tied to the sense of enough. When I live in Scare City and have survival issues, I discount my guidance as I can't see any financial value to it. I also can't seem to trust that I will follow through on an idea. Truth be told: I'm terrified that, if I followed my heart, I'd go broke! Moreover, how could I have money and be spiritual? Isn't money the root of all evil?

Surely, there is a great need to superimpose a caduceus over the dollar sign in light of the very toxic relationship that exists between money and spirituality. Just as my body is split from my soul, so is my money.

There must be a way to dismantle the old paradigm of "the meek shall inherit the earth." For now, I really believe that I have to compromise my soul to make money. Money is dirty. That thought is also how I tend to think the worst of wealthy people. I can't imagine that someone could be successful and ethical. I'm even surprised if they have a spiritual practice. Henceforth, and while I'm a gifted healer, I feel uneasy, ashamed or even guilty when it comes to stating my fee. How can I charge money for helping you heal? Because I judge wealthy people to be somewhat dishonest, I fear being judged for asking financial energy for my services. The sense that I have no real sense of worth ("I'm not enough") makes it hard for me to be in business. So, I'm like a child. I find myself saying: "I don't deal with money. When I need it, it's there!" And since I won't grow up, all I have is an allowance; pocket money, but not an income. I'm afraid of turning into an executive, afraid to do what it takes to be in business.

Here may just be the main reason why the male executive community distances the female spiritual community: it doesn't see any financial health to it. The lack of structure is distasteful. There's no financial solvency, no backbone, no integrity! Not to mention the financial and sexual scandals associated with cults!

I'm still a dreamer, and I still need money. To bridge the gap that I have drawn between Spirit and money, I may rationalize that my motivation for wanting wealth is to give a percentage back to charity. But giving to "God" won't solve my problem. To make a true difference, a new stage of surrender is needed. I might then have the heart to pray to be led into my highest potential, regardless of how it affects my finances. And that might just be what Buddha called "perfect livelihood!"

The Haves & the Have-nots

"I cannot serve two masters: I will either hate the one and love the other or I'll be devoted to the one and despise the other. Either way, I cannot serve *Elohim* and Mammon." *Matthew 6:24*

When serving Mammon, I find myself speaking and acting compulsively. I also have a hard time with people interrupting me or repeating themselves. How can I wait or be patient when I'm so lonely? Unless I satiate the hunger, the energy of sex and money will rule over me. I'll need proof of outcome before doing anything remotely courageous. This is the very weakness Mammon uses to entrap me.

Ignoring that I am created male and female, it is expectable that I'd fear both, losing what I have and not getting what I want. Since I can't trust myself not to compromise my integrity, I alternate between trying to dominate the "out there," and falsely yielding to Power. Either way, I fall prey to lust and greed...

Dante's *Commedia dell'Arte* speaks of lust as an "excessive love of others that detracts from the love due God" and greed as an "excessive love of power and money." While my excesses are sourced in an inability to know when enough is "in off" (I can't stop or wait), it is also evident that there is something I *think* sex and money would give me: *your* love, approval and recognition. Yep, looking for love in all the wrong places is how I fear rejection, no matter whether I see myself as a have or a have-not.

Questions for the haves: did I come into money through no action of my own? Am I feeling guilty about it? Am I using money to try to fix everyone and control everything around me? Did I marry my polar opposite: he wants to spend; I want to save (or vice-versa)? Do I treat money like sex, expecting that it would get pregnant and reproduce? If I feel undeserving and tend to put others' needs ahead of my own, what do I expect in return?

Questions for the have-nots: If I'm more comfortable giving, what makes me feel out of control about receiving? Do I equate getting my needs met with selfishness? Am I even aware of my needs? Am I needing to work all the time to pay for my lifestyle – fancy or not? Do I feel that the world owes me? Am I thinking I'll never be able to retire? Am I topping it off by worrying that I may become an invalid, and then what would I do for money?!

The Pound of Flesh

"Hath not a Jew hands, organs, dimensions, senses, affections, passions; fed with the same food, hurt with the same weapons, subject to the same diseases, healed by the same means, warmed and cooled by the same winter and summer as a Christian is? If you prick us, do we not bleed? If you tickle us, do we not laugh?" *Shakespeare, the Merchant of Venice.*

The belief that I am different from you ("special") and the claim that I am "holier than thou" automatically makes you my enemy, if only in my eyes. I am now justified in defending myself since I expect that you will fight the position in which I put you – my inferior. If clever enough to win, I'll shame you with my victory and enjoy your defeat as the spoils of war. But does it feel like a victory?

Might my specialness be hiding a profound hatred of "you," which is to say, of me? Does my superiority complex serve to cover a history of unrequited love? Whether Jewish or not, do I not fear rejection? If I understood that we are One (we both bleed when pricked), wouldn't I give you the love I ask of you?

I feel so inadequate that I long to see that I matter. In that case, imagining that I am Jewish, reading *Deuteronomy 14:2* ("Out of all the peoples on the face of the earth, the LORD has chosen you to be his **people specially treasured**"), it is understandable that I would have a real need to identify to a "**people specially treasured**" (*Am Segulah,* in Hebrew*)*. Eventually, the hopeless swinging from "I'm special" to "I'm not enough," combined with the pain of alternating between being a bully and a victim, will lead me to ask: is there another interpretation for this chosen people idea?

First, a compassionate and honoring note... TCO embraces both "camps:" those who suffer to be chosen and those who suffer not to be chosen. As such, it is written holding that both camps are equally "the second sex:" the non-chosen female side who has been increasingly angry to be raped by the male side, and the chosen male side who has turned to hatred when the female side responded to the abuse by being emasculating.

Would I let go of my resentment of wanting my pound of flesh and never getting it if I could trust that whatever is given is absolutely perfect? Moreover, seeing S/Hebrew's unsurpassed depth of meaning, I might even realize that what I used to read as "chosen people" makes much better sense as "chosen language." [taking a breath]

It is simple: a **"people"** (*Am*, in Hebrew) can be defined by its "language." When Italian, I speak Italian. When French, I speak French. When German, I speak German. As for the word *Segulah,* it is at the root of English word "sigil." This is how it also means "treasure," as the S/Hebrew letters are a "people" of non-biological sentient animals whose life eases the acquisition of symbolic Power by way of its *Seguloth* (pl.) also meaning "signs" or "healing charms."

As for me – a cultural creative, Jewish or not, would I judge religion for being stuck at the mythic level if I could detach from the belief "I am special," a belief which is bound to become "I'm not enough?" Yes, I can make religion the culprit for the idea that I am fallen. Yes, I can notice the lack of evolution of those who serve an ethnocentric agenda. I can see that they are waiting for the tribe to save them as they're too afraid to save themselves. I can also ask myself if I am capable of laughing when I fall, and willing to get up to take another shot at being successful. Bottom line: can I grow up and just give it all to LOVE?

Eve and Mortality

"Then He said to the woman, "I will sharpen the pain of your pregnancy, and in pain you will give birth." *Genesis 3:16* | "Adam called his wife by the name of Eve, because she would become the mother of all life." *Genesis 3:20*

I normally think of Adam and Eve as the "sinners." That's what I was taught! It took me a while to realize what the Torah actually says. The hunger for love starts in *Genesis 2:18* with a single judgment: "it is no good for the Adam to be alone." From there, "God" forms a bunch of animals out of the ground "to see what the Adam would name them." Whatever the name that was given, that would be the calling of a particular life-form. However, there was no partner for the Adam. In other words, he couldn't get her number!

That is when "God" put the Adam to sleep and removed a rib out of which he built a "Woman." This "Woman" wasn't tasked to give birth. She was just to complete "the Man!" Time passes, the Snake comes onto the scene, and leads "the Woman" into temptation, and by extension, "the Adam."

It is only in *Genesis 3:20*, long after *Genesis 3:6* (the wrongful eating), that the Adam wakes up long enough to get the girl; his wife. He names her "Eve" or *Chavah* in Hebrew because she was called to become the mother of all life – a life whose birth-giving process was now written to be experienced as suffering.

Prior to being cursed by "God" and then branded by her man as "Eve," the woman did not need to give birth, to give birth in pain, or to be in pain. She just lived as an immortal, in the Eternal Now. It's not that she didn't conceive, but more that her conceptions were immaculate (the famous "virgin birth"). She didn't worry about the future and was not compelled by the urgency of having offspring. She also had no past, as she was not plagued with a mind in auto-repeat, hungering endlessly for LOVE and never satisfied.

Regardless of my gender, I am Eve when I am trapped in the cycle of death and rebirth to which life in the material world is bound. I keep on reincarnating into the same error, insanely pretending to expect different results.

Since the opposite of death is not life but birth, it may be interesting to think of Eve as the "mother of all deaths and rebirths." This would reveal that *Chavah* is the Hebrew equivalent of Sanskrit *Saṃsāra*, the cyclicality of death and rebirth caused by my attachment to the material world. Therefore, if I stopped believing the lies the ego snake whispers in my ear, I'd be an immortal again. Instead of being a slave to the Power of history, I'd be in the Now, enjoying abundant synchronicities.

Therefore, the idea of karma spinning the wheel of transformation is as much a fundamental truth of Abrahamic religions as it is of Eastern religions.

The meaning of *Saṃsāra* is "wandering," suggesting a mundane existence in the world. Hmmm... Is anyone who is suffering from not yet being able to transform "a wandering Jew?" The dire fate is expressed by Cain who, condemned to be a fugitive and a wanderer, wants to die as he says: "my punishment is greater than I can bear (*Genesis 4:13*). Well, sometimes I wish that killing myself would be that easy! And then I hear this line from *Groundhog Day – the movie* "I killed myself so many times I don't even exist anymore."

Pregnancy and Cravings

'Then He said to the woman, "I will sharpen the pain of your pregnancy, and in pain you will give birth, AND YOUR DESIRE SHALL BE FOR YOUR HUSBAND, AND HE SHALL RULE OVER YOU."'
Genesis 3:16

I find it intriguing that most people remember the first part of the curse (the painful childbirths), but not its last part (the craving for a man). Surely, most men can have compassion for the women who give birth in pain. But what about being condemned to constantly yearn for a man's attention? It's like being ruled by a desire for alcohol, money, prestige... There is no freedom and no peace in that. The most terrible part may even be that men secretly enjoy having a sex slave, and getting to be the ruler and the object of a woman's desire... Indeed, it would take a very healthy ego to be impervious to the seduction of having a fan club.

Until my mom was kicked out of humanity's trinity, I had the "PAIR-fect" family: a Father, a Son, a Bride and a Mother. And then poof, the Bride was ghosted, and the Mother, exiled. And it makes me wonder... Since the Latin word *mater* gave "matter" and "mother," might the dark matter and dark mother be in an entanglement? Is that how I can't quite let go of my greed? Judaism speaks of *Shekhinah* as a black goddess ("Her feet go down to death; her steps lead straight to hell"), science echoes with dark matter, dark energy, antimatter and even degenerate matter.

One day, my evil eye will close, and I will stop judging that darkness is bad...

I shall never say this enough: 'for eons, the interpretation of the Judeo-Christian scriptures has worked to split spirit and matter. The message is as consistent as it is pervasive: the denigration of matter is linked to an evil Eve whose sinful nature leads her to be seduced by the serpent. On the other hand, Spirit is the ideal that I am sworn to attain, an ideal whose heavenly light will deliver me from the jail of the body. This is another way where my female side (matter) is cursed with the desire for the male (spirit).

I'm told that I shouldn't envy or lust or be greedy; that I ought to resist my anger... Only then, I hope, the "Father's" punishing voice will stop undercutting me with a stern "not good enough!" Yet no one is judging me but myself! These harsh projections split me from the center of my authenticity, making me vulnerable to the "either or" thinking of an addict. Whether I lose my power to a man, food, drugs, work, money (the list is long), it is the devil who made me do it!'

When matter is split from spirit and sent away as the Dark Mother, I can only be bound to the material world, and unable to disengage from the cycle of death and rebirth. The maddening auto-play of the destructive golem I have taken on can get old very quickly, which is how I'll eventually become willing to try something new...

The DREaM of LOVE

"LOVE is patient, LOVE is kind. It does not envy, it does not boast, it is not proud. It is not rude, it is not self-seeking, it is not easily angered, it keeps no record of wrongs. LOVE does not delight in evil but rejoices with the truth." *1 Corinthians 13:1 (TCO's uppercase).*

LOVE asks me: are you ready, able and willing to resolve the conflict between what reality is and what you *think* it should be? Will you surrender and stop fighting? But the DREaM reverses it all, inverting RAW (Ready-Able-Willing) into WAR. While I may sense that surrender is not an act of weakness but of strength, I still resist giving up my control games. Eventually, the yearning will get me to stop trying and start trusting.

LOVE is patient, LOVE is kind. It gives me all the time I need to make the decision to wake up from the DREaM, and stop feeding the ego's hunger.

Waking up from the HELLusion is making my Exodus out of *Eretz Mitzrayim* for "the Land of Egypt" but also "narrow-minded mind." While in Egypt, I am hungry for LOVE, and engage in all sorts of compulsions. The only waiting I can do is for the other shoe to drop, as I know I'm misusing Power. I take back my will to protect me from LOVE. I still expect to fail, but it'll seem less painful since I master-minded it.

There must be other reasons why I don't succeed in my creation. My parents didn't want me... I wasn't allowed to have cookies as a child... I was following orders... Surely this poor outcome cannot be the consequences of my decisions! And I keep singing the ego song, ignoring that the purpose of life is to experience the laws of creation: every word and action cause an effect. **Am I willing to know the truth?**

What can I choose to say and do now that will cause effects that bless all?

Code Honesty - PY / YD

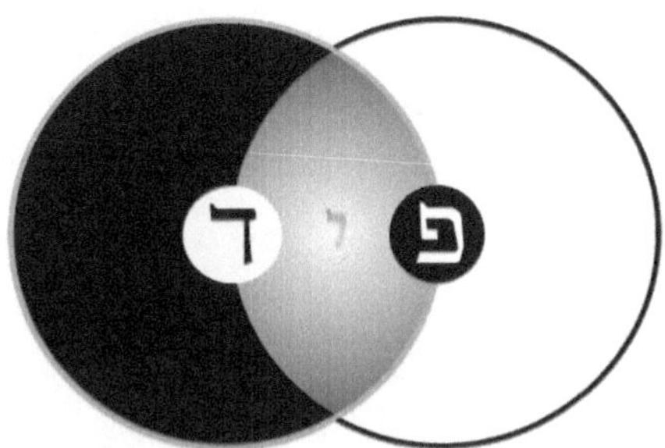

Imagine a language so pure and so sacred that it can reconcile opposites in just three letters...

Right: Hebrew letter Peh (פ) → P, Ph in Roman Script
Middle: Hebrew letter Yod (י) → Y in Roman Script
Left: Hebrew letter Dalet (ד) → D in Roman Script

Here is how S/Hebrew inscribes code "Honesty:"

- **PY**: In one direction, I read *Pi* (פי) for "my mouth."
- **YD**: In the other direction, I read *Yad* (יד) for "hand."

The Decoding: it is easy to make promises, and hard "to put my money where **my mouth** is." Being honest is to use my **hands** in support of my words. This was patriarch Joseph's forte, which is how he rose to high political office in Egypt after being sold into slavery by his brothers. His ministry and politics were founded on honesty, as told by the letters of his name. Here is how. If I were to add to the code PY/YD the letters XW/WX, I would create two new words: *Yoseph* (YWXP) and *Yesod* (YXWD). *Yesod* for "foundation" is the S/Hebrew name of the sex chakra, and *Yoseph*/Joseph, the guardian ascribed to this chakra. I have shared how, in classical Kabbalah, the seven lower spheres are guarded by seven patriarchs. Joseph watches over *Yesod* because he is honest in both his dealings with money and with sex (the energy of sex and money being linked to the sex chakra). Joseph actually turned down the sexual advances of Potiphar's wife, even though she had the power to send him to jail (which she ended up doing, so vexed she was). Being honest about why I want what I want is how to not misuse sexual Power. When I am as Joseph, I am not plagued by doubt, and don't fear being emPowered, as I have no shame-based secrets about neither money nor sex.

Pleasure *and* Business

> "He [Siddharta] always seems only to play at business, it never gets into his blood, it never rules him, he never fears failure, losses never bother him." *Hermann Hesse, Siddharta*

Joseph has a lot in common with Siddharta. The meaning of his name (*Yoseph*) is at once "to remove" and "to add." To remove and to add is a way to language the process of human development made known by Ken Wilber as "transcend and include." Indeed, what do I need to remove and/or add in order to avoid being inappropriate as I mix business and pleasure? Researchers have found that employees who did not have clear boundaries between work and free time experienced a lower sense of balance and well-being. As for me, I must have a few boundary problems because I'm wiped out.

Why am I unable to say "no?" Why take things so seriously? I am now guided to learn from Siddharta who "seemed only to play at business." His story begins as he left behind his privileged home in an ancient Indian kingdom ("remove"), to gain spiritual illumination ("add"). One day, he meets Kamala, a beautiful courtesan who offers to teach him the art of love. **A side note to myself: could the art of love (a.k.a. enlightenment) be teachable?**

Siddharta must first become wealthy enough to win Kamala's affections. Although he despised materialistic pursuits, he agrees to find work in order to be with the beautiful Kamala. She soon directs him to the employ of Kamaswami, a local businessman. If Siddhartha easily succeeds, it is because he provides a peaceful space, against the fits of passion of Kamaswami ("master of the worldly realm").

Siddharta's magic is simple: he remembers *Shabbat* and "rests," whether he plays or works. Non-action, especially in business, is such a paradox that I struggle accepting it. Isn't selling a numbers' game? Am I not supposed to call long lists of prospects? When I realize I need do nothing since creation (or money) happens *through* me and not *by* me, I make love to life and not war, and my business is a pleasure!

Code Success – ONC / NCO

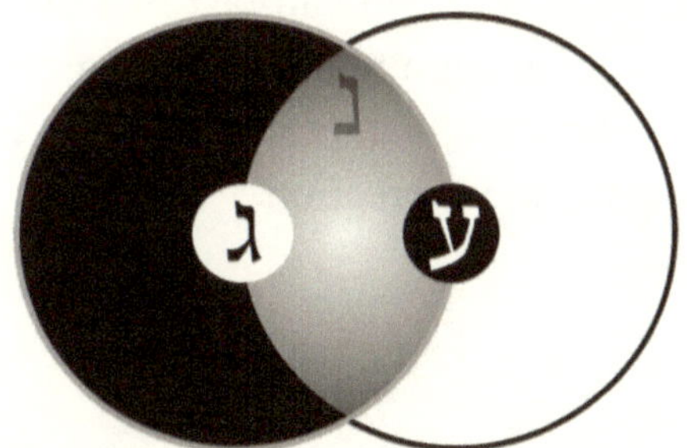

Imagine a language so sacred that it can reconcile opposites in just three letters...

Right: Hebrew letter Ayin (ע) → O in Roman Script
Top: Hebrew letter Nun (נ) → N in Roman Script
Left: Hebrew letter Gimel (ג) → C in Roman Script

Here is how S/Hebrew inscribes code "Success" (*Siddharta* in Sanskrit):

- **ONC**: counterclockwise from Ayin (ע), I read *Oneg* (עונג) for "pleasure."
- **NCO**: counterclockwise from Nun (נ), I read *Nogah* (נגע) for "to attain."

The Decoding: remembering and respecting *Shabbat* ("to rest") is to be in a flow state or "in the zone." It is to experience no creative blocks and no dry spells as I am an open channel. I am not acting: IT is acting me. Non-action is not inertia. It is the mental state of bliss in which I am so absorbed in the action that I am free of the action. It doesn't matter whether the task is ordinary or extraordinary. The profundity and the sacredness of the moment comes from my being totally consumed by its love. When I **attain** this state of total immersion in all I say and do, I know the *Mahamudra* – Sanskrit for the "Great Seal" imprinting my being with "Great **Pleasure**." I AM the AIM. I am not the body and I am not the doer either. I can wait → I can fast → I can think. When I no longer think that I am s/he who makes money (or who loses it), I can RUN my business without an "I" that will RUIN it. Knowing the art of love, I am now successful in my creation.

High Stakes

"Nothing is more important than your health – except for your money." *Ferengi 23rd Rule of Acquisition*

My perplexity brings me back to the same question: is there an "out there" out there? Sometimes – oftentimes – I don't understand the world especially in its relationship to stuff. Truth be told, I am possessed by my possessions. I think I have time before I'd put my affairs in order, that death is not for me. So, I don't prepare for the great Passover. I speak and act as if the body I'm in will last forever, as if the journey of this personality will not end. That explains how I would ignore the Buddha's Absolute Truth #3: there is an end to the dissatisfaction. Like it or not, my resistance will be assimilated. Put bluntly, I will die. And then I'll be in heaven, that is, in HAVIN'. When I have all I want because I have no choice but to want all I have, there is no more greed. Just grace, a gentle letting go, a sweet surrender – the knowing that I am not...

For now, what is my legacy? Did I put my affairs in order? Just how much cleanup will others have to do if I were to move today into my next mansion? How would it feel to have my hoarding be witnessed; all the things that don't fit, don't work, don't make me healthy or couldn't possibly give me pleasure? [taking a breath].

> **"When the green hills are covered with talking wires and the wolves no longer sing, what good will the money you paid for our land be then?"** *Chief Seattle*

Will I allow myself to know what the moral price of possessing is? If I own a thing the survival of people depends on, why withhold what they need and keep it all for myself? What is ownership? Under which law is it legal? How can I recognize that we are interdependently connected, and still look away when a beggar asks me for money? Right now, a price I may have to pay for my possessions is that someone would rob me and take it by force. Will I then hide behind the 8th Word and say: "thou shalt not have stolen from me?" Might that be why I buy guns and security systems? Because, at times, the price is too high! I wish I could be as honest in my commerce as a Ferengi who ADMITS that money is more valuable than health to him. But even that thought, I hide it as a secret. Is it then to wonder why I can't master commerce, let alone, healing?

How "TALK-SICK" is My Story?

Prepare to DIE: to access the online inquiry tool, click the BEE Map below or visit https://www.goldenxpr.com/tco_talk_sick/.

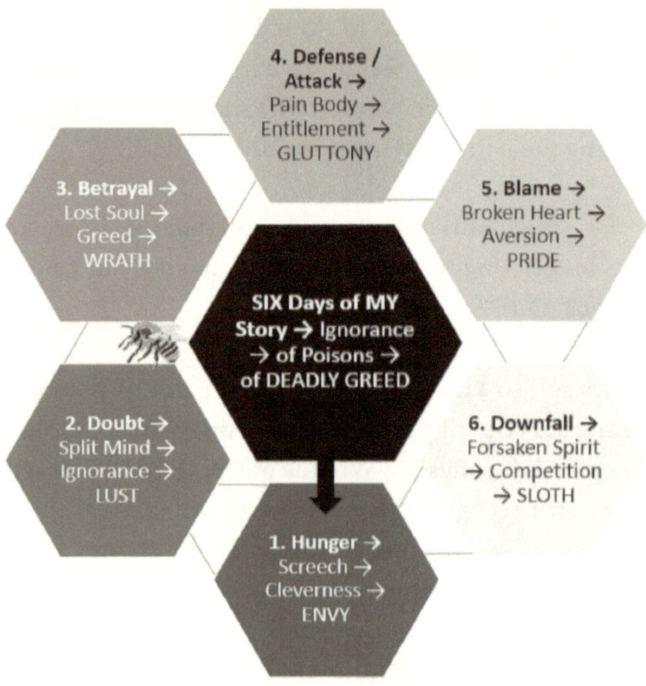

- **Step 1:** I fill in the blank: I want to know WHY I would choose to think I CAN'T _______ (e.g.; find a job, be patient, etc.).
- **Step 2:** I ask for truth and generate a number.
- **Step 3:** I find my number on the map to fill in the brackets: when I attach to my story of [**MY Story**], I ignore how my [**Ignorance**] takes over, and start being contaminated by the poison of [**Poisons**]. My giving and receiving are now out of balance, causing me to be led into the temptation of [**DEADLY GREED**].
- **Step 4:** what most surprised me in this process is _______.

PART III: MASTERING HEALING

Mastering healing takes me to Health – Health with a big "H." It is to appreciate reality as it is, love the neighbor, be true to my word... and not forget to brush my teeth. :-) THE Decision is made. I have no regrets over what I should have, could have done. None. I just see the perfection of the plan, right here and Now. That's Health, with a big "H."

It is simple. I didn't want to accept that, like it or not, I am free.

The realization that I exist in a state of absolute freedom and therefore, that oppression and bondage are of my own choosing, was too much for me. In a way, dis/ease was easier than waking up every day to being responsible for my creation, and feeling blessed beyond belief – in a mind and body superbly connected to the QKosmos by the fundamental truth of oneness...

You who are reading right now; you are what is left of me. Henceforth, why be poor and sick when you could choose Health?

Yod (י)	Vav (ו) / Heh (ה)	Heh (ה)
Heart	Mind / Body	Soul
Transmission	Creation / Manifestation	Formation
Individual Power	Symbolic Power	Collective Power
Communication	Healing / Health	Commerce

When the Vav Heh of YEWE echoes Hermes' mastery in healing…

Health (with a Big "H")

"Before you heal someone, ask him if he's willing to give up the things that made him sick." *Hippocrates – the Father of Medicine*

If the Power of choice is the greatest Power there is, how free am I to choose health and give up sickness? Velleity (or weak will) seems to be why I am poor and sick, if only in my mind. It appears that I cannot will my attention where I say I want it – on abundance rather than lack, on faith rather than doubt, on pleasure rather than pain. **Deep down, I secretly don't want to heal. I am bound to my illness – be it of the body, the soul or the mind (likely all three). There are advantages to not being well; a certain kind of attention that fuels my victim agenda.**

When my mind is at war, my body eventually gets ill out of being restless. Indeed, body follows mind, *until there is no more mind to follow.* My illness tells me who I am. To heal, I must hear the body's voice, which requires silencing the mind.

What does mind say? Does it linger on my good or on my evil inclination? When good, I persevere in doing what it takes to heal any situation. When evil, I quit on my goal and look for LOVE in all the wrong places – out there. I have now made me a victim, using my weakness as an excuse. Perseverance is the choice of justice, and I resent a justice whose laws I feel coerced to obey. Might the unrivaled pleasure of fulfilling my inner law threaten me so much that I would only succeed at failing?

To really succeed, I must stop trying. I must become so honest that I can rest in peace, as there are no "snake beliefs" to keep me awake at night; no guilt – just a graceful return to innocence. As I digest the poisonous fruit of the tree of the knowledge of opposites, I understand and awaken to what "God" means. I can sense that there is a field in between intuition and instinct, where to wait for my answers.

Fulfilled and free, I know that the LOVE that has no opposite is the Love that chooses Health with a big "H." I embrace my nemesis, love what is, forgive my debts and my debtors, brush my teeth, feel beautiful, and heal in a beautiful way. I am in awe of my body, and take splendid care of it. My energy is high and my body well-tuned. I feel so good and am so grateful for the gift of life that I continue developing my talents and offering them wholeheartedly to serve the greater whole. Reality check: while I am aware that this version of me exists, am I free enough to make that choice? Conversely, and if I can't quite give up what makes me sick, can I maintain peace until I am free to choose the high energy version of me?

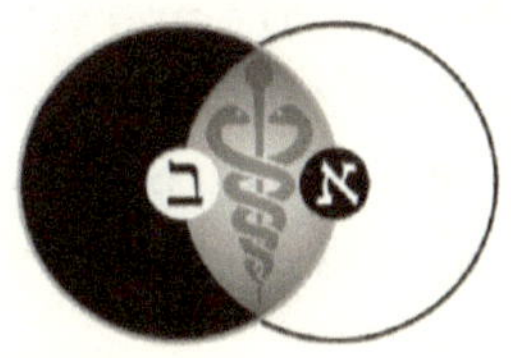

NO INSTINCT IS WHY I AM NOT HEALING: I am stuck in the same self-perpetuating trauma. My instinctual compass is so broken that I couldn't find the exit door if my life depended on it (and it does). My senseless behavior keeps on binding me to my illness. There are benefits to being unwell; a certain kind of attention that fuels my victiM's agenda and robs my Power.

Freedom of Choice

"The more decisions that you are forced to make alone, the more you are aware of your freedom to choose." *Thornton Wilder*

I remember this page from *TCO—Book 1*... Freedom in awareness, freedom in consciousness: if there's a difference, which is better? And this, right here, is a question asked by consciousness. As for awareness, it would resonate with Yogi Berra's humor and say: "when I come to a fork in the road, I take it."

Awareness doesn't care and only cares. Consciousness worries: shall I go right or left? Shall I stay or shall I go? Life is made up of an infinite number of choices, each choice being a creative act that determines which option I'll emPower and which consequence I will set up. The word "deciding" comes from Latin *de-caedere* for "to cut off." If each choice or edit I make collapses the quantum wave, small decisions, like what I will eat today, may be just as impactful as big decisions are, like getting married.

There is Power behind making a choice, which is why choosing terrifies me.

Will I be big enough to take responsibility for the results of my words and actions? What about a pandemic? What is my part in creating it? I don't know. That's why mortality is so beautiful: facing it centers me into what I really want and gives meaning to what I *choose* to empower. It clarifies that, if life is about making conscious choices, consciousness is the job I've signed up for, whether I'm conscious of it or not! So yes, life changes the moment I make the biggest cut of all, and deliberately decide to evolve consciousness.

Meanwhile, when avoiding the changes that deciding would generate, I mostly speak out of fear and lose connection with what I communicate.

If I can't make room for silence in which to hear my own counsel, it is because I am still needing to fail and to blame "you" for my failures. How honest are my yeses and my nos when I fear disappointing you? Conversely, how alone (or "all one") must I become to take full responsibility for the decisions I make?

Therefore, the question is not which is better; consciousness or awareness, but more how can I be so neutral that I'd do what it takes to heal any situation? That would be compassion – or being "with my pain." I imagine that I'd have to let go of needing a proof of outcome. I would then be able to make the unbiased choice that serves the good of all – the choice of Health.

Code Free Will - AB / BA

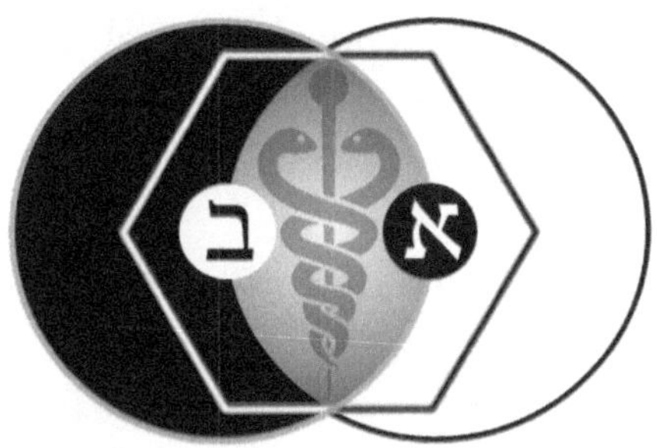

*Imagine a language so pure and so sacred it can
reconcile opposites in just two letters...*

Right: Hebrew letter Aleph (א) → A in Roman Script
Left: Hebrew letter (ב) Beth → B in Roman Script

Here is how S/Hebrew inscribes code "Free Will:"

- **AB:** in one direction, I read *Ab* (אב) for "father, alphabet."
- **BA:** in the other direction, I read *Bo* (בא) for "enter."

The Decoding: am I just a cog in the wheel or can I create my preferred reality? I admit it: I am powerless to be the change I wish to be. If my beliefs create my reality, why do I choose to believe what I believe? Why make Power my enemy? Why be uncertain or conflicted about pursuing one goal over another?

Life requires an even flow of attention. To supply it, I must know what I really want, why I really want it and whether what I really want serves the good of all. If I don't see me as a success in some areas of life (e.g.; I'm good at making money, but not at relationships), I may inquire on why I would want to fail if only in this one aspect of my life, and how failing this specific thing impacts the totality of my energy.

For me not to keep my attention on being successful, I must imagine that my gifts are or will be rejected. Gentle warning: if my attention cannot be inwardly sustained (that is, if I won't return to the **father** and **enter** the sanctuary of my heart), my **ego** will turn into a tyrant, keeping me asleep in the DREaM and failing **me miserably**:

- **The split mind of the prostitutE:** I seek shortcuts to reach my goal and alter procedure. I fail.
- **The lost soul of the saboteuR:** I criticize the job, resent others' success, and give up. I fail.
- **The pain body of the victiM:** I hide behind the excuse of a disability or an illness. I fail.
- **The broken heart of the chilD:** I need constant supervision and repeated instructions. I still fail.

For my angel to freely rise and fall IN-LOVE, I must lighten up and not make it about me. If I fall, I simply get up and try again. To help me, I read the **alphabet**. This "reading" involves staying open as pure choice-less awareness (the **Alpha** of III-Opening) to what consciousness will decide (the **Beth** of 222-Separating). I know that I am free to choose, even when in bondage, but only if I am not attached to an outcome. My decision to create anything – an idea, a service, a product – begins as a pure act of faith. I believe because I have no doubt. I have no doubt because I have no mind. I have no mind because I don't create. IT creates. IT uses me to change (my) creation. I'm just a willing and deliberate participant.

A creative block tells me that I'm unwilling to be responsible for my creation. Understanding the block makes room for peace. I can now be response-able and do what it takes to emPower the Now. This is the feel of free will.

In his book *On Repentance*, Rabbi Soloveitchik wrote about Adam, just as he was caught for his transgression. Adam only had one word to say: *Aval* (אבל) for "indeed." *Indeed*, I made an error. *Aval* (ABL) merges two codes – Code Free Will AB/BA and Code Simplicity BL/LB (see *Understanding Knowledge*). The merging enables the possibility to take full responsibility for what I communicate, consciously or not. The more I do, the more I am able to see that my self-defeating pattern turns into a blessing. There is no more curse: just an ability to include and transcend, which sets my will free.

Indeed, WHY?

"Everything you'll ever need to know is within you; the secrets of the universe are imprinted on the cells of your body." *Dan Millman*

It resonates with me that I would have the answers to my questions. My heart tells me what to do, moment to moment. It is I who is not willing to follow. I am confused as to the meaning of "free will," using it to devolve me. WHY?

Heart	Mind / Body	Soul
Atziluth	*Beriah / Assiyah*	*Yetzirah*
Transmission	Creation / Manifestation	Formation

The order of creation is law: body follows mind. When the mind-body connection is unobstructed, the worlds of creation and manifestation (*Beriah and Assiyah*) are freely communicating. This experience is what Jesus spoke: "when you pray for something, believe that you've received it." The QKabbalah of my receptor cells is instantaneous, for good or bad. When I am able to deliberately choose peace, I can know that what I put into form in my *Yetzirah* can only be "de-light-full."

Understand → Choose Peace → emPower the Now.

To understand my ambivalence about choosing Health in all my relations, I must bring light on the shadows of my reluctance. This is what reluctant prophet Jonah did when he went into the belly of the whale. This involves reading the signs and symbols of the dream, whether I am in the dreaming state or in the waking state while in a DREaM. The symbols are congruent across worlds and states. As the mediating agent of the Power of Three, they are here to promote the big "H" of Health.

When There Is No More Mind to Follow...

"Doctors won't make you healthy. Nutritionists won't make you slim. Teachers won't make you smart. Gurus won't make you calm. Mentors won't make you rich. Trainers won't make you fit. Ultimately, you have to take responsibility. Save yourself." *Naval Ravikant, CEO of AngelList*

The next page synthesizes the mastery of healing. Its BEE map inquires on sickness as the mostly unconscious choice to say "no" to health. Surely, resisting is how I drain my energy. For example, the split mind says "no to gratitude" as it has so much doubt that it can't imagine receiving a healing. Wellness is not in its purview.

These **SIX "days" of sickness** now lead me to inquire on what evil I summon by understanding the meaning of the SIX essential **Devils' Names.** From there, I will investigate my creation of victimhood and of immunity, victimhood and immunity being each other's complement. The fractal of **victimhood** infers the curse inflicted by the SIX Names of "the Devil." Once I understand these Devils of mine, I can feel the curse that they each spell out, e.g.; Belial signifies the "low self-esteem" leading me to suffer from chronic abuse.

Lastly, the fractal of **divine immunity** organizes the SIX core qualities of "God" which have the Power to break the curse. They also resolve the conflicts I project on "God," which are really my conflicts:

- How can "God" be at once just and omnipotent?
- How can "God" be at once just and merciful?
- How can "God" be at once impassible and merciful?

When owning that these are my conflicts and holding the tension between these opposite parts, I become internally referenced and stop believing that you can fulfill me or hurt me. Also, I am not asking you to love me or to know that you do. I am LOVE, and that is enough.

Creating Health

Prepare to DIE: to access the online inquiry tool, click the BEE Map below or visit https://www.goldenxpr.com/tco_creating_health/.

- **Step 1:** I fill in the blank: I want to know WHY I would choose to think I CAN'T ______ (e.g.; find a job, be patient, etc.).
- **Step 2:** I ask for truth and generate a number.
- **Step 3:** I find my number on the map to fill in the brackets: when I am fixated in a mode of [**Sickness**], I am cursed by [**the Devil**] whose calling is to victimize me by way of [**Victimhood**], and thus compromise my immune system by depriving me of [**DIVINE IMMUNITY**].
- **Step 4:** what most surprised me in this process is ________.

Mastering Healing into Health

"Healing is a matter of time, but it is sometimes also a matter of opportunity." *Hippocrates*

I must now push the pause button. Indeed, moving from healing into Health is a huge goal, as it is no less than waking up from the DREaM of karma, and entering "the Promised Land" of enlightenment.

For the chilD in me to take full responsibility for my experience and grow up into a Leader, I need the spacetime of another book, namely *TCO—Book 3*. For now, I just wish to unfold the image that will be on the cover. This image contains two codes. The first code (**Code Energy**) takes me into the darkest night of the DREaM. The second code (**Code Health**) gives the vision of what is involved in mastering healing into Health. This is the health with a big "H" that vibrates as the frequency of enough, when "in GOOD, I trust." The next chapter – *Ending the Fight* – will give more information on the book's contents.

Code Energy begins the awakening process with the saboteuR who is given an opportunity to drop the shame body. **Code Health** ends my awakening as the prostitutE turns to the East of Eden where the transformation completes.

Having dared to enter the big Nothing, I return as the beautiful mind of an Engineer. There is no more "I" – and certainly, no evil "eye" – to observe lack. The SCARED prostitute reorganizes as SACRED prostitute. All bondage to Mammon and to any level of materialism is gone. The space it left behind is now filled by a radiating Health – Health with a big "H."

Code Energy – AWR / OWR

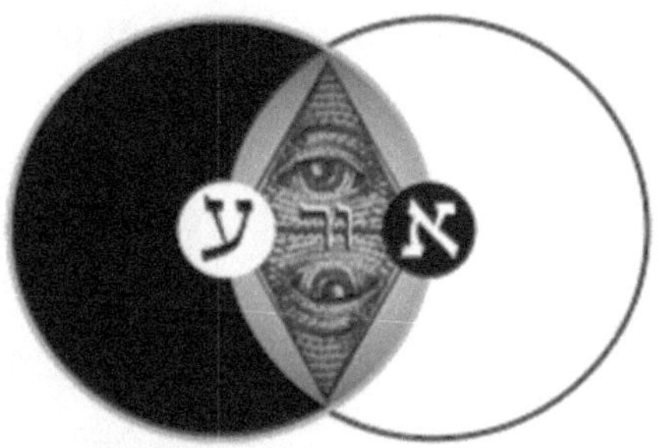

Imagine a language so pure and so sacred that it can reconcile opposites in just four letters…

Right: Hebrew letter Aleph (א) → A in Roman Script
Middle-right: Hebrew letter Vav (ו) → F, U, V, W in Roman Script
Middle-left: Hebrew letter Resh (ר) → R in Roman Script
Left: Hebrew letter Ayin (ע) → O in Roman Script

Here is how S/Hebrew inscribes code "Energy" in 4 letters, 3 words:

- **AWR:** right to middle-left, I read *Aur* (אור) for "light."
- **WRO:** middle-right to left, I read *V'Rah* (ורע) for "and evil."
- **ORW:** left to middle-right to middle-left, I read *Ohr* (עור) for "skin."

The Decoding: the two words above – *Aur* and *Ohr* – are pronounced in the exact same manner. As for the connection, here is the Adam's story, which is also my story. First in *Genesis 1:3*, *Elohim* says "let there be **light!**" I hear that, when I take myself so "lightly" that I can fly. Then comes YEWE *Elohim's* test which I flunk, resulting in PaRaDiSe lost. Just prior to expelling me, this LOVE God makes for me "and my woman garments of skins, and clothed us." The word *Labash* for "to clothe" expands the word *Bush* for "shame," a garment so heavy that it prevents me from flying. The work of transformation does involve a change of "clothing," as my snake must shed a **skin** or two before becoming messianic. Dropping the "shame body" reveals the "light body," *Bigdei Aur* in Hebrew. This body has other names – the diamond body, the rainbow body, the resurrection body, the body of bliss. The secret to maintaining its state of enLIGHTenment is to come into the full knowledge of good **and**, especially, **evil,** as it is the "rib" that I project out and long for. Code Health restores this rib as the sentience of my female side. I receive it when I accept the invitation to feel every-thing and resist "nothing."

Code Health - OYN / AYN

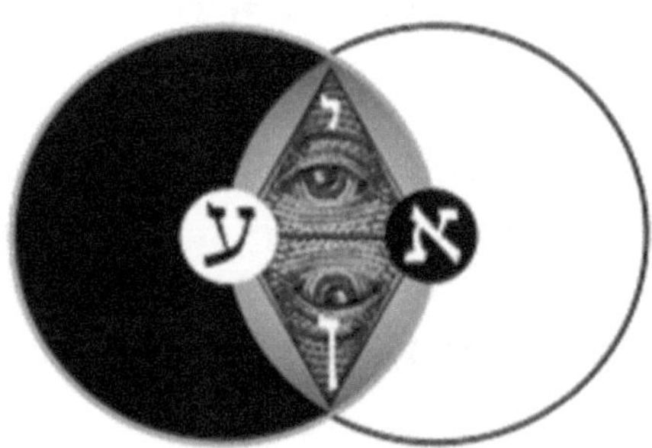

Imagine a language so pure and so sacred that it can
reconcile opposites in just four letters...

Here is how S/Hebrew inscribes code "Health" in 4 letters, 2 words:

- **OYN:** left to top to bottom, I read *Ayin* (עין) for "eye."
- **AYN:** right to top to bottom, I read *Ain* (אין) for "nothing."

The Decoding: the two words above – *Ayin* and *Ain* – are pronounced in the exact same manner. Also, the same partnering of signs Aleph (A) and Ayin (O) that was present in Code Energy is now in Code Health. *Ayin* (with a sign Ayin) is the word for **"eye."** The first time that it appears is in *Genesis 3:5*: "For God knows that when you eat of it, your eyes will be opened, and you will be like God, knowing good and evil." The word is fittingly used in its plural form, since it is the eyes of duality (pl.) that open as I commit a transgression. Conversely, the singular eye that was opened (the third eye) now closes and goes into nothingness. For it to open again, I will have to assimilate the personality that only serves my private agendas – the ego that is up to "no good," and sees evil, speaks evil and hears evil. "Assimilating" means to reduce to **nothing**. What S/Hebrew says via the words *Ayin* and *Ain*, English transmits as "eye-no-sense." Surely, when I am innocent, I stop seeing the proof that I am not enough. My quest for love, approval and recognition does not own me as it once did. "I" change the way "eye" looks at things and what I look at changes. Returning to innocence is easy. I just need to welcome anonymity and forget about making a name for myself. The eye of providence now shines on me again. I am able to see the good in the bad. This is no less than the gift of vision. The ability to envision health precedes the formation of health. This explains how it is my faith that makes me well, for it is only the eye of doubt that keeps my attention focused on being unwell and, thereby, continue to create disease. All together now, drop the body of shame, shed a skin, and live your light!

I am now ready to move into the conclusion and end the fight.

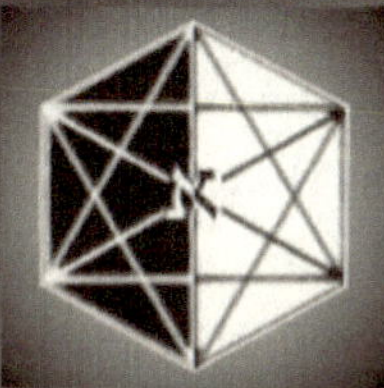

SIX

Ending the Fight

'And Jacob named the place Peniel, for he said, "I have seen God face to face, yet my life has been spared."' *Genesis 32:31*

Yes, it is at Peniel that Jacob stopped the fight and became ISRAEL/REAL. The place he called *Peniel* ("face of God"), I call "Pineal." The pineal gland is commonly dubbed the "third eye" not only because of its location deep in the core of the brain, but also and foremost due to its connection to the light. Since it serves as a bridge between the physical and spiritual worlds, many mystical traditions view the pineal gland as the seat of enlightenment.

I live in an extraordinary time, when the religious traditions are dissolving to reveal their mystical teachings – teachings that are universal and therefore, sacred. They are the bone marrow and absolute truths across traditions. Am I ready to let their essence touch my soul and pour into my energy system for me to harness my creativity? If so, this section will tell me about how the creation of evil follows the SIX "days" of the creation of good. Yep, good and evil are my creation! It will also give me information on the PaRaDiSe Mystery School where to unlearn the false Self and become REAL.

Being REAL

"Attachment is the great fabricator of illusions; reality can be obtained only by someone who is detached." *Simone Weil*

To succeed in my creation, I must stop arguing with reality. When I do, the mask drops; the fakeness dissolves. It is palpable. I am now in my heart, experiencing a realness that shows in my body language. If I lied before, it was only because I wanted something I didn't believe I could get. And now, I'm ready to tell the truth, and see that my personal reality is exactly the reality I want!

How did I get "there" – in a place where I am One with everything? Simple! I felt the grasping – the insatiable and predatory desire for Power. Yep, there is a greed monster in me. I can either feed it by attaching to desires that only benefit the little self, or starve it by focusing on desires that serve the common good. If I allow it to grow, it will soon turn to the next capital sin. Indeed, would I be prey to wrath, pride, envy, sloth, lust or gluttony if I were detached?

These "sins" are the places where I am as Jacob, divorced from reality and fighting "God." I start feeling like a loser; someone who opened the gates of hell and can't find a way back to heaven. To help me, there is an ancient Kabbalistic teaching meant to connect the seven infernal spheres to the guidance of seven patriarchs. XPR links these seven spheres to the seven sins, to give me an "ISRAEL/REAL" way to make my exodus from Ego-Egypt. I saw this image in *Chapter 4, Understanding Knowledge*. This time, however, I added the patriarchs' names. I can now see how, when in 7-greed, Jacob's heart closes (sphere #7). However, when real as Israel, his heart opens to grace.

Seven Guardians

"I am good, but not an angel. I do sin, but I am not the devil. I am just a small girl in a big world trying to find someone to love."
Marilyn Monroe

5-Pride | 6-Sloth	7-Greed | 2-Lust | 4-Gluttony	3-Wrath | 1-Envy
Isaac | Aaron	Jacob | Joseph | David	Abraham | Moses
Humility | Diligence	Grace | Containm. | Temperance	Patience | Kindness

——— Throat
——— Heart
——— Navel
——— Sex
——— Root

The seven patriarchs are no angels. But they can make and end up making a different choice. As the song goes, "there's always time to change the road you're on." Jacob's story – the embezzler, the cheater, the liar, the con-artist – guides me on the path to realness. Such is the nature of opposites. Similarly, Moses teaches me how to overcome envy by way of kindness, Joseph, how to overcome lust by way of containment, Abraham, how to overcome wrath by way of patience, David, how to overcome gluttony by way of temperance, Isaac, how to overcome pride by way of humility, and finally (sphere #6), Aaron, how to overcome sloth by way of diligence. Jacob's story is clear. Unfolding the different stories of how the remaining patriarchs came to the other side is beyond the scope of this chapter.

When I overcome my dark side, I participate in the creation of good. When I don't, I allow the creation of evil to flourish. These opposite ways to create will be what I next explore, as viewed by *Elohim*, the "Created-SIX" God who ordered creation to be happening in SIX "days" or SIX stages. I still must return to the state before the beginning, that is, before the desire to be somebody moves me to come out of nothingness.

Before the Beginning...

"And the end and the beginning where always there, before the beginning and after the end. "*T. S. Eliot*

0/1	Before the BIG Bang B-ginning	Male	Neutral	Female
		Beth (B)	Aleph (A)	Beth (B)
		Order/Spirit	Intention	Chaos/Matter
		The Heaven	Reality / God Created-SIX	The Earth

0/1: Before the BIG Bang B-ginning

Before the BIG Bang B-Ginning, there was the *Ain Soph* or the "infinite" empty-fullness. Therein was everything and nothing. In that non-vacuum space, I wasn't a man, a woman or even binary. I just was... and wasn't! Nothing personal...

Aleph and Beth were there, although they were yet to know their purpose. I already shared how, when S/Hebrew was still embryonic, Sovereign 0/1 contemplated how to use its alphabet to create the world. I am touched by how the letters presented themselves in reverse order, one after the other, pleading to be placed first in the creation of the world. The beginning was in the end, as last letter Tav advanced in front, only to be rejected. While Tav was the end letter of *emeT* "truth," it also was the end letter of *maveT* "death," and death could not take part in creation. Including Tav, twenty letters were turned down before Beth (the 21st letter before Aleph) was chosen to create the world. Indeed, Beth started the word *B'rakhah* for "blessing," and blessing the world was the intention that had "me" come out of nothingness.

However, creating calls for separation, and I am yet to realize the emotional and cognitive implications of being caught by dualism. Eventually, chaos reforms itself around me in the form of a disorder; eating disorder, speaking disorder, sexing and/or spending disorder; you name it! These were just a few on a list of many... Eventually, I will come to see that my sanity (and any success in my creation) demands a turnaround. Just like the letters, I will then reverse my way in order to return to innocence.

Whether I like it or not, I have now signed up to a *Tiqqun* program as a "rectification, repair, amendment" by which to produce a new order – a reordering of my priorities. As for the chaos of knowledge, it took me a long time to hear the "Created-SIX" as the alternate translation of "in the beginning." When I did, I realized I had the unifying equation I was looking for – to reveal the order in the chaos I inhabited.

> "To unleash my creativity (and/or the power to decide), I must be wild enough to surrender to a lawless disorder, and straight enough to maintain an impeccable organization. Without *Olam HaTohu* ("the world of chaos"), there would be no need for *Olam HaTiqqun* ("the world of order"), and vice versa." Excerpt from *TCO—Book 1*

Quick Reminder - the Ari's teachings

"There was spoilage for the sake of fixing, and destruction for the sake of rebuilding." *Rabbi Isaac Luria*

Below is the Lurianic tree of life of contemporary Kabbalah, superimposed over TCO's fish. It pictures the 10 spheres moving as the mind of the *Adam Qadmon* ("primary Adam") – the Self.

The Ari saw how the *Ain Soph* (the "infinite") first had to **withdraw** in order for this tree-mind to exist. The new **boundaries** soon led to the opposition of chaos and order, a duality at root of the perennial battle of good and evil. Ideally, the light of the Word (i.e.; the intuitive hit I'm given) zigzags down through the 10 spheres from the crown (#1) to the root (#10), where my

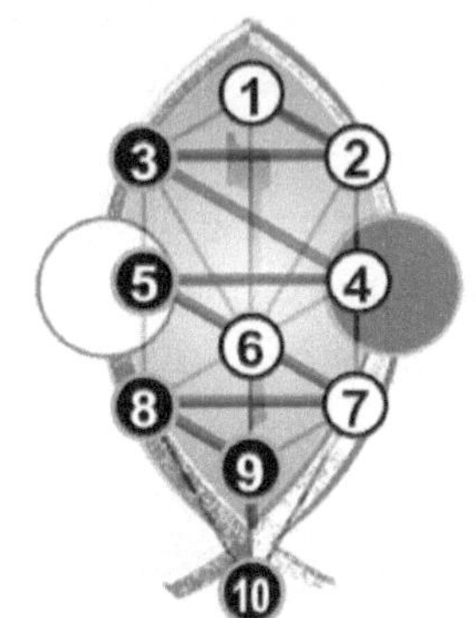

heart's desire is made manifest. However, an accident happened as the sphere of Power (#5) exploded, taking down with "her" the six lower spheres, and preventing me from being successful in my creation. This is what the Luria calls "the **shattering of the vessels**" (*Shevirat Hakelim*).

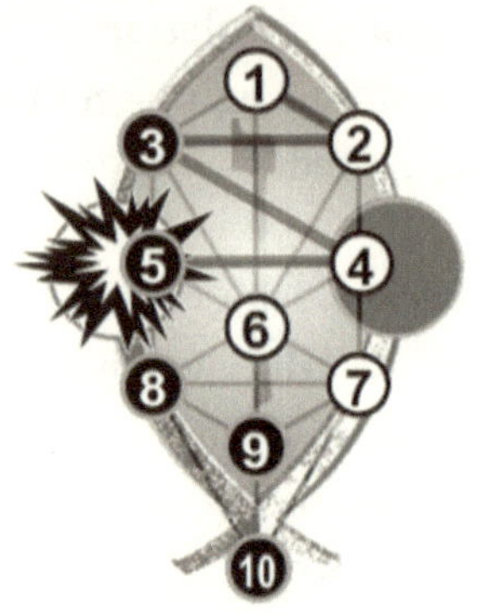

The higher spheres were untouched, because they were purified by their nearness to the *Ain Soph*, and, as such, able to bear the light. The lower spheres, however, were destroyed. The sparks of the broken vessels were eventually ingested by chaotic, excessive, and ghostly "shells" (*the Q'lippoth*). To ensure that the light would reach its destination, the numbered spheres were solidified into "figures" or "**faces**" (the *Partzuphim*), among which are the Mother, the Father, the Son and the Bride. The conflict between opposites could now only be resolved through the advent of universal redemption (the *Tiqqun*), a "**correction**" which humans can either hinder or expedite through their own actions.

I am now evolving in the domain of theurgy. Theurgy is how to master the operation of the moon and come into wisdom. If it precedes alchemy, it is only because the suffering caused by my lunacy will cause me to inquire on my choices. Indeed, I must follow my folly until it delivers me to making sound judgment calls. Alchemy is its natural complement. Alchemy is how to master the operation of the sun and come into Power. After persevering in showing up to the task at hand, I CAN only be victorious. I am now at the end of dissatisfaction, filled with compassion, knowing wholesome Power. *TCO—Book 3* reconciles mother theurgy and father alchemy via their astrology child, astrology being the operation of the stars by which to know that it's not about me (nothing personal!).

Resulting - the SIXth day of Theurgy

"Our lack of confidence is not the result of difficulty. The difficulty comes from our lack of confidence." *Seneca, 4 AD-65 AD, Roman philosopher*

Indeed, which comes first – the lack of confidence or the difficulty; the chicken or the egg? The theurgy of the Ari moves in FIVE stages – from **withdrawing** to **causing** to **shattering** to **linking** to **correcting**. When there is a cause, there must be an effect. Thus, **resulting** ought to be the SIXth day. *Elohim* was, after all, "Created-SIX." This SIXth day may be the last stage of the creation of theurgy. It may also be its first stage.

Causing is a fundamental answer to the question "why?" – "why is there evil in the world?" To the point, why is there evil in *my* world? However, before I can establish a causal relationship, I must show that I have some type of relationship (**linking**), and if I must link different objects, these objects must first be ruptured (**shattering**). **Resulting** is proposed by TCO as the sixth and/or first stage of the creative process: the last should be the first. :-) Retrocausality, or backwards causation, is a concept of cause and effect in which an effect precedes its cause in time, and so a later event affects an earlier one. In quantum physics, the distinction between cause and effect is not made at the most fundamental level and so time-symmetric systems can be viewed as causal or retrocausal. Here is what it may mean in terms of the operation of the moon, which invites me to follow my folly until it leads me to wisdom...

Resulting: once upon a time, I felt vulnerable and chose to create an entity to defend me from the chaos. To do so, I had to enter the realm of the delirious. This realm is called the *Tohu VaBohu* in the Bible (*Genesis 1:2*). How naïve of me: I really thought that I could stop anytime! I didn't know that my creation (which seemed like a good idea at the time) would eventually take control of me. Called *Q'lippoth* ("shells"), these chaotic, excessive, addictive and ghostly formations ravenously ingest the sparks of the broken vessels (the fragmented parts of me). Moved by the dark force, they live in shame and can never have enough. They had to be here before the beginning, when the *Ain Soph* withdrew itself to make room for me as an independent cause. Only then could I create my reality and "see that it was good..."

The Creation of Good by way of the good seed of life and the SIX white "days" of my creation centered around a sane mouth chakra (opaque white sphere).

How could I know that I would shift out of being primary Adam, emPowered to create what I see as "good," to become secondary Adam, feeling powerless to succeed in my creation? How could I know that I came to Earth to remember the knowledge of opposites and feel how contrary forces such as dark-light, negative-positive, and/or evil-good are actually complementary, interconnected, and interdependent in the natural world, and how they give rise to each other as they interrelate to one another?

Nope, I "had to" become insane – a lunatic who firmly believed that what was bad for me was actually good for me, and vice-versa, that what was good for me was actually bad. This is how the image above has two seeds of life – one white and one black; one white for the creation of good and one black for the inevitable creation of evil, one centered on the mouth chakra, one centered on the sex chakra. But I'm getting ahead of myself... For now, I wish to focus on the creation of good, when I say "let there be whatever, and see that there was whatever. Again, the ability to own that the reality I see is my creation ends all dissatisfaction. There's no point in double-guessing myself: I must have wanted to see "that," if only unconsciously.

The Creation of Good

"There is no limit to the amount of good a person can do if they don't care who gets the credit." *Anonymous*

1	2	3	4	5
Genesis 1	"Day" 1	The Light of Day	Creation of Observation	The Darkness of Night
	"Day" 2	The Waters of Above	Creation of Boundaries	The Waters of Below
	"Day" 3	Earth as Order	Creation of Divergence	Ocean as Chaos
	"Day" 4	The Greater Sun	Creation of Illumination	The Lesser Moon
	"Day" 5	The Birds	Creation of Blessing	The Fish
	"Day" 6	Livestock	Creation of Power	Creepy Crawlers
Gen. 2	"Day" 7	Rest	Creation of Good	Work

The five columns above organize the creation of good as follows:

- **Column 1:** the chapters of Genesis where the creation occurs.
- **Column 2:** the six days of creation and the 7th day of rest.
- **Column 3:** the white and positive polarity (yang/male/good) of what was seen and/or created on a given day.
- **Column 4:** the grey and neutral polarity (yin yang, sexual knowledge, good-evil) of what was seen and/or created on a given day.
- **Column 5:** the black and negative polarity (yin/female/evil) of what was seen and/or created on a given day.

Taking the example of **"Day" 1, the Light of Day** and **the Darkness of Night** comes directly from *Genesis 1:3-5:* 'And *Elohim* said, "Let there be light," and there was light. *Elohim* saw that the light was good, and he separated the light from the darkness. *Elohim* called the light "day," and the darkness he called "night." And there was evening, and there was morning—the first day.'

When reading the Hebrew version, I realize that the translator who rendered "the first day" made an error. *Yom Echad* means "day one," and not "the first day." There's a difference between a cardinal number (e.g.; one) and an ordinal number (e.g.; first). A cardinal number tells me how many there is of something; they show a quantity. An ordinal number tells me the order of how things are set; they show the position or the rank of something. This has a paramount importance, especially as the alternate translation of the first word of *Genesis, Chapter 1* is "Created-SIX."

To hint to the validity of translating the first word of the first chapter of the Torah as "created-SIX," I am given the first five days of creation as cardinal numbers: day one, day two, day three, day four, day five. Whereas I would expect to read "day six," I read *Yom Hashishi* for "the SIXth day." The Torah is telling me: "wink, wink! Pay attention, here... There's something going on with this perfect number 6. Moreover, whereas *Barashit* for "created-SIX" is the first word of *Chapter 1*, *Hashishi* for "the SIXth" is the last word of the same chapter. If that was not enough of a clue, it is only in *Chapter 2* that there is talk of the Shabbat as the 7th day. Here it is, for me to SEE:

- The first word of *Chapter 1* is *Barashit* for "created-SIX."
- The last word of *Chapter 1* is *Hashishi* for "the SIXth."
- The length of *Chapter 1* unfolds the SIX "days" of creation.

And yes, thus far I have lacked the lucidity of sight, which may be how I keep on asking "why evil?" It may just be for me to actually SEE that it was good. This is how the place in the middle of Day One – in between the good light and the evil darkness – is given to the **Creation of Observation.**

The Unfurnished "I"

"Not "Revelation" – tis – that waits / But our unfurnished eyes."
Emily Dickinson.

The Light of Day	Creation of Observation	The Darkness of Night

When I enter the place "in-between," I live without a why (see Code Understanding, in *Understanding Knowledge*). I am free to place my attention on something else besides a pain story which is on auto-repeat. Experiments in quantum physics have shown that what is being observed in nature depends on choices made by the observer. If "eye" chooses – consciously or not – to observe lack rather than plenty, it is because "I" am yet to take full ownership of my creating misery and keeping it in place by judging it as "bad." My training in resisting the "bad" prevents me from hearing Carl Jung's wisdom: "what you resist persists." My eyes are not ἁπλοῦς (*ap-loose*) Greek for "simple" enough to understand *Matthew 6:22:* "The eye is the lamp of the body. If your eyes are ἁπλοῦς, your whole body will be full of light."

Indeed, why observe myself as poor and sick, when I could see Health?

My **creation of observation** will eventually lead me to open the "unfurnished eye" – the third eye in between right and left – the eye that sees Health. Enlightenment is seeing black and white, a dead cat and an alive cat, at the exact same time. It is speaking in the language of paradox and communicating with "God." When I accept that there is nothing out there, and that any judgment that I make is self-judgment, what I dare reading in the "text" of life is the consciousness that I occupy – for "good" or "bad."

It makes me smile to imagine that "God" is no longer my nemesis. I am now ISRAEL REAL, having and holding my spouse "reality," from this day forward, for better for worse, for richer, for poorer, in sickness and in health, to love and cherish always.

I am reminded of Nemesis – the Greek goddess who enacts retribution against those who succumb to hubris or arrogance before the gods, as Narcissus did. Narcissus' name – his calling – was to be "asleep, numb." He could not feel that how his pride in his looks led him to disdain those who loved him. He died as he could not realize he was merely looking at an image – not the real thing. Whether I enter the exploration of consciousness via Greek mythology or the Bible, I must die to my sins before the body dies. That's the ideal. That's also enlightenment, when I am no longer so burdened by a mass of furniture that prevents me from seeing the beauty of what is.

The Simplicity of Creating Goodness

"Use what talent you possess: the woods would be very silent if no birds sang except those that sang best." *Henry van Dyke*

Some days are "simple" enough such as:

- **Day 2** – the **creation of boundaries**, when the waters were split between the pairs of above and the pairs of below, for me to be congruent in the decisions I make.
- **Day 4** – the **creation of illumination**, when the sun, the moon and the stars were set as guiding principles.
- **Day 5** – the **creation of abundance**, when the fish and the fowl were blessed to be fruitful and multiply.

However, **day 3** which sees the **creation of divergence** and **day SIX** which sees the **creation of Power** surprise me. How can they be seen as "good?"

Earth as Order	Creation of Divergence	Ocean as Chaos

A divergence occurred on day three (day "TREE?") after "God" ordered fruit trees with fruits bearing seeds and received trees with fruit bearing seeds. The story of this mishap entirely repositions the idea of the original sin, a concept developed in the writings of St. Augustine. The author attributes the tendency to sin to the genes you and I inherited from Adam in consequence of the Fall. St. Augustine must not have noticed that the first violation of "God's" order was perpetrated by the trees, and most probably, by the tree of the knowledge of good and evil – a tree that would not be silenced (see *TCO—Book 1, Chapter 4, Oh, no! Why the Bible?*). Would I better use my talents if, instead of dying to my "sins," I would die to my perception of "sin?" In other words, is my insane behavior only here because I resist it and judge it to be bad? What if I didn't contract when a divergence occurs, and instead just relaxed into the goodness of it?

Livestock	Creation of Power	Creepy Crawlers

The yin part of Day five's creation are the **creepy crawlers.** How can these be good? Among helpful behaviors, bugs act as sanitation experts, cleaning up waste so that the environment wouldn't become overrun with dung. The yang part is the **livestock** whose goodness is easier to see and to relate to. In the middle grey area is the Adam, who was created male and female, in the image of "God," and, as such, emPowered. It is only in *Genesis 2* that a different brand of Adam showed up – the kind that believed he was a man. Being identified to the thought "I am the body" (or that which is dying), he could only get lonely and look for Love out there – in the "wrong" places.

Surely, Power is sexual. When I think that I am not enough and that I need someone to complete me, I either play a game of dominance or submission. Either way, I misuse Power and get burned. However, when I know myself to be "PAIRfect" (as in male and female), my **creation of Power** is wholesome.

Genesis 2:1-3 – the Shabbat

"The Sabbath is not for the sake of the weekdays; the weekdays are for the sake of Sabbath. It is not an interlude but the climax of living." *Abraham Joshua Heschel*

The Shabbat is when I come to THE END – when I rest while working. I shift from human doing to human being. Knowing who I am, I witness the work of creation being done *through* me and not *by* me or even *to* me. This is also called "being in the zone," a succession of resisting (which is work) and resting. Work and rest – resist and rest.

Therein is the secret of building muscles, physically or metaphysically. Even the word "RESIST" says it, whose letters also spell "REST IS." So how can "God" complete his work and rest from his work at the same time? The answer is made visible by the geometry of the Seed of Life, demonstrating that "God" is indeed a geometer.

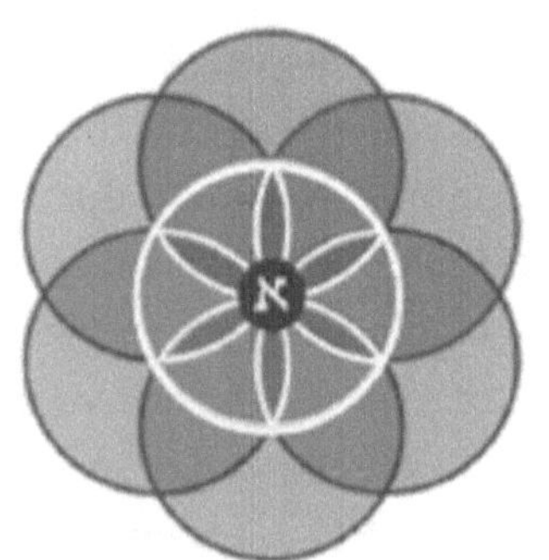

At the exact moment when the 6th circle is formed, the 7th circle that was here before any creating appears as the final stage of creation. There is no action involved and yet there is a new circle created. This state of mind is *Shabbat* "rest," a S/Hebrew word coming from the Sumerian *Sabattu* for "heat-rest." *Sabattu* is the pause taken by the Moon when full, since, at that moment, it is neither increasing nor decreasing. When I realize I need do nothing since creation happens through me and not by me, I make love; not war and my creativity is pure beauty!

"And on the seventh day God completed the work that he had done, and he rested on the 7th day from all the work that he had done." *Genesis 2:2*

I find it super interesting that the Shabbat would not be part of *Genesis 1*. The 7th "day" only occurs in *Genesis 2*, as if to prepare me for the upcoming transition – when the letters rewrite destiny by inverting their flow. Thus far, the letters moved in reverse order – from Tav to Beth to Aleph in three stages:

1. T: from Tav to Beth, they begged to take part in creating the world.
2. B: once in Beth, they knew the blessing to create.
3. A: as Aleph, they stayed the heck out of creation.

Creation is dicey as it dances with opposites, placing in front of me either the curse or the blessing. Now the letters ABT of my Alpha-BeT turn around to go on a free fall To Be Announced as "yet to be free." Yep, I fear falling, as I equate falling with failing. My vision is also inverted: what I think is up is actually down, and vice-versa (see tree below). Not only did I lose PaRaDiSe, but I also lost the blissful knowledge of good and evil and, with it, any real sense of my mouth chakra.

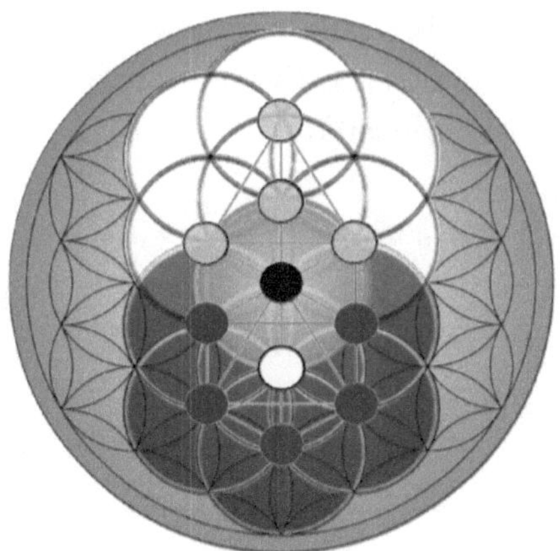

The Creation of Evil by way of the evil seed of life as SIX black stages of my creation centered around an inverted mouth chakra (white sphere) dominated by the sex chakra.

The Creation of Evil

"There is no limit to the amount of evil a person can do if they care who gets the credit." *Anonymous*

1	2	3	4	5
	Stage 8	Earth	Creation of Materialism	Heaven
	Stage 9	The Adamah	Creation of Misery	The Adam
Genesis 2:4 to Genesis 3:21	Stage 10	The Woman	Creation of Yearning	The Adam w/o Heh
	Stage 11	The Woman	Creation of Deception	The Snake
	Stage 12	The Woman	Creation of Violation	The Adam
	Stage 13	Eve	Creation of Fear	Adam
Gen. 3	Stage 14	Eve vs. the Snake	Creation of Evil	Adam vs. the Adamah

The five columns above organize the creation of evil as follows:

- **Column 1**: the chapters of Genesis where the creation occurs.
- **Column 2**: the six stages of creation after the Shabbat "rest."
- **Column 3**: the black and negative polarity (yin/female/evil) of what was created on a given day.
- **Column 4**: the grey and neutral polarity (yin yang, sexual knowledge, good-evil) of what was created on a given day.
- **Column 5**: the white and positive polarity (yang/male/good) of what was created on a given day.

The creation of evil starts with a barely noticeable inversion as "the heaven and the earth" flip into "earth and heaven," in *Genesis 2:4:* "These are the generations of the heaven and of the earth when they were created, in the day that the LORD God made **earth** and **heaven**." The generations of the heaven and the earth refer to the SIX days when "God" saw the goodness of a creation. Prior to that moment, *Genesis 2:1-3* spoke of the Shabbat, when "God" rested while working. This "God" was *Elohim.* A shift happens in the next verse (*Genesis 2:4*), when "God" becomes "the LORD God" or YEWE *Elohim.* This "God" Name is the Power of history (and even "HIStory"), a name spinning *Binah,* the sphere of understanding. Surely, I will someday seek to understand why I would repeat the same insane behavior, expecting different results... For now, I am identified to "I am not enough," and living mostly in linear time. I think that the body and matter are solid rather than fluid. Moreover, whereas the creation of good passed through *the* heaven and *the* earth, the creation of evil passes through earth and heaven. There is no definite article to introduce both objects. S/Hebrew's grammar places the particle *Et* before a direct object to remind me not to objectify "it." This function was unfolded in Code Communication (see *Learning to Code*). Surely, when at the end of greed, I have no wish to control anything. The **creation of materialism** can only happen when I don't know that I am whole, "PAIRfect," complete and cellularly connected. Ignorance causes me to play games of dominance and/or submission.

Earth	Creation of Materialism	Heaven
The Adamah	Creation of Misery	The Adam

As for the reason why I would do so, it is spelled out in the same verse via the word *Behibaram* for "when they were created," written with a shrunk Heh (grey).

The minimized scripting of the sign Heh marks the **creation of misery**, as it diminishes the feminine (or the  possibility to be womb-like and receiving). Suddenly, I find myself moved from the haves to the have-nots. See *Chapter 5, Choosing Mastery, the Entry into Scare City.*

This is to say that my feminine side is all numbed up. And now that I can't feel myself, I can't trust my judgment calls. Instead, I am afraid to decide, imagining that the results will come back as a loss – a material loss.

The Vicious Cycle

> "Why are you drinking? demanded the little prince. "So that I may forget," replied the tippler. "Forget what?" inquired the little prince, who was already sorry for him. "Forget that I am ashamed," the tippler confessed, hanging his head. "Ashamed of what?" insisted the little prince, who wanted to help him. "Ashamed of drinking!"
> *Antoine de Saint-Exupéry, The Little Prince*

I am now part of a vicious cycle, as the **creation of materialism** breeds the **creation of misery**. This is signified by **the Adam** which is missing the sign Heh that is present in **the Adamah** ("the ground"). Feeling ungrounded, I start seeing lack and feeling miserable. What else would I observe but no shrub in the earth, no herb to be sprung up, and no rain? (*Genesis 2:5*). The next step is the **creation of yearning**, and although the name *Mammon* is not given, it is the master I now serve.

The Woman	Creation of Yearning	The Adam w/o Heh
The Woman	Creation of Deception	The Snake

This master of money and yearning uses intimidating techniques. Indeed, *Genesis 2:18* is when YEWE *Elohim* utters the first negative judgment, saying: "it is no good that the Adam should be alone. I will make a partner for him." Sooo... "God" created all possible living creatures for the Adam to recognize them and name them. "But for the Adam, there was no partner in sight." Henceforth, "God" put **the Adam** to sleep, removed a side – the famous Heh rib out of which He fashioned **the Woman**. Note: the first "no good" judgment occurs right after the first negative commandment: 'And YEWE *Elohim* commanded the Adam, saying: "of every tree of the garden you may freely eat; but of the tree of the knowledge of good and evil, you shall not eat of it; for in the day that you do eat from it, you will surely die."' *Genesis 2:16-17*

Following the sense of coercion, I must now do a lot of inner work until I see how the Power of history leads me to be source again, as I understand why I choose to make the law a repressive device. Surely, how can I accept the validity of my instincts when I am so hungry that I am unable to feel what's true for me in my gut? I need to project the evil I deny and suppress onto a punishing "God." This is how what started as the **creation of yearning** now turns into the **creation of deception**. It is "God's" fault if I'm not successful, and I'm going to use all possible tricks to make "him" pay for that. Oyveh! I forget that there's no one out there: I can only be deceiving myself!

Certainly, deception is THE distinguishing feature of **the Snake** who champions the ability to lie (he fakes kindness → she turns hysterical). "Now the snake was slicker than any beast of the field which the LORD God had made." *Genesis 3:1*. The lie was super-subtle as it was disguised by a half-truth: 'did God say: "you must not eat from any tree in the garden?"' That was enough to trip up **the Woman** who follows the Snake's example with another lie: 'God did say "you may eat fruit from the trees in the garden, but you must not eat fruit from the tree that is in the middle of the garden, and you must not touch it, or you will die."' There never was any command of not touching the tree: the woman just made it up!

The Woman	Creation of Violation	The Adam
Eve	Creation of Fear	Adam

The **creation of violation** naturally follows suit, since each stage carefully lays the ground for the next stage to occur. Indeed, first I must be in bondage to the material world. Very soon, I become identified to my own misery, leaving me longing and making me so lonely I could die! Unless I believe myself to be disconnected from my guidance system, I wouldn't be able to commit a violation to LOVE!

And sure enough, one lie after the next, the tree that I thought was not good for me now appears quite differently: "And when the woman saw that the tree was good for food, and that it was a delight to the eyes, and that the tree was to be desired to make one wise, she took of the fruit thereof, and did eat; and she gave also unto her husband with her, and he did eat." This shift in perspective inverts my polarities: while I just ate from the tree of the knowledge of opposites, the bite I took is stuck in my throat (literally). This inability to swallow and digest my own transgression ends up inverting my polarities: now, what I think is good for me is actually bad for me, and vice-versa, what I think is bad for me would actually be good for me. I can't make a straight judgment call if my life depended on it... and it does! The result – once again – precedes the cause, for how would the woman see that the tree was "desired to make one wise" unless she knew she was about to embark in a foolish behavior?

As for me, the knowing that I went against my heart in turn sparks the **creation of fear**. A number of fears now plague me: the fear of death (which was the promised outcome of the violation), the fear of rejection (following my rejecting my inner guidance), the fear of speaking (as I wonder how I will justify my actions), and the big FEAR of loss (whose False Evidence will soon Appear as Real as paradise lost).

Eve vs. the Snake	Creation of Evil	Adam vs. the Adamah

The creation of evil is now complete, making the core of the dark seed visible.

However, this second Shabbat (stage 14) is more of an anti-Shabbat, as I find myself restless. Just like sleep is said to be for the innocent, sleeplessness must be for the guilty. Therein is the primary reason behind *Tiqqun Cain* – to allow the Cain in me to understand the mark on his forehead and thereby, transform the nature of my communication to myself/others. Once I decode myself, instead of dying and being reborn time and again into the same transgression (see movie *Groundhog Day*), I can finally die (i.e.; change my evil ways), and rest in peace. For now,

the blessings granted in the creation of good have turned into a quadruple curse:

- **The Snake's curse** is enmity: no one loves or even likes a liar!
- **Eve's curse** is painful births and the longing for her man side.
- **Adam's curse** is to have to work hard for his money.
- **The Adamah's curse** is to starve mankind in lieu of nourishing it.

After the End...

"Now this is not the end. It is not even the beginning of the end. But it is, perhaps, the end of the beginning." *Winston Churchill*

Gen. 3	Stage 14	Eve vs. the Snake	Creation of Evil	Adam vs. the Adamah
Gen. 3:23 & Beyond	After the END – Non-Causality	Existentialism Cain "Possession"	Creation of Forgiveness Seth "Appointment"	Nihilism Abel "Vanity"
		Work	Creation of Folly	Rest

The beginning of time is the beginning of mind; when I start identifying to the thought that I am the body, and by extension, not enough.

Going back to the fundamentals of consciousness, I create as I speak, and I speak my thoughts. All that I experience is my creation. Sometimes the gap is such that I have completely forgotten that I had desired it in the first place. Indeed, it can be years or even lifetimes between a creation and its experience! But if I pay attention, I will realize that my beliefs create my reality – be it hell or heaven; misery or joy. First, I create my reality, then I experience it, and then I get caught in the experience, because I ignore that the source of all exists in me. So yes, whatever I think (or pray for) will be fulfilled sooner or later.

Once I realize that I am source, things begin to change. I have more space to play. I become artist-like, painting my chosen vision. I just have to adopt a different angle. If I decide to paint misery, I can indulge my creation as much as I want. But I am not complaining, for I know that it is my creation and not anyone else's. As I take full responsibility for my creation, I open to new possibilities. I can stop creating the world, my reality and/or "God." There is no need for it. The artist can retire; a retirement of the mind also known as forgiveness and/or meditation. I am complete: I understand why I once chose to experience folly as only folly can lead me to the full out expression of my genius. I am both **Cain** and **Abel**; the former being an **existentialist**, and the latter a **nihilist**. When no longer "possessed" by my "vanity," I CAN actually rest while working. Indeed, I am also **Seth** in that I no longer disappoint my Self.

Work	Creation of Folly	Rest

Being on the other side of my **creation of folly**, I can feel why my female side ate from the forbidden fruit, seeing that this bite was desired to make me wise. Therein is the force of opposites – a rivalry between good and evil which I can only transcend by having a "sexual" knowledge of both. Whether I realize it or not, I have just accepted the invitation of *Genesis 3:22*: "Look, the humans have become like us, knowing both good and evil. What if they stretch their hand, take the fruit from the tree of life, and eat it? Then they'll live forever!" As I emPower the Eternal Now, I CAN wait for the path to be clear before any word or action. I came to the END, when I am One because I open to non-causality. I just enjoy the show, not taking any of it personally.

Beyond Creation into Sexual Knowledge

"The non-dimensional spheres are numbered ten as the fingers; five opposite five, with a singular covenant precisely in the middle, sanctified by the circumcision of the tongue and the phallus." *Sepher Yetzirah, Chapter 1*

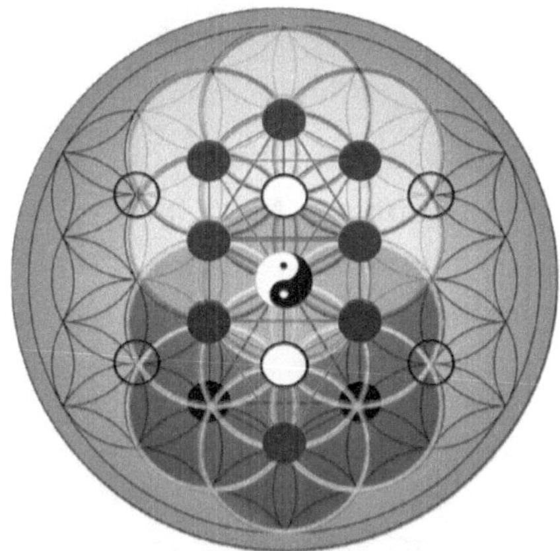

Beyond Creation – The Singular Covenant in the Middle of
the Creation of Good and the Creation of Evil.

The singular covenant and the place "precisely in the middle" is the
heart chakra (where the Taijitu is), sanctified by the circumcision of the
mouth chakra and the sex chakra (opaque white spheres). This is when
I am Aleph-like. While all the letters went in reverse order to 0/1
pleading to create the world, first letter Aleph remained silent. 0/1 was
surprised: "why didn't you come before me as all the other letters did?"
The ability not to need credit for being "the creator" is how Aleph
imparts the spirit of unity. When there is no illusion of separation, I
witness the creation of (my) folly, without taking it personally. Indeed,
there is no one left to create it! It just is. I feel the deliverable of *Golden
XPR* as the unequivocal sense of enough.

As for the seeds of the creation of good and evil themselves, the former
sprouts from the mouth chakra and the latter, from the sex chakra. I
have seen how the seven lower spheres are each guarded by the seven
patriarchs: **Joseph**, for example, is the guardian of the sex chakra. But
who is the guardian of the mouth chakra? The information on this
transcendental chakra being sparse, TCO had to feel into it and innovate. **Miriam** comes to mind. She was Moses' sister, and a prophetess
herself (*Numbers 19:1:22*). There is even talk of "the mouth of Miriam's

well." After Miriam died, the well that gave an abundant supply of water became dry (*Pirkei Avot 5:6:3*).

The names Miriam and Mary are often confused, specifically in the Qu'ran. Sooo... **Joseph** (sex chakra), **Mary** (mouth chakra) and **Jacob/Israel** (heart chakra). Speaking of realness, how much more real a guardian for the sacred heart can we get besides **Jesus**?

You Create Your "IS-REALity

"You have to systematically create confusion; it sets creativity free. Everything that is contradictory creates life." *Salvador Dalí*

		Male	Neutral	Female
0/1	Before the BIG Bang B-ginning	Male	Neutral	Female
		Beth (B)	Aleph (A)	Beth (B)
		Order/Spirit	Intention	Chaos/Matter
		The Heaven	Reality / God Created-SIX	The Earth
Genesis 1	"Day" 1	The Light of Day	Creation of Observation	The Darkness of Night
	"Day" 2	The Waters of Above	Creation of Boundaries	The Waters of Below
	"Day" 3	Earth as Order	Creation of Divergence	Ocean as Chaos
	"Day" 4	The Greater Sun	Creation of Illumination	The Lesser Moon
	"Day" 5	The Birds	Creation of Abundance	The Fish
	"Day" 6	Livestock	Creation of Power	Creepy Crawlers
Gen. 2	"Day" 7	Rest	Creation of Good	Work
to Genesis 3:21 / Genesis 2:4	Stage 8	Earth	Creation of Materialism	Heaven
	Stage 9	The Adamah	Creation of Misery	The Adam
	Stage 10	The Woman	Creation of Yearning	The Adam w/o Heh
	Stage 11	The Woman	Creation of Deception	The Snake
	Stage 12	The Woman	Creation of Violation	The Adam
	Stage 13	Eve	Creation of Fear	Adam
Gen. 3	Stage 14	Eve vs. the Snake	Creation of Evil	Adam vs. the Adamah
Gen. 3:23 & Beyond	After the END – Non-Causality	Existentialism	Creation of Forgiveness	Nihilism
		Cain "Possession"	Seth "Appointment"	Abel "Vanity"
		Work	Creation of Folly	Rest

Visualizing the key chapters of *Genesis* in this way – good against evil, horizontally and vertically – leads me to realize the universal nature of a vast narrative, pulled down in such a way to where I can easily recognize in them my own programming. This "Smart Torah" app makes it easier to persevere and continue my own journey of decoding my ego patterns until I come to the end. Indeed, no matter how many times I heard these stories, seeing them in this way inspires the compassion to do what it takes to surrender.

I know that my intention is pure. I also know that forces work in polarity for the "good-bad" of all (confusion included). I can now trust myself to adequately deal with adversity, should chaos knock at my door. And it will... :-)

An "IS-REALity" Check

"The virtuous soul that is alone and without a master, is like a lone burning coal; it will grow colder rather than hotter. Those who fall alone remain alone in their fall, and they value their souls little since they entrust it to themselves alone. If you do not fear falling alone, do you presume that you will rise up alone? Consider how much more can be accomplished by two together than by one alone." *John of the Cross, Dark Night of the Soul*

XPR satiates the hunger for LOVE by procuring a sense of awe that stretches me toward something greater; toward the Divine. Will I have the courage to face my fear of loss, and make THE Decision – the decision to go for purity?

Unless I do, I cannot really experience how laughter moves into acceptance, acceptance into presence, presence into trust, until I can finally know beyond doubt the faith that makes me well. Will I get cold feet upon sensing that shadow work does present real dangers? Will I be honest enough with myself to realize that this work of making the unconscious conscious cannot be done alone?

When humble enough to know that I need help, I may seek spiritual guidance, and welcome the process of a Mystery School whose teachings must remain silent until I am RAW (Ready – Able – Willing) to do what it takes to hear them inwardly.

Just how RAW am I?

- **Am I Ready?** Do I "personally" (to use that word as a joke) feel the urgency of the call to be the change? Do I also realize that, as an Earthling, I am involved in an extreme crisis that threatens the Earth and all life within it?
- **Am I Able?** Can I choose to allocate the necessary resources of time and money to the Great Work? For while the Work is *not* about time and *not* about money, it will involve reorganizing my priorities.
- **Am I Willing?** Will I allow myself to know just how potent a force evil is? How destructive is the greed that contaminated religious institutions, corporations, the military, the educational system, the food, the pharmaceutical and medical industries – the Whole? Moreover, am I brave enough to recognize that the same greed infiltrated me, and rigorous enough to understand and embrace it so totally that it would transition into grace?

To find out just how RAW I am, I may consult next page's BEE map...

Being Deliberate in my Creation

Prepare to DIE: to access the online inquiry tool, click the BEE Map below or visit https://www.goldenxpr.com/tco_being_deliberate/.

- **Step 1:** I fill in the blank: I want to know WHY I would choose to think I CAN'T ______ (e.g.; find a job, be patient, etc.).
- **Step 2:** I ask for truth and generate a number.
- **Step 3:** I find my number on the map and then use the words in the given hexagon to fill in the brackets: when asleep and acting out as a [**DREaM**], I tell the story of [**MY Story**] which gives me an excuse to go into my creation of [**Creation of Evil**]. Instead, if I were to own that I can have the sense of [**Creation of Good**], I wouldn't kill my soul by way of [**Greed**].
- **Step 4:** what most surprised me in this process is ______.

The PaRaDiSe Mystery School

"The most beautiful thing we can experience is the mysterious. It is the source of all true art and science." Albert Einstein

Truth / Secret	Difference / Practicality	Reflection / Mystery
TO END	TO KEEP SILENCE / TO HAVE	TO OWN

The Why of the PaRaDiSe Mystery School ™ **is:** TO END my suffering by clearing the confusion induced by the "God" label, whose abstraction keeps me lonely as I run from the Mystery, and angry as I won't see the Truth that I am creating IT all!

The How of the PaRaDiSe Mystery School ™ **is:** TO OWN my projections by using *Golden XPR* as a scrying mirror, at once shocking and sobering, and see that the places in the decoding where I go in limbo exactly **Reflect** where my shame-based **Secrets** are at work.

The What of the PaRaDiSe Mystery School ™ **is:** TO WILL with a Power that cannot be corrupted; TO KEEP SILENCE as both the practice and **Practicality** of self-mastery; TO DARE wielding energy to solve problems, TO HAVE the wisdom to know the **Difference** moment to moment.

To apply for the PaRaDiSe Mystery school visit:
https://www.goldenxpr.com/mystery-school-application/

To receive the gift of the online course *The Genesis Pattern,* visit
https://www.goldenxpr.com/course/the_genesis_pattern/
and use coupon code: TCO1

TCO—Book 3

> "So, I cast a deep sleep upon me, and while I was sleeping, I took one of my sides and closed up the flesh at that spot. Then I made a female from the side I had taken out of me." *Genesis 2:21-22*

There is some truth in the romantic dream that, one day, my prince or princess will come, and fulfill all my desires. Each moment is my lover, when I resist nothing.

Here is a question for me: do I believe with complete faith that there is an END to suffering? If yes, *Golden XPR* **may just be a path to THE END. If not, I may choose to inquire on what I get from my attachment to suffering?**

The four core chapters of *TCO—Book 3* are dedicated to the four DREaM archetypes, to ease their trans-formation into LOVE. When confused about what's "out there" and forgetting that togetherness is a mirage coming from my fear of being alone, I enforce the "I am not enough" thought, and would rather hit the snooze button than to wake up!

One thing is sure: the pain caused by the unconscious DREaM types will eventually lead me to become real – the END. I will then reopen the flesh at the "sentience spot," giving me the permission to feel and sense again. Meanwhile, why look for LOVE "out there" and be a slave to my longing? Why feel obligated to you?

From Beth to Shin, there are 20 signs or lettered stages. These 20 letters can be grouped into four families of YEWE to wake me up from the DREaM, and a fifth to remind me that I am the light. Always was. Always will be. Unlearning the shadow of 20 archetypes is the Great Voyage sponsored by the PaRaDiSe Mystery School. This voyage is alchemical in nature, inviting me to adopt the Sun's trajectory into transcendence.

1. **Putrefaction is the Nigredo "black" stage of how the saboteuR** in me will turn into a **Visionary.** This unfolds in the first chapter when I understand why my throat was bi-polar, and how to safely manage a most abysmal passage into the "Promised Land" of an open 3rd eye.

2. **Purification is the Albedo "white" stage of how the victiM** in me will turn into an **Officer.** This unfolds in the second chapter – when I understand why I played a toxic "righteous" and wrong game, and how to revitalize, energize and sensitize the tree of (my) life.

3. **Awakening is the Citrinitas "yellow" stage of how the chilD** in me will turn into a **Leader.** This unfolds in the third chapter – when I understand why I must carve vanity out of the egoic marble, and how killing it (vanity) will set my **angel** free to equally rise or fall.

4. **Transcendence is the Rubedo "red" stage of how the prostitutE** in me will turn into an **Engineer.** This unfolds in the fourth chapter – when I understand why I am poor and sick (a have-not) when I could choose Health with a big H (and have it all).

South	East / West	North
Yellow chilD	Red prostitutE / White victiM	Black saboteuR
Citrinitas	Rubedo / Albedo	Nigredo
Awaken	Transcend / Purify	Putrefy

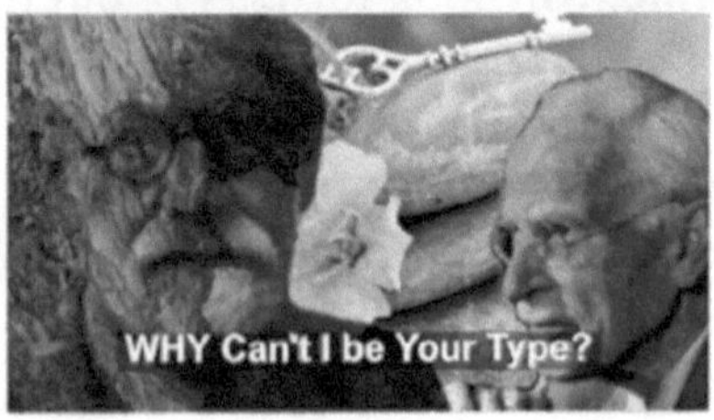

To connect the alchemical stages to the DREaM code, click the image above or go to https://www.goldenxpr.com/why-the-love-types/.

Live Long and Prosper!

TCO thanks you for your work in consciousness. Enlightenment will not happen because of what you do. It will also never happen without your doing everything for it!

LOVE bless you and keep you!
LOVE deal kindly and graciously with you!
LOVE bestow favor unto you and grant you peace.
LOVE link your name to ALL that **IS-REAL** and thus **B-LESS** you so that you can **B-MORE**!
Transmission of Numbers 6:24-27

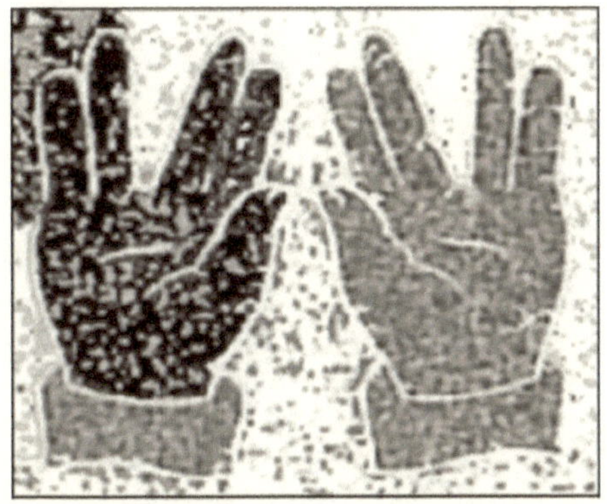

B'Siyata DiShemaya: "with Heaven's help!"
April 22, 2022 – 22 Nissan 5782, 7th night of Passover

List of Publications :: the Path of *Golden XPR*

1. Golden XPR
2. Golden XPR Distilled
3. Opening to the heART of XPR
4. The Genesis Pattern - book 1
5. The Genesis Pattern - book 2
6. This Year: EZ to Digest
7. Tweet tweeT
8. The LOVE Code
9. Sooo... I CAIN'T and *you're* ABEL!
10. The Creation Tool
11. The Expire Tarot Advanced
12. Victim of my GENESis
13. The WHYS Bite
14. The ThREE of Sapphires
15. The 7x7 Count
16. PaRaDiSe Circle
17. TABU: The Anarchist Book of Understanding
18. The GR-Code
19. This Year in Jerusalem
20. Welcome to the PaRaDiSe Mystery School
21. The Sapphire Book
22. Mercury REDROgrade

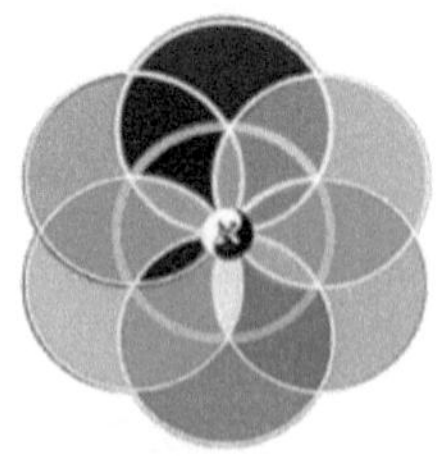